Cybersecurity Education and Training

Razvan Beuran

Cybersecurity Education and Training

 Springer

Razvan Beuran
Next-Generation Digital Infrastructure
Research Area
Japan Advanced Institute of Science
and Technology
Nomi, Ishikawa, Japan

ISBN 978-981-96-0554-5   ISBN 978-981-96-0555-2   (eBook)
https://doi.org/10.1007/978-981-96-0555-2

This Springer imprint is published by the registered company Springer Nature Singapore Pte Ltd.
The registered company address is: 152 Beach Road, #21-01/04 Gateway East, Singapore 189721,
Singapore

If disposing of this product, please recycle the paper.

To my family and two cats =˄.˄=

Preface

In the early 2000s, as a fresh Ph.D. student living in France, I returned back to my home country, Romania, for the holidays. Naturally, I took with me the laptop that I had recently purchased and used for a while already. Once I arrived home, I almost immediately connected it to the Internet—via dial-up access, naturally—to read my emails. Almost instantly I noticed some strange network activity, and by some sort of reflex, I disconnected the modem cable. Alas, it was too late, as a virus had already infected my laptop, and every minute or so the computer would keep rebooting itself. What was I to do?!

The only solution I could come up with was to visit one of the early Internet cafés that had popped up in Bucharest and investigate the problem. Luckily, I was able to find some instructions on how to remove that virus by deleting a specific file in the system directory. I then rushed home and used the interval between reboots to follow those instructions as quickly as I could. Imagine my relief when, lo and behold, the virus was gone. Only then I was able to use again my computer normally (after enabling the firewall this time, of course).

Fast forward 20+ years, and I am now doing research on cybersecurity in Japan, one of my topics being cybersecurity education and training. Times have changed, and nobody in their right mind would connect to the Internet on a computer that doesn't have some security software installed. Malware has also evolved, and the chances that you can remove an infection yourself by simply deleting one file are pretty slim. Given the emergence of advanced persistent threats, you'll probably not even notice that your computer is infected. But despite all these changes, my vision of cybersecurity is still driven by that early experience I had when connecting my first laptop to a dial-up network in Romania, as doing practical things by yourself is definitely a *sine qua non* of this field.

Fortunately, I was able to put into play this vision as a member of the Cyber Range Organization and Design (CROND) endowed chair at Japan Advanced Institute of Science and Technology (JAIST) that was established with the support of NEC Corporation from April 2015 until March 2021. The goal of CROND was to advance the field of cybersecurity education and training, especially through conducting research on cyber ranges, the network environments that are typically used for the hands-on training activities that any cybersecurity professional must undertake.

This book was conceived as a culmination of our research at CROND and I intend it to be a practical instrument that cybersecurity educators and training experts can use to guide their work. To achieve this goal, the book provides a thorough view on cybersecurity education and training, in which theoretical descriptions are interspersed with practical details. Consequently, readers can gain both the theoretical understanding, and the practical information, needed to develop and conduct cybersecurity training activities.

The first part of the book systematizes all the aspects related to cybersecurity education and training methodologies, starting with technical cybersecurity training for professionals, which is discussed in much detail. Moreover, issues related to IoT security training, and the cybersecurity awareness training targeted at regular IT users, are also mentioned. This makes it possible for readers to understand the requirements of developing effective training activities that help participants learn how to deal appropriately with cybersecurity incidents.

The second part of the book focuses on the presentation of actual cybersecurity training platforms, such as Capture The Flag (CTF) platforms and cyber ranges. This is followed by a detailed case study on the integrated cybersecurity training framework CyTrONE that we developed at CROND, and a discussion of training platform capability assessment. Thus, the second part provides all the practical know-how needed to effectively set up cybersecurity training activities.

I hope that readers will find this book useful when addressing the many challenges related to cybersecurity education and training, and I am looking forward to the progress that their own contributions to this field will bring—a progress that is absolutely necessary to fill the significant cybersecurity workforce gap that we are currently faced with.

Nonoichi, Japan   Razvan Beuran
August 2024

Acknowledgements

This book would not have been possible without the support of many people. First and foremost, I would like to thank Prof. Yoichi Shinoda and Prof. Yasuo Tan, who gave me the opportunity to come to JAIST as a postdoc in 2005, and later to return as research associate professor in 2015. In this context, I would also like to mention Prof. Ken-ichi Chinen, who has been my main collaborator at the Cyber Range Organization and Design chair at JAIST. Many of the ideas presented in this book were born through the stimulating discussions I had with them.

In addition, I cannot forget all the students in my lab at JAIST who contributed to the many research projects whose accomplishments laid the foundation for this book. They are listed next in chronological order of their study period: Cuong Pham, Dat Thanh Tang, Takuya Inoue, Jidong Wang, Zheyu Tan, Min Zhao, Liangwen Yuan, Zhe Zhang, Youmeizi Zeng, Zhenguo Hu, Tan Duy Le, Sian En Ooi, Quyen Van Nguyen, and Thanh Phuong Huynh Nguyen. Thank you all!

Furthermore, several Chinen lab students, such as Fumikazu Awa, Masanori Sunagawa and Gen Komatsu, as well as minor research project or internship students, such as Muhammad Harith bin Noor Azam, Chunqi Du, Lei Jiang, Kien Chi Vu, Wataru Mishima, Yuichiro Sakamoto, and Yoshiki Makino, have made important contributions to our research projects, and I am also very grateful to them.

Last but not least, I would like to wholeheartedly thank Assoc. Prof. Jan Vykopal, Prof. Herve Debar, and Prof. Youki Kadobayashi, who have been so kind as to review this manuscript. The insightful comments and suggestions they have provided have helped me significantly improve the book.

Contents

1   **Introduction** 1
    1.1   Background and Motivation 1
    1.2   Book Outline 2
    1.3   Existing Literature 3
    1.4   Key Contributions 4
    1.5   Intended Audience 4
    References 5

Part I   Cybersecurity Education and Training Methodologies

2   **Cybersecurity Education and Training** 9
    2.1   Education Versus Training 9
       2.1.1   Term Connotations 9
       2.1.2   Education and Training for Cybersecurity 10
    2.2   Cybersecurity Training Categories 11
       2.2.1   Technical Cybersecurity Training 12
       2.2.2   Cybersecurity Awareness Training 14
       2.2.3   Training Category Comparison 16
    References 18

3   **Technical Cybersecurity Training** 19
    3.1   Technical Cybersecurity Training Taxonomy 19
       3.1.1   Training Purpose 19
       3.1.2   Training Approach 21
       3.1.3   Training Characteristics 24
       3.1.4   Theoretical Training 26
    3.2   Cybersecurity Skill Overview 27
       3.2.1   Workforce and Skill Frameworks 27
       3.2.2   Cybersecurity Skill Analysis 31

3.3   Training Effectiveness 33
        3.3.1   Effectiveness Requirements 33
        3.3.2   Necessary Implementation Features 34
3.4   Case Study: Hardening Project 35
        3.4.1   Program Overview 35
        3.4.2   Spin-Off Programs 37
        3.4.3   Taxonomy-Based Analysis 37
References 39

4   Attack Training 41
4.1   Attack Training Overview 41
        4.1.1   Overall Methodology 41
        4.1.2   Approach Interdependency 42
4.2   Attack Training Types 43
        4.2.1   Fundamental Attack Training 43
        4.2.2   Pentesting Training 47
4.3   Related Information 52
        4.3.1   Attack Knowledge Bases 52
        4.3.2   Security Testing Guidelines 64
        4.3.3   Attack Training Tools 65
        4.3.4   Attack Training Platforms 66
4.4   Discussion 68
        4.4.1   Main Advantages 68
        4.4.2   Potential Issues 70
References 71

5   Forensics Training 73
5.1   Forensics Training Overview 73
        5.1.1   Overall Methodology 74
        5.1.2   Approach Interdependency 74
5.2   Forensics Training Types 75
        5.2.1   Fundamental Forensics Training 76
        5.2.2   Forensic Methodology Training 81
5.3   Related Information 85
        5.3.1   Forensic Knowledge Bases 85
        5.3.2   Forensic Methodology Guidelines 86
        5.3.3   Forensics Training Tools 89
        5.3.4   Forensics Training Platforms 92
5.4   Discussion 92
        5.4.1   Main Advantages 92
        5.4.2   Potential Issues 93
References 95

6 Defense Training 97
   6.1   Defense Training Overview 97
       6.1.1   Overall Methodology 97
       6.1.2   Approach Interdependency 98
   6.2   Defense Training Types 99
       6.2.1   Fundamental Defense Training 100
       6.2.2   Defense Methodology Training 108
   6.3   Related Information 111
       6.3.1   Defense Knowledge Bases 111
       6.3.2   Defense Methodology Guidelines 118
       6.3.3   Defense Training Tools 123
       6.3.4   Defense Training Platforms 126
   6.4   Discussion 127
       6.4.1   Main Advantages 127
       6.4.2   Potential Issues 129
   References 130

7 IoT Security Training 133
   7.1   IoT Security Training Challenges 133
       7.1.1   IoT Device Diversity 134
       7.1.2   IoT Device Risks 135
       7.1.3   Developer Issues 136
       7.1.4   End User Issues 137
   7.2   IoT Security Training Approaches 139
       7.2.1   Hands-On Training 139
       7.2.2   Theoretical Training 141
       7.2.3   Approach Comparison 142
   7.3   Case Study: IoTrain-Sim and IoTrain-Lab 144
       7.3.1   IoTrain-Sim 144
       7.3.2   IoTrain-Lab 147
       7.3.3   System Comparison 149
   References 151

8 Cybersecurity Awareness Training 153
   8.1   Cybersecurity Literacy 153
   8.2   Cybersecurity Awareness Training Approaches 154
       8.2.1   Reading Materials 154
       8.2.2   Training Videos 155
       8.2.3   E-Learning 156
       8.2.4   Simulation 158
       8.2.5   Gamification 159
       8.2.6   Approach Comparison 161
   8.3   Case Study: CyATP 163
       8.3.1   CyATP Overview 164
       8.3.2   Concept Map Based Learning 164

8.3.3   Content Generation 166
8.3.4   Crossword Puzzle Quiz 168
References 169

Part II   Cybersecurity Training Platforms

9   Cybersecurity Training Platform Overview 173
9.1   Training Platform Model 173
9.1.1   Model Outline 173
9.1.2   Component Overview 176
9.2   Training Content 179
9.2.1   Training Content Types 180
9.2.2   Content Type Comparison 182
9.2.3   Education Aspects 184
9.3   Training Environment 186
9.3.1   Training Environment Types 186
9.3.2   Environment Type Comparison 190
References 191

10   Capture the Flag Platforms 193
10.1   CTF Platform Overview 193
10.1.1   Jeopardy-Style CTF 194
10.1.2   Attack-Defend CTF 195
10.1.3   CTF-Type Comparison 196
10.2   Online CTF Platforms 198
10.2.1   Jeopardy-Style Platforms 198
10.2.2   Hybrid Platforms 201
10.2.3   Online Platform Comparison 203
10.3   Open-Source CTF Platforms 206
10.3.1   Jeopardy-Style Platforms 206
10.3.2   Hybrid Platforms 210
10.3.3   Open-Source Platform Comparison 214
10.4   Discussion 216
10.4.1   Potential Issues 216
10.4.2   Additional Resources 218
References 218

11   Cyber Ranges 221
11.1   Cyber Range Overview 221
11.1.1   Cyber Range Significance 222
11.1.2   Cyber Range Categories 222
11.2   General Cyber Ranges 223
11.2.1   Government Cyber Ranges 223
11.2.2   Private-Sector Cyber Ranges 228

11.2.3   Academia Cyber Ranges 237
11.2.4   General Range Comparison 238
11.3   Specialized Cyber Ranges 242
11.3.1   IoT Cyber Ranges 243
11.3.2   ICS/SCADA Cyber Ranges 245
11.3.3   Critical Infrastructure Cyber Ranges 247
11.3.4   IoMT and Healthcare Cyber Ranges 249
11.3.5   Specialized Range Comparison 250
11.4   Discussion 255
11.4.1   General Cyber Ranges 255
11.4.2   Specialized Cyber Ranges 256
11.4.3   Overall Recommendations 256
References 257

12   Detailed Case Study: CyTrONE 261
12.1   Motivation and Target 261
12.2   Framework Overview 262
12.2.1   CyTrONE Architecture 262
12.2.2   Training Platform Model Mapping 267
12.3   CyTrONE Training Content 268
12.3.1   Training Content Representation 269
12.3.2   Training Content Examples 273
12.4   CyTrONE Training Environment 277
12.4.1   Cyber Range Description 277
12.4.2   Cyber Range Examples 283
12.5   Lessons Learned 288
12.5.1   Modular Architecture 289
12.5.2   Moodle LMS Reliance 290
12.5.3   YAML Representation 291
12.5.4   Other Concerns 293
References 294

13   Training Platform Capability Assessment 295
13.1   Capability Assessment Overview 295
13.1.1   Motivation and Background 295
13.1.2   Cybersecurity Training Platform Stakeholders 296
13.1.3   Capability Assessment Perspectives 297
13.2   Capability Assessment Methodology 298
13.2.1   Methodology Outline 298
13.2.2   Capability Assessment Criteria 299
13.2.3   Assessment Procedure 303
13.3   CyTrONE Capability Assessment 305
13.3.1   Training Content Representation 305
13.3.2   Network Environment Management 307
13.3.3   Training Activity Facilitation 308

13.4 Capability Assessment Applications 308
    13.4.1 For Developers 309
    13.4.2 For Organizers 309
    13.4.3 For Trainees 313
References 313

14 Conclusion 315
14.1 Book Summary 315
    14.1.1 Part I: Training Methodologies 315
    14.1.2 Part II: Training Platforms 316
14.2 Key Takeaways 317
14.3 Toward the Future 318
    14.3.1 Cybersecurity Training Prospects 318
    14.3.2 Cybersecurity Training in the Age of AI 320
    14.3.3 From Cybersecurity to Trustworthiness 322
References 323

Chapter 1
Introduction

*Know the small rather than the big, reach the deep rather than
the shallow.*
*Miyamoto Musashi, "The Book of Five Rings," 1645, translated
by the author.*

This chapter discusses first the motivation for this book, as well as its two-part structure. Then, the main characteristics of the existing literature related to cybersecurity education and training are outlined, followed by a summary of the key contributions the book makes in this respect. The chapter ends with a discussion of the intended audience of the book.

1.1 Background and Motivation

The *Cybersecurity Workforce Study 2023* report published by ISC2, which is the world's leading association for cybersecurity professionals, concluded that the global cybersecurity workforce had an 8.7% year-over-year (YoY) growth compared to the results reported in 2022, to reach approximately 5.5 million professionals [3]. However, it was reported that the workforce gap has increased even more, specifically by 12.6% YoY, to reach a number of almost 4 million professionals that organizations require in addition in order to secure themselves appropriately.

This dire situation is not new, however. Thus, a 2013 report by the National Center of Incident Readiness and Strategy for Cybersecurity in Japan (NISC), formerly known as the Information Security Policy Council, revealed that the existing cybersecurity personnel was insufficient and not well-enough trained. In particular, it was reported that, although there was a total of about 265,000 individuals with cybersecurity-related jobs in Japan at that time, there was also a potential deficiency

R. Beuran, *Cybersecurity Education and Training*,
https://doi.org/10.1007/978-981-96-0555-2_1

of 80,000 such security personnel. Moreover, of the existing cybersecurity personnel, those who actually possessed the required level of skills were considered to be around 105,000, meaning that additional education and training was deemed necessary for the remaining 160,000 individuals [5].

This led to the creation of several cybersecurity education and training programs in Japan that were meant to support the development of future security experts. One such program is CYber Defense Exercise with Recurrence (CYDER), which was created in 2013 by the Ministry of Internal Affairs and Communications (MIC) with the goal of improving the capabilities of local government agencies to cope with cyberattacks. For this purpose, MIC conducted practical cyber defense exercises at several locations throughout Japan until 2015. However, since 2016 CYDER is operated by the National Institute of Information and Communications Technology (NICT), and the scope and frequency of the activities have been extended. Thus, starting from 2018 all the 47 prefectures in Japan are covered, and more than 100 training events are held each year [6].

In addition to the training programs, several endowed chairs were created in Japanese universities to promote cybersecurity education and training activities. One of these endowed chairs was Cyber Range Organization and Design (CROND) that operated at Japan Advanced Institute of Science and Technology (JAIST) from April 2015 to March 2021 with the support of NEC Corporation. The goal of CROND was to advance the field of cybersecurity education and training, especially through conducting research on *cyber ranges*, the network environments that are typically used for hands-on training activities.

As one of the core members of CROND, the author conceived this book as a summary of the knowledge that was created, and the research results that were produced by the endowed chair. Consequently, he hopes it will serve as a helpful guideline for cybersecurity educators and training experts worldwide.

1.2 Book Outline

This book provides a comprehensive overview on cybersecurity education and training methodologies. The book uses a combination of theoretical and practical elements in order to address both the abstract and concrete aspects of the discussed concepts.

The book is structured into two parts. The main focus of the first part of the book is on technical cybersecurity training approaches. Following a general overview on cybersecurity education and training, technical cybersecurity training and the three types of training activities in this context—attack training, forensics training, and defense training—are discussed in detail. In addition, we present specific issues related to the particular case of IoT security training, which has its unique challenges that must be addressed. Lastly, cybersecurity awareness training, also known as end-user training or IT literacy, is also discussed in order to provide a thorough view on cybersecurity education and training methodologies.

The second part of the book describes the main characteristics of cybersecurity training platforms, which are the systems used to conduct the technical cybersecurity training activities. We start by introducing a generic training platform architecture, as well as key elements of the architecture, such as training content and training environments. This is followed by a wide-ranging analysis of actual cybersecurity training platforms, with focus on various CTF[1] systems and cyber ranges that are currently being used worldwide. To better illustrate the concepts discussed in the book, a detailed study of an open-source cybersecurity training platform is also included, namely the integrated cybersecurity training framework CyTrONE [2]. Finally, a cybersecurity training platform capability assessment methodology is introduced as a way to make it possible for the organizations that want to deploy or develop training platforms to objectively evaluate them.

1.3 Existing Literature

The current literature regarding cybersecurity education and training consists mainly of books that are dedicated to teaching practical low-level cybersecurity skills, such as penetration testing and hacking. One example in this category is *Penetration Testing: A Hands-On Introduction to Hacking* by Weidman [8], who is a penetration tester and security researcher. Another example is *Handbook for CTFers* by Nu1L Team [7], which is one of China's top CTF teams. Yet another example is *Network Security Assessment* by McNab [4]. And many other similar books can be easily found through a simple online search.

While such books are useful from the practical perspective of beginners who want to learn this type of low-level skills, they do not discuss the higher-level principles behind cybersecurity education and training. Therefore, such books lack the information that is required to understand how to organize training activities in an effective manner, and how to develop training content or training platforms in order to meet specific training goals.

A more unique perspective is provided in the book *Cyber Security Education: Principles and Policies* by Austin [1]. This is the closest to our book in terms of subject matter, but its main focus is on cybersecurity education principles seen from a mostly theoretical angle. In contrast, our book also discusses practical aspects related to training, thus providing a more concrete view on the topic, as well as readily applicable information that readers can use to plan and conduct various forms of training activities.

---

[1] CTF (Capture The Flag) is a type of cybersecurity competition in which participants are faced with a number of challenges in which they need to retrieve pieces of information, named "flags," to prove they have managed to solve those challenges.

In addition, the aforementioned book is a contributed one, that gathers the various perspectives of the contributing authors on cybersecurity education. Consequently, the book fails to provide a unified view on cybersecurity education and training similar to the one we present in this book.

1.4 Key Contributions

Based on the above considerations, we conclude that our book fills an important gap in the current literature by taking a middle-ground approach to discussing cybersecurity education and training. Thus, the book provides enough theoretical background and practical details so that it can be used by readers as a comprehensive guideline that makes it possible to effectively address all the issues related to planning and conducting cybersecurity education and training activities.

The key contributions of the present book are summarized below; the corresponding related chapters are also mentioned for reader's convenience:

1. Provides a thorough view on cybersecurity education and training methodologies and tools, focusing on the technical perspective that covers attack, forensics, and defense training (Chaps. 2 through 6).
2. Introduces other specific types of cybersecurity training, such as IoT security training and non-technical awareness training (Chaps. 7 and 8).
3. Discusses a generic cybersecurity training platform architecture, as well as a set of specific CTF and cyber range platforms (Chaps. 9 through 11).
4. Analyzes in detail a case study of an actual cybersecurity training platform, named CyTrONE, emphasizing its features and applicability for particular training activities (Chap. 12).
5. Describes a cybersecurity training platform capability assessment methodology that makes it possible to objectively evaluate training platforms in view of deployment or development (Chap. 13).

1.5 Intended Audience

The intended audience of this book covers the following areas:

- The main audience is cybersecurity education and training practitioners and professionals, both in the academia and industry, who will gain knowledge about how to organize meaningful cybersecurity training activities, and how to practically conduct those activities.
- Another category of potential readers are researchers and postgraduate students working in the area of cybersecurity training, who will gain insights about the current state-of-the-art in this field and will be able to build upon the information presented to extend their research and find new research topics.

- University lecturers and tutors, as well as undergraduate students, will also gain knowledge helping them make better use of the cybersecurity education classes they are tutoring or taking.
- Last but not least, corporate and academic libraries may decide to purchase this book in order to support the cybersecurity education and training activities of the professionals and students in those organizations.

As for the cybersecurity education and training activities that will be discussed, they are mainly related to work roles that have a strong practical component, such as incident responders, system architects, developers, digital forensics investigators, and penetration testers. However, even if the necessary training for certain work roles, such as legal, policy, and compliance officers, is not directly addressed, many of the issues discussed apply to those roles as well, although additional knowledge is required in those cases, e.g., with regard to laws and regulations.

References

1. Austin G (ed) (2020) Cyber security education: principles and policies. Routledge, London
2. Cyber Range Organisation and Design (CROND). CyTrONE GitHub page. https://github.com/crond-jaist/cytrone. Accessed 1 July 2024
3. ISC2 (2023) Cybersecurity workforce study 2023. https://media.isc2.org/-/media/Project/ISC2/Main/Media/documents/research/ISC2_Cybersecurity_Workforce_Study_2023.pdf. Accessed 1 July 2024
4. McNab C (2016) Network security assessment, 3rd edn. O'Reilly Media Inc, Sebastopol
5. National Center of Incident Readiness and Strategy for Cybersecurity (NISC), Japan (2013) Cybersecurity strategy. https://www.nisc.go.jp/eng/pdf/cybersecuritystrategy-en.pdf. Accessed 1 July 2024
6. National Institute of Information and Communications Technology (NICT), Japan. Cyber defense exercise with recurrence (CYDER) (in Japanese). https://cyder.nict.go.jp/. Accessed 1 July 2024
7. Nu1L Team (2022) Handbook for CTFers. Springer, Heidelberg
8. Weidman G (2014) Penetration testing: a hands-on introduction to hacking. No Starch Press, San Francisco

Part I
Cybersecurity Education and Training Methodologies

Part I of the book discusses in detail various aspects related to cybersecurity education and training methodologies. The main focus is on technical cybersecurity training, and the three types of training activities in this context: attack training, forensics training, and defense training. The specificities of IoT security training are also examined, followed by a discussion of cybersecurity awareness training.

Chapter 2
Cybersecurity Education and Training

This chapter discusses first the manner in which we use in this book the concepts of education and training in the context of cybersecurity. Then, an overview of the two main categories of training, technical cybersecurity training and cybersecurity awareness training, is provided, including a discussion of specific issues for each of them. The chapter ends with a comparative analysis of the main characteristics of the two training categories.

2.1 Education Versus Training

The terms education and training are sometimes used interchangeably, especially in relation with cybersecurity, and in this section, we will clarify what are the meanings that we will give to these two concepts in the present book.

2.1.1 Term Connotations

According to the Random House Kernerman Webster's College Dictionary, one definition of *education* is "the act or process of imparting or acquiring general knowledge and of developing the powers of reasoning and judgment." We believe that this is one of the most commonly agreed upon meanings of the word, which equates education with acquiring knowledge, as well as generic reasoning skills.

Another definition given in the same dictionary for the word *education*, however, considers it to be "the result produced by instruction, training, or study." This clearly positions training as one of the methods through which education is achieved.

As for *training*, in the same Random House dictionary, it is defined as "the education, instruction, or discipline of a person or thing that is being trained." Interestingly, this situates education as a methodology that is used for training, which is the opposite of the connotation mentioned above.

A more accurate definition for the word *training*, in our opinion, is to be found in the Collins English Dictionary, which defines training as "the process of bringing a person, etc., to an agreed standard of proficiency, etc., by practice and instruction," since it emphasizes the important of practice in the context of training.

We can thus say that, in a general context, there is no clear relationship between education and training, and they are sometimes used with very similar meanings. Let us analyze next this issue in the context of cybersecurity.

2.1.2 Education and Training for Cybersecurity

Cybersecurity is one of the fields that requires its practitioners to master both a vast amount of knowledge and a large range of technical skills. For this purpose, cybersecurity education and training programs must first teach the required theoretical knowledge, such as network protocols, operating systems, and cryptography. This must then be complemented with hands-on practice in order to instill the related technical skills: how to use network protocols, how to secure operating systems, how to configure encryption algorithms, etc.

In the book *Cyber Security Education: Principles and Policies*, even though the word education is used in the title, many of the actual book chapters discuss practical aspects as well. For example, several chapters discuss methods for developing cybersecurity skills, such as complementing in-class curricula with experiential activities to apply the learned concepts and skills in real-world settings [1]. We conclude that, in the mentioned book, cybersecurity training is conceived as an intrinsic component of cybersecurity education. However, this begets the question of how to refer to that part of cybersecurity education that is not training.

To simplify the discussion and eliminate the confusion that appears to reign in dictionary definitions and common understanding regarding the relationship between education and training, in this book we will use the term *education* to refer to the act of imparting knowledge, whereas *training* will be used to refer to the use of practice to bring a person to a target level of proficiency.

Since education sciences are already well established, this book will focus mainly on practical aspects related to cybersecurity training. Nevertheless, educational aspects will also be discussed as needed, since many of the cybersecurity training methodologies and platforms include education content, as well as rely on various instructional strategies in order to augment the information retention rate, or to improve trainee motivation, for example.

We note that a challenge in this context is how to design the overall cybersecurity educational program, and the general methodology proposed in [8] is a possible starting point for addressing this issue. Thus, the methodology integrates an educational framework based on institutional, user, and external dimensions, with a set of pedagogical methods based on learning type, learning level, and informal learning techniques, to provide a thorough but flexible design strategy.

As an indication of the wide variety of approaches that are currently used in the area of cybersecurity education and training, the *Computer Security Education Resource Collection* is a helpful source of information [6]. An important aspect of this collection is that each entry is tagged according to its characteristics, such as "CTF/contest," "curriculum content," "concept framework," or "pedagogical learning objectives," making it easy to determine the type of a resource at a glance.

We also note that, although we can assume that all nations consider cybersecurity capacity building to be of high priority, differences between countries were observed, mainly deriving from differences in economic development and the scale of Internet use [3]. Moreover, countries that had greater and lower levels of maturity in capacity building than expected only on the basis of their development and scale of Internet use were also identified in that study. This signifies that, in the long term, social and cultural differences must also be considered when designing cybersecurity education and training programs.

2.2 Cybersecurity Training Categories

We live in a network-centric society, with most people using IT systems on a regular basis—either in schools, for work, and also after retirement. Thus, ITU estimates that approximately 5.4 billion people, that is 67% of the world population, have used the Internet in 2023 [7]. This means that the current number of regular IT users is really huge. Moreover, they come from various societal backgrounds. Consequently, we can expect that the security-related knowledge and skills of regular IT users are relatively low in general.

The IT infrastructure itself is managed by professionals, who due to the nature of their work must possess at least a medium level of cybersecurity skills in order to be able to carry out their work-related tasks. In addition, a number of security experts make sure that the cybersecurity risks regarding the IT infrastructure are minimized. Such highly skilled experts are also called upon when the need to handle cybersecurity incidents arises.

When considering the need for cybersecurity education and training, it becomes obvious that participant background and skill level are important in determining the most suitable kind of training for a given type of participant. Thus, education and training activities can be broadly divided into two categories:

- Technical cybersecurity training.
- Cybersecurity awareness training.

The relationship that exists between participant type, their skill level, and the corresponding cybersecurity training category is illustrated in Fig. 2.1, and details on each category are provided in the following sections.

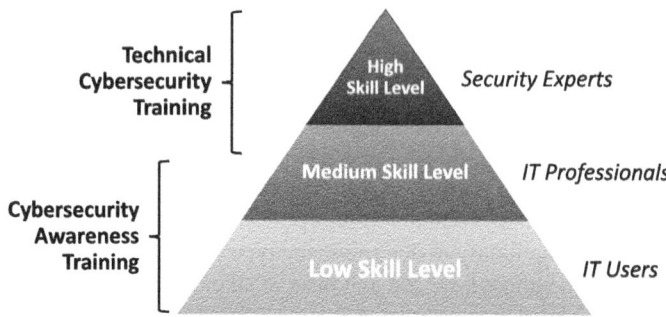

Fig. 2.1 Cybersecurity training approach dependency on participant background and skill level

2.2.1 Technical Cybersecurity Training

We use the term *technical cybersecurity training* to refer to that class of training activities that are aimed at improving the technical knowledge and abilities of high-to-medium skill level participants, such as security experts and IT professionals who are involved in security operations. The goal for this type of training is to make it possible for the trainees to handle efficiently the technical cybersecurity issues that they will encounter in real life.

Since technical security training is aimed at improving the technical skills of the participants, hands-on practice is often included in the training. For this purpose, trainees make use of training environments that are built specifically for cybersecurity training purposes, named cyber ranges. Therefore, conducting training activities is a challenging process, and important preparation is needed on the organizer side. This is the reason why training is not only a service that is provided by academia and commercial companies, but national governments are also getting involved.

For example, the U.S. Cybersecurity and Infrastructure Security Agency (CISA) supports the training and education of the cybersecurity workforce in the U.S. for many categories of personnel: federal employees, critical infrastructure operators, private-sector cybersecurity professionals, as well as the general public. This is achieved by making available a large selection of training exercises, including those that use virtual training environments [11].

From the perspective of an organization that wants to conduct training activities, or even to develop a training platform, it is important to note that the way in which the training environments are configured, and the actual content of the training depend on a series of conditions. These include, for example, issues such as what aspects of cybersecurity training are being targeted, what are the characteristics of target systems, or how motivated the trainees are, as it will be discussed next.

2.2.1.1 Training Aspects

The three aspects or facets of technical cybersecurity training are attack, forensics, and defense [2]. Attack training consists mainly in teaching *ethical hacking* or *penetration testing* (also called *pentesting*) techniques. Different from a malicious attack, pentesting is an authorized simulated cyberattack on an organization network conducted in order to assess the cybersecurity posture of that organization. Forensics training refers to learning the skills needed to investigate the consequences of cyberattacks, so that trainees which can determine relevant information, such as how an attack was started, what mechanisms were used, what assets were affected, and so on. As for defense training, it refers to making the trainees capable of protecting and defending a system from cyberattacks, both via the preliminary steps of securing the system, as well as by responding to an actual live attack.

We note that learning how to pentest also helps with the development of forensics skills. In addition, by leveraging the perspective of pentesters, trainees can deeply understand the practical mechanisms of cyberattacks—a steppingstone that makes it possible to later design and build defense mechanisms. It can be said, therefore, that pentesting training is an entry point for cybersecurity training, and this is the reason why security experts often start training via such activities.

A similar vision is shared by the author of *Network Security Assessment*, Chris McNab, who states that the best way to find out how to secure a network is "to attack it, using the same tactics attackers employ to identify and exploit weaknesses." The author proceeds then to demonstrate common security vulnerabilities, and the steps used to identify them by describing a methodology for performing network-based penetration testing in a structured manner [9].

More details about technical cybersecurity training will be provided in Chap. 3, with each specific training aspect being detailed in Chaps. 4 through 6.

2.2.1.2 Target System Characteristics

Technical cybersecurity training is usually conducted in relation with typical computer networks. In this case, the creation of the appropriate training environments is relatively straightforward in terms of the technologies to be used.

However, the advent of the Internet of Things (IoT) has led to a significant rise in security incidents related to IoT networks and technologies. Given that IoT devices and protocols have different characteristics compared to regular computers and network protocols, such as lack of displays, lower processing capabilities, and simplified features, creating an IoT security training platform poses different challenges. Consequently, such platforms need to consider the specificities of IoT systems, and new training methodologies and content must be developed.

Given the many issues related to IoT security training and the importance of the topic in the wider field of technical cybersecurity training, we will discuss in detail the methodologies for IoT security training in Chap. 7.

2.2.1.3   Trainee Motivation

Given that the target of technical cybersecurity training are mainly IT professionals who want to improve their skills, it is assumed, in general, that they are highly motivated to take part in the training activity. Consequently, instructors create the training content by focusing on the technical elements that are required to help participants acquire the desired skills.

However, not all trainees are equally motivated, and participants to some technical cybersecurity training programs can be young people who have just started taking an interest in cybersecurity. Therefore, in order to increase the motivation of such trainees, educators may create training content that balances the technical elements with other elements that will make it more fun to take part in the training activity. This is because motivated trainees are more willing to actively participate in the training, and also to return for future training activities.

A typical example in this context is the case of Capture The Flag (CTF) competitions. In CTFs, the technical aspects are split into small, focused tasks, and score tables and badges are introduced to keep the participants interested and motivated. The CTF type of training was popularized by the annual DEF CON cybersecurity conference, where it was first introduced in 1996 [5], but CTF events are currently being held in most countries and for a wide range of participants, including starting at elementary school level in some cases.

It is, therefore, obvious that the way in which the training content for technical cybersecurity training is created and how it is presented plays an important role in increasing trainee motivation. The various challenges regarding content creation will be discussed in more detail in Chap. 9, in particular in Sect. 9.2.

2.2.2   Cybersecurity Awareness Training

The wide public of regular IT users, as well as those IT professionals who do not require security skills, are not in need of technical cybersecurity knowledge and skills. Instead, they must acquire basic knowledge about IT and security, which is sometimes called *IT security literacy* to emphasize its importance in the modern society. Such knowledge and skills enable IT users to handle correctly any cybersecurity issues they may encounter during their typical use of IT technology.

Given how wide the public to which this type of education is addressed is, national governments have taken steps to ensure that such training takes place at the needed scale and with the necessary scope for it to be effective. For example, the U.S. Congress has introduced in 2021 the *American Cybersecurity Literacy Act*, which requires the administration to develop and conduct a cybersecurity literacy campaign with the goal of increasing the knowledge and awareness of the best practices needed to reduce cybersecurity risks [10].

In this book, we will use the term *cybersecurity awareness training* to refer to that class of training activities that focus on providing the basic knowledge and abilities to medium-to-low skill level participants, such as regular IT users and those IT professionals that are not directly involved in security tasks. The goal of this type of training is to minimize the cybersecurity risks that the trainees will have to face during their daily life and work activities.

Given the difference in training methodology and target learners compared to technical cybersecurity training, cybersecurity awareness training faces additional challenges in regard to training content creation and trainee motivation.

2.2.2.1 Training Content Creation

Typically, the content of cybersecurity awareness training courses is created manually by educators, who try to include materials about all the areas of knowledge that they consider the training should cover. The creation is, therefore, a time-consuming process that also leads to the possibility of having outdated content. This can happen, for example, due to the evolution of security concepts, the appearance of new security issues, and so on. In particular, the fact that manually created training content is potentially updated only rarely can become a serious issue in the quickly evolving field of cybersecurity.

Automating the creation of training content is a potential solution for this issue. For example, Natural Language Generation (NLG) techniques could be employed to automatically generate the training content based on various knowledge bases, such as publicly available data from Wikipedia. Such automatic generation comes with several challenges about the quality of the generated training content. However, these challenges can be addressed by leveraging the recent advances in the NLG field, such as Large Language Models (LLMs).

2.2.2.2 Trainee Motivation

We have mentioned already that trainee motivation issues can occur for technical cybersecurity training. However, regular IT users are typically even less motivated than technical personnel when conducting training. This is because cybersecurity awareness training courses can be perceived as an unnecessary burden added to the normal work tasks of the trainees, especially when taking the courses is mandated by their organization.

Various approaches can be used to make the training activity more attractive and effective, and one such possibility is the *serious game* approach. Serious games are a type of games that incorporate pedagogic elements, and that are not intended to be played primarily for amusement purposes. Whereas the concept of serious games has been initially introduced in the context of role-playing in the 1970s [4], it has been since extended to computer games as well. By using the process called *gamification* to incorporate game elements into cybersecurity awareness training, it becomes possible to increase the motivation of the learners; improvements in the retention rate are also to be expected.

Moreover, the automatic content generation mentioned above also makes it possible to create training content that is more attractive than the manually generated one. For example, game-like components, such as crossword puzzles, can be introduced into the training as an addition to or replacement of the typical quizzes that are used in IT literacy training. Consequently, automatic training content generation as well has the potential of making the overall cybersecurity awareness training process more enjoyable.

More details about cybersecurity awareness training methodologies, including specific approaches for increasing trainee motivation, will be provided in Chap. 8, where a related case study will also be discussed.

2.2.3 Training Category Comparison

Before proceeding to the in-depth discussion in subsequent chapters of the various aspects related to technical cybersecurity training and cybersecurity awareness training, we will compare here the fundamental properties of these two methodologies. Table 2.1 summarizes this comparison, which we conducted from several perspectives, as follows:

- Target audience: Who is the training addressed to?
- Training method: How is the training conducted?
- Main challenge: The most significant issue regarding that training category.

2.2.3.1 Target Audience

Regarding the target audience of the two types of training, while security experts and regular IT users are the obvious targets for technical cybersecurity training and

Table 2.1 Comparison of technical cybersecurity training and cybersecurity awareness training

Feature	Technical training	Awareness training
Target audience	Security experts, IT professionals with security involvement	Regular IT users, IT professionals without security involvement
Training method	Hands-on training that is conducted either on-site or online	E-learning (with quizzes), video training, reading materials, etc.
Main challenge	Create technical content suited for the participants to learn the target skills	Ensure that participants are motivated and can apply the knowledge in real life

cybersecurity awareness training, respectively, IT professionals can benefit of both types of training, depending on what is the scope of their work.

On the one hand, those IT professionals who are also involved with security issues, as it often happens in smaller companies, for example, should make sure to take technical cybersecurity training courses. On the other hand, those IT professionals who have no security involvement, as it may happen in larger companies, where the separation of professional roles is stronger, can limit themselves to taking cybersecurity awareness training courses only, even though they could also benefit from technical training.

2.2.3.2 Training Method

Technical cybersecurity training focuses on teaching skills; hence, it is conducted via hands-on activities in which participants can exercise their existing skills and learn new ones via solving practical problems. These hands-on activities can be conducted on-site, in which case the educators and staff can be involved more closely in the training process, assisting the participants as needed. Alternatively, the hands-on activities can also be conducted online when the focus is more on self-learning via the tasks included in the training.

Currently, cybersecurity awareness training is often conducted via e-learning methods that typically include quizzes to evaluate participants' knowledge and to determine if they have achieved a passing score or need to repeat the training. However, video training or even just reading materials are also used sometimes, which was the initial manner in which cybersecurity awareness training was conducted. Moreover, such training methods are easier to manage and deliver. Nevertheless, this type of passive activities has a lower engagement of the participants and does not allow for evaluating their knowledge.

2.2.3.3 Main Challenge

Each training category has its own specific challenges that we will discuss in more detail in the following chapters. For the purpose of this comparison, however, we will focus on what we consider to be the main challenge instructors are faced with in each case.

Thus, for the case of technical cybersecurity training, content creation is the biggest challenge from our point of view due to two main issues. First of all, the complexity of the technical training content hinders automation, and content creation itself is done manually by educators/instructors; hence, it is a tedious process that requires creators to master a significant amount of knowledge and skills. Furthermore, malware and security threats evolve rapidly, meaning that new content needs to be created relatively frequently in order to be able to train additional skills that are applicable to current security issues.

As for cybersecurity awareness training, content creation typically requires simply writing explanation text and creating visual aids, hence no technical knowledge is required. This also means that content can be updated, if needed, with relatively less effort. Moreover, automated content generation techniques can be used to create and update the content with limited human intervention. However, while security experts are usually motivated to learn new skills, regular IT users often perceive awareness training as uninteresting, especially if it is a work-mandated type of training. Therefore, we consider that the main challenge in the case of cybersecurity awareness training is to create such training content and organize such training activities that keep the participants interested and motivated. In addition, the new knowledge that is gained via the training activity must be structured in such a manner that it is readily applicable to practical situations.

References

1. Austin G (ed) (2020) Cyber security education: principles and policies. Routledge, London
2. Beuran R, Chinen K, Tan Y, Shinoda Y (2016) Towards effective cybersecurity education and training. Tech. Rep. IS-RR-2016-003, Japan Advanced Institute of Science and Technology
3. Creese S, Dutton WH, Esteve-González P (2021) The social and cultural shaping of cybersecurity capacity building: a comparative study of nations and regions. Pers Ubiq Comput 25(5):941–955. https://doi.org/10.1007/s00779-021-01569-6
4. Cruz-Cunha MM (2012) Handbook of research on serious games as educational. Business and research tools. IGI Global, Hershey
5. DEF CON Cybersecurity Conference: DEF CON website. https://defcon.org/. Accessed 1 July 2024
6. Denning T (2024) Computer security education resource collection. https://securityeducationresourcecollection.net/. Accessed 1 July 2024
7. International Telecommunication Union, Telecommunication Development Sector (ITU-D): ITU-D ICT statistics. https://www.itu.int/en/ITU-D/Statistics/Pages/stat/default.aspx. Accessed 1 July 2024
8. Kim E, Beuran R (2018) On designing a cybersecurity educational program for higher education. In: Proceedings of the 10th international conference on education technology and computers, pp 195–200. https://doi.org/10.1145/3290511.3290524
9. McNab C (2016) Network security assessment, 3rd edn. O'Reilly Media Inc, Sebastopol
10. U.S. Congress: American cybersecurity literacy act. https://www.congress.gov/bill/117th-congress/house-bill/4055. Accessed 1 July 2024
11. U.S. Cybersecurity and Infrastructure Security Agency (CISA): Cybersecurity training & exercises. https://www.cisa.gov/cybersecurity-training-exercises. Accessed 1 July 2024

Chapter 3
Technical Cybersecurity Training

This chapter discusses technical cybersecurity training from several perspectives. First, we define a taxonomy for cybersecurity training programs that is based on training purpose, training approach, and other features. We also discuss several frameworks in relation with cybersecurity workforce skills. Then, the effectiveness of training programs is analyzed in terms of relevant requirements and necessary implementation features. Lastly, we present the Hardening Project competition as a case study of applying our training taxonomy in practice.

3.1 Technical Cybersecurity Training Taxonomy

Technical cybersecurity training is a complex activity, and many methodologies and combinations thereof are used, depending on the goal of a particular activity. Therefore, our presentation will begin by detailing a taxonomy of the methodologies currently used in technical cybersecurity training. The taxonomy will be based on the following three aspects:

- Training purpose: What is the goal of the training in terms of the knowledge and skill set to be acquired?
- Training approach: What methods and techniques are used when conducting the training activities?
- Other features: Various other features that can be used to provide a more comprehensive view on a training activity.

3.1.1 Training Purpose

Real-world security incidents typically start with the exploitation of a software vulnerability, which represents the attack vector of the incident. Once the attack is detected, it is analyzed to understand its mechanisms, which makes it possible for security experts to design defense mechanisms. Finally, during the incident response phase, those defense mechanisms must be implemented, so that the attack is countered; on longer term, this can also include actions such as patching the software vulnerability, so that it cannot be exploited again.

This pattern of actions related to security incidents leads us to define three main forms of cybersecurity training:

1. Attack training: Give trainees the experience of recreating vulnerability exploitation techniques by including activities such as penetration testing, which make use of the same tools and methodologies that attackers employ.
2. Forensics training: Cultivate in trainees a deeper understanding of the phenomena related to vulnerability exploitation and patching, including in relation with the identification of targeted attack campaigns, etc.
3. Defense training: Focus on the design and implementation of attack prevention mechanism, such as vulnerability protection, in order to prevent cyberattacks.

The three forms of technical cybersecurity training above are not mutually exclusive, and it is only through their combination that cybersecurity personnel can achieve the state of *readiness* that is required to make it possible to handle effectively and in a timely manner security incidents. The relationship between the phases of real-world cybersecurity incidents and the forms of training activities based on their purpose is depicted in Fig. 3.1. More details about each training form will be provided in Chaps. 4 through 6.

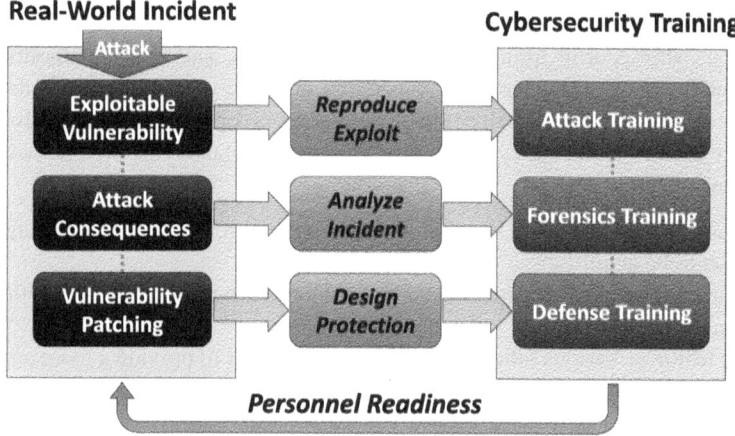

Fig. 3.1 Relationship between real-world cybersecurity incident phases and forms of training depending on the purpose of the training activity

3.1.2 Training Approach

Another perspective on technical cybersecurity training can be had by considering what is the particular approach used for the associated hands-on activities. The target trainee skills are perhaps the most important guiding factors when designing a technical cybersecurity training activity. Consequently, we will use the skill perspective to discuss several aspects that we consider to be the defining elements of every technical cybersecurity training approach, as follows:

- Content type: The kind of content used during the training.
- Environment type: The kind of environment used during the training.
- Training cost: The cost of organizing and providing the training.

In what follows, we will first examine the range of skills related to cybersecurity. Then, we will analyze the aforementioned aspects, and their influence on the approaches used in cybersecurity training activities contingent upon the skills that those activities are targeting.

3.1.2.1 Cybersecurity Skills

The type of training approach that is used in a cybersecurity training activity is very much related to the kind of skills a given training program aims to develop in the trainees. Therefore, let us consider the three types of cybersecurity skills (for a more detailed discussion of cybersecurity skills, see Sect. 3.2):

- Individual skills: Standalone cybersecurity techniques.
- Team skills: Abilities needed to become part of an effective cybersecurity team.
- CSIRT skills: Advanced team skills needed for the adequate operation of a Computer Security Incident Response Team (CSIRT).

Individual Skills Being able to solve security issues requires first of all mastering a series of fundamental standalone cybersecurity techniques. When individual skills are targeted, then the goal of the training activity is to teach trainees how to conduct basic cybersecurity activities, such as network sniffing, vulnerability scanning, and password cracking.

Team Skills The handling of cybersecurity incidents is often done in teams, because the wide area of potential security issues means that cybersecurity professionals have most of the expertise in specific areas, such as web application development and firewalls; and system and network administration.

Since team members work together on a common problem, in addition to basic technical skills, they must also be able to communicate about the issues in their specific area, and to cooperate in order to solve that common problem. Therefore, soft skills, such as communication and cooperation, are needed in order to build an effective cybersecurity team.

CSIRT Skills A CSIRT is a group of experts put together in a large organization with the purpose of handling cybersecurity incidents in a comprehensive and holistic manner. Members of a CSIRT must, therefore, be able take part in more advanced activities, as needed in order to solve the incident. This includes, for example, the deployment of external resources for solving the issues (e.g., via the outsourcing of aspects that cannot be handled within the organization), dealing with the possibility of attack escalations activities that can worsen the consequences of the attack, managing issues related to the supply chain for that particular organization, etc.

Consequently, in order to prepare trainees to become part of a CSIRT, the training activity must allow them to practice and develop a wide range of advanced team skills, as those mentioned above. Only in this manner, it becomes possible to get them ready to be effective CSIRT members that are able to handle the specific tasks that are required in this context.

3.1.2.2   Content Type

When targeting individual skills, then training activities that are based on simple tasks, such answering questions or solving basic problems, are most of the time sufficient. For example, the trainees may be asked to determine information about computers (e.g., IP address), to analyze network packet traces, to determine the vulnerabilities of a host, etc.

However, for team skill training more complex and realistic scenarios are required, that ask trainees with different backgrounds (or different roles in the training scenario) to solve a problem together.

Finally, when targeting CSIRT skills, training activities should be based on *continuous scenarios* in which team members are faced with conditions that evolve continuously and to which they have to react by communicating with staff that is not part of the team (e.g., reporting the incident to organization leaders, outsourcing forensics to external parties, etc.). This type of scenario represents the most realistic type of training activity, that ensures participants will be able to handle security incidents in the real world.

3.1.2.3   Environment Type

The other important characteristic of a training activity is the type of environment used therein. The most basic type of training environment for cybersecurity purposes is a desktop computer, on which the trainees conduct all their training. Because of its simplicity, this is one of the most often used types of training environment for individual skills.

On the other hand, by utilizing virtualization technologies, it is possible to construct training environments that are built of multiple Virtual Machines (VMs). In addition, by using more and more realistic settings for the VMs and the network topology they form, it is possible to reproduce in detail actual computer and network topology settings. Such elaborate training environments make it possible to train more advanced skills in more complex scenarios. As the realism of the training environment increases, so does the effectiveness of the training, as the trainees are placed in situations similar to real-world incidents; hence, the skills they develop will be readily applicable in real life.

3.1.2.4 Training Cost

While not an intrinsic characteristic of a training activity, it is obvious that increasing the complexity of the training environment leads to cost increases, as equipment and environment setup costs become larger. This is the reason why most training activities are conducted on one computer, typically provided by the trainees, as this is the least expensive solution.

For more advanced forms of training, which are conducted in more complex environments, the costs naturally increase, thus creating a barrier to entry for participants. As a side comment, training environment setup currently requires advanced security knowledge and a significant amount of manual configuration; this leads to the fact that for really complex training environments the setup cost may actually exceed the equipment cost, especially in the long term.

3.1.2.5 Training Approach Analysis

There is a strong relationship between the target skills of a training activity, and the various training aspects and design elements that need to be incorporated into it in terms of training scenarios and environment types, and these choices affect the training cost. This relationship is summarized in Fig. 3.2.

Finding the most suitable combination of design elements for a training activity basically requires a trade-off between the realism of the training and its cost, given a certain set of target skills. For individual skill training, scenarios based on problems and questions are sufficient in most cases, and a desktop-based training environment can typically be used to implement such scenarios. Consequently, the training cost will be relatively low.

When moving toward targeting team skills, the complexity of the training scenarios must be increased to make them more realistic, and the complexity of the training environment will increase accordingly, for example, through the use of basic VM environments or even more complex virtual network environments. This will also drive up the cost of the training activity, as setup becomes more difficult.

Finally, for training CSIRT skills, complex continuous scenarios are required, which can only be put into practice through the use of network emulation techniques, or real network environments. The costs associated with setting up such environments, including the development and run-time support of the appropriate scenarios, are high, as expected. Network emulation is a powerful technique in this

Fig. 3.2 Relationship between the various characteristics of technical cybersecurity training: target skills, content type, environment type and training cost

context, since its hybrid approach makes it possible to create realistic environments, while lowering the deployment costs (see [1] for an introduction to this topic).

3.1.3 Training Characteristics

In addition to training purpose and training approach, there are several other characteristics of technical training activities that we consider important for fully defining a certain cybersecurity training program, as follows:

- Target participants: Who is the program mostly addressed to?
- Prerequisite ability: What is the expected ability level of the target participants?
- Barriers to entry: Is training participation subject to restrictions?
- Training frequency: What is the frequency of the training events?

3.1.3.1 Target Participants

The way in which a cybersecurity training program is designed depends strongly on the type of participants that it is mainly addressed to. By considering the background of the trainees, one can ensure that they benefit as much as possible from the training.

For example, some training programs are targeted at students and should take into account their initial lack of skills, whereas other programs are mainly targeted at professionals, for whom honing their already existing skills is the main goal, hence the training content should be more challenging.

3.1.3.2 Prerequisite Ability

Somewhat related to the type of the target participants is their expected ability level. This influences, for instance, the manner in which the instructors design training content, as content that is too easy or too difficult compared to the ability level of the participants decreases their motivation.

Even within a certain class of participants, let us say university students, it may be advantageous to assess their skill level on an individual basis. Then, the participants can be split into groups, for example, beginner, medium, and advanced, so that the content can be tailored accordingly.

3.1.3.3 Barriers to Entry

When differentiating between cybersecurity training programs, it is useful to know whether participation to the program is subject to any barriers to entry. There can be many kinds of restrictions, such as age limitations (for example, only participants under 25 years old can attend), any type of membership requirements, etc.

Financial cost as well can be considered a potential barrier to entry, since expensive training programs are more difficult to attend, especially if the trainees must bear the cost themselves. Therefore, lowering the cost of training programs can be considered as an important objective for organizers.

3.1.3.4 Training Frequency

Another characteristic of cybersecurity training programs is the frequency of the training events or sessions that are held. Most training programs, especially those organized on-site, take place according to a predefined schedule, being held, for example, several times a year.

Some training programs, however, can be held on demand. This is the case for most online programs, but it can also happen when an organizing institution offers an on-demand training service to its customers. The training frequency of a program determines the number of opportunities participants have for taking that program, hence, its availability.

3.1.4   Theoretical Training

In this book, we use the term technical cybersecurity training to refer mainly to those training activities that include hands-on aspects. However, for the sake of completeness, we will discuss here some approaches to cybersecurity education and training that focus on knowledge, as opposed to the practical skills gained through hands-on training.

While we consider theoretical training to be mostly outside the scope of this book, we deem it to be a very important aspect of cybersecurity education, that complements the practical training activities, hence it needs to be discussed at least briefly. In particular, the two such types of theoretical cybersecurity training that we will examine are the following:

- Online courses.
- Tabletop exercises.

3.1.4.1   Online Courses

The online courses in this area are typically introductory courses that present the basic concepts regarding cybersecurity. Usually, they are considered as the first step toward becoming a cybersecurity professional, with more practice-oriented training following in the later years.

One example in this category is the course entitled *Foundations of Cybersecurity* that is available on the Coursera platform [3]. The course content is implemented by Google as the first part of the *Google Cybersecurity Professional Certificate* course series. There are four modules in the course, starting with an introduction to the world of cybersecurity, followed by information about the evolution of cybersecurity, and how to protect systems against threats, risks, and vulnerabilities. The last module covers cybersecurity tools and programming languages. The course consists of videos, reading materials, videos, quizzes, and discussion prompts, and it is provided in an instructor-led manner. The estimated completion duration is approximately 20 h.

In addition to the aforementioned course, the *Google Cybersecurity Professional Certificate* course series available on Coursera includes seven other courses, many of them having more practical content, such as how to use Linux commands to manage the file system, or how to automate cybersecurity tasks using Python [4].

3.1.4.2   Tabletop Exercises

One disadvantage of online courses is that learners' involvement is relatively low, as they are mostly passively receiving information, with occasional quizzes to check knowledge retention. As a way to address this issue, another type of theoretical training that became popular in the area of cybersecurity is tabletop training. A tabletop exercise consists of a discussion-based training session in which the participants discuss their roles and responses in a given situation or scenario, such as cybersecurity incident response.

The tabletop approach makes it possible to involve the trainees actively, for instance in the decision process needed to solve the challenges presented during the training. Nevertheless, tabletop exercises do not have built-in learning features, nor do they include technical hands-on exercises. Therefore, they are mostly useful once other forms of education and training have been completed, such as related cybersecurity education courses available in universities or online.

As an example, tabletop training is being promoted by the U.S. Cybersecurity and Infrastructure Security Agency (CISA) as an effective way to conduct planning exercises on a wide range of threat scenarios. For this purpose, CISA makes available more than 100 tabletop exercise packages that include all the resources needed for stakeholders to be able to conduct exercises by themselves. The threat vector scenarios cover several important cybersecurity areas, such as ransomware, insider threats, phishing, and so on [11].

3.2 Cybersecurity Skill Overview

While cybersecurity skills can be classified broadly into individual, team, and CSIRT skills, as mentioned in Sect. 3.1.2.1, a more precise categorization is required in order to be able to define what specific skills a training program should address. Such categorizations are included in frameworks related to the cybersecurity workforce and skills, as it will be detailed next.

3.2.1 Workforce and Skill Frameworks

Organizations in various countries have proposed frameworks which specify the skills and knowledge that are relevant for various cybersecurity tasks, known as *workforce frameworks* or *skill frameworks*. In what follows, we briefly introduce the most well-known frameworks of this kind.

3.2.1.1 NICE Framework

The U.S. NIST Workforce Framework for Cybersecurity (NICE Framework) is a framework that provides the building blocks needed to describe the Tasks, Knowledge, and Skills (TKS) that are needed to perform cybersecurity work by individuals or teams [10]. Organizations can use these building blocks to develop their cybersecurity workforces. In addition, learners can use them to explore various cybersecurity domains and to engage in learning activities for developing their capabilities. The main elements of the NICE Framework will be described next based on v1.0.0 of the framework released in March 2024.

Work Role Categories Conceptually, at the top level of the NICE Framework lie the work role categories, which are used to classify the possible work roles in the cybersecurity domain. In particular, a total of seven categories are defined, as follows:

1. Oversight and Governance.
2. Design and Development.
3. Implementation and Operation.
4. Protection and Defense.
5. Investigation.
6. Cyberspace Intelligence.
7. Cyberspace Effects.

Work Roles For each of the above work role categories, a series of concrete work roles are specified in the framework, for a total of 52 work roles. For example, the work roles in the *Protection and Defense* category are:

- Defensive Cybersecurity.
- Digital Forensics.
- Incident Response.
- Infrastructure Support.
- Insider Threat Analysis.
- Threat Analysis.
- Vulnerability Analysis.

Tasks, Knowledge, and Skills At the lowest level of the NICE Framework are its building blocks, which are tasks, knowledge, and skills statements (2280 in total):

- Task Statements: Descriptions of cybersecurity actions that are to be accomplished by professionals (1084).
- Knowledge Statements: Descriptions of the understanding needed to be able to complete the associated task (640).
- Skills Statements: Descriptions of the skills that must be demonstrated in order to be able to complete the associated task (556).

An essential aspect of the NICE Framework is the list of associations provided between each work role and a set of task, knowledge, and skill statements that are relevant for that particular work role.

Competency Areas Competencies represent mechanisms by which organizations are able to assess learners. The framework defines a set of 11 such areas, which represent clusters of related knowledge and skill statements that correlate with the capabilities of a person to perform the tasks that are required in a given cybersecurity domain. For example, the *Operating Systems (OS) Security* competency area is defined as follows [10]:

This Competency Area describes a learner's capabilities to install, administer, troubleshoot, backup, and conduct recovery of Operating Systems (OS), including in simulated environments.

3.2.1.2 ECSF Framework

The European Cybersecurity Skills Framework (ECSF) is a framework created by the European Union Agency for Cybersecurity (ENISA) [5]. We will provide an overview of this framework below by referring to ECSF v1, which was published in October 2022.

Role Profiles ECSF defines a total of 12 cybersecurity role profiles that represent the possible work roles in this domain, as follows:

1. Chief Information Security Officer (CISO).
2. Cyber Incident Responder.
3. Cyber Legal, Policy & Compliance Officer.
4. Cyber Threat Intelligence Specialist.
5. Cybersecurity Architect.
6. Cybersecurity Auditor.
7. Cybersecurity Educator.
8. Cybersecurity Implementer.
9. Cybersecurity Researcher.
10. Cybersecurity Risk Manager.
11. Digital Forensics Investigator.
12. Penetration Tester.

Tasks, Knowledge, and Skills ECSF also specifies a set of tasks, knowledge, and skills (275 in total), as follows:

- Task statements: Descriptions of relevant tasks (125).
- Knowledge statements: Descriptions of required knowledge (67).
- Skill statements: Descriptions of required skills (83).

Each task, knowledge, and skill statement is associated with one or more of the previously defined role profiles. However, no direct correspondence between the task, knowledge, and skill statements themselves seems to be included, as it is done in the NICE Framework.

E-Competences E-competences are those competencies that professionals matching a given role profile must have, and they are classified into five categories: *Plan*, *Build*, *Run*, *Enable*, and *Manage*. Each e-competence category includes a number of e-competences (41 in total), such as the following ones for the *Build* category:

- Application Development.
- Component Integration.
- Testing.

- Solution Deployment.
- Documentation Production.
- ICT Systems Engineering.

For each e-competence, the level that is required for a given role profile is specified on a scale from 1 to 5. For example, for the *Build* category mentioned above, the role *Cyber Incident Responder* requires a level 2 e-competence for *Component Integration*, and level 3 e-competences for *Testing* and *Documentation Production*.

Deliverables Deliverables are high-level outcomes that a professional with a given role profile must produce, with a total of 22 deliverables being specified. For example, for the CISO role profile, ECSF defines the following two deliverables, *Cybersecurity Strategy* and *Cybersecurity Policy*.

3.2.1.3   SecBoK Framework

Security Body of Knowledge (SecBoK) is a framework created by the Japan Network Security Association that specifies the required knowledge and skills for a series of cybersecurity work roles [7]. The latest version, released in May 2021, aims to shift the focus of the framework from simple skill development to achieving a coordination between skills, tasks, and roles. The description we provide below is based on this latest version, also referred to as SecBoK 2021.

Work Roles SecBoK 2021 defines a total of 16 work roles in connection with cybersecurity, as follows:

1. Chief Information Security Officer (CISO).
2. Point of Contact (POC).
3. Notification.
4. Commander/Triage.
5. Incident Manager/Incident Handler.
6. Curator.
7. Researcher.
8. Self-assessment/Solution Analyst.
9. Vulnerability Diagnostician.
10. Education/Public Awareness.
11. Forensic Engineer.
12. Investigator.
13. Legal Advisor.
14. IT Planning Department.
15. IT Systems Department.
16. Information Security Auditor.

We note that SecBoK 2021 also includes a mapping of the work roles it specifies into the work roles defined in the NICE Framework.

Human Resources Skill Map The core of SecBoK is represented by the human resources skill map, which establishes the relationship between knowledge, skills and abilities, and the work roles mentioned above. The total number of knowledge, skill and ability items is 1145, with the most notable aspects in the skill map regarding these items being as follows:

- The knowledge domain and subdomain an item belongs to are indicated, with 18 knowledge domains being defined; for some items, even a knowledge sub-subdomain is specified.
- The required work experience level for mastering a particular knowledge or skill item is defined, with the following possible values:

  - Low: Can be handled even with less than 3 years of experience.
  - Medium: Requires more than 3 years of experience or related training.
  - High: Requires more than 10 years of experience or advanced training.
  - Pending: Items related to information gathering and intelligence that are not subject to level assignment at this time.

- The required knowledge, skill, or ability for a particular role is specified via three possible choices, each being assigned a numerical code:

  - Prerequisite (1): Knowledge and skills considered as a premise for being able to perform that role.
  - Required (2): Knowledge and skills required to actually perform that role.
  - Reference (0.5): Knowledge and skills that are not required to perform that role, but are desirable.

Regarding the relationship between the *prerequisite* and *required* labels mentioned above, it is mentioned in SecBoK that if an organization can secure personnel having the prerequisite skills and provides them with education and training regarding the required skills, then it can be considered that the personnel will be able to handle their role in a satisfactory manner.

3.2.2 Cybersecurity Skill Analysis

In what follows, we will first compare the discussed workforce and skill frameworks, and then provide suggestions on how the target skills of a given cybersecurity training program can be evaluated based on such frameworks.

3.2.2.1 Framework Comparison

In order to compare the three frameworks that we have introduced, we will look at their main elements, as follows:

Work Roles The NICE Framework defines the largest amount of work roles, 52, which means its level of detail is much higher compared to the 12 role profiles in ECSF, and the 16 work roles in SecBoK. While some correspondence can be established between the work roles defined in each of the three frameworks, as it is done between SecBoK and NICE, it appears that no complete consensus can be reached, as there are a number of conceptual differences between them.

TKS Statements The NICE Framework also defines the largest amount of TKS statements, 2280 in total, followed by SecBoK with a total of 1145 statements (although no tasks are included). The lowest number appears in ECSF, only 275 in total, meaning that those statements are made at a relatively higher abstraction level. Nevertheless, it can be said that all the three frameworks have a reasonable amount of TKS statements in relation with the number of work roles they define. Although the ratio of statements over roles is relatively high for SecBoK, we reiterate that no tasks are defined in that framework, which includes ability statements, however.

Competencies For competencies, ECSF has the largest number, with a total of 41 e-competences, followed by SecBoK with 18 knowledge domains. There are only 11 competencies defined in the NICE Framework. It is also important to note that ECSF associates a competency level to the e-competences it specifies, which is not done for the other frameworks.

Specific Elements Even though the three frameworks we discussed have many elements in common, there are several specific aspects that differentiate them even further, such as

- Deliverables are a specific element of ECSF, corresponding to high-level outcomes that are not considered in NICE and SecBoK, but that can be useful from a cybersecurity education and training perspective.
- SecBoK defines required work experience levels for each knowledge, skill and ability item, which provides an estimate about how much effort is required to master that particular item.
- When mapping knowledge, skill and ability item to work roles, SecBoK also defines whether that item is prerequisite, required, or desirable for that role, a very useful piece of information for making training-related decisions.

3.2.2.2   Target Skill Evaluation

Each of the three frameworks we presented was conceived with a certain goal in mind; therefore, despite their similarities, there are several differences regarding their scope, not to mention the use of different naming conventions. Consequently, we suggest learners focus on the framework that is most suitable for the geographic area in which the training activity takes place, or in which the job position they aim for is located. The corresponding skill classification can then be used to make various decisions about training programs and platforms, as we will discuss next.

Let us consider first the case of a potential learner who needs to decide whether a given training program is suitable for them or not. By checking which of the skills associated with their current or intended work role can be acquired or improved via the program, they can determine if that program is indeed appropriate. Note that several of the existing cyber range platforms provide information about the coverage of their exercises with respect to a workforce framework such as the NICE Framework, as it will be seen in Chap. 11.

Another possible scenario is when a training organization needs to decide what kind of training content to create. In that case, by starting from the work roles of the target participants, the organization can develop training content that covers as many as possible of the TKS statements corresponding to those target work roles. We consider that similar strategies can be used in many other situations, which makes the workforce and skill frameworks we discussed a very practical tool for cybersecurity education and training.

In this context, we would also like to mention the Cybersecurity Skills Alliance REWIRE project that aims to develop a blueprint for the cybersecurity industry and a concrete European cybersecurity skills strategy [6]. The still-ongoing project is expected to end in October 2024, when all its deliverables will become available, providing a wealth of relevant information, with the deliverables of *WP3: Design of the European Cybersecurity Blueprint* being of particular interest in our opinion.

3.3 Training Effectiveness

As we have seen so far, there are many approaches to cybersecurity training, each with its different characteristics. This begs the question of how to determine the effectiveness of a particular training approach or training program, as well as how to improve this effectiveness, which we will investigate below.

3.3.1 Effectiveness Requirements

The taxonomy of technical cybersecurity training that we discussed so far, as well as the more detailed comparative analysis of a diversity of training programs presented in [2], makes it possible to formulate a series of requirements that must be met in order to ensure the effectiveness of the training activity. Thus, in order for a training program to be effective, we consider that it must satisfy the following conditions:

1. The difficulty of the training content should match the target audience in terms of knowledge and ability levels.
2. The training content should be created in accordance with the skills that the program aims to develop.

3. The training program should use hands-on activities for developing practical skills, thus ensuring that trainees can handle real-life security issues.
4. The training program should reach as large an audience as possible in order to have a significant impact on the cybersecurity readiness of the workforce.
5. The training program should have good cost/performance characteristics, leading to long-term sustainability.

Deciding whether one of the above requirements is met or not is not necessarily straightforward, but for some of them objective decisions can be made relatively easily. For instance, training content can be considered effective (requirement #2) if it provides learners with the opportunity to practice all the skills and validate all the knowledge required in connection with a given training goal. To determine what these skills and knowledge are, a workforce framework such as those discussed in Sect. 3.2.1 can be used as reference.

3.3.2 Necessary Implementation Features

Although there are various ways to ensure that the above requirements are met in practice, we note that they all refer to two key aspects of any cybersecurity training program, namely the training content used in that program, and the hands-on activities that are included in it.

Therefore, in terms of practical implementation, the above requirements can be converted into two necessary features for the creation of an effective technical cybersecurity training platform:

1. Ability to easily modify the training content and to add new content.
2. Ability to automatically create and manage the training environment.

3.3.2.1 Training Content Aspects

The first necessary feature that we identified—easy modification and addition of training content—addresses the need for producing content that is suitable for the training audience and the target skills of the program.

Such an ability would solve an issue that many current training programs have in common, namely that training content, such as training activity description, questions and answers, or related training environment configurations, is fundamentally hard coded within the training activity. This implies that training organizers cannot easily adapt the content to match the actual circumstances of a given event, such as trainee background and level, or to add variation to the included tasks. Moreover, they cannot easily add new training content into the platform, for instance, in order to extend an existing activity so as to address emergent security issues, etc.

3.3.2.2 Training Environment Aspects

As for the second necessary feature—automatic creation and management of the training environment—it addresses the need for hands-on training activities that are organized and conducted in manner that is scalable and cost-effective.

This ability aims to solve the other significant issue of many training programs, namely that the training environment is predominantly set up by experts, either via manual settings or by using custom or proprietary scripts and tools. This drawback impacts the scalability of the program, hence its ability to address a large audience, and also leads to poor cost/performance characteristics.

3.3.2.3 Content and Environment Dependencies

We note that the training content and the training environment are interdependent. This is because for an instructor to be able to add new training content, typically the training environment must be updated as well. This is also true in the opposite direction: when a training environment gets updated (e.g., via software package or operating system updates), the training content may need to be modified as well to match the characteristics of the training environment.

Consequently, the facilitation and automation of both update tasks play a crucial role regarding the usability of a training platform. In Chap. 12, we will discuss the approach we have taken to address these requirements in practice when developing the integrated cybersecurity training framework CyTrONE.

3.4 Case Study: Hardening Project

There are many examples of cybersecurity training programs that target individual skills since most CTF competitions are included in this category. Therefore, in this section we will conduct a case study analysis from the perspective of the taxonomy discussed so far by focusing on a program that targets team and CSIRT skills, namely Hardening Project.

3.4.1 Program Overview

Hardening Project is a two-day training event organized by the Web Application Security (WAS) Forum in Japan starting from 2012 [12]. This training activity in the form of a cybersecurity competition is being held twice a year, and its main goal is to maximize the strength of the defensive cybersecurity techniques of its participants. This led to name of the event, since in the field of cybersecurity, the term *hardening* denotes the process of securing a system by reducing its vulnerability surface.

3.4.1.1 Organization and Infrastructure

The attendees of Hardening Project are divided by the event organizers into several teams before the competition starts, typically based on their self-declared skills, as well as their previous experience with this competition (or lack thereof). This differs from regular CTF events in which the participants form their own teams in advance, and creates additional challenges in term of the soft skills the participants must put into use during the event.

As for the training content, Hardening Project recreates a very realistic scenario, which could very easily be encountered in the real world. Thus, the participants are tasked with dealing with security incidents and patching vulnerabilities of a virtual e-commerce website created for the purpose of the event—all these being skills that are readily applicable to real-life situations. Those security incidents are caused by red teams composed of event staff members who try to exploit vulnerabilities that were planted on purpose when the training environment was created.

The training environment built for the Hardening Project hands-on activities is an emulated network environment created on the large-scale network experiment testbed StarBED [9]. The emulated environment is realistic in terms of its composition and content, with more than a dozen servers (running as virtual machines on the physical StarBED hosts) allocated to each participant team. The architecture of each network environment mimics a typical e-commerce site in terms of server composition and network topology.

3.4.1.2 Hardening Day

On the first day of the event, called *Hardening Day*, the teams compete for approximately eight hours in terms of the security hardening they can provide for the virtual e-commerce website used in the event. The winning team is decided based on the total amount of virtual sales their website generated during the entire duration of the competition. Additional score tables are used to keep track of other aspects related to the training, such as the technical proficiency of the teams, in a manner similar to other competitions.

Using the sales amount to decide the winner is the main factor distinguishing Hardening Project from other security events. Whereas many security events focus solely on accomplishing technical tasks, for the purpose of the Hardening Project competition, the sales amount is considered to be an objective and realistic measure of the overall effectiveness of the hardening activity of the participants. This teaches them that in a business context cybersecurity tasks must always be addressed while considering not only the direct result of an action, but also its consequences on business performance indicators.

3.4.1.3 Softening Day

The second day of the Hardening Project event is called *Softening Day*, and it is the education-oriented part of the competition. During this second day, the organizers provide feedback to participants regarding the previous day activities, so that they can fill in whatever knowledge and ability gaps they may have had. The winners of the competition are also announced on that day.

While there is no hands-on practice on the second day of the event, the information provided helps participants understand the weaknesses of the strategies that they followed on the first day. It also teaches them about attack actions that took place in the training environment, the consequences of which they may have not even realized. Overall, it increases the motivation of the participants to apply their skills in their everyday activities and to attend next training events to further hone their cybersecurity skills.

3.4.2 Spin-Off Programs

Starting in 2015, a shorter version of the training program, called *MINI Hardening Project*, was organized several times a year until 2021[1] [13]. This mini event had similar rules with the main training activity; however, in order to improve its accessibility, both its location and duration were modified. Thus, instead of the rather remote locations in Japan where most of the Hardening Project competitions are held, the mini event was held in Tokyo or other large cities. Moreover, the duration of the competition was also changed to be only three hours, which contributes to creating a more intense and focused event.

Another spin-off event, called *Micro-Hardening*, is being conducted since 2018 [8]. This is a smaller-scale event that offers 45-min training sessions that are repeated three times. The attacks are fully automated during these sessions, and the participants are awarded points based on the number of attacks they could ward off. The entire experience, thus, benefits of gamification techniques in similar manner to CTF competitions; however, the participant tasks are defensive, not offensive, in this case. The training sessions are usually repeated several times, so that participants can have the opportunity to learn from their mistakes and improve their scores (and skills) in subsequent sessions.

3.4.3 Taxonomy-Based Analysis

In Table 3.1, we summarize our analysis of the characteristics of the Hardening Project training program from the perspective of the training activity taxonomy pre-

---

[1] This alternative competition seems to be discontinued at present.

Table 3.1 Analysis of the Hardening Project training program from the perspective of the training activity taxonomy presented in this chapter

Main aspect	Details	Characteristics
Training purpose	Main purpose	Defense training via network hardening
	Additional purpose	Forensics training to augment the defense training
Training approach	Target skills	Individual, team, CSIRT
	Scenario type	E-commerce company network management
	Environment type	Virtual network environment with dozens of hosts
	Cost	Event supported by sponsors, free to attend
Other features	Target participants	Anyone can attend: students, professionals, etc.
	Prerequisite ability	Participants with any ability level accepted
	Barriers to entry	Low due to the lack of participation restrictions
	Training frequency	Twice a year (more if including the spin-off events)

sented in this chapter. Note that this analysis can also be considered as an example of how any other training program can be evaluated in terms of the features it provides, for example in view of deciding whether it is suitable (or valuable) to attend it.

Regarding training purpose, defense training is the main purpose of Hardening Project, and forensics is used to assist participants in understanding the attacks and devising defense methods. However, attack training is not included, the rationale for this being that the actual cybersecurity tasks of a professional have more to do with defense and forensics, than with attacks.

As for the training approach, the team-based participation makes it possible to address all skills, from individual ones to CSIRT ones. The training scenario is a realistic e-commerce company network hardening scenario, with the company network being recreated via a virtual network environment with dozens of hosts per team. The event organization costs are supported by sponsors, making Hardening Project free to attend (aside from transportation and accommodation fees).

Lastly, regarding the other features in the taxonomy, we note that anyone can attend this competition, and no prerequisite abilities are needed. Moreover, the barriers to entry are low given the free attendance and lack of restrictions on occupation and abilities. The twice a year frequency of the event, or even more if including the spin-off events, makes it also easy to attend.

Given all of the above, we note how large is the coverage of Hardening Project in terms of the characteristics discussed in this chapter, including those shown in

Fig. 3.2. This emphasizes the wide range of applicability and benefits of this cybersecurity competition, which was the main reason why we selected it as the subject of the case study.

Acknowledgements The author would like to thank the organizers of the Hardening Project program for providing the opportunity to attend several training events, both as observer and as participant. The firsthand experience with these training activities proved invaluable in developing the training program analysis methodology presented in this chapter.

References

1. Beuran R (2012) Introduction to network emulation. Jenny Stanford Publishing, Singapore
2. Beuran R, Chinen K, Tan Y, Shinoda Y (2016) Towards effective cybersecurity education and training. Tech. Rep. IS-RR-2016-003, Japan Advanced Institute of Science and Technology
3. Coursera. Foundations of cybersecurity. https://www.coursera.org/learn/foundations-of-cybersecurity. Accessed 1 July 2024
4. Coursera. Google cybersecurity professional certificate. https://www.coursera.org/professional-certificates/google-cybersecurity. Accessed 1 July 2024
5. European Union Agency for Cybersecurity (2022) European cybersecurity skills framework (ECSF). https://www.enisa.europa.eu/topics/education/european-cybersecurity-skills-framework (2022). Accessed 1 July 2024
6. Japan Network Security Association. Cybersecurity skills alliance—a new vision for Europe (REWIRE). https://rewireproject.eu/. Accessed 1 July 2024
7. Japan Network Security Association (2021) SecBoK 2021—security body of knowledge. https://www.jnsa.org/en/reports/secbok.html. Accessed 1 July 2024
8. Kawaguchi H. Micro Hardening (in Japanese). https://microhardening.connpass.com/. Accessed 1 July 2024
9. National Institute of Information and Communications Technology, Japan. Hokuriku StarBED Technology Center. https://starbed.nict.go.jp/en/index.html. Accessed 1 July 2024
10. Petersen R, Santos D, Wetzel KA, Smith MC, Witte G (2020) Workforce framework for cybersecurity (NICE framework), NIST special publication 800-181 revision 1. https://doi.org/10.6028/NIST.SP.800-181r1
11. U.S. Cybersecurity and Infrastructure Security Agency (CISA). CISA tabletop exercise packages. https://www.cisa.gov/resources-tools/services/cisa-tabletop-exercise-packages. Accessed 1 July 2024
12. Web Application Security Forum. Hardening Project (in Japanese). https://wasforum.jp/hardening-project/. Accessed 1 July 2024
13. Web Application Security Forum. MINI Hardening Project (in Japanese). https://minihardening.connpass.com/. Accessed 1 July 2024

Chapter 4
Attack Training

This chapter discusses in detail the attack training form of cybersecurity training, starting with an overview of the training methodology. The two main attack training types, fundamental attack training and pentesting training, are presented next from the perspective of teaching or learning the corresponding skills. Some related information is also provided, such as attack knowledge bases and attack training tools. Finally, the main advantages and potential issues of attack training are discussed from the trainee and organizer points of view.

4.1 Attack Training Overview

In this book, we use the term attack training to refer to those cybersecurity training activities that mainly focus on teaching offensive techniques. This form of training gives trainees the opportunity to learn how malicious actors conduct real-world attacks. Such skills make it possible for them to take professional roles of ethical hackers, who test (with permission) the security level of computer and network systems with the goal of identifying their weaknesses.

This type of testing makes it possible for companies to proactively strengthen the security of their systems instead of waiting for actual attacks to occur. Consequently, many companies offer ethical hacking courses and certifications, including some free online courses, such as that provided by Cybrary [1].

4.1.1 Overall Methodology

The methodology for conducting attack training activities depends on the goals of the training, such as teaching basic skills or more complex ones. The first important criterion relates to the use or not of a training environment:

© The Author(s), under exclusive license to Springer Nature Singapore Pte Ltd. 2025   41
R. Beuran, *Cybersecurity Education and Training*,
https://doi.org/10.1007/978-981-96-0555-2_4

- No training environment: At a minimum, preparing a set of files could be enough to perform attack training, such as encrypted files that the trainees must decrypt. In this case, no training environment per se is required, although training platforms may have some kind of user interface to facilitate the training.
- Simple training environment: For teaching more advanced skills, some simple forms of training environments are required, such as websites with vulnerabilities that the trainees will try to exploit.
- Realistic training environment: Placing the trainees in realistic situations is the most effective form of training. In this case, full-fledged network environments should be made ready, that the trainees can attack in order to practice their skills.

Another important distinction is regarding any defense mechanisms that could be included during the training, as follows:

- No/passive defense: Most attack training activities involve no defense mechanisms (such as for the files to be decrypted, or the websites to be attacked). However, in the case of network environments, passive defense mechanisms, such as the use of firewalls, can be utilized to make the activity more challenging.
- Active defense: Some attack training activities may involve participants whose role is to defend the systems under attack, typically called the *blue team* (versus the *red team* made of attackers). This type of active defense not only makes the training more challenging, but also more realistic.

The above discussion makes it clear that there is an interdependency between attack training and the other forms of training, as it will be discussed next.

4.1.2   Approach Interdependency

As mentioned in Chap. 3 (cf. Fig. 3.1), attack training is complemented by two other forms of training, forensics training and defense training, which refer to the other types of cybersecurity skills that a security professional needs to master. The interdependency that exists between these three forms of training, illustrated in Fig. 4.1, is an essential aspect of cybersecurity training.

Thus, attack training makes it possible for trainees to get into the mindset of attackers and gain their skills. This firsthand in-depth understanding of attack techniques is a valuable asset when conducting forensics training, which teaches how to analyze the evidence related to attacks. The knowledge acquired through forensics training can then be leveraged in attack training to obtain insights into how attack traces and indicators can be concealed.

The hands-on practice that is done during attack training enables trainees to master various attack mechanisms. These skills are very important during defense training, which teaches how to prevent the attacks, since such knowledge can be used to design and implement more effective defense mechanisms. By getting again into

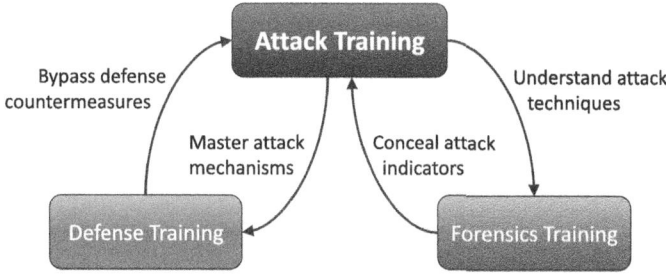

Fig. 4.1 Interdependency of attack training with respect to the other forms of training, forensics training and defense training

the mindset of attackers, the abilities acquired through defense training can then be utilized to further refine one's attack skills, for example, to find ways to bypass defense countermeasures.

Consequently, although the three forms of cybersecurity training can be considered separately and often are used as such during training, it is important to understand their strong interdependency. The type of synergetic continuous training that we described above is the only way for trainees to keep up to date with real-life situations, in which attackers also keep refining their techniques, bringing thus forth the need to mimic such conditions during training.

4.2 Attack Training Types

The potential attack surface of real computer and network systems is very large, and hence attack training must cover a wide area of topics. In what follows, we will discuss in more detail the manner in which attack training is conducted by classifying the training activities into two types:

- Fundamental attack training.
- Pentesting training.

4.2.1 Fundamental Attack Training

Fundamental attack training refers to teaching essential techniques that can be employed for offensive purposes and that should be part of the arsenal of any cybersecurity expert. Many of these fundamental skills are the target of challenges included in Capture The Flag (CTF) competitions; therefore, various guidelines pertaining to CTFs, such as [2] and [14], are useful references in this context. For the purpose of our discussion, we will separate the fundamental attack skills into two classes:

- Individual attack skills.
- Complex attack skills.

4.2.1.1   Individual Attack Skills

Individual attack skills are typically categorized by the area of cybersecurity they refer to. CTF competitions often use such categories to indicate to participants what type of skills are required to solve a given challenge (or which is the main required skill type, in case multiple skills are needed). Below we will review the skill categories that are most encountered in practice, shown next in alphabetical order:

- Cryptography.
- Operating systems.
- Networking.
- Web.

Cryptography This category includes various skills related to cryptography, such as ciphers and cryptographic protocols. In the context of attack training, trainees must learn how to exploit the weaknesses of existing solutions to decrypt the data they are presented with. This can include several types of exercises, such as decrypting password hashes or encrypted messages, or cracking the encryption keys of vulnerable wireless network protocols, e.g., Wired Equivalent Privacy (WEP).

Operating Systems This category includes various skills related to operating systems, especially in regard to the use of low-level commands and cybersecurity-related tools to achieve various offensive goals. Examples include manipulating file systems, accessing log files, executing various commands to obtain detailed information about the running processes, etc. Given the multitude of existing operating systems, training should cover widely used OSs, such as Linux and Windows.

Networking This category includes various skills related to network systems, especially with respect to network protocols. A fundamental area in this context is for trainees to become able to understand the formatting of network packets and to extract information from them. This is typically achieved by learning how to capture and analyze network traffic, for example, by using tools such as the Wireshark network protocol analyzer.

Web This category includes various skills related to web applications, and how vulnerabilities in the design of a web application can be exploited in order to obtain information that the original programmer did not intend to make accessible. This category encompasses a broad area of topics and is very often encountered in CTF competitions. The most typical web exploitation techniques are as follows:

- SQL injection: Using vulnerabilities in user input validation to inject SQL commands that allow the unauthorized retrieval of content stored in the web application database.
- Command injection: Using vulnerabilities in user input validation to submit system commands that will be executed remotely in an unauthorized manner on the website host.
- Directory traversal: Using vulnerabilities in user input validation to freely change the path of the displayed web page in order to access sensitive information.
- Cross Site Scripting (XSS): Using vulnerabilities that allow inserting code, such as JavaScript, in a given application, so that it is executed in the browser of another user of the same application.
- Cross Site Request Forgery (CSRF): Using the session hijacking mechanism, i.e., changing the state of a web browser session for an authenticated user, in order to perform unauthorized actions in the name of that user.
- Server Side Request Forgery (SSRF): Using web server vulnerabilities to cause a web application to send a forged request that makes it possible to obtain information that would not be accessible otherwise.

4.2.1.2 Complex Attack Skills

Being able to use attack techniques also requires more complex skills, and next we review several such categories:

- Binary exploitation/pwning.
- Programming.
- Reconnaissance.
- Sandbox escape.
- Specific skills.

Binary Exploitation/Pwning This category includes various skills related to the way in which a binary program can be used either to break out of the program and obtain access to a command shell or to otherwise modify its functionality for malicious purposes. The term *pwning* is often used for the first meaning in our definition, as it refers to the act of getting unauthorized access to a computer. In its most basic form, pwning can indeed mean to make a program crash so that one gets access to the command shell. However, more complex forms of pwning require writing exploits, which are small programs that take advantage of various vulnerabilities (either in applications, but also in various APIs, such as those of services running on a computer) to achieve a malicious goal.

To master binary exploitation and pwning techniques, trainees must learn about binary program structure and operation, such as registers, stack and heap, calling conventions. Moreover, they should learn about ways in which vulnerabilities can be exploited, such as via buffer overflow and format string vulnerability exploitation techniques. Due to the need to have low-level knowledge about binary code and debugging tools, this is one of the most demanding categories of skills, which explains why exploit development by itself is one type of standalone cybersecurity certification [12]. Note, however, that there are available tools, such as the Metasploit penetration testing framework, that include a large set of exploit modules, which can be used to conduct exploit actions without any knowledge of the inner workings of that exploit (see Sect. 4.3.3.2). In this case, trainees must learn instead how to use this type of frameworks.

Programming Many attack techniques can only be performed successfully if one masters various programming skills. This requires trainees to learn several programming languages, depending on the area to which they want to apply the attack. For web-related techniques, mastering relevant languages, such as JavaScript and PHP, is important. For application-related techniques, such as binary exploitation, C/C++, as well as assembly language, are required.

Other attacks require scripting; hence, shell script or Python knowledge are useful in that case. In addition, understanding deeply the intrinsic weaknesses and potential sources of vulnerabilities of each particular programming language is also essential.

Reconnaissance This class of skills, also known as open-source intelligence (OSINT), typically refers to gathering information about a target person or company from public sources, such as social media, company websites, and public records. Consequently, trainees must learn how to retrieve information from web pages, both that which is readily available, and that which is not immediately accessible (e.g., metadata in HTML files).

In addition, reconnaissance can also refer to gathering technical information regarding a target host or network, such as open ports and IP addresses. A very useful tool for this purpose is Nmap, which can be used to retrieve most of this host and network-related information (see Sect. 4.3.3.1). Moreover, they should learn how to obtain information from network traffic, for example, via the use of the networking skills described in Sect. 4.2.1.1.

Sandbox Escape Another category of attack skills that require mastering a wide range of techniques is that related to escaping from a sandbox, also known as *jailbreaking*. For simple sandboxes, such as Python jails, deep knowledge of a certain programming language may be sufficient.

However, to escape from a complex sandbox, such as a virtual machine, the ability to identify vulnerabilities in the various virtualization APIs is required. Consequently, trainees must acquire deep knowledge of a large number of libraries, as well as skills related to writing exploits that target the identified vulnerabilities.

Specific Skills In this category, we include those sets of skills that refer to specific topics pertaining not to a given skill category, but to a certain attack target. For example, if one wants to target the Android OS, one needs skills related to the various programming languages used in this OS, such as Java, Kotlin, C/C++, Rust, and also knowledge about the file structure, API, and so on, of Android. Similarly, to target CPU architectures such as ARM and MIPS, one requires a deep understanding of those architectures, their instruction sets, binary code representation, etc. We note that many CTF competitions have a challenge category named *Misc* which groups miscellaneous challenges that span several basic categories and/or require specific skills, such as those mentioned here.

4.2.2 Pentesting Training

Once trainees become proficient at using fundamental attack skills, the training should continue by placing them in more realistic situations, and penetration testing (pentesting) is one of the most realistic types of attack training. When conducting pentesting, most of the core skills that are used are fundamentally the attack skills that we have discussed so far.

However, to become competent pentesters, trainees must learn how to concatenate those fundamental skills in order to attain a complex goal in a real-life scenario. Learning about pentesting best practices as well teaches trainees to follow an established sequence of pentesting stages, so that the goal is reached in an optimal manner. Furthermore, acquiring non-technical knowledge on how to organize the overall pentesting activity is another must.

One example of a best practice sequence of pentesting steps is the *Penetration Testing Execution Standard* that was created by a group of information security practitioners from various industry areas, such as financial institutions, service providers, and security vendors [15]. Note that although the guideline does not contain technical details, a thorough technical guide is also included as reference for the mechanisms that can be used to achieve the objective of each stage. In what follows, we will use the sequence in this guideline to describe the related pentesting training activities according to the following stages:

1. Pre-engagement interactions.
2. Intelligence gathering.
3. Threat modeling.
4. Vulnerability analysis.
5. Exploitation.
6. Post-exploitation.
7. Reporting.

While we consider that the above guideline is most suitable from an attack training perspective, we note that pentesting is not officially standardized though, and there are several other resources that are useful for gaining knowledge on the pentesting process. One valuable book in this context is *Professional Red Teaming: Conducting Successful Cybersecurity Engagements* by Oakley [11]. In this book, the author leverages his practical cybersecurity expertise to cover a variety of important topics, such as the rules of engagement and execution methodology for pentesting, an outline of the reporting process, various risk assessment considerations, how to evaluate offensive security processes, and so on.

Another useful resource regarding pentesting, although its scope is limited to web technologies, is the *Web Security Testing Guide* (WSTG) released by the OWASP foundation [13]. WSTG provides a framework for testing the security of web applications and services. The perspective of the guideline is very practical, with actions split into several phases: before development begins, during definition and design, during development, during deployment, and during maintenance and operations. A thorough description of testing techniques for various aspects related to web applications and services, such as identity management, authentication, authorization, and input validation, are also included.

4.2.2.1   Pre-engagement Interactions

The pre-engagement stage refers to all the communications held between the pentesting individual or company and the organization that wishes to use their service. To prepare for this initial stage of pentesting, trainees should learn about various aspects, such as

- How to define the pentesting activity scope and duration?
- What questions the organization must answer before deciding the contract terms?
- How to establish secure communication lines and emergency contacts?
- How to define the rules of engagement (timeline, legal considerations, etc.)?

4.2.2.2   Intelligence Gathering

Before an actual pentesting engagement, pentesters must perform reconnaissance in order to gather intelligence about the target organization, which will become helpful during the actual pentesting. For this purpose, the skills in the *Reconnaissance* category mentioned previously should be employed. However, in order to be able to deal with real targets, trainees must learn various additional aspects, such as

- How to establish the actual scope of the pentesting target (e.g., the web server domains of an organization)?
- What type of information gathering method is most suitable for a particular case (e.g., passive, semi-passive, or active)?
- How to determine the actual hosts that are within the scope of the engagement and their properties (also known as *footprinting*)?
- How to identify what protection mechanisms the organization has in place (network-based, host-based, application-level, etc.)?

4.2.2.3 Threat Modeling

Once enough information about the target has been gathered, pentesters should model the threats regarding the target systems in order to be able to determine the best course of action. This stage involves considering two sides, those of business assets and threat agents, each with their specific sets of required skills:

- Business asset side

  - How to analyze business assets in order to determine what are the potential targets based on organizational data, employee and customer data, personnel assets, etc.?
  - How to analyze business processes to identify their mapping onto business assets, to establish which are the critical versus non-critical processes, etc.?

- Threat agent side

  - How to identify the threat agents, including modeling their possible motivations, while making the distinction between internal agents (management, engineers, etc.) versus external ones (competitors, contractors, etc.)?
  - How to determine the threat capabilities of the agents identified in the previous step in terms of the available tools, exploits, communication mechanisms, etc., including via a survey of incidents that occurred in similar organizations?

4.2.2.4 Vulnerability Analysis

The next stage of the pentesting process refers to discovering what system and application flaws could be exploited by an attacker. The scope of this analysis is defined based on the information gathered in the previous stages. Many of the skills required to complete the analysis are fundamental attack skills, but the way in which they are put into practice when targeting real systems, and additional information corroboration aspects must be mastered by trainees, as follows:

- How to conduct active testing by using various types of vulnerability scanners, including general scanning, service-based, specific scanning (web applications, network protocols), and so on?
- How to conduct passive testing by using methods that do not create any traffic, such as file metadata analysis and traffic monitoring, to gather further information?
- How to validate the discovered vulnerabilities by suitable methods, such as correlating the data obtained from various tools, manual and protocol-specific testing, and how to link them together in an attack tree?
- How to find ways in which the discovered vulnerabilities can be exploited by gathering related information from vulnerability databases, vendor-issued security advisories, exploit databases and framework modules, etc.?

4.2.2.5   Exploitation

The results of the vulnerability analysis stage are used to perform exploitation, through which the vulnerabilities are utilized in a deliberate and precise manner to attempt to gain access to the target assets. The development of actual exploits is done by relying on fundamental attack techniques, but trainees must also learn how to deal with several situations that are expected in real-life situations, such as

- How to handle the potential countermeasures that can be in place in the target network, such as anti-virus software, data execution prevention (DEP) mechanisms, and web application firewalls (WAF)?
- How to conduct evasive actions to avoid triggering additional defense mechanisms, such as intrusion detection and/or prevention systems (IDS, IPS, IDPS)?
- How to execute zero-day attacks in case standard exploit methods fail by relying on techniques such as fuzzing and source code analysis to build custom exploits?

4.2.2.6   Post-exploitation

Once the exploitation phase ends, the pentester achieves control over a number of business assets of the target organization. In the post-exploitation stage, various actions will be carried out in order to assess how valuable each compromised host is and to make sure they can be used to expose further assets in the target network. While some of the techniques used in this phase are fundamental, trainees should also learn a series of specific methodologies to ensure the safety of the process:

- How to protect the day-to-day operation of the target organization by making sure that no critical systems are affected (unless previously agreed upon), that all changes are dully documented, that collected data is properly safeguarded, etc.?
- How to protect oneself by ensuring that the contract contains all the necessary provisions needed for the post-exploitation stage, that no laws or regulations are violated in the process, etc.?
- How to conduct a thorough analysis of the compromised hosts in order to identify additional targets based on information obtained already with regard to network configuration, network services, etc.?
- How to extract information from the compromised hosts according to the pentesting goals, or in order to further penetrate the network, such as installed programs and available services (file sharing, database servers, directory/name servers, virtualization, messaging, backup systems, etc.), as well as sensitive data, user information, and system configuration?
- How to create and test paths through which sensitive data can be exfiltrated from the compromised hosts to the servers controlled by the pentester in order to simulate actual exfiltration activities of the threat agents, and to validate whether the mechanisms set in place by the organization to block sensitive information export work correctly?

- How to conduct pivoting, that is penetrating the target network even deeper by either executing actions on the compromised hosts (service enumeration, abuse of compromised credentials, etc.) or by using them as stepping stones (via port forwarding, execution of remote exploits, etc.)?
- How to thoroughly cleanup the compromised systems once the pentesting ends by removing all the added files (executables, scripts, etc.), restoring the original values for all the modified system settings and configuration parameters, removing any installed backdoor or rootkit, removing any created user accounts, etc.?

4.2.2.7 Reporting

Reporting is the last phase of penetration testing, and being able to write a report that contains all the necessary information requires trainees to learn how to structure it correctly. In general, the following are the types of information that need to be included into the two logical sections of a pentesting report:

- Executive summary: Describes the specific goals of the pentesting, and its high-level findings to those who oversee the security aspects of the target organization, and any other members who may be impacted by those findings

  - What was the overall pentesting purpose, and the detailed goals established in the pre-engagement phase?
  - To what extent those goals were achieved, and a summary of the identified issues, including risk rating metrics.
  - What recommendations can be made in order to solve the identified issues, and an estimate of the efforts needed to do that, possibly accompanied by a detailed resolution roadmap?

- Technical content: Details the test scope, gathered information, attack paths, test impact, and remediation suggestions in technical terms

  - Who conducted the test, what was its scope, and how it was conducted?
  - What information was gathered, and how that was accomplished (passive versus active intelligence, and corporate versus personnel intelligence)?
  - What were the findings of the vulnerability assessment, including both technical and logical vulnerabilities, and the severity of those exposures?
  - What were the results of the exploitation and vulnerability confirmation actions, with details about the way in which exploitation was conducted, such as direct versus indirect attacks?
  - What was the demonstrated impact of the vulnerabilities on the organization, such as acquisition of critical information, access to core systems and protected datasets, ability for persistence and exfiltration; moreover, what was the effectiveness of the security countermeasures that were in place in the organization?

– What are the estimated risks for the organization assessed, for example, by evaluating the probable incident frequency, strength of the countermeasures, required level of skills and access, etc.; in addition, what is the estimated magnitude of losses, and what is the root cause of the risks?

We note that the main role of the executive summary is to inform the decisions of the personnel with management roles in the organization to conduct the necessary changes for improving the security posture of the organization. As for the technical content, which outlines the objective evidence that served as basis for creating the executive summary, it is addressed mainly to the personnel with technical roles in the organization and supports their actions for implementing the decided changes.

4.3 Related Information

Attack training is a very complex activity that challenges the trainees to a high degree. In what follows, we will review several resources that we consider particularly helpful in the context of attack training, first in terms of additional information sources, such as knowledge bases and security testing guidelines. Then we will discuss some more practical aspects, such as tools that trainees can use during the attack training activity, and examples of attack training platforms.

4.3.1 Attack Knowledge Bases

While practical skills are undoubtedly an essential part of cybersecurity training, a vast amount of knowledge is also required in order to be able to apply those skills in practice effectively. Fortunately, the cybersecurity field benefits of the existence of a variety of knowledge bases that can be searched as needed in order to retrieve information about a particular topic of interest.

Such knowledge bases are not only a rich source of information that trainees can use to learn new things or simply as reference, but they can also be extremely valuable for cybersecurity training organizers. Thus, organizers can use them as guidance and inspiration when creating training content that targets real cybersecurity issues which are widely relevant.

4.3.1.1 ATT&CK

ATT&CK is one of the most comprehensive knowledge bases regarding the attack tactics and techniques used by real-world cyber adversaries [7]. The knowledge base is managed by MITRE Corporation, and it outlines attack tactics, techniques, as well as mitigation methods, but also the relationships between all these elements, which makes it a very powerful tool. ATT&CK has many uses, such as helping defenders develop threat models and methodologies, but also red teaming and security assessment. In what follows, we will illustrate its utilization from an attack training perspective. For the examples provided below, we rely on ATT&CK v15.1 that was released in May 2024.

Tactics At the top level of ATT&CK are situated the attack tactics. The knowledge base uses a meta structure based on context, such as Enterprise, Mobile, and ICS, that makes it possible to filter only the relevant entries for that context. By selecting a context, the relevant matrix of entries is displayed.

There are currently 14 tactics specified in the knowledge base for the Enterprise matrix, as summarized in Table 4.1. For each tactic, we include its brief description, which explains what adversaries are trying to do when using a certain tactic, and a count of techniques that are included in that tactic. We note that the *Defense Evasion* and *Discovery* tactics include a very large number of techniques, emphasizing the large array of methods available to attackers in those two cases.

The order in which the tactics are presented in ATT&CK follows the generally accepted order of the steps in a cyberattack. For each tactic, the knowledge base also includes a detailed explanation regarding the scope of that tactic. For example, for the *Lateral Movement* (TA0008) tactic, the detailed explanation is as follows [7]:

> Lateral Movement consists of techniques that adversaries use to enter and control remote systems on a network. Following through on their primary objective often requires exploring the network to find their target and subsequently gaining access to it. Reaching their objective often involves pivoting through multiple systems and accounts to gain. Adversaries might install their own remote access tools to accomplish Lateral Movement or use legitimate credentials with native network and operating system tools, which may be stealthier.

Readers will recognize some of tactic names in Table 4.1 as phases of the pentesting process discussed in Sect. 4.2.2. This is why by studying the information regarding a given tactic, trainees are able to learn practical information about how to execute the corresponding pentesting stage.

Techniques On the second layer of the ATT&CK knowledge base are situated the attack techniques, with more than 600 techniques and sub-techniques being currently defined, where sub-techniques are sub-components of an attack technique that provide more specific information for a particular use case. By studying the techniques of interest, trainees are able to learn about practical attack mechanisms.

Each tactic covers a set of techniques. For instance, the *Lateral Movement* tactic contains nine techniques, as shown in Table 4.2. Techniques do not have brief descriptions, only detailed explanations, as it will be explained below. The numbers shown in the table indicate how many sub-techniques each technique has. Most of the techniques in our example have no sub-techniques, but *Remote Services*, for instance, has eight, each referring to a specific remote service, such as Remote Desktop Protocol, SSH, VNC, and the way in which those specific services can be used as attack vectors.

Table 4.1 Overview of the tactics in the ATT&CK knowledge base

Name	Tactic description	Count
Reconnaissance	The adversary is trying to gather information they can use to plan future operations	10
Resource Development	The adversary is trying to establish resources they can use to support operations	8
Initial Access	The adversary is trying to get into your network	10
Execution	The adversary is trying to run malicious code	14
Persistence	The adversary is trying to maintain their foothold	20
Privilege Escalation	The adversary is trying to gain higher-level permissions	14
Defense Evasion	The adversary is trying to avoid being detected	43
Credential Access	The adversary is trying to steal account names and passwords	17
Discovery	The adversary is trying to figure out your environment	32
Lateral Movement	The adversary is trying to move through your environment	9
Collection	The adversary is trying to gather data of interest to their goal	17
Command and Control	The adversary is trying to communicate with compromised systems to control them	18
Exfiltration	The adversary is trying to steal data	9
Impact	The adversary is trying to manipulate, interrupt, or destroy your systems and data	14

Similar to tactics, each technique is given an identifier,[1] and includes an explanation of its scope. For example, the detailed explanation for the *Exploitation of Remote Services* (T1210) technique is as follows [7]:

---

[1] Note that some techniques use the same name but a different identifier, depending on the context. For instance, *Exploitation of Remote Services* (T1210) is defined for the Enterprise context, and *Exploitation of Remote Services* (T1428) for the Mobile context.

Table 4.2 Overview of the techniques for the *Lateral Movement* tactic in the ATT&CK knowledge base

Technique name	Count
Exploitation of Remote Services	0
Internal Spearphishing	0
Lateral Tool Transfer	0
Remote Service Session Hijacking	2
Remote Services	8
Replication Through Removable Media	0
Software Deployment Tools	0
Taint Shared Content	0
Use Alternate Authentication Material	4

Adversaries may exploit remote services to gain unauthorized access to internal systems once inside of a network. Exploitation of a software vulnerability occurs when an adversary takes advantage of a programming error in a program, service, or within the operating system software or kernel itself to execute adversary-controlled code. A common goal for post-compromise exploitation of remote services is for lateral movement to enable access to a remote system.

An adversary may need to determine if the remote system is in a vulnerable state, which may be done through Network Service Discovery or other Discovery methods looking for common, vulnerable software that may be deployed in the network, the lack of certain patches that may indicate vulnerabilities, or security software that may be used to detect or contain remote exploitation. Servers are likely a high value target for lateral movement exploitation, but endpoint systems may also be at risk if they provide an advantage or access to additional resources.

There are several well-known vulnerabilities that exist in common services such as SMB and RDP as well as applications that may be used within internal networks such as MySQL and web server services.

Depending on the permissions level of the vulnerable remote service an adversary may achieve Exploitation for Privilege Escalation as a result of lateral movement exploitation as well.

Procedure Examples Another aspect of techniques in ATT&CK that is particularly useful from an attack training perspective is that many of them include examples of procedures, that is practical ways in which a particular type of attack technique was previously executed in the real world. Each such procedure includes not only a brief outline, but also references to technical reports that detail the attack mechanisms that were actually used.

The *Exploitation of Remote Services* technique, for instance, includes more than 20 procedure examples. Some of them refer to higher-level strategies used by threat groups, such as *APT28* (G0007), but many refer to actual software used to conduct a certain type of attack, such as *Bad Rabbit* (S0606). The current version of ATT&CK includes almost 800 references to such software. Procedure examples are, therefore, very valuable for the study of penetration testing techniques.

Table 4.3 Overview of the mitigations for the *Exploitation of Remote Services* technique in the ATT&CK knowledge base

Name	Mitigation description
Application Isolation and Sandboxing	Make it difficult for adversaries to advance their operation through exploitation of undiscovered or unpatched vulnerabilities by using sandboxing [...]
Disable or Remove Feature or Program	Minimize available services to only those that are necessary
Exploit Protection	Security applications that look for behavior used during exploitation such as Windows Defender Exploit Guard (WDEG) and the Enhanced Mitigation Experience Toolkit (EMET) can be used to mitigate some exploitation behavior [...]
Network Segmentation	Segment networks and systems appropriately to reduce access to critical systems and services to controlled methods
Privileged Account Management	Minimize permissions and access for service accounts to limit impact of exploitation
Threat Intelligence Program	Develop a robust cyber threat intelligence capability to determine what types and levels of threat may use software exploits and 0-days against a particular organization
Update Software	Update software regularly by employing patch management for internal enterprise endpoints and servers
Vulnerability Scanning	Regularly scan the internal network for available services to identify new and potentially vulnerable services

Mitigations So far, we have focused on the information in the ATT&CK knowledge base that refers to offensive actions. However, the defined attack techniques also include lists of mitigations that can be used to counter those attack techniques in various manners. The current version of ATT&CK contains a total of 43 such mitigations in the Enterprise matrix. For example, the *Exploitation of Remote Services* technique mentions eight possible mitigations, as shown in Table 4.3, which provides a brief description for each mitigation (some descriptions were shortened for clarity).

Mitigations, as well, use an identifier and include a detailed description of the mitigation mechanism, but also link back to all the attack techniques they are relevant with respect to. For instance, the mechanism for the *Network Segmentation* (M1030) mitigation is described as follows [7]:

Architect sections of the network to isolate critical systems, functions, or resources. Use physical and logical segmentation to prevent access to potentially sensitive systems and information. Use a DMZ to contain any Internet-facing services that should not be exposed from the internal network. Configure separate virtual private cloud (VPC) instances to isolate critical cloud systems.

To use the same mitigation example, *Network Segmentation* links back to more than 20 attack techniques. While such information is mostly useful from a defense perspective, trainees can also use it as reference for the type of defense mechanisms that are expected in a pentesting engagement for those attack techniques and try to consider appropriate ways of bypassing those countermeasures.

Detection Most attack techniques also include information about how one could detect those attacks. In particular, the data sources and data components to be used, as well as the actual detection mechanism are specified. For instance, the *Exploitation of Remote Services* (T1210) technique mentions two data sources: *Application Log* and *Network Traffic*. In its turn, the description of how *Network Traffic* (DS0029) and its content can be used to detect T1210 attacks is as follows [7]:

> Use deep packet inspection to look for artifacts of common exploit traffic, such as known payloads.

While attack detection information is again mostly useful from a defense perspective, trainees can also use it as reference for the types of detection mechanisms that are expected in a pentesting engagement, and try to determine the corresponding evasion methods they could employ.

4.3.1.2 CAPEC

Common Attack Pattern Enumeration and Classification (CAPEC) is a list of known attack patterns that are employed by adversaries to exploit known weaknesses in computer systems [8]. CAPEC too is managed by MITRE Corporation with the goal of providing a tool that can help security analysts, software developers, testers, and educators to gain a better understanding of the cyberattack patterns and improve their defense techniques. The content of CAPEC can be viewed in two main ways:

- Mechanisms of Attack: A view that organizes attack patterns hierarchically based on the most common mechanisms used to exploit a vulnerability, with each category representing different techniques employed to attack a system.
- Domains of Attack: A view that organizes attack patterns based on the attack domain, with the following six domains being defined: *Software, Hardware, Communications, Supply Chain, Social Engineering, Physical Security*.

Attack Pattern Categories At the top level of each view of CAPECs are situated in the attack pattern categories. Thus, there are nine categories in the *Mechanisms of Attack* view, as shown in Table 4.4. Note that, for clarity, we have included only partial descriptions in the table, and the knowledge base should be referred to for details. Each category represents an attack mechanism, and trainees can consult the

Table 4.4 Overview of the attack pattern categories for the *Mechanisms of Attack* view in the CAPEC knowledge base

Name	Attack pattern category description
Engage in Deceptive Interactions	Attack patterns within this category focus on malicious interactions with a target in an attempt to deceive the target and convince the target that it is interacting with some other principal and as such take actions based on the level of trust that exists between the target and the other principal
Abuse Existing Functionality	An adversary uses or manipulates one or more functions of an application in order to achieve a malicious objective not originally intended by the application, or to deplete a resource to the point that the target's functionality is affected
Manipulate Data Structures	Attack patterns in this category manipulate and exploit characteristics of system data structures in order to violate the intended usage and protections of these structures
Manipulate System Resources	Attack patterns within this category focus on the adversary's ability to manipulate one or more resources in order to achieve a desired outcome
Inject Unexpected Items	Attack patterns within this category focus on the ability to control or disrupt the behavior of a target either through crafted data submitted via an interface for data input, or the installation and execution of malicious code on the target system
Employ Probabilistic Techniques	An attacker utilizes probabilistic techniques to explore and overcome security properties of the target that are based on an assumption of strength due to the extremely low mathematical probability that an attacker would be able to identify and exploit the very rare specific conditions under which those security properties do not hold
Manipulate Timing and State	An attacker exploits weaknesses in timing or state maintaining functions to perform actions that would otherwise be prevented by the execution flow of the target code and processes
Collect and Analyze Information	Attack patterns within this category focus on the gathering, collection, and theft of information by an adversary
Subvert Access Control	An attacker actively targets exploitation of weaknesses, limitations and assumptions in the mechanisms a target utilizes to manage identity and authentication as well as manage access to its resources or authorize functionality

explanation of that mechanism during attack training to learn how to conduct the corresponding types of attacks.

Attack Patterns On the second level of CAPECs are situated the attack patterns. Each category includes a number of concrete attack patterns that correspond to it logically. CAPEC distinguishes three types of attack patterns, depending on the abstraction level of their mechanism:

- Meta: Most abstract of the attack patterns, which describe a general methodology, but lack specific technology or implementation information (e.g., *Content Spoofing*); they are meant to provide an understanding of a high-level approach and are useful for threat modeling at design level.
- Standard: Attack patterns that describe a specific methodology or technique, and represent a singular piece of a fully executed attack (e.g., *Intent Spoof*); they are meant to provide sufficient details to understand the specific techniques and how they work, being specific types of meta-level attack patterns.
- Detailed: Attack patterns that provide low-level details, which leverage specific techniques and target specific technologies, and which express a complete execution flow (e.g., *Checksum Spoofing*); they are more specific than meta and standard attack patterns and often leverage a number of different standard attack patterns chained together to accomplish a goal.

For example, the *Engage in Deceptive Interactions* category in the *Mechanisms of Attack* view includes six meta attack patterns, as shown in Table 4.5. Note that, for clarity, we have included only partial descriptions in the table, and the CAPEC knowledge base should be referred to for details.

Each attack pattern includes various information fields, such as description, typical severity, prerequisites, required resources, mitigations, and related weaknesses. For example, the description for the *Checksum Spoofing* (CAPEC-145) detailed attack pattern is as follows [8]:

> An adversary spoofs a checksum message for the purpose of making a payload appear to have a valid corresponding checksum. Checksums are used to verify message integrity. They consist of some value based on the value of the message they are protecting. Hash codes are a common checksum mechanism. Both the sender and recipient are able to compute the checksum based on the contents of the message. If the message contents change between the sender and recipient, the sender and recipient will compute different checksum values. Since the sender's checksum value is transmitted with the message, the recipient would know that a modification occurred. In checksum spoofing an adversary modifies the message body and then modifies the corresponding checksum so that the recipient's checksum calculation will match the checksum (created by the adversary) in the message. This would prevent the recipient from realizing that a change occurred.

By analyzing the fields of various attack patterns of interest, trainees can learn how to design an attack, what weaknesses can be exploited to realize that attack, what mitigations can be expected, and so on. This makes CAPEC a very useful resource for attack training, especially in terms of learning how to devise effective attack strategies.

Table 4.5 Overview of the meta attack patterns for the *Engage in Deceptive Interactions* category in the CAPEC knowledge base

Name	Meta attack pattern description
Content Spoofing	An adversary modifies content to make it contain something other than what the original content producer intended while keeping the apparent source of the content unchanged
Identity Spoofing	Identity Spoofing refers to the action of assuming (i.e., taking on) the identity of some other entity (human or non-human) and then using that identity to accomplish a goal
Resource Location Spoofing	An adversary deceives an application or user and convinces them to request a resource from an unintended location
Action Spoofing	An adversary is able to disguise one action for another and therefore trick a user into initiating one type of action when they intend to initiate a different action
Manipulate Human Behavior	An adversary exploits inherent human psychological predisposition to influence a targeted individual or group to solicit information or manipulate the target into performing an action that serves the adversary's interests
Metadata Spoofing	An adversary alters the metadata of a resource (e.g., file, directory, repository, etc.) to present a malicious resource as legitimate/credible

4.3.1.3 CWE

Common Weakness Enumeration (CWE) is a list of weaknesses that are commonly encountered in software and hardware, which is also maintained by MITRE Corporation [9]. The term *weakness* is used here to refer to a condition in a system component that, under certain circumstances, could contribute to the introduction of vulnerabilities. The goal of CWE is to serve as a common language for describing security weaknesses and to support the efforts regarding their identification, mitigation, and prevention. The content of the CWE database can be accessed based on three types of views, as follows:

- Software Development: A representation intended for software developers and educators that groups weaknesses around concepts that are frequently encountered in software development.
- Hardware Design: A representation intended for hardware designers and educators that groups weaknesses around concepts that are frequently used in the area of hardware design.

Table 4.6 Selected weakness categories in the CWE knowledge base

Name	Weakness category description
API/Function Errors	Weaknesses in this category are related to the use of built-in functions or external APIs
Audit/Logging Errors	Weaknesses in this category are related to audit-based components of a software system
Authentication Errors	Weaknesses in this category are related to authentication components of a system
Authorization Errors	Weaknesses in this category are related to authorization components of a system
Bad Coding Practices	Weaknesses in this category are related to coding practices that are deemed unsafe and increase the chances that an exploitable vulnerability will be present in the application
Behavioral Problems	Weaknesses in this category are related to unexpected behaviors from code that an application uses
Business Logic Errors	Weaknesses in this category identify some of the underlying problems that commonly allow attackers to manipulate the business logic of an application
Communication Channel Errors	Weaknesses in this category are related to improper handling of communication channels and access paths
Complexity Issues	Weaknesses in this category are associated with things being overly complex
Concurrency Issues	Weaknesses in this category are related to concurrent use of shared resources

- Research Concepts: A representation intended for academic researchers, vulnerability analysts, and assessment tool vendors that organizes weaknesses according to abstractions of behaviors.

Weakness Categories At the top level of each CWE view are situated the weakness categories. There are currently about 40 categories in the *Software Development* view, which are organized in alphabetical order. The first 10 such categories are shown in Table 4.6 for illustration purposes. Note that, for clarity, we have included only partial descriptions of the categories in the table, and the CWE knowledge base should be referred to for details.

Each weakness category represents a class of related weaknesses, and trainees can consult this information during attack training to learn what are the issues that can be exploited to conduct a certain type of attack.

Table 4.7 Overview of the base weaknesses for the *API/Function Errors* category in the CWE knowledge base

Name	Base weakness description
Use of Inherently Dangerous Function	The product calls a function that can never be guaranteed to work safely
Use of Function with Inconsistent Implementations	The code uses a function that has inconsistent implementations across operating systems and versions
Undefined Behavior for Input to API	The behavior of this function is undefined unless its control parameter is set to a specific value
Use of Obsolete Function	The code uses deprecated or obsolete functions, which suggests that the code has not been actively reviewed or maintained
Use of Potentially Dangerous function	The product invokes a potentially dangerous function that could introduce a vulnerability if it is used incorrectly, but the function can also be used safely
Use of Low-Level Functionality	The product uses low-level functionality that is explicitly prohibited by the framework or specification under which the product is supposed to operate
Exposed Dangerous Method or Function	The product provides an Applications Programming Interface (API) or similar interface for interaction with external actors, but the interface includes a dangerous method or function that is not properly restricted

Weaknesses On the second level of CWE are located the actual weaknesses. Each category includes a number of concrete base weaknesses that can be linked to vulnerabilities. Thus, the first weakness category in the *Software Development* view, *API/Function Errors*, includes the seven base weaknesses, as shown in Table 4.7.

Each weakness includes many fields, such as description and extended description, relationship, and mapping information. For example, the extended description for the *Use of Inherently Dangerous Function* (CWE-242) weakness is [9]:

> Certain functions behave in dangerous ways regardless of how they are used. Functions in this category were often implemented without taking security concerns into account. The gets() function is unsafe because it does not perform bounds checking on the size of its input. An attacker can easily send arbitrarily sized input to gets() and overflow the destination buffer. Similarly, the >> operator is unsafe to use when reading into a statically allocated character array because it does not perform bounds checking on the size of its input. An attacker can easily send arbitrarily sized input to the >> operator and overflow the destination buffer.

Of particular interest from an attack training perspective is the fact that examples are provided for each weakness, both in terms of how the weakness itself is introduced, and in which context it was observed. Moreover, potential mitigation and detection methods are also proposed. By studying these details, trainees can understand how to recognize weaknesses in source code, and how they could be exploited, but also how those weaknesses could be fixed.

For the case of *Use of Inherently Dangerous Function* (CWE-242), for example, two source code fragments regarding the C function `getc()` are provided as demonstrative examples. In addition, the vulnerability CVE-2007-4004 is provided as an observed example with the following description:

> FTP client uses inherently insecure gets() function and is setuid root on some systems, allowing buffer overflow.

As potential mitigations regarding CWE-242, banning the use of dangerous functions, and the replacement with their safe equivalent are suggested for the implementation/requirements phase. Moreover, the use of `grep` or static analysis tools to spot the use of dangerous functions are suggested as mitigations for the testing phase. Finally, with regard to detection, automated static analysis, also known as Static Application Security Testing (SAST), is recommended as highly effective.

4.3.1.4 Vulnerability and Exploit Databases

Learning about actual vulnerabilities is an important component of attack training. Some very useful resources in this context are the following:

- Common Vulnerabilities and Exposures (CVE)[2]: A standard for identifying, defining, and cataloging publicly disclosed cybersecurity vulnerabilities operated by MITRE Corporation. The associated database, named CVE List, is very large, containing detailed records on more that 240,000 vulnerabilities at the time of writing.
- National Vulnerability Database (NVD)[3]: A repository of standards-based vulnerability management data operated by the U.S. NIST. All vulnerabilities in the NVD have an associated CVE identifier. Moreover, the Common Vulnerability Scoring System (CVSS) is used to supply a qualitative measure of the severity of each vulnerability.
- Exploit-DB[4]: A fully searchable CVE-compliant archive of public exploits and vulnerable software maintained by the Offensive Security (OffSec) cybersecurity training company. The database is intended for use by pentesters and vulnerability researchers. Its extension, the Google Hacking Database (GHDB), is an index of search queries that are designed to uncover potentially sensitive information available on the Internet.
- Exploit DB[5]: A repository of computer software exploits and exploitable vulnerabilities maintained by the Rapid7 cybersecurity company. The database contains

---

[2] https://www.cve.org/.

[3] https://nvd.nist.gov/.

[4] https://www.exploit-db.com/.

[5] https://www.rapid7.com/db/.

technical details for over 180,000 vulnerabilities and 4000 exploits that are made available for security professionals and researchers. All the exploits are included in the Metasploit framework, meaning that they are readily available for pentesting and similar activities.

The information in the CVE and NVD databases mentioned above represents basic knowledge that is extremely useful for trainees to understand the potential attack surfaces for a system. The CVSS score mentioned in connection with NVD, and the detailed metrics associated with each CVSS score value (exploitability, impact, exploit code maturity, etc.) can then be used to determine the vulnerabilities that are potentially easier to exploit, or that have a potentially greater impact. Last but not least, the exploits from the mentioned exploit databases can be used as basic tools to attempt to take advantage of those vulnerabilities during attack training.

We note that navigating the complex ecosystem of cybersecurity-related knowledge bases, such as those mentioned so far, can be quite challenging. One resource that is specifically helpful in this context is BRON, a project that automatically unifies several information sources to create an aggregate graph representation [4]. In particular, BRON is able to integrate the information made available in ATT&CK, CAPEC, CWE, NVD, Exploit-DB, as well as several other knowledge bases.

4.3.2   Security Testing Guidelines

We have seen that pentesting training is an important component that prepares trainees for real-life situations. However, security testing is an even broader field, and it is important to follow standard methodologies in order to ensure that the testing is done thoroughly and correctly. Below we describe two examples of such standard methodologies that interested readers can consult for further information.

4.3.2.1   Technical Guide to Information Security Testing and Assessment

The *Technical Guide to Information Security Testing and Assessment* is a guideline pertaining to basic technical aspects related to conducting information security assessments developed by the U.S. National Institute of Standards and Technology (NIST) [17]. The goal of the guideline is to help organizations develop assessment policies and methodologies, plan and safely execute the assessment, handle the technical data correctly, and translate the findings into risk mitigation actions for improving their security posture.

The guideline starts by providing an overview on security testing and assessment. This is followed by technical details on the three main categories of security testing and assessment techniques, which trainees can refer to in order to understand what the best practices in this domain are:

1. Review techniques: A class of techniques that includes review of documentation, logs and system configuration, network sniffing, and file integrity checking.
2. Target identification and analysis techniques: A class of techniques that includes network discovery, network port and service identification, vulnerability scanning, and wireless scanning.
3. Target vulnerability validation techniques: A class of techniques that includes password cracking, penetration testing, and social engineering.

The NIST guideline also contains recommendations about the planning and execution of security assessment, as well as post-testing activities. Such information can serve for trainees as a complement to their technical knowledge, so that they can become more effective security professionals.

4.3.2.2 Open Source Security Testing Methodology Manual

The *Open Source Security Testing Methodology Manual* (OSSTTM) is a comprehensive methodology that addresses the full spectrum of penetration and security testing, security analysis and operational security assessment [5]. OSSTTM, for which version 3 was released in 2010, was developed by the Institute for Security and Open Methodologies (ISECOM) with the goal of breaking the complex overall process of testing into elemental processes. The manual also defines suites of tests for verifying those elemental processes, as well as metrics that ensure the methodology has been carried out correctly and make it possible to grade the result of applying the methodology.

The guideline starts by introducing general concepts, such as an overview of security analysis and testing, operational security metrics, and trust analysis. Then details are provided on the actual security testing from several perspectives: human, physical, wireless, telecommunications, and data networks. Finally, issues such as compliance and regulations, and the security testing audit report are discussed. This comprehensive guideline provides a wealth of targeted knowledge that can support trainees in becoming more effective security professionals.

4.3.3 Attack Training Tools

Trainees must be able to master a wide range of tools in order to become effective at attack training exercises. For example, the Kali Linux distribution includes about a dozen meta installation packages that are related to offensive actions, with names such as `kali-tools-exploitation` or `kali-tools-passwords`, comprising a total of more than 100 relevant tools.

An exhaustive presentation of such tools is out of our scope, but we briefly discuss two representative examples below to illustrate the overall nature of the tools used in this context. For interested readers, a large amount of technical details about related tools can be found in *Handbook for CTFers* [10].

4.3.3.1   Nmap

Network Mapper (Nmap) is one indispensable tool used during attack training [6]. Nmap is an open-source utility that is employed for discovering the properties of hosts and services present in a computer network. This tool is often used for security auditing, but also for network inventory and various other purposes.

Nmap works by sending packets from a host into the networks that host is connected to and analyzing the responses to those packets in order to gather information about the connected hosts and services that are running on them. Nmap has a huge list of features, with the most important ones being as follows: host discovery, port scanning, service and version detection, and OS detection. Nmap also has other specific features, such as support for a scripting engine, as well as firewall and IDS evasion and spoofing mechanisms.

4.3.3.2   Metasploit

Metasploit, which is described as the "world's most used penetration testing framework" [16], is one of the most widely used tools for attack training activities. This applies in particular to those situations when complex actions need to be performed, such as exploitation.

The main strength of the Metasploit framework is represented by the large number of modules that it includes, totaling more than 5500 at the time of writing. The Metasploit modules are grouped into several classes, based on their purpose, as shown in Table 4.8. For each class, we included in the table a description of the functions that can be performed using the modules in that class, as well as an approximate count of the number of modules in it.

4.3.4   Attack Training Platforms

For illustration purposes, we provide below two examples of platforms that we consider particularly useful for attack training. The examples are selected from the CTF platforms discussed in Chap. 10, since the online nature of CTF platforms makes them easily accessible:

Table 4.8 Overview of the Metasploit module classes

Name	Module class description	Count
Auxiliary	Perform tasks such as manipulating a target machine, analyzing and gathering data, DoS attacks, scanning operations, running support servers, etc.	1200
Encoder	Encode data via algorithms such as bitwise XOR, for example, before it is transmitted over the network	50
Evasion	Generate evasive payloads without the need of external tools, for instance, to avoid anti-virus software	10
Exploit	Leverage vulnerabilities in order to execute a provided payload consisting of arbitrary code	2400
Nop	Generate 'no operation' instructions, such as those that are typically used to perform stack overflow attacks	10
Payload	Encapsulate arbitrary code that is to be later used as payload in an exploit	1400
Post	Gather, collect and enumerate data from a host that has been compromised	400

- Hack The Box (HTB) [3]: A gamified cybersecurity platform with skill improvement, certification, and ability assessment features. The platform content provides both basic CTF challenges, as well as more complex exercises relying on virtual machines. The following training categories are especially relevant from an attack training perspective: *Crypto, Hardware, Mobile, Pwn, Recon, Web* (see Sect. 10.2.2.1 for details).
- W3Challs [18]: An online CTF platform that hosts a large number of challenges that cover various areas of hacking, and which are mostly related to offensive hacking. A very useful feature of W3Challs is a fine-grained challenge tagging mechanism that makes it possible to filter challenges based on difficulty level, challenge category, but also the actual type of skills required to solve a given challenge, such as Android, ARM, Java, PHP, and Python. The following training categories are the most related to attack training: *Crypto, Misc, Pwn, Web* (see Sect. 10.2.1.6 for details).

4.4   Discussion

In what follows, we will discuss what are the main advantages of attack training, but also what potential issues are to be expected when conducting such training activities. Since it is important to consider both the trainee and organizer perspectives on these topics, we will examine them independently for each of them.

4.4.1   Main Advantages

Attack training is the most common among the three main forms of cybersecurity training, as demonstrated by the popularity of Capture The Flag (CTF) platforms. Thus, in a CTF competition, most of the challenges basically ask trainees to use different offensive techniques to retrieve flags from a target system (for a more detailed discussion of CTF platforms, see Chap. 10).

4.4.1.1   Trainee Perspective

To understand the reasons for the popularity of attack training, we will first examine its positive aspects from a trainee perspective.

Entertainment Value We consider that the entertaining nature of attack training is one of its main attractions. For example, being able to successfully conduct an attack is immediately rewarding from a trainee perspective. Gamification features used by training platforms, such as scoreboards and badges, further increase the entertainment value of attack training, as these features make it possible to quantify trainee progress in an easy-to-understand manner.

Psychological Appeal Due to the way in which hacking is represented in popular culture, such as movies, hackers have an aura of mystery and coolness that we believe to be very appealing, especially for the younger trainees. For them, it can be stated that the idea of becoming a successful hacker represents a strong psychological motivation to participate in attack training activities. Moreover, the profession of ethical hacker or pentester makes it possible to use offensive skills for non-malicious goals, hence it is a socially sanctioned way of putting into practice such skills.

Financial Rewards Many companies nowadays have bug bounty programs that provide not only public recognition, but also financial compensation to anyone who reports bugs in their products, especially in connection with security vulnerabilities. Consequently, becoming a successful ethical hacker can also have financial benefits.

While bounties usually start from amounts of hundreds of dollars, large companies have committed to provide rewards in excess of one million U.S. dollars for certain high-risk vulnerabilities. For example, Apple will provide such high rewards for demonstrating a network attack without user interaction that makes possible zero-click kernel code execution with persistence.[6]

Easy to Get Started Since there are presently many opportunities for basic attack training, for instance, by using online CTF platforms, the barrier to entry is relatively low for this form of training. Moreover, learning individual attack techniques is not particularly difficult, especially for the fundamental skills. Therefore, many trainees start with attack training, compared to other forms of cybersecurity training, due to its wider availability, and the initially straightforward learning experience.

4.4.1.2 Organizer Perspective

Let us review now what makes coordinating attack training activities attractive from an organizer perspective.

Strong Demand Given all the reasons discussed above, it is clear that attack training has a great appeal with trainees. It is natural, therefore, that organizers are willing to meet this demand by organizing such activities. Having a strong demand means that both for the free training activities, and also for the paid one, there will always be participants willing to take part. Many training companies actually provide a free tier for attracting initial customers, some of whom will also use the paid tiers for additional benefits, such as more targeted learning resources or certifications.

Easy Environment Setup Attack training is relatively easy to organize in terms of set-up overhead, especially when compared to defense training. As mentioned in Sect. 4.1.1, for many aspects of attack training there is no need to set up a training environment, or only basic environments are required, such as websites with vulnerabilities that the trainees try to exploit. Even for the more realistic training environments, while the setup procedure can be more complex, the environments are *static*. This means that once they are up and running, nothing else needs to be done, and a simple reset is enough to bring them back to the initial state before the start of a new training session.

Other features used in attack training, such as scoring, are also relatively easy to implement by using the flag concept from CTFs to determine whether a trainee was able to solve a challenge or not. In conclusion, the overall low organization overhead constitutes another aspect that makes attack training a preferred form of cybersecurity training from an organizer perspective too.

---

[6] https://security.apple.com/bounty/categories/.

4.4.2   Potential Issues

Despite the many arguments in favor of attack training that we discussed so far, this form of training can also lead to several potential issues. In what follows, we discuss those issues by using again the two perspectives of trainees and organizers.

4.4.2.1   Trainee Perspective

We consider that the issues that attack training can cause for trainees come mainly from a psychological perspective, as explained next.

Information Overload Even though learning individual offensive skills may not be very difficult when considering each skill in itself, becoming proficient at hacking requires trainees to master a large number of technical skills from a variety of areas, as demonstrated by the many challenge categories of CTF platforms. Therefore, as the training progresses, a state of information overload can occur, as some of the trainees may reach their limits when trying to learn more and more attack skills.

As a way to cope with this issue, many trainees begin to specialize in certain areas they are more successful or feel more comfortable working in. This is the reason why in many CTF competitions participation is done as teams, with each team member having a certain area of expertise.

High Competitiveness Attack training, especially when it is done in public forms, such as CTFs, is highly competitive. Accordingly, the training activity in itself can become quite stressful, which associated with the information overload issue mentioned above can lead to a burnout of the trainees.

Occasionally, the stress can also lead to the use of bad manners and even forms of abuse and harassment that may discourage other participants from attending the training. While CTFs typically have policies against this type of harmful conduct, one solution is to organize competitions that target certain groups, such as CTFs for women, with the goal of minimizing the potential for abuse.

4.4.2.2   Organizer Perspective

Next we will review several potential issues that attack training organizers may be faced with, and some possible solutions for these issues.

Ethical Issues Attack training teaches trainees how to conduct offensive actions that are intrinsically dangerous. As a consequence, it is important that organizations understand the risks associated with such training activities and find ways to mitigate them in order to avoid unwanted consequences.

For online settings, this can be achieved by withholding high-risk content from free tiers of the training platforms and verifying the identity of (and possibly vetoing) the participants in the paid tiers. Another solution, which can be used, for example, when training is conducted in educational institutions, is to conduct interviews with the candidates to evaluate their motivations and psychological fitness before accepting them into a training program. In some cases, one can imagine even running background checks on the candidates, similar to security clearance procedures.

Training Environment Isolation The training environments used in cybersecurity training can also lead to several issues if they are not correctly isolated from production networks and the Internet. A lack of isolation may make it possible for trainees, either by mistake or on purpose, to use the attack tools in the training environment on external systems. In addition to potentially serious security consequences to the hosts on the production networks and/or Internet, this also decreases the credibility of the training organizers, both at personal and institutional levels.

Isolation is important from another point of view as well, since for attack training activities the training environment typically contains security vulnerabilities. In case the environment is not isolated from external networks, it could also be subjected to attacks from the outside. This would at a minimum affect the quality of the training, but it could also enable the attackers to use the training environment as a steppingstone to penetrate the internal network of the hosting organization.

Content Creation Issues Despite the fact that content for individual training exercises is not very difficult to create, attack training requires a large amount of practice. Therefore, content creation can become a problem, as overall it requires a large amount of human effort, as well as deep knowledge of cybersecurity. Several possible solutions can be envisaged. The simplest one would be to have training ecosystems that would allow sharing of training content created by different parties. However, this solution is not feasible from a commercial perspective, since training organizations usually try to differentiate from each other, and specific content can become one of such differentiating factors.

A very modern alternative would be to employ automatic content generation techniques, for example, by using machine learning, as it has been done already in the context of cybersecurity awareness training [19]. We envisage that the rapid progress of Large Language Models (LLMs), which are now able to generate not only natural language text, but also programming language code, will make it possible in the near future to have them also generate attack training content. Such as system could, for instance, use an entry from the CVE or NVD vulnerability databases to generate the corresponding attack training content that asks the trainees to exploit that particular vulnerability.

References

1. Cybrary. Penetration testing and ethical hacking. https://www.cybrary.it/course/ethical-hacking. Accessed 1 July 2024
2. Fauzi F. CTF playbook. https://fareedfauzi.gitbook.io/ctf-playbook. Accessed 1 July 2024
3. Hack The Box. Hack The Box website. https://www.hackthebox.com/. Accessed 1 July 2024

4. Hemberg E, Turner MJ, Rutar N, O'Reilly UM (2024) Enhancements to threat, vulnerability, and mitigation knowledge for cyber analytics, hunting, and simulations. Digital Threats 5(1):8. https://doi.org/10.1145/3615668
5. Institute for Security and Open Methodologies (ISECOM). Open source security testing methodology manual (OSSTMM). https://www.isecom.org/research.html. Accessed 1 July 2024
6. Lyon G. Nmap security scanner. https://nmap.org/. Accessed 1 July 2024
7. MITRE Corporation. ATT&CK knowledge base. https://attack.mitre.org/. Accessed 1 July 2024
8. MITRE Corporation. Common attack pattern enumeration and classification (CAPEC) list. https://capec.mitre.org/. Accessed 1 July 2024
9. MITRE Corporation. Common weakness enumeration (CWE) list. https://cwe.mitre.org/. Accessed 1 July 2024
10. Nu1L Team (2022) Handbook for CTFers. Springer, Heidelberg
11. Oakley JG (2019) Professional red teaming: conducting successful cybersecurity engagements. Apress Media, LLC, New York
12. Offensive Security (OffSec). Cybersecurity certificate programs. https://learn.offsec.com/cybersecurity-certification-paths. Accessed 1 July 2024
13. Open Worldwide Application Security Project (OWASP). Web security testing guide. https://owasp.org/www-project-web-security-testing-guide/. Accessed 1 July 2024
14. OSIRIS Lab. CTF handbook. https://ctf101.org/. Accessed 1 July 2024
15. Penetration testing execution standard (PTES). http://www.pentest-standard.org/index.php/Main_Page. Accessed 1 July 2024
16. Rapid7, Inc. Metasploit: the world's most used penetration testing framework. https://www.metasploit.com/. Accessed 1 July 2024
17. Scarfone K, Souppaya M, Cody A, Orebaugh A (2008) Technical guide to information security testing and assessment. National Institute of Standards and Technology Special Publication 800-115
18. W3Challs. W3Challs website. https://w3challs.com/. Accessed 1 July 2024
19. Zeng Y (2021) Content generation and serious game implementation for security awareness training. Master's thesis, Japan Advanced Institute of Science and Technology

Chapter 5
Forensics Training

This chapter discusses in detail the forensics training form of cybersecurity training, beginning with an overview of the training methodology. The two main forensics training types, fundamental forensics training and forensic methodology training, are presented next to illustrate how to teach and learn the corresponding skills. Some related information is also provided, such as forensic methodology guidelines and forensics training tools. Lastly, the main advantages and potential issues of forensics training are discussed from the trainee and organizer points of view.

5.1 Forensics Training Overview

Forensics training refers to those cybersecurity training activities that focus on teaching trainees how to conduct digital forensic procedures, i.e., how to collect and analyze in a systematic manner the digital evidence necessary to fully understand what occurred in the case of a cybersecurity incident. Such skills make it possible for trainees to take professional roles of forensic examiners or investigators, and there are several organizations that offer certifications in this field, both in vendor-neutral and vendor-specific forms [1].

Reconstructing the steps of a cyberattack enables forensic experts to carry out several complementary tasks, such as assisting the incident responders, supporting the remediation efforts, providing evidence in case of legal actions, preparing documentation for external auditors, etc. These are all critical components of the cybersecurity strategy of an organization, hence the strong need for having an effective forensics training methodology.

R. Beuran, *Cybersecurity Education and Training*,
https://doi.org/10.1007/978-981-96-0555-2_5

5.1.1   Overall Methodology

The methodology for conducting forensics training depends on the goals of the training activities, such as teaching only fundamental skills, or focusing on more complex skill sets. The first important criterion to consider relates to the use or not of a training environment:

- No training environment: At a minimum, simply preparing some files may be enough to perform forensics training, for instance, for trainees to analyze their metadata in order to extract date/time or location information. In this case, no training environment is required, even though training platforms may have a user interface to facilitate the training activity.
- Simple training environment: For teaching more advanced skills, virtual machines can be used as training environments, for example, to make it possible for trainees to locate and extract by themselves specific data, such as browser history, log files, or registry content, before analyzing it.
- Realistic training environment: Placing the trainees in realistic situations is the most effective form of training in the case of forensics too. By using full-fledged network environments, trainees can attempt to trace the sequence of attack steps across several hosts, as it would be done in a real-world scenario.

Another important distinction that needs to be made is regarding the presence or absence of live attacks during the training, as follows:

- No attacks: Most forensics training activities are done in settings that assume that an incident has already taken place. Therefore, no attack is occurring during the training, and trainees simply have to investigate post factum the circumstances and consequences of the incident.
- Live attacks: More realistic forensics training conditions can be achieved by organizing live attacks (for example, conducted by a *red team*) while the training takes place. This makes it possible for trainees to learn how to determine if an attack is in progress, for instance, based on suspicious connection attempts, unexpected activity, etc. Note that attack detection is one aspect of forensics training that is tightly related to defense training.

It is clear from the above discussion that there is a strong interdependency between forensics training and the other forms of training, as it will be discussed next.

5.1.2   Approach Interdependency

As it was pointed out in Chap. 3 (cf. Fig. 3.1), forensics training is complemented by the two other forms of training, namely defense training and attack training. This interdependency is a key aspect of cybersecurity training, since it makes it possible for trainees to improve their corresponding skills in a mutually correlated manner, as illustrated in Fig. 5.1.

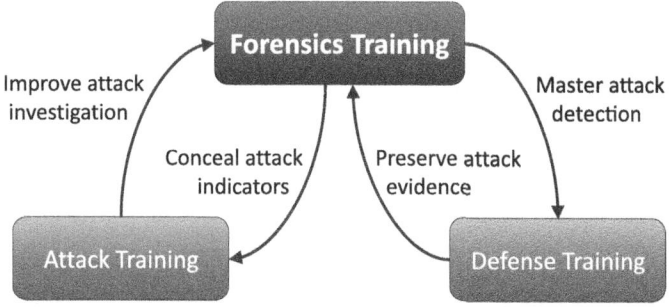

Fig. 5.1 The interdependency of forensics training with respect to the other forms of training, defense training and attack training

One of the main outcomes of forensics training is that trainees become able to detect the signs of cyberattacks based on how they are reflected in system log files, network activity, or even memory content. This understanding is extremely valuable for defense training, since attack detection represents the first step of any set of countermeasures. Furthermore, the knowledge gained via defense training in regard to possible defense mechanisms for various attacks augments the forensics training process, as it provides insights into how attack traces and evidence can be preserved and retrieved even when defense countermeasures are used.

As for the relationship with attack training, the skills acquired via forensics training makes it possible for trainees to devise ways in which the attack traces and indicators can be concealed, so that both attack detection becomes harder, and the amount of evidence left is smaller. In its turn, all the knowledge and skills gained through attack training can be fed back into forensics training, helping trainees improve their overall attack investigation skills.

The above discussion emphasizes once more the need to consider the three forms of cybersecurity training not as independent aspects of cybersecurity training, but as complementary ones. Therefore, only by continuously going through the three forms of training security professionals can improve their knowledge and skills in order to be effective in handling cybersecurity issues in real circumstances.

5.2 Forensics Training Types

In order to distinguish between teaching basic forensic techniques, and teaching the methodology of the full forensic process, we classify the forensics training activities into two types:

- Fundamental forensics training.
- Forensic methodology training.

5.2.1 Fundamental Forensics Training

Fundamental forensics training refers to teaching essential techniques that can be
employed for digital forensics and related purposes. Many CTF challenges require
trainees to use this type of basic skills for solving them. Consequently, various guidelines aimed at CTF participants, such as [2] and [7], are particularly useful references
in this context. For the purposes of this chapter, we will separate the fundamental
forensic skills into two main classes:

- Digital forensics skills.
- Reverse engineering skills.

5.2.1.1 Digital Forensics Skills

Digital forensics skills are what could be considered the most standard type of forensic skills, and many CTF competitions include a challenge category named *Forensics*
that targets these skills. The topics that refer to fundamental digital forensic skills
can be classified into three main categories:

- File analysis.
- Memory analysis.
- Network analysis.

File Analysis This is the most basic type of analysis, in which the content of files is
analyzed from a forensics perspective. Given of many types of files that exist, this
category is in fact rather broad, and it includes various subclasses, such as:

- Log analysis: Analyze system logs in order to identify suspicious activity or anoma-
  lous events.
- Database analysis: Employ specific techniques to analyze the content of databases.
- File system analysis: Analyze a file system at binary level, for instance, in order
  to retrieve files that might have been deleted on purpose by an attacker (e.g., in
  order to hide their tracks).

   In what follows, we will discuss several important issues with regard to file analysis that trainees need to consider. We note, however, that not all file analysis techniques must necessarily be mastered, and proficiency in only some areas, such as log
analysis, may be sufficient for certain work roles.

OS Specific Files Given the multitude of operating systems in current use, trainees
must be able to conduct the analysis of files that are specific to given OSs, such as:

- For Linux: System log files (e.g., in relation with remote access attempts via the
  SSH protocol, or code execution), programs configuration files (e.g., settings of
  sensitive programs, such as the remote connection server sshd), etc.

- For Windows: Event log entries and registry entries that contain important information about system events (e.g., administrative events that indicate important changes to the system) and program configuration (e.g., application settings that may indicate a malicious behavior), etc.

File Related Concepts When learning about file analysis techniques, it is also important for trainees to comprehend the following concepts:

- File formats: While file extensions are typically used to identify a file type, binary files also include a piece of information called *file signature* that allows programs that support those file types to check their validity. This information is used in forensics to identify the format of an unknown file (e.g., via the command `file`) in order to determine what tools to utilize for further analyzing it. A hexadecimal editor, which is a computer program used to view and edit the raw binary data of a file, can also be used to examine binary files in detail in case no suitable tool can be identified, or to correct corrupted file data.
- File metadata: Metadata refers to information that is associated with a file and that provides additional details about the file itself or its content. We distinguish two main cases in this context:

  - Embedded metadata: Most often, the metadata is embedded into the file itself. For example, digital photographs include EXIF (Exchangeable Image File Format) data that can be used to determine not only photography-related information, such as camera settings, but also information useful from a forensics perspective, such as when the photo was taken, and its GPS location. For this purpose, utilities such as ExifTool are used (see Sect. 5.3.3.1).
  - File system metadata: In other cases, the metadata about a file is saved in the file system. Of particular interest is the time information associated to files, such as when a file was created, modified or accessed. Using this information makes it possible to reconstruct timelines regarding the ways in which a file was used, a potentially significant piece of evidence.

- Disk imaging: This represents the process of creating the binary image of a disk, in order to make it possible to analyze that binary image without risking that the original data is tampered with. Such tampering can happen even unwillingly, for instance, with respect to file metadata such as access time, since this type of information is updated automatically by the operating system whenever a file is accessed. A potentially useful tool in this context is Foremost,[1] which uses file header and footer information, as well internal data structure, in order to recover deleted files from a binary image.

Steganography The concept of steganography, which means "concealed writing," refers to the act of hiding data in binary files, such as images or audio, typically in

---

[1] https://foremost.sourceforge.net/.

order to convey a message or some other data in an undetectable manner.[2] For example, the change caused by modifying the least significant bits in the representation of a pixel color of an image is not perceptible to the human eye, but the method can be used to hide some information in that image.

Due to the wide range of possibilities that exist in terms of steganography techniques, it is difficult to uncover messages concealed in this manner, unless there is a strong suspicion that a message is hidden in a given file. This is why CTF competitions usually have a separate category, named *Steganography* in addition to *Forensics*, dedicated to this particular type of challenge. For steganography challenges, the flag is typically hidden using simple techniques, such as making some text nearly invisible; various image filters can then be used unmask it. In other cases, a text flag can be hidden inside a binary file, for instance, in the file metadata, or by appending it at the end of the file. Metadata utilities or hexadecimal editors can be used in those cases to extract the hidden information.

In practice, one reason why malicious actors may use steganography is to exfiltrate data from a system in an undetectable manner. Especially for binary data, manipulating the least significant bits of a file representation is perhaps the most effective manner. Encrypting the message before hiding it makes retrieval even more difficult. Another use of steganography is to hide parts of ransomware or malicious JavaScript code, conceal encrypted URLs used to deliver attack payloads, and so on [8]. From a defense perspective, detecting such attacks directly is very difficult, hence analyzing software behavior is a more reliable solution in this case.

Memory Analysis While the information needed for digital forensics is typically stored on permanent storage media (hard disks, memory cards, etc.), there are cases when the necessary information is only present in the volatile memory of the system. This can happen for ongoing attacks, for instance. Hence, it is important for trainees to familiarize themselves with memory analysis techniques, so that they can retrieve any attack indicators that are present in the memory.

For real-time memory analysis, various command-line tools can be used to retrieve information about the running processes. For example, the utility `ps` can be run to examine the actual command used to launch a certain program, and the command arguments. Moreover, the utility `top` can be executed to display further details, such as the CPU and memory utilization for each process.

However, similar to the case of file systems, the state of the memory changes over time, and can also be altered by the actions of the forensics investigator. Consequently, a better approach when conducting forensics is to save the content of the RAM memory into a binary image file, typically referred to as a *memory dump*. The saved memory content can be examined via specialized tools, such as Volatility (which will be described in Sect. 5.3.3.3) to retrieve for further analysis not only information about the running processes, but also their internal data.

---

[2] A related technique is *digital watermarking*, for which the goal, however, is to mark the binary file for specific purposes, such as ownership identification and copyright.

The steps that a trainee should typically follow for the analysis of a memory dump are the following:

1. Determine the type of the memory dump (OS name, version, etc.); this is especially necessary during training exercises, when only the memory image file is provided, without any additional information.
2. List the running processes that appear in the memory dump, and look for any suspicious signs, such as unusual process names.
3. Extract the memory data related to any suspicious process that was identified at the previous step.
4. Analyze the extracted process data for indicators of malicious activity, either via simple analysis techniques, such as the `strings` command that will extract all the text from the data, or by relying on more complex procedures, such as reverse engineering (see Sect. 5.2.1.2).

Network Analysis Network activity plays an important role in the forensics process, as it can reveal how a network-based attack took place (as opposed to physical attacks that are conducted by having physical access to a system, for example, via malicious USB devices). Network analysis makes it possible to accomplish various tasks, such as identifying the type of the attack, understanding the attack techniques, and determining the scope of the incident.

Since the number of cybersecurity incidents for which the entry point is in the network is considerable large, network analysis techniques are important to master. From a learner perspective, we distinguish two subclasses in this context:

- Network traffic analysis: This refers to the analysis of actual network traffic, be it live traffic, or most typically based on a traffic capture file that contains the network packet information of interest. The network traffic mentioned here refers not only to user-generated traffic, but also to network management traffic, such as related to IP address assignment, routing, etc.
- Network activity analysis: This refers to the analysis of network-related user activity, such as web browsing, emailing, and so on, which is conducted by examining the corresponding files in the operating system, such as the web browser cache or email software storage.

For network traffic analysis, specialized analysis tools are needed, with the most often utilized tool being Wireshark (see Sect. 5.3.3.4). Such a network analysis tool makes it possible to display details about the network packets, filter them according to various criteria of interest, analyze the network traffic based on the characteristics of specific protocols, compute statistics about the network packets, and so on.

Note that, although for most internet traffic the TCP/IP protocol is used, there are instances when other protocols such as UDP, ARP, and so on, are also used, hence a broad knowledge of protocols may be required. Moreover, especially in IoT and industrial environments, completely different protocols may also appear, such as the CAN bus controller area network vehicle bus protocol, or the Modbus protocol for communication between industrial electronic devices.

We also note that some of the techniques used for network activity analysis are related to those described in the File Analysis paragraph above. Thus, for analyzing web browsing activity, trainees must be able to retrieve the browsing history and cache data, any saved cookies, etc. Then, this data must be examined based on file analysis techniques to extract the relevant information for further processing.

In this context it is important to stress that analyzing application data often requires investigating and correlating data obtained from multiple sources. For example, many applications use data files, may alter the configuration of the system, and often generate some form of network traffic. In such cases, all the techniques mentioned in the File Analysis, Memory Analysis and Network Analysis paragraphs may need to be used jointly in order to be able to draw meaningful conclusions.

5.2.1.2   Reverse Engineering Skills

The digital forensics techniques that we have discussed so far are mainly used to detect the occurrence of cybersecurity attacks, and to discover the sequence of steps that was used to conduct those attacks. However, to really understand the actual mechanisms of an attack, the malicious files used to execute that attack need to be analyzed in depth as well.

Reverse engineering is the process through which a binary (compiled) program is analyzed so that its functionality can be understood. In the context of forensics training, this refers to examining the behavior of a malicious program to identify the attack mechanisms that are embedded in it. Since this is a critical task in forensic investigations, CTF challenges often include a category named *Reversing* which covers this kind of exercises.

With regard to the practical techniques used for reverse engineering purposes, we distinguish three main classes of methods:

- Direct analysis.
- Execution analysis.
- Decompilation.

Direct Analysis The most straightforward way to analyze a binary program is to examine directly the representation of the program in assembly language, which is a human-readable representation of machine code instructions. The conversion of machine code into assembly language is typically achieved via a utility named *disassembler*. The de facto standard utility employed for this purpose in forensics is called IDA[3] (Interactive Disassembler), which is a software with a rich set of features applicable to reverse engineering.

Once a binary program is disassembled, trainees can examine the assembly language code to try to understand its functionality. Although this is in principle difficult for complex programs, for simpler programs, if one has enough knowledge of assembly language, it is not an impossible task. In order to better understand

---

[3] https://hex-rays.com/ida-free/.

the correspondence between C language and assembly language code, trainees can use the Compiler Explorer[4] online tool that shows the C and assembly language representations side by side for comparison and study purposes.

Execution Analysis The direct analysis approach only works for relatively simple programs. In more complex cases, executing the machine code helps with understanding the program behavior. To achieve this, a utility named *debugger* is used to execute the code step by step and examine how it behaves. The standard tool used for this purpose is the GNU Debugger, also known as gdb. For reverse engineering purposes, enhancing the functionality of the standard gdb with the Pwndbg[5] plugin, which has a more user-friendly interface, yields a superior and more effective debugging experience.

Debugger programs such as gdb typically have built-in disassembly functionality, and they also enable trainees to perform many other useful actions. This includes viewing the state of the CPU registers, setting execution breakpoints, executing a program one step at a time, examining internal program data and structures, changing the values of program data, and so on. Another valuable feature of gdb is that it makes it possible to attach the debugger to an already running process, so that the internal state of that live process can be analyzed.

Decompilation For programs that have complex logic, even performing execution analysis may not provide sufficient insights into the behavior of a program. In that case, as a last resort, *decompilation* can be used, which is the process of converting machine code back into a high-level programming language such as C. While decompilation cannot generate the original source code, the high-level representation that is produced makes the code analysis much easier. One utility that can be used in practice to decompile a program is Ghidra, which also provides disassembly, assembly, graphing, and scripting capabilities (see Sect. 5.3.3.2).

The main challenge with decompiled code is that variable names are automatically generated, and typically have no connection with the role that a variable plays in the program. Therefore, trainees need to try to deduce the role of variables based on the way in which they are used. Converting the decompiled C language code to a simpler programming language, such as Python, can help in this respect, since it allows trainees to focus on the functionality of each block of code.

5.2.2 Forensic Methodology Training

In order to be able to successfully conduct a forensic investigation in real life from start to finish, experts should follow a standardized methodology or process that prescribes the sequence of phases that should be followed, and the detailed actions for each phase. One common model for the forensics process is that presented in the

---

[4] https://godbolt.org/.

[5] https://pwndbg.re/.

NIST *Guide to Integrating Forensic Techniques into Incident Response* [4], and we will rely on this model for the phases discussed in this section.

In order to master the forensic process, trainees must first understand what its phases are, then study in detail the specificities and techniques corresponding to each phase. Based on the aforementioned model, forensic methodology training should cover the following four phases:

1. Collection: In this phase, various types of media sources are inspected to identify, label, record and collect the data relevant to a certain event, while making sure that data integrity is preserved.
2. Examination: In the second phase, the collected data is processed using suitable forensic tools and techniques to identify and extract all relevant information, while ensuring that information integrity is protected.
3. Analysis: Next, the extracted information is analyzed to derive the evidence related to the event of interest that is required to address all the questions pertaining to the forensics investigation.
4. Reporting: In the last phase, the obtained evidence and the actions that were performed are described in detail, along with any recommendations that can be formulated regarding the improvement of related policies, procedures, etc.

We note that the phases described above consecutively transform the available media sources into data, then into information, and finally into evidence. Remembering this sequence of transformations is important for grasping what is the input and output of each of the forensic process phases.

5.2.2.1 Collection

In order to prepare for the first phase of the forensic process, collection, trainees must learn how to perform the following types of tasks:

- How to identify the possible sources of data, both from permanent storage media and volatile memory?
- How to reliably acquire the data by following a plan that takes into account collection priorities, such as data value, volatility, amount of required effort?
- How to verify the integrity of the acquired data?
- How to document each step of the data acquiring process for future reference, including what specific tools were used?
- For ongoing incidents, how to collaborate with the incident response team, especially in terms of incident containment strategies that mitigate the evolving risks while preserving data integrity.

5.2.2.2 Examination

The second phase of the forensic process is examination, which requires trainees to learn how to perform the following actions:

- How to assess and extract the relevant pieces of information from the data collected in the previous phase?
- How to handle any system features that may hinder access to data and code, such as data compression, encryption, and access control mechanisms?
- How to identify the data sources that contain the information of interest, and how to filter any extraneous information that is also included in the data?

To accomplish the actions presented above, various technical solutions are needed that further require trainees to learn practical skills that are necessary in connection with specific tasks, such as:

- How to use text and pattern searches to identify the relevant data (e.g., which mentions a particular subject, refers to a given email address, etc.)?
- How to distinguish between types of data files, so that those that are of no interest for the examination can be excluded from the examination?
- How to inspect network traffic data, including that originating from multiple sources that must be correlated for a meaningful examination?
- How to identify the point of origin of an attack, in particular when faced with evasive techniques such as IP address spoofing, multiple or no longer valid IP addresses, etc.?
- How to examine application data by correlating several heterogeneous sources, such as file systems, memory content, and network traffic?

Many of the tasks mentioned above are the focus of fundamental forensics training, which should provide the required amount of practice for trainees. Mastering the relevant forensic tools, such as those mentioned in Sect. 5.3.3, is also important for being able to successfully accomplish these tasks.

5.2.2.3 Analysis

Analysis is the third phase of the forensic process, with its goal being to reach appropriate conclusions based on the available data (or to determine that no conclusions can be drawn). For the purpose of forensic analysis, trainees should learn how to perform the following actions:

- How to identify what are the key elements concerning an incident, such as people, items, events, etc.?
- How to determine the relations between the identified elements in view of reaching a conclusion, typically by correlating data among multiple sources?
- How to identify the various types of changes made to a system, for example, by comparing system characteristics to a known baseline?

As discussed already for the examination phase, trainees must clearly understand that when analyzing application data is of utmost importance to be able to analyze data from multiple sources, and to correlate the events across sources. This is because most modern applications use data files, alter the system configuration, and also generate network traffic, making for highly complex scenarios.

5.2.2.4   Reporting

The last phase of the forensic process, reporting, is much less technical than the previous stages. Nevertheless, the forensic report is a very significant part of the process, as it summarizes the conclusions of the analysis phase, and a report of poor quality undermines all the work that was done up to that point.

The reporting phase is not covered in fundamental forensic training; hence, trainees must make additional efforts for learning how to master it. The information to be included in a forensic report typically includes:

- Description of the actions that were conducted as part of the forensic process.
- Explanation of the selection of the tools and procedures used in the process.
- Detailed description of the results of the forensic analysis.
- Additional actions that may need to be performed (examining additional data sources, patching the identified vulnerabilities, improving the existing security controls, etc.).
- Recommendations regarding the improvement of the policies, procedures, and tools, as well as any other aspects of the forensic process.

Being able to clearly describe all the above elements is an important non-technical skill that trainees must learn. The main challenges they should be aware of in the context of forensic reporting are:

- Alternative explanations: For some incidents, several explanations may be possible; all those explanations should be considered carefully, and attempts to prove or disprove each of them should be made.
- Audience considerations: Reports must contain the kind of information that is expected by its audience, such as copies of all evidence in case of law enforcement personnel, network data for system administrators, visual representations for senior management, etc.
- Actionable information: The information extracted from data should be included in the report in an actionable form, so that it can be used for further processing or follow-up purposes (e.g., to prevent future incidents that are made possible by a discovered vulnerability).

Identifying any problems that need to be remedied in the future, and proposing possible improvements to guidelines and procedures that the forensics team should implement are very important aspects of reporting. Once such changes are carried out, all team members should be informed, and the changes should be tracked via formal mechanisms to make it possible to identify the current versions of each process and procedure document. This also represents an opportunity for team members to improve their skills, for instance, by learning how to use tools and techniques that address the latest forensic techniques.

5.3 Related Information

Forensics training is a type of training activity that requires trainees to have deep technical knowledge. In what follows, we will review several resources that we consider particularly helpful in this context, first in terms of additional information sources, such as knowledge bases and forensic methodology guidelines. Then we will discuss several tools that trainees can use during the forensics training activity, and examples of forensics training platforms.

5.3.1 Forensic Knowledge Bases

Different from attack training and defense training, forensics training does not benefit from the existence of dedicated knowledge bases. Nevertheless, some efforts were recently made to integrate a series of related standards and guidelines by using an ontological model into a knowledge base that unifies the relevant concepts in order to assist the activity of forensic investigators [5].

In addition, the interdependency between the three forms of cybersecurity training makes it possible to reuse knowledge bases related to the other forms of training in the forensics context. Below we illustrate this possibility with two knowledge base examples that are discussed more extensively in other chapters.

5.3.1.1 ATT&CK

ATT&CK is a comprehensive knowledge base that includes a wide variety of information items regarding cyberattacks, as follows (see the attack training related discussion in Sect. 4.3.1.1 for details):

- Attack tactics used by real-world adversaries.
- Attack techniques corresponding to each attack tactic.
- Procedure examples for each attack technique.
- Mitigation methods for countering each attack technique.
- Information on how to detect each attack technique.

From a forensics training perspective, we consider that the following two aspects of the ATT&CK knowledge based are most relevant for trainees:

- Procedure examples provide practical information on how certain attacks are conducted, hence the trainees can analyze them to determine what potential traces a given attack may leave in the system.
- The information related to attack detection includes valuable knowledge on how an attack manifests itself, hence for which type of signs one needs to look for to investigate that attack, for instance, via network traffic analysis.

5.3.1.2 D3FEND

D3FEND is a knowledge graph of cybersecurity countermeasures that serves as basis for the design and enactment of defense operations, such as (see the defense training related discussion in Sect. 6.3.1.1 for details):

- Defense tactics used to classify the possible defensive methods.
- Defense technique categories corresponding to each defense tactic.
- Defense techniques within each defense technique category.
- Additional information for each defense technique, including relationships with various digital artifacts, mapping to ATT&CK techniques, references to related documents, etc.

We consider that the following two aspects of D3FEND are the ones that trainees should mostly pay attention to in the context of forensics training:

- The defense techniques categories that are part of the *Detect* tactic, such as *File Analysis* and *Network Traffic Analysis*, are directly related to the corresponding aspects of forensics. Studying them in detail, for example, via the referenced documents, would provide useful background information to trainees.
- The mapping of defense techniques to the cyberattack techniques described in the ATT&CK knowledge base makes it possible to understand their mutual relationship, and how various forensic techniques can be applied in order to investigate a given attack type.

5.3.2 Forensic Methodology Guidelines

Given that digital forensic techniques are often used as part of the legal process, various standardization organizations have published guidelines regarding the associated methodology. In what follows, we will review several such guidelines.

5.3.2.1 Guide to Integrating Forensic Techniques into Incident Response

The *Guide to Integrating Forensic Techniques into Incident Response* is a guideline on how to perform computer and network forensics that was developed by the U.S. National Institute of Standards and Technology (NIST) [4]. One specific aspect of this guide is that it uses an IT perspective on forensics and provides practical information on how to effectively perform forensics activities. Therefore, we consider it to be one of the most important guidelines in the area of digital forensics, and we followed it when designing the forensics training methodology described in Sect. 5.2.2.

The guide starts with advice on how to establish forensics capabilities in an organization. Then it reviews the forensics process and its four phases: data collection, examination, analysis, and reporting. However, the most significant part of the guideline, and its key contribution to the practical aspects of forensics training, is the detailed presentation of the procedures required for handle the various types of data during a forensics investigation, as follows:

- Data from files.
- Data from operating systems.
- Data from network traffic.
- Data from applications.
- Data from multiple sources.

Another useful aspect of this guideline is that it includes the description of eight realistic scenarios that make it possible to practice the concepts presented in the guide via tabletop exercises. A general list of suggested questions for such exercises, as well as additional questions for each scenario are also provided. We consider that these scenarios could also be used by training organizers as a source of inspiration for designing practical exercises in regard to forensic techniques.

5.3.2.2 Related ISO/IEC Standards

The International Organization for Standardization (ISO) and International Electrotechnical Commission (IEC) have published several joint standards pertaining to forensics that we will briefly examine below.

ISO/IEC 27037:2012 *Guidelines for identification, collection, acquisition and preservation of digital evidence* This standard provides guidance on how to conduct the activities related to the handling of digital evidence, namely identification, collection, acquisition, as well as preservation of potential digital evidence. The devices and circumstances covered by this standard include:

- Digital storage media, such as hard drives and memory cards.
- Mobile phones, Personal Digital Assistants (PDAs).

- Digital still and video cameras.
- Computers with network connectivity.

ISO/IEC 27041:2015 *Guidance on assuring suitability and adequacy of incident investigative method* This standard provides guidelines on the mechanisms to be used in order to ensure that the methods and processes used during the investigation of an information security incident are suitable for that purpose. In particular, the following aspects are covered by this standard:

- How to capture and analyze the functional and non-functional requirements in relation with an incident investigation?
- How to validate the investigation processes to assure their suitability?
- How to assess the required levels of validation for given circumstances?
- How to integrate external testing and documentation into the validation process?

ISO/IEC 27042:2015 *Guidelines for the analysis and interpretation of digital evidence* This standard provides guidance on how to analyze and interpret digital evidence, while addressing the continuity, validity, reproducibility, and repeatability aspects related to this process. The best practices put forward in this standard include:

- How to justify the selection of a given method for a particular analysis task, and how to show its equivalence with the methods used by other investigators?
- How to demonstrate that new methods devised for the examination of digital evidence are suitable for that purpose?
- How to interpret the digital evidence processed by a certain method, depending on the exact specificities of that method?

ISO/IEC 27043:2015 *Incident investigation principles and processes* This standard provides generic guidelines for common incident investigation processes, ranging from pre-incident preparation to investigation closure, with application to various incident investigation scenarios related to digital evidence. The processes and principles described in this standard refer to forensic investigations in relation with typical cybersecurity incidents, such as:

- Unauthorized access.
- Data corruption.
- System crashes.
- Information security breaches.

The ISO/IEC standards we examined above provide less low-level technical details compared to the NIST guideline mentioned previously. Nevertheless, they do include important guidance on the general methodology to be used in forensic investigations that trainees must necessarily become familiar with if they want to conduct such investigations professionally.

5.3.3 Forensics Training Tools

There are many tools and utility programs that can be used in forensics training. Some of them are very basic, such as the `file` command that returns the type of a file and basic information about it (e.g., PNG image with a certain size and encoding), or the `strings` command that will extract all the strings from a binary file.

However, trainees should master the utilization of many other tools in order to become proficient at digital forensics. For example, the meta installation package named `kali-tools-forensics` for the Kali Linux distribution includes a list of about 70 such tools. Note that trainees must also be aware of the characteristics of anti-forensic tools, which malicious actors can utilize to conceal or destroy data, thus hindering forensic investigations.

Below we discuss some representative examples of forensic tools, especially in connection with the fundamental forensics training methodology in Sect. 5.2.1.

5.3.3.1 ExifTool

ExifTool is a utility for reading and writing meta information for a wide variety of files produced by digital cameras from many manufacturers, such as Canon, FujiFilm, Nikon, Sony, etc. The operation of ExifTool is based on the concept of tags, which are predefined labels that denote the type of meta information stored about the file, and the associated meta information.

Many tags in photographs are related to camera settings, such as image size, focal length, shutter speed, flash use, etc. From a forensics perspective, some of the most relevant tags are those related to the following types of meta information:

- Camera information: Camera make, model name, firmware version, etc.
- File information: File name and type, modification date/time, access date/time, changed date/time, etc.
- GPS information: Altitude, date/time, latitude, longitude, etc.
- Comment: A description of the image that preview software typically displays.

Some of these tags can also be utilized to embed malicious information in an image file. For example, comment tags can potentially be used for command-injection purposes. Moreover, many forensics-related CTF challenges provide image files to participants, asking them to discover flags that are hidden in the modifiable tags of those files, and ExifTool can be used to accomplish such tasks.

Another use for ExifTool is to remove tags from images in order to protect the privacy of the author. This is a significant issue given the widely spread use of photo uploading to social networks, and many online platforms automatically scrub the metadata of the uploaded photos to prevent privacy violations.

5.3.3.2   Ghidra

Ghidra is an open-source software reverse engineering suite of tools developed by U.S. National Security Agency (NSA) [6]. Ghidra is implemented in Java, and can be used on Windows, Linux and macOS platforms. Ghidra has many features for the analysis of compiled code, including disassembly, assembly, decompilation, graphing, and scripting, as summarized below:

- Disassembler functionality that displays the assembly language representation of a machine code program.
- Decompiler functionality that displays the automatically generated C language source code corresponding to a machine code program.
- Visualization of various components of a program, such as program tree, symbol tree, function call graph, etc.
- Analysis functionality for various components of a programs, such as defined strings, references to functions or addresses, etc.
- Version tracking capabilities for analyzing the differences between several versions of a program.
- Support for a variety of processor instruction sets and executable formats.
- Support for multiple users working together on a single project via the use of the Ghidra Server component.
- Optional extension components can be used to integrate other tools with Ghidra (such as Eclipse or IDA), or to add user-contributed plugins.

We consider that the visualization features and the program analysis features of Ghidra are most relevant for forensics training, especially for trainees who do not have much experience with reverse engineering.

5.3.3.3   Volatility

Volatility, which is presented as the "world's most widely used memory forensics platform" [9], is a memory analysis framework that makes it possible to conduct forensics investigations based on the content of system memory. Volatility is mainly used to extract digital artifacts from RAM memory images of computer systems, so that the runtime state of those systems can be examined.

The supported memory image formats in Volatility correspond to a wide range of Windows, Linux and Mac operating system versions. However, for acquiring the actual memory images, external tools need to be utilized, such as the dd utility; alternatively, special files can be used, such as hibernation files or crash dump files.

The power of Volatility in the context of forensics training comes from the very large set of plugins that it includes, which the trainees can use to perform very specific tasks with regard to the memory image content. In Table 5.1 we present, for illustration purposes, the categories of plugins available for Linux, with several representative commands mentioned for each category.

Table 5.1 Overview of the Linux plugin categories available in Volatility

Name	Command examples
Processes	`linux_pslist`, `linux_pstree`, `linux_lsof`
Process Memory	`linux_memmap`, `linux_bash`
Kernel Memory and Objects	`linux_lsmod`, `linux_moddump`
Rootkit Detection	`linux_check_tty`, `linux_keyboard_notifier`
Networking	`linux_arp`, `linux_ifconfig`, `linux_netstat`
System Information	`linux_cpuinfo`, `linux_dmesg`, `linux_mount`
Miscellaneous	`linux_volshell`, `linux_yarascan`

5.3.3.4 Wireshark

Wireshark, which is described as the "world's most popular network protocol analyzer" [11], is one of the most widely used tools for network analysis, and consequently for network forensics purposes. Although the tool can be used to analyze live network traffic or capture it for further analysis, in forensics training the most common use of Wireshark is for the analysis of network packet capture files in the standard format named PCAP (e.g., produced via command-line tools such as `tcpdump`). In CTF challenges, as well, PCAP files are provided to participants for investigation and flag retrieval.

The Wireshark features that we consider most important in the context of forensics training are as follows:

- Display network packets with details about each protocol layer embedded in them (e.g., Ethernet, IP, UDP, etc.).
- Filter network packets based on many criteria, such as source and destination IP address, source and destination ports, etc.
- Colorize the displayed packets based on various filters for the easy identification of each protocol or packet type.
- Analyze network packets based on the characteristics of specific protocols, such as TCP data and control flows, etc.
- Create various statistics about the network packets, such as packet counts for each type of protocol, network statistics, etc.

5.3.4   Forensics Training Platforms

For illustration purposes, we provide below two examples of platforms that we consider particularly useful for forensics training. The examples are selected from the CTF platforms discussed in Chap. 10, since their online nature makes them easy to access and use:

- HackThisSite [3]: A free online training platform with content divided into two main categories: basic Jeopardy-style challenges that are aimed at beginners, and realistic missions that ask participants to target training websites with built-in security flaws via a role-playing game approach. The training categories most relevant from a forensics training perspective are *Forensics* and *Steganography*, with the latter being important, as HackThisSite is one of the few platforms that has a distinct category for this type of challenges (see Sect. 10.2.1.3 for details).
- W3Challs [10]: A free online CTF platform that hosts a large number of challenges, and which includes a fine-grained challenge tagging mechanism. The tags make it possible for participants to filter challenges, including based on the actual type of skills required to solve them, such as Android, ARM, Java, Python, etc. The training categories that are most related to forensics training are *Forensics* and *Reversing*, with W3Challs being one of the few platforms that includes reverse engineering challenges[6] (see Sect. 10.2.1.6 for details).

5.4   Discussion

Similar to how we proceeded for attack training, in this section we will discuss what are the main advantages of forensics training, but also what potential issues can be expected when conducting this kind of training activities. Again, we will examine both the trainee and organizer perspectives, so as to provide a well-rounded view regarding this topic.

5.4.1   Main Advantages

Due to its characteristics, forensics training presents several advantages compared to the other forms of cybersecurity training, as discussed next.

---

[6] The Hack The Box platform too includes a reverse engineering category (see Sect. 10.2.2.1).

5.4.1.1 Trainee Perspective

First, we will discuss some of the advantages that we consider specific to forensics training from a trainee perspective.

Low Stress Aside from live incident detection, forensics training only involves various types of investigations of incident traces. Consequently, we judge it to be a more stress-free form of training compared to attack and defense training. This aspect can appeal to some of the trainees, who may find this kind of stress-free training experience more comfortable.

Career Opportunities Cybersecurity experts can work in a wide variety of environments. However, forensics experts have the specific opportunity to work in governmental agencies and law enforcement related professions. This type of careers may be very attractive for some trainees, and certifications such as Certified Computer Examiner (CCE) or Certified Cyber Forensics Professional (CCFP) are only a few of the relevant certifications that can help them achieve these goals.

5.4.1.2 Organizer Perspective

As for the organizer perspective, here are some of the advantages of forensics training compared to other forms of training.

Certification Demand As it was mentioned above when discussing career opportunities from a trainee perspective, working in governmental agencies and law enforcement is one of the appeals of digital forensics. However, in order to be able to join such professions, certification from a recognized authority is required. This leads to a corresponding demand for forensics training, and organizers can definitely benefit from such a demand. Moreover, such certifications typically need to be renewed regularly, which creates further opportunities for organizers.

Easy Training Setup The vast majority of forensics training exercises, especially with regard to fundamental skills, simply require preparing files that the trainees need to analyze. Hence the setup process for a forensics training activity is relatively easy compared to attack and defense training.

Even for more complex types of forensics training, in which realistic network environments that trainees will investigate must be prepared, their generally static nature, without events that need to be managed in real time, makes training environment setup relatively easy in this case as well.

5.4.2 Potential Issues

Forensics training can also lead to several potential issues that we will discuss below, first from a trainee and then from an organizer perspective.

5.4.2.1   Trainee Perspective

The most important issues that trainees can expect when conducting forensics training are examined below.

Acquiring Non-technical Skills Being able to conduct a forensic investigation requires from trainees a series of non-technical skills. Some of them are tightly related to personal aptitudes, such as the ability to think analytically, to organize one's activity, to draw conclusions about data, to pay attention to detail throughout the investigative processes. Learning such skills may be challenging for some trainees, who may even end up finding this type of work too tiresome.

Other phases of the forensics methodology, in particular reporting, requires trainees to possess excellent written and verbal communication skills, and to be able to explain complex information in a clear and concise manner. This type of abilities are easier to learn, but sufficient practice is required to master them at a satisfactory level.

Task Complexity When attempting a forensic analysis, trainees need to consider many possibilities and scenarios, as cybersecurity incidents can occur in a variety of patterns. Therefore, being able to locate and put together the necessary information for understanding the incident can be a challenging task. Although some trainees may consider this variety as a positive and motivating factor, we consider that becoming proficient at forensics requires an important amount of learning. Nevertheless, the learning curve can be greatly improved by leveraging any previous experience with cybersecurity incidents a trainee may have.

5.4.2.2   Organizer Perspective

From an organizer perspective, some of the challenges related to forensics training are as follows.

Teaching Non-technical Skills The challenge related to acquiring non-technical skills mentioned above for trainees is also relevant from an organizer perspective. This is because organizers must devise ways through which this kind of skills, such as analytical thinking, can be taught. However, a lack of a standardized methodology in this field makes the task difficult. We consider that the best approach to tackle this issue is that instructors explain their own thought processes to trainees, then help them practice via non-technical exercises as needed.

Accreditation Requirements As mentioned previously, forensics experts have the opportunity to work in governmental agencies and law enforcement jobs. This aspect creates constraints on training organizers who want to target such trainees, as the training programs must then be aligned with the requirements of those professions. Moreover, in order that their certifications are recognized in these domains, the training programs themselves need to be accredited/approved by a government entity, such as the ANSI National Accreditation Board (ANAB) in the U.S. These requirements create a management and financial overhead that the organizers should be aware of before attempting to set up such training programs.

References

1. Bowcut S (2014) In-demand digital forensics certifications. https://cybersecurityguide.org/programs/cybersecurity-certifications/digital-forensics/. Accessed 1 July 2024
2. Fauzi F. CTF playbook. https://fareedfauzi.gitbook.io/ctf-playbook. Accessed 1 July 2024
3. HackThisSite. HackThisSite website. https://www.hackthissite.org/. Accessed 1 July 2024
4. Kent K, Chevalier S, Grance T, Dang H (2006) Guide to integrating forensic techniques into incident response, NIST special publication 800-86. https://doi.org/10.6028/NIST.SP.800-86
5. Matijević Gostojić M, Vuković Ž (2023) A knowledge-based system for supporting the soundness of digital forensic investigations. Forensic Sci Int Digital Invest 46:301601
6. National Security Agency. Ghidra website. https://ghidra-sre.org/. Accessed 1 July 2024
7. OSIRIS Lab. CTF handbook. https://ctf101.org/. Accessed 1 July 2024
8. SentinelOne. Hiding code inside images: how malware uses steganography. https://www.sentinelone.com/blog/hiding-code-inside-images-malware-steganography/. Accessed 1 July 2024
9. Volatility Foundation. Volatility website. https://volatilityfoundation.org/. Accessed 1 July 2024
10. W3Challs. W3Challs website. https://w3challs.com/. Accessed 1 July 2024
11. Wireshark Foundation. Wireshark website. https://www.wireshark.org/. Accessed 1 July 2024

Chapter 6
Defense Training

This chapter discusses in detail the defense training form of cybersecurity training, starting with an overview of the training methodology. The two main defense training types, fundamental defense training and defense methodology training, are presented next from the perspective of teaching or learning the corresponding skills. Some related information is also provided, such as defense knowledge bases and defense training tools. Finally, the main advantages and potential issues of defense training are discussed from the trainee and organizer points of view.

6.1 Defense Training Overview

Defense training refers to those cybersecurity training activities that focus on teaching trainees how to defend network systems from cyberattacks. To achieve this goal, a multidimensional approach is required that comprises the implementation of security controls and verification of their effectiveness, effective security operations and analysis, reliable security architectures and engineering, and so on. By mastering such skills, trainees are able to take various roles in an organization, such as members of a Cybersecurity Operation Center (CSOC), architects of security and risk management solutions, etc.

6.1.1 Overall Methodology

The methodology used to conduct defense training activities depends on the specific goals of the training, such as teaching fundamental skills or more complex ones. However, differently from attack and forensics training, having a training environment is inherently always necessary when conducting defense training. This is because,

© The Author(s), under exclusive license to Springer Nature Singapore Pte Ltd. 2025   97
R. Beuran, *Cybersecurity Education and Training*,
https://doi.org/10.1007/978-981-96-0555-2_6

apart from general knowledge and best-practice information gained through study, actual defense skills need to be practiced. The complexity of the environment can be adjusted to the training goal, though, as follows:

- Simple training environment: For teaching basic skills, such as those related to the configuration and settings that are required to harden a system, simple forms of training environments are sufficient, such as virtual machines with the target operating system and applications installed.
- Realistic training environment: For more complex skills, especially those that are related to networking aspects, such as network intrusion prevention or network traffic filtering, full-fledged network environments are needed, so that trainees can practice their skills in realistic conditions.

Another important distinction is that regarding live attacks that could be included during the training, with two main possibilities:

- No attacks: For many defense training activities, having a passive environment is sufficient for practicing a wide variety of skills. Trainees can use such environments to make certain that they have the required practical abilities related to specific defense mechanisms, for instance, how to configure firewalls, how to harden the operating system and communication settings, etc. Note, however, that passive environments do not make it possible to test the effectiveness of the defense techniques the trainees use.
- Live attacks: To determine how effective the defense skills of a trainee are, live attacks are needed, as their success or failure can be used to judge whether a defense technique was used correctly or not. Most often, live attacks are conducted by a *red team*, as part of the training activity. However, emulated live attacks can also be used as a lower-cost approach that, in addition, ensures the reproducibility of training conditions.

Next, we will proceed to discuss in more detail the interdependency that exists between defense training and the other forms of training.

6.1.2   Approach Interdependency

As indicated in Chap. 3 (cf. Fig. 3.1), defense training is complemented by two other forms of training, namely attack training and forensics training. These three forms of training, combined, cover all the cybersecurity skills that a security professional needs to master. However, the interdependency between these three forms of training, as illustrated in Fig. 6.1 from a defense training perspective, is important to keep in mind in the overall context of cybersecurity training.

The main outcome of defense training is, obviously, that trainees are able to master a wide variety of defense mechanisms that they can apply in practice to block and mitigate attacks. This in-depth understanding is extremely valuable when conducting

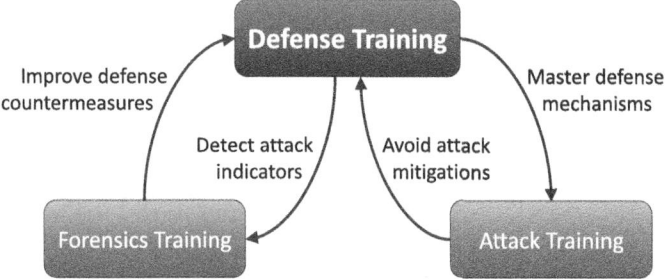

Fig. 6.1 The interdependency of defense training with respect to the other forms of training, attack training and forensics training

attack training, as trainees can then switch to an attacker mindset, and try to devise techniques that make it possible to avoid those attack mitigations; thus, trainees can further improve the effectiveness of their attack skills.

Via defense training, trainees also become proficient at detecting the key attack indicators for various categories of attacks. This knowledge is beneficial for forensics training, of which attack detection is an important component. Moreover, forensics training informs trainees on how to improve the defense countermeasures, so that in turn their defense skills improve as well. In fact, Digital Forensics and Incident Response (DFIR) is a cybersecurity specialization that addresses the identification, investigation, and remediation of cyberattacks. This specialization further emphasizes the tight connection that exists between forensics and defense training.

As mentioned already, even though we have discussed the three forms of cybersecurity training in separate chapters, and often training activities are conducted separately as well, it is essential to recognize their strong interdependency. By continuously going back and forth between all the three forms of training, trainees are able to form a comprehensive view on cybersecurity and master the full range of skills needed in a wide variety of related jobs.

6.2 Defense Training Types

In order to distinguish between teaching basic defense techniques, and teaching the detailed procedure corresponding to the full cyber defense methodology, we classify the defense training activities into two types:

- Fundamental defense training.
- Defense process training.

6.2.1 *Fundamental Defense Training*

Fundamental defense training refers to teaching essential techniques that can be employed for cyber defense purposes. In what follows, we will examine the fundamental defense skills from two perspectives, as follows:

- Types of skills, examined based on the abilities required to use the skills.
- Purposes of skills, considered based on the intended function of the skills.

For the discussion of the fundamental defense skills, we will make reference to two sources of information. When considering skills based on their type, we will refer to the mitigations in the MITRE ATT&CK knowledge base (see Sect. 6.3.1.3 for details). Then, when discussing the skills from the perspective of their purpose, the defense tactics, categories and techniques in the D3FEND knowledge graph (see Sect. 6.3.1.1 for details) will be used as reference. At the end, we will also conduct a comparison of the two perspectives, which will provide some interesting insights.

6.2.1.1 Fundamental Defense Skills by Type

From the point of view of the trainees learning them, the easiest way to consider skills is in a bottom-up manner, in which the skills are classified based on their type, as this makes it simpler for trainees to target a given skill in order to learn it. We identified four types of skills from this perspective, as shown next:

- Configuration skills: Abilities regarding how to perform configurations and settings related to security.
- Tools use skills: Abilities with regard to the use of software tools and utilities related to security.
- Mechanisms use skills: Abilities related to employing specific security mechanisms and techniques.
- Awareness skills: General practices and knowledge important in a defense context.

When discussing below these four types of defense skills, we will mention the corresponding mitigations from the MITRE ATT&CK knowledge base. Trainees can use them as reference in order to obtain practical information about each mitigation, and the way in which it can be implemented for specific attack techniques.

For this purpose, all the 43 MITRE ATT&CK mitigations currently available in the Enterprise matrix are presented in Table 6.1 in alphabetical order, the same order in which they are displayed in the knowledge base. The table also includes the identifiers for each mitigation, as well as our classification by skill type in the third column. Note that the right-hand portion of the table presents information about the defense tactics, categories and techniques from the D3FEND knowledge graph corresponding to those mitigations, which will be referred to in Sect. 6.2.1.3.

Configuration Skills The ability to correctly configure the operating system and applications is a key defense skill. Since the range of the types of configurations and

Table 6.1 Required types of skills, and mapping into corresponding D3FEND tactics, categories and techniques, for the ATT&CK mitigations in the Enterprise matrix

Id	ATT&CK mitigation	Skill type	D3FEND tactic	Cat./Tech.
M1036	Account Use Policies	Configuration	Harden	D3-CH*
M1015	Active Directory Configuration	Configuration	Isolate	D3-MAC
M1049	Antivirus/Antimalware	Tools	Detect	D3-FCOA
M1013	Application Developer Guidance	Awareness	–	–
M1048	Application Isolation and Sandboxing	Mechanisms	Isolate	D3-KBPI
M1047	Audit	Mechanisms	Model	~D3-SYSVA
M1040	Behavior Prevention on Endpoint	Tools	Detect	D3-PA*
M1046	Boot Integrity	Configuration	Harden	D3-TBI
M1045	Code Signing	Configuration	Harden	D3-AH*
M1043	Credential Access Protection	Tools	Harden	D3-CH*
M1053	Data Backup	Tools	–	–
M1057	Data Loss Prevention	Tools	Model	~D3-DI
M1042	Disable or Remove Feature or Program	Configuration	Harden	D3-AH*
M1055	Do Not Mitigate	Awareness	–	–
M1041	Encrypt Sensitive Information	Mechanisms	Harden	D3-MENCR
M1039	Environment Variable Permissions	Configuration	Harden	D3-SCP
M1038	Execution Prevention	Configuration	Isolate	D3-EDL
M1050	Exploit Protection	Tools	Detect	D3-PA*
M1037	Filter Network Traffic	Mechanisms	Isolate	D3-NTF
M1035	Limit Access to Resource Over Network	Mechanisms	Isolate	D3-NI*
M1034	Limit Hardware Installation	Configuration	Harden	D3-PH*
M1033	Limit Software Installation	Configuration	Harden	D3-PH*
M1032	Multi-Factor Authentication	Configuration	Harden	D3-MFA
M1031	Network Intrusion Prevention	Tools	Detect	D3-NTA*
M1030	Network Segmentation	Mechanisms	Isolate	D3-NI
M1028	Operating System Configuration	Configuration	Harden	D3-PH*
M1027	Password Policies	Configuration	Harden	D3-SPP
M1056	Pre-Compromise	Awareness	–	–
M1026	Privileged Account Management	Configuration	Harden	D3-UAP
M1025	Privileged Process Integrity	Configuration	Isolate	D3-EI*
M1029	Remote Data Storage	Tools	Harden	D3-AH*
M1022	Restrict File and Directory Permissions	Configuration	Harden	D3-LFP
M1044	Restrict Library Loading	Configuration	Harden	D3-DLIC
M1024	Restrict Registry Permissions	Configuration	Harden	D3-SCP
M1021	Restrict Web-Based Content	Configuration	Harden	D3-AH*
M1054	Software Configuration	Configuration	Harden	D3-ACH
M1020	SSL/TLS Inspection	Tools	Detect	D3-FC
M1019	Threat Intelligence Program	Awareness	–	–
M1051	Update Software	Mechanisms	Harden	D3-SU
M1052	User Account Control	Configuration	Harden	D3-UAP
M1018	User Account Management	Configuration	Harden	D3-UAP
M1017	User Training	Awareness	–	–
M1016	Vulnerability Scanning	Tools	Model	D3-SYSVA

settings is wide, a significant amount of knowledge is required for that. We review below the most important types of settings that need to be performed:

- Operating system configuration: Settings related to application integrity verification (M1045), unnecessary software use prevention (M1042), environment variable modification permissions (M1039), undesired application execution prevention (M1038), limiting installation of unapproved software (M1033), mechanisms for hardening the operating system (M1028), restricting access to files and directories (M1022), protection of processes with high privileges (M1025), library loading restrictions (M1044), and registry/configuration restrictions (M1024).
- Account configuration: Settings related to user account management (M1018), multi-factor authentication (M1032), policies related to user accounts (M1036), policies regarding passwords (M1027), management of privileged accounts (M1026), and management of user account elevation mechanisms (M1052).
- Application/service configuration: Settings related to Active Directory service management (M1015), restrictions on access to web-based content (M1021), and mechanisms for hardening applications and services (M1054).
- Host-level configuration: Settings related to secure booting (M1046), and limiting installation of unauthorized hardware, including USB devices (M1034).

Based on the large number of mitigations referenced above—21 in total, which makes almost half of the total number of mitigations in the MITRE ATT&CK Enterprise matrix—it is clear that this type of skill is very important. Most of the necessary settings have to be done at the operating system level (10 in total), hence good knowledge of operating systems is important for defense training. In addition, many settings are related to account configuration (6 in total), as this represents a key defense mechanism. Mastering techniques for hardening applications and services, as well as securing hosts is also important.

Tools Use Skills To be effective, trainees must also master the use of various software tools and utilities that are employed for cyber defense purposes. These tools cover a wide variety of aspects, such as:

- Execution prevention: Software tools with functionality related to virus/malware detection (M1049), suspicious behavior prevention (M1040), protection from exploits (M1050), and network intrusion prevention (M1031).
- Access and loss prevention: Software tools with capabilities related to credential access prevention (M1043), data loss prevention (M1057), remote storage or backup of security logs and sensitive files (M1029), and the inspection of encrypted traffic for adversary activity (M1020).
- General security purposes: Software tools with capabilities related to scanning systems for vulnerabilities (M1016), and data backup (M1053).

From the list above—in which a total of 10 skills were mentioned—it is obvious that execution and access/loss prevention are key defense mechanisms, with 8 skills in total being included in those two areas, and trainees must necessarily master the utilization of the related software tools. However, abilities related to software tools that implement two fundamental security best practices, namely vulnerability scanning and data backup, are also important.

Mechanisms Use Skills This category includes a number of specific mechanisms and techniques—corresponding to a total of 7 skills—which are employed to ensure the security of a system, and that the trainees should necessarily learn how to employ, as described below:

- Application isolation and sandboxing: Using isolation and sandboxing techniques makes it possible to restrict code execution to virtual environments in order to lower the associated security risks (M1048).
- Auditing: To be able to identify any existing potential weaknesses, it is important for trainees to know how to conduct audits and scans of systems, permissions and configurations (M1047).
- Encryption: The encryption of sensitive information is a critical aspect of any defense strategy, being one of the strongest methods in this context from a theoretical/mathematical perspective (M1041).
- Traffic filtering/limitation: Filtering network traffic is an important defense mechanism, and trainees must master skills and knowledge related to the use of network appliances and/or endpoint software for filtering network traffic (M1037), and for limiting remote access to network-connected resources, such as files shares, data base systems, and so on (M1035).
- Network segmentation: Network segmentation refers to designing the topology of a network in such a manner that critical functions and resources are isolated (M1030); this can be done physically or logically, via architectures such as DMZ (Demilitarized Zone), or mechanisms such as VPC (Virtual Private Cloud).
- Software updates: As an important aspect of any defense strategy, all software should be regularly updated (M1051); a challenge in this context is identifying how to avoid impacting the operations of the organization, and suitable update strategies should be designed for this purpose.

Awareness Skills In this category we include those defense best practices that are not related to actual technical skills, but rather to knowledge that is necessary for a comprehensive approach to defense. The items in this category are as follows:

- Training activities: Trainees must acknowledge the need for defense-related training activities; this includes guidance and training for application developers (M1013), as well as training for regular users (M1017).
- Threat intelligence: Given the importance of threat intelligence, having an internal threat intelligence program can significantly improve the defense capabilities of an organization (M1019).
- Mitigation limitations: Trainees should be aware that for certain attack techniques, such as execution guardrails, mitigations may actually increase the damage. Therefore, choosing *not* to mitigate is the recommended approach in such cases (M1055); moreover, pre-compromise attack techniques, i.e., those that precede initial access, such as reconnaissance, are often difficult to mitigate (M1056).

Although only 5 elements in total are included in the awareness category, their wide scope shows that this type of knowledge is also important in the context of defense training and should be taken into account by trainees.

6.2.1.2   Fundamental Defense Skills by Purpose

Once trainees master several types of skills, it is important to also consider what is the function of those skills, that is, for what purpose they are to be used, in a top-down perspective. This makes it possible for trainees to reason about the ways in which specific skills are to be used not only individually, but as a combination, in order to achieve a certain defense goal.

For the presentation of the fundamental defense skills based on their purpose, we will rely on the defense tactics presented in the D3FEND knowledge base (see Sect. 6.3.1.1). Those defense tactics are listed below, where we also mention the number of corresponding techniques and technique categories for each tactic, based on the information in Table 6.2, to give an indication of their respective weight in the overall model:

- Modeling (27 techniques).
- Hardening (33 techniques).
- Detection (77 techniques).
- Isolation (23 techniques).
- Deception (11 techniques).

Table 6.2 Overview of the tactics in the D3FEND knowledge graph

Name	Tactic definition	Count
Model	The model tactic is used to apply security engineering, vulnerability, threat, and risk analyses to digital systems. This is accomplished by creating and maintaining a common understanding of the systems being defended, the operations on those systems, actors using the systems, and the relationships and interactions between these elements	27
Harden	The harden tactic is used to increase the opportunity cost of computer network exploitation. Hardening differs from Detection in that it generally is conducted before a system is online and operational	33
Detect	The detect tactic is used to identify adversary access to or unauthorized activity on computer networks	77
Isolate	The isolate tactic creates logical or physical barriers in a system which reduces opportunities for adversaries to create further accesses	23
Deceive	The deceive tactic is used to advertise, entice, and allow potential attackers access to an observed or controlled environment	11
Evict	The eviction tactic is used to remove an adversary from a computer network	12
Restore	The restore tactic is used to return the system to a better state	12

- Eviction (12 techniques).
- Restoration (12 techniques).

We suggest that readers refer to Table 6.1 as a complement to the discussion below. Of particular note is the fact that, the mitigations in the ATT&CK knowledge base that we considered in Sect. 6.2.1.1 refer to one of the following D3FEND tactics: *Harden, Detect, Isolate,* and *Model.* Consequently, the corresponding ATT&CK mitigations can be used to obtain more practical details about the skills required for those four purposes. This also means, however, that trainees should also pay a special attention to the other tactics mentioned next, in order to gain a more thorough understanding of defense training aspects that were not yet covered.

Modeling Modeling refers to the creation of a logical model that reflects the common understanding of all the elements related to an organization: the systems to be defended, their operations, and the actors using them. The tasks that are involved for this defense aspect are as follows:

- Create an inventory of all the assets of interest in terms of configuration, data, hardware and software components, network nodes, etc.
- Map all the network resources, both regarding logical and physical links, and including any associated traffic policies.
- Map all operational activities of the organization, such as access modeling, dependency and organization mapping, risk assessment.
- Map all the information related to systems, such as data exchange modeling, service and system dependency mapping, vulnerability assessment.

Hardening Hardening refers to all the steps that should be taken before making a system available online and operational. The purpose of this category of skills is to strengthen the system, so that it becomes more difficult to exploit from an adversary perspective. Some examples of tasks in this category are:

- Update all applications and software packages, patch all known vulnerabilities.
- Configure the firewalls, including web application firewalls, to allow the minimum set of traffic types that are required for the system to operate correctly.
- Ensure that users have only the minimum set of permissions needed to perform their tasks, and that suitable authentication policies are in place.

Detection Detection refers to discovering the occurrence of a cyber incident as early as possible. For this purpose, a wide range of techniques are required that consider various aspects of the system or network that is to be defended. Below we provide some examples of relevant tasks in this category:

- Monitor files and processes for signs of suspicious activity (although utilities such as anti-virus software can be relied on for this purpose during normal operation, manual analysis may be required once suspicious activity is detected).
- Monitor network traffic for signs of suspicious activity (as mentioned above, even though utilities such as intrusion detection systems can be used during normal operation, manual analysis may be need if suspicious activity is detected).

- Monitor user activity for signs of suspicious activity (again, utilities for monitoring behavior patterns can be relied on during normal operation, but manual analysis may be required in case any suspicious activity is detected).

Isolation Isolation techniques are those techniques used to restrict the possibilities of an adversary expanding their control over a system in case of an incident. There are two main types of tasks in this context:

- Isolate processes by creating restrictions on what processes can be executed, what resources they can access, etc.
- Isolate hosts by introducing restrictions on what network resources they can access, the types of traffic they can send and receive, etc.

Deception Deception represents a class of modern defense techniques that attempt to make potential attackers target a controlled environment in order to reduce the risk to the organization, and to be able to observe their malicious behavior (for a more detailed discussion of this approach, see Sect. 6.3.1.2). The main tasks in this context are as follows:

- Create a decoy environment that will become the target of the attack, such as a honeynet connected to the enterprise network that emulates certain functionality in order to attract adversaries.
- Create decoy objects that will become attack targets or vectors, such as files, network resources, session tokens or user credentials, etc.

Eviction Eviction refers to those defense techniques that are used to remove attackers from a system. For this purpose, defenders must strive to eradicate the effects of attacker activity, as illustrated next:

- Eliminate credentials that were used by attackers by techniques such as locking of the compromised accounts, invalidation of the authentication cache, revoking of credentials, etc.
- Eliminate files that were used by attackers, such as malicious artifacts or programs, malicious emails, etc. (the files may, however, be stored securely for future purposes, such as forensics).
- Eliminate processes that are related to an attack by suspending or terminating those processes, shutting down or rebooting the compromised hosts, etc.

Restoration In order to return a system to its operational state, various restoration techniques must be used. This category includes skills that aim to:

- Restore access to all the compromised components, such as network access, and user account access.
- Restore all the compromised objects, such as configurations, databases, files, and software, as well as reissue credentials.

6.2.1.3 Training Perspective Comparison

None of the two perspectives we discussed so far is intrinsically better or worse than the other. However, considering the fundamental defense skills based on their type (i.e., bottom up), or considering them based on their purpose (i.e., top down), as we did in Sects. 6.2.1.1 and 6.2.1.2, respectively, have each their own advantages and disadvantages in terms of ease of learning.

Nonetheless, the type-based skill classification makes more sense for trainees who start defense training, and in this section, we will use this perspective to compare the two approaches. Based on the mapping that we conducted in Table 6.1, we note several interesting insights, as follows:

- Most ATT&CK mitigations are mapped into the *Harden* D3FEND tactic—22 in total—emphasizing the significance of hardening for both perspectives.
- The other ATT&CK mitigations are mapped into the *Isolate, Detect, Model* D3FEND tactics—7, 5, and 3 mitigations, respectively—showing both the importance of those tactics, and the fact that the overlap between the two knowledge bases is not very strong.
- A total of 6 ATT&CK mitigations could not be mapped at all into D3FEND tactics; most of them refer to the *Awareness* category that we discussed, which D3FEND, being oriented toward immediate practical measures, does not cover.
- The mapping process of ATT&CK mitigations was not straightforward when reaching the level of D3FEND techniques, further emphasizing that the two knowledge bases each contain specific information that could be used to complement each other. Some of the difficulties we encountered were:

  - Some mitigations, such as *Privileged Account Management, User Account Control*, and *User Account Management* had to be mapped into the same D3FEND technique, *User Account Permissions* (D3-UAP), showing that the level of detail of the knowledge bases can be different in some instances.
  - For several mitigations, no suitable D3FEND technique could be identified, and we used a suitable technique category instead; for example, we mapped *Account Use Policies* into the generic *Credential Hardening* (D3-CH) technique category. In such cases, the suffix '*' was used to denote that the mapping is a category, not a technique.
  - In a few occasions, the D3FEND technique corresponding to an ATT&CK mitigation covered only partially the scope of the mitigation; for instance, we consider that the *System Vulnerability Assessment* (D3-SYSVA) technique has a narrower scope than the *Audit* mitigation. For these situations, the prefix '~' was used to denote that the mapping is approximate.

6.2.2 Defense Methodology Training

For the outline of the training methodology with regard to the overall defense process, we will rely on the functions defined in the NIST Cybersecurity Framework (CSF) that will be detailed in Sect. 6.3.2.1, as they cover all aspects of a well-rounded defense methodology. The functions refer to the following aspects and expected outcomes of the defense process:

1. Govern: Manage the overall organization cybersecurity risk management strategy.
2. Identify: Determine what are the relevant cybersecurity risks for the organization.
3. Protect: Safeguard the organization assets so as to manage the identified risks.
4. Detect: Find and analyze potential cybersecurity attacks and compromises.
5. Respond: Take the necessary actions in order to mitigate a cybersecurity incident.
6. Recover: Restore all the organization assets and operations that were affected by a cybersecurity incident.

We note that there is some overlap between the methodology presented here and the D3FEND tactics discussed in Sect. 6.2.1.2. This is because this CSF-based methodology also takes a top-down view on defense. However, a complete defense process needs to consider the overall perspective of an organization, not only a technical defense point of view. Consequently, trainees should keep in mind this generic methodology for a comprehensive overview of all the defense-related activities and refer as needed to D3FEND tactics for technical details.

6.2.2.1   Govern

The initial factors to consider regarding the defense of an organization are the overall governing aspects regarding risk management. Although this function is not technically oriented, it is essential for several cybersecurity work roles, such as Chief Information Security Officer (CISO) or cybersecurity risk manager. Therefore, trainees who aim to work in such roles should learn how to address the following issues in relation with an organization:

- How to determine the context (mission, expectations, requirements, etc.) surrounding the cybersecurity risk management decisions?
- How to formulate the strategy (priorities, constraints, assumptions, etc.) regarding risk management, and how to use it to support the decision process?
- How to establish and communicate the relevant roles, responsibilities, and authorities regarding cybersecurity?
- How to establish, communicate and enforce the cybersecurity policy?
- How to leverage the oversight of risk management activities to continuously improve the risk management strategy?
- How to establish and monitor the supply chain risk management processes?

6.2.2.2 Identify

From an operational perspective, the first step in defining the risk management is to understand what the current cybersecurity risks in an organization are. This requires trainees to master a series of techniques, as follows:

- How to identify and manage the organization assets (data, systems, services, etc.) in accordance with the organization objectives and risk strategy?
- How to assess the risks regarding the organization, its assets and individuals from all the relevant perspectives (vulnerabilities, threats, etc.)?
- How to formulate improvements to the risk management processes, procedures and activities based on evaluation, testing, activity oversight, etc?

6.2.2.3 Protect

Once the cybersecurity risks regarding an organization are identified, the next step is to put in place the necessary safeguards for managing those risks. This requires considering a wide variety of aspects, such as:

- How to manage identities and credentials, as well as authentication and access control mechanisms?
- How to provide cybersecurity awareness and training to personnel, depending on their roles and tasks?
- How to manage data security consistent with the organization's risk strategy for all the possible data states: data-at-rest, data-in-transit, and data-in-use?
- How to manage platform security (hardware, software, services, etc.) consistent with the organization's risk strategy?
- How to ensure the resilience of the technology infrastructure in the event of threats and adverse situations?

The actual tasks to be conducted in relation with this outcome are more technical in nature, and trainees can refer to the Informative References and Implementation Examples provided alongside CSF (see Sect. 6.3.2.1) for more practical information. Moreover, trainees should also leverage the techniques learned during fundamental defense training for this purpose.

6.2.2.4 Detect

All the goals discussed so far regarded mainly the defense preparation of the organization. However, pro-active measures must be taken in order to find and analyze potential cybersecurity attacks and compromises. These tasks too are relatively technical in nature, and they address the following issues:

- How to monitor the organization assets (networks, physical environment, personnel, etc.) continuously so as to identify any anomalies, indicators of compromise, and adverse events?
- How to analyze the identified anomalies, indicators of compromise, and adverse events to characterize them and detect possible cybersecurity incidents?

We note that from a technical perspective several tasks in this category, especially those concerning event analysis, are closely related to the digital forensics skills discussed in connection with forensics training in Sect. 5.2.1.1.

6.2.2.5 Respond

In case a cybersecurity incident was actually detected, various actions must be taken to mitigate it. This is a very important phase of the defense methodology, since it is critical in ensuring that the resulting damage is minimized. The most important aspects that trainees must consider in this context are as follows:

- How to manage competently the response actions with regard to the detected cybersecurity incidents?
- How to leverage incident analysis to ensure an effective response, as well as to support the forensics and recovery activities?
- How to notify the relevant stakeholders, and how to publicly share information about the incident?
- How to prevent incident escalation via containment techniques, and how to mitigate incident effects?

Incident containment and mitigation techniques are most important from an operational perspective, and trainees should make sure to master the relevant technical skills that allow them to carry out these tasks. A high proficiency in this area is needed because these tasks must be completed not only effectively, but also in a timely manner, given the critical need to respond to incidents as soon as possible.

6.2.2.6 Recover

Last but not least, after a cybersecurity incident takes place, all the organization assets and operations that were affected by it must be restored. From an organization perspective this is a very important phase as well, as it allows the organization to resume its normal operation. Typical tasks in this context include:

- How to perform the restoration activities according to the incident recovery plan to ensure that the systems and services affected by the cybersecurity incident are again operational?
- How to communicate and coordinate with all the related internal and external parties (stakeholders, the general public, etc.) regarding the recovery activities?

While the restoration activities themselves are technical in nature and depend significantly on the nature of the systems and services in an organization, the communication and coordination activities require trainees to make use of communication skills in order to be able to successfully accomplish such tasks.

6.3 Related Information

Defense training is a type of training activity that requires participants to master a wide variety of knowledge and skills. In what follows, we will review several resources that we consider particularly helpful in this context, first in terms of additional information sources, such as knowledge bases and defense methodology guidelines. Following that, we will discuss several tools that trainees can use during defense training, and some examples of defense training platforms.

6.3.1 Defense Knowledge Bases

There are a number of sources of knowledge that trainees can leverage in order to gain a deeper insight into how cybersecurity defense is to be conducted. In what follows, we will review the most important of them to illustrate what type of information is readily available for defense training purposes.

6.3.1.1 D3FEND

D3FEND is a knowledge graph of cybersecurity countermeasures that is intended as a basis for the design and enactment of defense operations [8]. Specifically, D3FEND includes the following information:

- Defense tactics used to classify possible defensive methods.
- Defense technique categories corresponding to each defense tactic.
- Defense techniques within each defense technique category.
- Additional information for each defense technique, including relationships with various digital artifacts, mapping to ATT&CK techniques (see Sect. 4.3.1.1), references to related documents, etc.

In what follows, we will illustrate the utilization of the D3FEND knowledge graph from a defense training perspective. For the examples provided below we will rely on D3FEND v0.15 that was released in April 2024.

Tactics At the top-level of D3FEND are situated the defense tactics, each of them representing one aspect of the defense methodology that trainees must be aware of.

Table 6.3 Overview of the technique categories for the *Isolate* tactic in the D3FEND knowledge graph

Name	Category definition	Count
Execution Isolation	Execution isolation techniques prevent application processes from accessing non-essential system resources, such as memory, devices, or files	7
Network Isolation	Network isolation techniques prevent network hosts from accessing non-essential system network resources	14

Differently from ATT&CK, D3FEND tactics are not assigned an identifier; however, definitions of their scope are provided for each tactic.

There are currently seven tactics specified in the knowledge graph, which are used to categorize a total of about 200 defense techniques. In Table 6.2 we summarize the D3FEND tactics by showing the name of each tactic, its definition, as well as the number of techniques that it includes.

Technique Categories D3FEND has a hierarchical structure, and at the second level are included defense technique categories, which can be considered as a sort of abstract defense technique. Technique categories have associated an identifier, a definition, and a graph of relationships with regard to digital artifacts for that category, which is an important source of information.

For instance, the *Isolate* tactic includes the technique categories shown in Table 6.3, for which we mention their corresponding definitions and technique count. If we consider the *Network Isolation* (D3-NI) technique category as an example, D3FEND describes for it the types of traffic that are blocked (e.g., DNS network traffic) or filtered (e.g., email) using this technique category, and also what this technique category can be used to isolate (e.g., intranet network).

From a defense training perspective, the main role of categories is to help trainees conceptualize the defense techniques at a high abstraction level in preparation for learning about the practical techniques we will discuss next.

Techniques Each technique category in D3FEND includes a number of techniques that are more practical from an operation point of view. These techniques as well have associated an identifier, a definition, and a graph of digital artifact relationships. For some of the techniques, specific sub-techniques are also defined that represent particular cases of application of a given technique.

As an example, in Table 6.4 we summarize the techniques and sub-techniques in the *Network Isolation* (D3-NI) category. The symbol '–' is used as prefix to identify those sub-techniques that are subclasses of a given technique. For instance, the *Network Traffic Filtering* technique in the lower part of the table includes three sub-

Table 6.4 Overview of the techniques and sub-techniques for the *Network Isolation* category in the D3FEND knowledge graph

Name	Category definition
Broadcast Domain Isolation	Broadcast isolation restricts the number of computers a host can contact on their LAN
DNS Allowlisting	Permitting only approved domains and their subdomains to be resolved
DNS Denylisting	Blocking DNS network traffic based on criteria such as IP address, domain name, or DNS query type
– Forward Resolution Domain Denylisting	Blocking a lookup based on the query's domain name value
– Reverse Resolution Domain Denylisting	Blocking a reverse DNS lookup's answer's domain name value
– Hierarchical Domain Denylisting	Blocking the resolution of any subdomain of a specified domain name
– Homoglyph Denylisting	Blocking DNS queries that are deceptively similar to legitimate domain names
– Forward Resolution IP Denylisting	Blocking a DNS lookup's answer's IP address value
– Reverse Resolution IP Denylisting	Blocking a reverse lookup based on the query's IP address value
Encrypted Tunnels	Encrypted encapsulation of routable network traffic
Network Traffic Filtering	Restricting network traffic originating from any location
– Inbound Traffic Filtering	Restricting network traffic originating from untrusted networks destined toward a private host or enclave
– Email Filtering	Filtering incoming email traffic based on specific criteria
– Outbound Traffic Filtering	Restricting network traffic originating from a private host or enclave destined toward untrusted networks

techniques, which specify whether the filtering is done in the inbound or outbound directions, and whether the filtered traffic type is email.

From a practical perspective, the sub-techniques in the D3FEND knowledge graph are the most relevant for defense training. This is because, in addition to the details mentioned above, other useful information is included for them, such as how each sub-technique works, various considerations about their use, as well as tools that can be used to put them into practice.

Nevertheless, we consider that the level of technical detail is lower compared to that available in the ATT&CK knowledge base. Hopefully, this will improve as new versions of D3FEND are released. The list of ATT&CK techniques related to a D3FEND technique is also an experimental feature that, while already useful to some extent, is expected to improve as the knowledge graph grows.

6.3.1.2 Engage

Another framework developed by MITRE is *Engage* [9]. Its goal is to support adversary engagement operations, which represent a modern cyber defense methodology. During such operations, an organization provides deceptive artifacts and systems with the goal of exposing adversaries in the organization network, affecting their ability to operate, and gathering information about their Tactics, Techniques and Procedures (TTPs). Also known as *cyber denial* or *cyber deception*, this type of adversary engagement operations have three phases:

1. Prepare: Determine all the details regarding the engagement, such as operational objective, expected adversary reactions, success criteria, etc.
2. Operate: Execute the actual engagement operation.
3. Understand: Process the data into actionable intelligence, analyze the points of success and failure, etc.

In what follows we will focus on the most technical phase, namely *Operate*, which includes the actual engagement actions, i.e., those cyber denial and deception activities used to make progress toward the engagement objectives.

Goals At the top level of each phase in the Engage framework are situated the goals, which represent the objectives of a phase component. In particular, the *Operate* phase is composed of three goals, as shown in Table 6.5. Each goal refers to a different aspect of the engagement, such as revealing adversary operations for *Expose* (EGO0001), or negatively affecting their operations for *Affect* (EGO0002).

Approaches At the second level of each phase in Engage are located the approaches. For example, the *Affect* (EGO0002) goal includes three approaches, as shown in Table 6.6. Each approach refers to an overall method that can be used to achieve a given goal. For instance, the *Disrupt* (EAP0005) methodology should be used to reduce the ability of an adversary of conducting their planned attack.

Table 6.5 Overview of the goals for the *Operate* phase in the Engage framework

Name	Goal description
Expose	Reveal the presence of ongoing adversary operations
Affect	Negatively impact the adversaries operations
Elicit	Learn about adversaries tactics, techniques, and procedures (TTPs)

Table 6.6 Overview of the approaches for the *Affect* goal in the Engage framework

Name	Approach description
Prevent	Stop all or part of the adversary's ability to conduct their operation as intended
Direct	Encourage or discourage the adversary from conducting their operation as intended
Disrupt	Impair an adversary's ability to conduct their operation as intended

Table 6.7 Overview of the activities for the *Disrupt* approach in the Engage framework

Name	Activity description
Isolation	Configure devices, systems, networks, etc. to contain activity and data, thus preventing the expansion of an engagement beyond desired limits
Lures	Deceptive systems and artifacts intended to serve as decoys, breadcrumbs, or bait to elicit a specific response from the adversary
Network Manipulation	Make changes to network properties and functions to achieve a desired effect
Software Manipulation	Make changes to a system's software properties and functions to achieve a desired effect

Activities At the lowest level in the Engage framework are situated the activities. For example, the *Disrupt* (EAP0005) approach includes the activities presented in Table 6.7. Each activity represents a concrete technique that can be used to put a given approach into practice, such as *Isolation* (EAC0020) to prevent the expansion of an engagement beyond the desired limits, or *Lures* (EAC0005) to elicit a specific response from adversaries.

Note that some Engage activities appear in several approaches. For instance, *Isolation* (EAC0020) is part not only of the *Disrupt* (EAP0005) approach, but is also included in the *Prevent* (EAP0003), since isolation techniques can also be used to hinder the ability of an adversary to conduct operations as intended.

The information that is provided for Engage activities is richer than for the other components of the framework. Thus, in addition to descriptions and detailed definitions, which are provided for all the components, the following specific information is included for most activities:

- A list of references to relevant research papers and technical documents that provide more details regarding a particular activity.
- A list of related ATT&CK tactics, alongside an explanation of the vulnerabilities that those tactics reveal about the adversaries using them.

We consider that this additional information is particularly important from a defense training perspective, as trainees can use it to expand their practical knowledge.

6.3.1.3 ATT&CK Mitigations

We have already discussed the ATT&CK knowledge base [6] in the context of attack training in Sect. 4.3.1.1. At that point we mentioned that the knowledge base includes a series of mitigations that are associated to attack techniques. These mitigations are security concepts and classes of technologies that one can use to prevent an attack technique from being successfully executed. Since mitigations are core components of any defense strategy, we will consider them in more detail here.

There are currently 43 mitigations in the ATT&CK knowledge base, and we display in Table 6.8 a selection of 10 representative mitigations for illustration purposes, with focus on the network domain. It can be seen from our example that some mitigations, such as *Software Configuration*, refer to best practices regarding configuration and settings. Others, such as *Exploit Protection*, relate to best practices regarding defense mechanisms. Finally, some mitigations, such as *Application Developer Guidance*, refer to best practices regarding personnel training.

The categorization of mitigations based on their scope is important for determining which mitigations are important from a technical and operational perspective, and which are more relevant from a management perspective. For a discussion of how mitigations can be categorized, and the practical application of such a classification to automated secure system design, readers can consult [12].

Furthermore, the ATT&CK knowledge base also provides additional details about the actual mechanisms required to implement a certain mitigation depending on what specific threat one tries to address. As an example, in Table 6.9 we show several of the suggested mechanisms for implementing the mitigation *Application Isolation and Sandboxing* in the case of several attack techniques. Note that, for many of these mechanisms, the knowledge base also includes links to documents that contain more detailed technical information, which trainees can use as practical reference in the context of defense training.

6.3.1.4 Cyber Analytics Repository

The Cyber Analytics Repository (CAR) [7], which is also made available by MITRE Corporation, is a knowledge base of analytics that were developed as mechanisms for detecting the adversary behaviors described in the ATT&CK knowledge base. Consequently, the information included in the CAR repository is greatly relevant from an attack detection perspective.

The procedure that was taken to develop the CAR analytics involves the following four steps:

Table 6.8 Selected mitigations from the ATT&CK knowledge base

Name	Mitigation description
Application Developer Guidance	This mitigation describes any guidance or training given to developers of applications to avoid introducing security weaknesses that an adversary may be able to take advantage of
Application Isolation and Sandboxing	Restrict execution of code to a virtual environment on or in transit to an endpoint system
Encrypt Sensitive Information	Protect sensitive information with strong encryption
Exploit Protection	Use capabilities to detect and block conditions that may lead to or be indicative of a software exploit occurring
Filter Network Traffic	Use network appliances to filter ingress or egress traffic and perform protocol-based filtering. Configure software on endpoints to filter network traffic
Network Intrusion Prevention	Use intrusion detection signatures to block traffic at network boundaries
Network Segmentation	Architect sections of the network to isolate critical systems, functions, or resources. Use physical and logical segmentation to prevent access to potentially sensitive systems and information. Use a DMZ to contain any internet-facing services that should not be exposed from the internal network. Configure separate virtual private cloud (VPC) instances to isolate critical cloud systems
Privileged Account Management	Manage the creation, modification, use, and permissions associated to privileged accounts, including SYSTEM and root
Software Configuration	Implement configuration changes to software (other than the operating system) to mitigate security risks associated to how the software operates
User Account Control	Configure Windows User Account Control to mitigate risk of adversaries obtaining elevated process access

Table 6.9 Selected mitigation mechanisms for the *Application Isolation and Sandboxing* mitigation in the ATT&CK knowledge base

Target technique	Mitigation mechanism
Escape to Host	Consider utilizing seccomp, seccomp-bpf, or a similar solution that restricts certain system calls such as mount. In Kubernetes environments, consider defining pod security standards that limit container access to host process namespaces, the host network, and the host file system
Exploitation for Credential Access	Make it difficult for adversaries to advance their operation through exploitation of undiscovered or unpatched vulnerabilities by using sandboxing. Other types of virtualization and application microsegmentation may also mitigate the impact of some types of exploitation. Risks of additional exploits and weaknesses in these systems may still exist
Inter-Process Communication	Ensure all COM alerts and protected view are enabled

1. Identify and prioritize the adversary behaviors that should be addressed.
2. Identify what data is necessary to detect those adversary behaviors.
3. Identify or create a "sensor" utility for collecting the necessary data.
4. Develop the analytic used to detect the identified adversary behaviors.

For each CAR analytic, the ATT&CK techniques it refers to, possible implementation solutions, and the applicable platforms are described. Currently, there are about 100 entries in the analytics database. However, CAR contains not only analytics, but also a model to represent the observable data used to run the analytics, as well as information about sensor utilities that can be used to collect that data. All these are extremely useful instruments from a defense training perspective.

6.3.2 Defense Methodology Guidelines

From an organization perspective, cyber defense is the most important aspect in relation with cybersecurity. Consequently, government institutions have taken the necessary steps to create guidelines that organizations can use to make sure their cyber defense activities are as effective as possible. This is because, only by following standard methodologies an organization can ensure that it is taking a thorough and correct approach to address potential cyber threats. Next, we will introduce two examples of such guidelines that readers can refer to for this purpose.

6.3.2.1 NIST Cybersecurity Framework

The U.S. NIST *Cybersecurity Framework* (CSF) is a guideline regarding the management of cybersecurity risks that provides a taxonomy of high-level cybersecurity outcomes that can be used by organizations to understand, assess, prioritize, and communicate their cybersecurity efforts [11]. While the framework does not contain technical information on how these outcomes are to actually be achieved in practice, several relevant resources are provided alongside CSF to help in this context in an online, regularly updated form:

- Informative References: Links to sources of guidance regarding each outcome that were selected among relevant global standards, guidelines, frameworks, regulations, policies, etc.
- Implementation Examples: Practical advice that explains potential ways in which each outcome can be achieved, expressed in a concise, action-oriented manner.

The essential part of CSF is represented by the *CSF Core* taxonomy, whose components are a hierarchy of Functions, Categories, and Subcategories that detail each outcome in a manner that is independent from business sector, country, and technology aspects. This makes it possible for organizations to address their unique risks, technologies, and mission considerations. For the component description that follows, we will rely on the content of CSF 2.0, released in February 2024.

Functions At the top of the CSF framework are the functions, which are the representation at the highest level of the desired cybersecurity outcomes. For each function, a unique alphabetic identifier, and a description of the function meaning are provided. Table 6.10 summarizes the CSF functions, and specifies the number of categories for each function. Note that the *Govern* function is new in CSF 2.0, and is conceived as an all-encompassing function that informs how an organization will implement the other five ones.

Categories Each CSF function includes a number of categories that provide a more detailed description of the expected outcomes for various aspects of that function. For example, the *Protect* (PR) function includes the categories shown in Table 6.11, ranging from asset management and training to infrastructure resilience, which are all important aspects of safeguarding an organization.

Subcategories At the lowest level in CSF are subcategories, with each CSF category containing a number of such subcategories. The role of subcategories is to establish more practical controls that make it possible to assess the cybersecurity posture of an organization from a specific point of view. Subcategories do not have names, just alphabetic identifiers, but a description is provided for each of them.

For instance, the *Platform Security* (PR.PS) category includes the subcategories shown in Table 6.12. For illustration purposes, we have also included in the table an implementation example for each subcategory. These examples were selected from the Implementation Example document published alongside CSF. This type of detailed information is particularly relevant for defense training, as trainees can use it to define actionable strategies for achieving a certain goal.

Table 6.10 Overview of the functions in the CSF 2.0 framework

Name	Function description	Count
Govern	The organization's cybersecurity risk management strategy, expectations, and policy are established, communicated, and monitored	6
Identify	The organization's current cybersecurity risks are understood	3
Protect	Safeguards to manage the organization's cybersecurity risks are used	5
Detect	Possible cybersecurity attacks and compromises are found and analyzed	2
Respond	Actions regarding a detected cybersecurity incident are taken	4
Recover	Assets and operations affected by a cybersecurity incident are restored	2

6.3.2.2 Security and Privacy Controls for Information Systems and Organizations

The U.S. NIST *Security and Privacy Controls for Information Systems and Organizations* guideline is a comprehensive catalog of security and privacy controls for information systems and organizations [10]. The term *controls* is used in this guideline to denote "descriptions of the safeguards and protection capabilities appropriate for achieving the particular security and privacy objectives of the organization and reflecting the protection needs of organizational stakeholders."

The controls mentioned above are intended as support for the protection of organizational operations and assets from a diverse set of threats and risks. These risks include hostile attacks, human errors, natural disasters, structural failures, foreign intelligence entities, and privacy risks. Although not all the aspects in this guideline are directly related to defense training, there are many relevant controls, and for this reason we will next briefly introduce its components.

Control Families At the top level of this guideline are control families, which group all the controls related to a certain topic. There are currently 20 control families, and we present a selection of some of those most relevant for defense training in Table 6.13. For each control family, we show its alphabetic identifier, as well as the number of base controls in that family.

Table 6.11 Overview of the categories for the *Protect* function in the CSF 2.0 framework

Name	Category description	Count
Identity Management, Authentication, and Access Control	Access to physical and logical assets is limited to authorized users, services, and hardware and managed commensurate with the assessed risk of unauthorized access	6
Awareness and Training	The organization's personnel are provided with cybersecurity awareness and training so that they can perform their cybersecurity-related tasks	2
Data Security	Data are managed consistent with the organization's risk strategy to protect the confidentiality, integrity, and availability of information	4
Platform Security	The hardware, software (e.g., firmware, operating systems, applications), and services of physical and virtual platforms are managed consistent with the organization's risk strategy to protect their confidentiality, integrity, and availability	6
Technology Infrastructure Resilience	Security architectures are managed with the organization's risk strategy to protect asset confidentiality, integrity, and availability, and organizational resilience	4

Base Controls At the second level of the guideline are situated the base controls, which refer to a specific aspect that an organization must consider. For each control, a list of related controls, both in the same and in other families, is also provided. In addition, references to other relevant standards and guidelines are included as sources of technical information on how to implement a given control.

The *System and Communications Protection* (SC) control family has the largest number of such controls amongst the control families that we selected, namely 47, so we will use it next as an illustrative example. Thus, in Table 6.14, we present a selection of several base controls from the SC family, displaying for each of them their identifiers and descriptions.

Control Enhancements At the lowest level of the guideline are situated the control enhancements, which are meant to add functionality or specificity to a base

Table 6.12 Overview of the subcategories for the *Platform Security* category in the CSF 2.0 framework

Id	Subcategory description	Implementation example
PR.PS-01	Configuration management practices are established and applied	Review all default configuration settings that may potentially impact cybersecurity when installing or upgrading software
PR.PS-02	Software is maintained, replaced, and removed commensurate with risk	Perform routine and emergency patching within the timeframes specified in the vulnerability management plan
PR.PS-03	Hardware is maintained, replaced, and removed commensurate with risk	Replace hardware when it lacks needed security capabilities or when it cannot support software with needed security capabilities
PR.PS-04	Log records are generated and made available for continuous monitoring	Configure all operating systems, applications, and services (including cloud-based services) to generate log records
PR.PS-05	Installation and execution of unauthorized software are prevented	Verify the source of new software and the software's integrity before installing it
PR.PS-06	Secure software development practices are integrated, and their performance is monitored throughout the software development life cycle	Protect all components of organization-developed software from tampering and unauthorized access

control, or to increase its strength. They are mainly intended for systems and environments of operation that require greater protection than that provided only by the base controls. For instance, the *Transmission Confidentiality and Integrity* (SC-8) base control includes five control enhancements, as shown in Table 6.15, together with their identifiers and descriptions.

We consider that the level of detail included for base controls in general, and control enhancements in particular, is most useful from a defense training perspective, as trainees can obtain from them practical information on what measures are to be taken for a given purpose, as illustrated by the examples in Table 6.15.

Table 6.13 Selected control families from the *Security and Privacy Controls for Information Systems and Organizations* guideline

Id	Control family name	Count
AC	Access Control	23
AT	Awareness and Training	5
CA	Assessment, Authorization, and Monitoring	8
IA	Identification and Authentication	12
IR	Incident Response	9
MP	Media Protection	8
RA	Risk Assessment	9
SC	System and Communications protection	47
SI	System and Information Integrity	22
SR	Supply Chain Risk Management	12

6.3.3 Defense Training Tools

Defense training relies on several tools and utilities for accomplishing the technical tasks related to the various defense actions that are required to safeguard a system. For instance, the Kali Linux distribution makes available several related meta installation packages that are organized based on the CSF functions discussed in Sect. 6.3.2.1. The packages are named accordingly, such as `kali-tools-identify`, `kali-tools-protect`, `kali-tools-detect`, `kali-tools-respond`, `kali-tools-recover`, and include a total of around 40 utilities. In what follows, we will introduce some representative examples of defense training tools that illustrate the capabilities trainees can expect from such utilities.

6.3.3.1 `iptables`

`iptables` is a utility program for configuring filter rules of the Linux kernel firewall, and is part of the netfilter.org project [13]. We use here the mentioned utility name generically, but in practice the `iptables` command is used only in relation with IPv4 traffic, whereas other commands, such as `ip6tables`, `arptables` and `ebtables`, are used in relation with IPv6, ARP and Ethernet traffic, respectively. The same project also develops a successor for `iptables`, named `nftables`, which provides additional scalability and flexibility.

The key architecture element of `iptables` are the *chains* of rules that are to be applied to network traffic packets. Using the chains makes it possible to design a

Table 6.14 Selected base controls for the *System and Communications Protection* control family in the *Security and Privacy Controls for Information Systems and Organizations* guideline

Id	Name	Base control description
SC-2	Separation of System and User Functionality	Separate user functionality, including user interface services, from system management functionality
SC-3	Security Function Isolation	Isolate security functions from nonsecurity functions
SC-8	Transmission Confidentiality and Integrity	Protect the confidentiality and/or integrity of transmitted information
SC-23	Session Authenticity	Protect the authenticity of communications sessions
SC-26	Decoys	Include components within organizational systems specifically designed to be the target of malicious attacks for detecting, deflecting, and analyzing such attacks
SC-35	External Malicious Code Identification	Include system components that proactively seek to identify network-based malicious code or malicious websites
SC-39	Process Isolation	Maintain a separate execution domain for each executing system process

wide variety of actions. While the chains are mainly used to filter traffic, other uses are possible, such as Network Address Translation (NAT), and even modifications of the IP header of the packets. The five chains of rules available in `iptables` are the following:

- PREROUTING: Chain where packets enter before a routing decision is made.
- INPUT: Chain for packets that are to be delivered locally.
- FORWARD: Chain for packets that are to be routed.
- OUTPUT: Chain for packets sent from the local host.
- POSTROUTING: Chain where packets enter after a routing decision was made.

Although the actual firewall utility used and its features depend on the operating system of a computer host, learning about `iptables`, and how it can be used to configure the Linux firewall, represents a very good introduction for trainees to the general concept of firewalls. Moreover, the fact that `iptables` configurations can be saved into and loaded from files makes it possible to reuse configurations for multiple hosts, which is another powerful feature of this utility.

Table 6.15 Overview of the controls enhancements for the *Transmission Confidentiality and Integrity* base control in the *Security and Privacy Controls for Information Systems and Organizations* guideline

Id	Name	Control enhancement description
SC-8(1)	Cryptographic Protection	Implement cryptographic mechanisms to prevent unauthorized disclosure of information; and/or detect changes to information during transmission
SC-8(2)	Pre- and Post-Transmission handling	maintain the confidentiality and/or integrity of information during preparation for transmission and during reception
SC-8(3)	Cryptographic Protection for message externals	Implement cryptographic mechanisms to protect message externals unless otherwise protected by alternative physical controls
SC-8(4)	Conceal or Randomize Communications	Implement cryptographic mechanisms to conceal or randomize communication patterns unless otherwise protected by alternative physical controls
SC-8(5)	Protected Distribution System	Implement a protected distribution system to prevent unauthorized disclosure of information; and/or detect changes to information during transmission

6.3.3.2 Greenbone OpenVAS

Greenbone OpenVAS is a vulnerability scanning and management utility that is currently being developed by the company Greenbone AG [3]. OpenVAS has many features, including unauthenticated and authenticated scanning, support for various internet and industrial protocols, efficient large-scale scanning capabilities, as well as a powerful custom language that can be used to implement vulnerability tests.

The scanning functionality of OpenVAS is supported by feeds that are updated daily with information on how to detect new vulnerabilities. It is said that more than 160,000 vulnerability tests are currently available by means of these feeds.

Vulnerability scanning is an essential component of the risk assessment process, since it makes it possible to understand what possible attack points exist in an network system. Consequently, trainees should learn how to use such scanning tools as part of the risk assessment process.

6.3.3.3 Snort

Snort is an open-source network Intrusion Detection System (IDS) and Intrusion Prevention System (IPS) that is currently being developed by Cisco [1]. To achieve the IDS/IPS functionality, Snort relies on a series of rules that characterize malicious network activity. When a match is found against those rules, Snort generates an alert regarding the possible detected intrusion. In addition to the detection capabilities, Snort also can be used to stop the malicious network traffic packets, thus enabling the prevention functionality.

The rules available in Snort are powerful enough to allow the utility to perform complex protocol analysis, as well as content searching and matching. Moreover, a machine learning-based detection engine for Snort, named SnortML, has been released in 2024.

Snort can also be used for packet sniffing, i.e., to display network traffic, and for packet logging, that is, to save network packets into a file. This specific functionality makes it possible to use Snort for the debugging of network applications. Consequently, Snort is a very powerful tool in the context of defense training, and mastering it is an essential need for trainees.

We note that several other powerful open-source tools with similar functionality exist, such as the network analysis and threat detection software Suricata[1] or the network security monitoring tool Zeek[2].

6.3.4 Defense Training Platforms

There seem to be a relatively small number of training platforms that are explicitly aimed at defense training. Even a platform such as CyberDefenders[3], which defines itself as a "blue team training platform for SOC analysts, threat hunters, security blue teams and DFIR professionals," seems to be mainly geared toward forensics training. Thus, from the 142 free and pro tier training labs available at the time of writing, 111 of them—that is, almost 80%—are related to forensics (malware analysis, network forensics, endpoint forensics, etc.). Only the remaining 31 labs—that is, 20% of the total number—are related to topics that are actually defense oriented, such as threat intel and threat hunting, and detection engineering.

---

[1] https://suricata.io/.

[2] https://zeek.org/.

[3] https://cyberdefenders.org/.

However, even though most publicly available platforms are generally targeted at attack training, several of them allow attack-defend type of exercises. This makes it possible for trainees to also practice their defense skills, as illustrated in the following two examples of such platforms:

- TryHackMe [14]: A browser-based gamified cybersecurity training platform that provides learning content for various skill level participants. The most important feature from a defense training perspective is the support for attack-defend competitions in the "king of the hill" format. In this case, participants must prevent other players from compromising a target machine, for example, by patching its vulnerabilities. Furthermore, the amount of points awarded to other players can be minimized by evicting them from that machine (see Sect. 10.2.2.2 for details).
- Facebook CTF [2]: An open-source CTF platform developed by Facebook [2] that can be used to organize competitions with hundreds of participants. The attack-defend type of challenge, named *Bases*, is also a "king of the hill" type of game. Similarly to TryHackMe, participants must both harden the bases to prevent their capture, and also attempt to evict other players to limit the number of points awarded to them (see Sect. 10.3.2.2 for details).

Although not a training platform, we also want to remind readers in this context about the Hardening Project competition that we reviewed in detail in Sect. 3.4. During that competition, participants have to deal with security incidents and patch vulnerabilities of a virtual e-commerce website created for the purpose of the event. Such defense skills are readily usable in real-life situations, and we consider that Hardening Project is one of the best examples of how to conduct an effective defense training with immediate practical application.

6.4 Discussion

As we did for the cases of attack and forensics training, in this section we will discuss the main advantages of defense training, but also the potential issues that can be expected when conducting this kind of training activities. These aspects will be examined both from the trainee and organizer perspectives, so as to facilitate a full understanding of the matter.

6.4.1 Main Advantages

Defense training has several advantages compared to the other forms of cybersecurity training, as we will discuss next.

6.4.1.1   Trainee Perspective

We will start with the trainee perspective in order to see what can make defense training attractive from their point of view.

Career Opportunities Perhaps the most important advantage of defense training for trainees is that defense skills open considerable career opportunities. All organizations need cybersecurity personnel who are capable of defending them from cyber threats. Hence, defense training builds highly requested abilities that enable trainees to find employment in various environments.

One of the most recognized certifications in this area is CISSP[4] (Certified Information Systems Security Professional), which is a way for candidates to prove their knowledge regarding security practices and principles. CISSP certification is required or recommended for a wide variety of cybersecurity job positions, including Security Analyst, Security Manager, Security Architect, etc.

Growth Potential Related to career opportunities, it is important to note that given the vast amount of knowledge and skills related to cyber defense, the training process is usually done in stages. This means that, after acquiring a sufficient amount of skills, trainees can already start working in job positions such as entry-level Cybersecurity Operation Center (CSOC) analyst, for example.

Such security analyst roles are usually available as a multi-tier system, with growing responsibilities once one acquires more experience via the on-the-job exposure to real cyber threats and cybersecurity tools. Such growth potential is a very attractive aspect of defense training.

6.4.1.2   Organizer Perspective

As for the organizer perspective, some of the most important advantages of defense training are as follows.

Trainee Maturity Trainees who seek to conduct attack training, and to some extent basic forms of forensics training, are often young and inexperienced. However, defense training programs are usually attended by candidates who are more mature, and sometimes even experienced professionals, as defense skills are mainly required for organization employees. These characteristics of the trainees makes it easier to conduct training activities, as those trainees possess not only a wide variety of technical skills, but also job know-how, sense of responsibility, etc.

Moreover, trainees with professional experience can also contribute via feedback to organizers, thus helping to improve the training activity. For instance, examples of incidents from their own organizations, and information about the practical defense needs of those organizations, can assist training organizers in designing more suitable and targeted training content.

---

[4] https://www.isc2.org/Certifications/CISSP.

Workforce Contribution As mentioned in the beginning of this book, there is a huge worldwide workforce gap in the area of cybersecurity [5]. Professionals with defense training represent a significant contribution to this workforce, and this type of contribution can be considered a strong motivating factor for organizers to conduct defense training programs.

We believe that efforts such as Hardening Project [15] are huge steps in this direction. We hope that such examples of ways in which defense training can be effectively performed will inspire organizers to create new programs that make possible defense training activities in an accessible manner and at a wider scale.

6.4.2 Potential Issues

As with the other forms of cybersecurity training, defense training is also associated with several potential issues that we will examine next.

6.4.2.1 Trainee Perspective

First we will discuss the trainee point of view, and see what difficulties they may encounter in the case of defense training.

Defense Challenges Being proficient at cyber defense is a difficult task, as defenders have to face many challenges. This is because, in order for an attack to be successful, it is enough if an adversary manages to identify and exploit a single vulnerability. On the other hand, in order for the defense process to be effective, defenders must harden the overall system and patch all its vulnerabilities.

Moreover, defense requires a wide range of skills—not only the specific defense abilities that we discussed in this chapter, but also forensics-related skills that are typically associated with forensics training. Consequently, trainees need a strong motivation in order to fully benefit of defense training.

Acquiring Non-technical Skills Similarly to forensics training, defense training also requires trainees to learn various non-technical skills. A clear example in this sense is the *Govern* function of the CSF framework (see Sect. 6.3.2.1), which is related to establishing, communicating and monitoring the cybersecurity risk management strategy, expectations and policy of an organization.

Accordingly, trainees who do not have enough professional experience may find it difficult to grasp and learn such advanced non-technical skills. Nevertheless, some of these skills are part of the typical workplace skills that are required in any professional environment and mastering them presents additional advantages for trainees.

6.4.2.2   Organizer Perspective

Organizers are also faced with various issues in relation with defense training, which we will examine next.

Environment Setup Issues Making available a realistic environment is a key component for the success of defense training. One aspect is, of course, that the training environment mimics as closely as possible a real network, so that trainees can easily transfer the skills they have learnt to real-life situations. However, the most challenging part for defense training is to orchestrate live attacks that give trainees the opportunity to validate their practical abilities.

In some cases, such as the Hardening Project competition mentioned before, the live attacks are conducted by white-hat hackers who belong to supporting organizations [15]. This requires dedicating those experts to the task and is also associated with large financial and time costs. We consider that the live attack orchestration challenge explains perhaps best why defense training exercises are not organized as often as those related to attack or forensics training.

An alternative solution is to leverage the advances in Machine Learning (ML) techniques, and to deploy ML-based autonomous penetration testing agents as replacement for the human red team. The Deep Reinforcement Learning (DRL) based agents described in [4] could be used for this purpose, for example. However, such autonomous agents do not have yet an equivalent performance with human experts, so future improvements are required.

Teaching Non-technical Skills The potential issue mentioned above for trainees in relation with acquiring non-technical skills is also relevant from an organizer perspective. Teaching high-level topics, in particular, such as how to consider the risk management strategy of an organization, requires instructors to have deep professional knowledge about organizations as well.

Nevertheless, this teaching task is simplified when trainees have some professional experience, as it happens in many cases for defense training, since they are often already familiar with many of the organization-level concepts.

References

1. Cisco: snort website. https://www.snort.org/. Accessed 1 July 2024
2. Facebook, Inc. Platform to host capture the flag competitions. https://github.com/facebookarchive/fbctf. Accessed 1 July 2024
3. Greenbone AG. Greenbone openVAS. https://openvas.org/. Accessed 1 July 2024
4. Hu Z, Beuran R, Tan Y (2020) Automated penetration testing using deep reinforcement learning. In: IEEE European symposium on security and privacy workshops (EuroS&PW 2020), workshop on cyber range applications and technologies (CACOE'20), pp 2–10
5. ISC2 (2023) cybersecurity workforce study 2023. https://media.isc2.org/-/media/Project/ISC2/Main/Media/documents/research/ISC2_Cybersecurity_Workforce_Study_2023.pdf. Accessed 1 July 2024
6. MITRE corporation: ATT&CK knowledge base. https://attack.mitre.org/. Accessed 1 July 2024

7. MITRE corporation: cyber analytics repository. https://car.mitre.org/. Accessed 1 July 2024
8. MITRE corporation: D3FEND knowledge base. https://d3fend.mitre.org/. Accessed 1 July 2024
9. MITRE corporation: Engage framework. https://engage.mitre.org/. Accessed 1 July 2024
10. National institute of standards and technology (NIST) (2020) Security and privacy controls for information systems and organizations, NIST special publication 800–53. https://doi.org/10.6028/NIST.SP.800-53r5
11. National institute of standards and technology (NIST) (2024) The NIST cybersecurity framework (CSF) 2.0. https://doi.org/10.6028/NIST.CSWP.29
12. Ooi SE, Beuran R, Kuroda T, Kuwahara T, Hotchi R, Fujita N, Tan Y (2023) Intent-driven secure system design: methodology and implementation. Comput Secur 124:102955
13. The netfilter.org project: netfilter: firewalling, nat, and packet mangling for Linux. https://www.netfilter.org/. Accessed 1 July 2024
14. TryHackMe: TryHackMe website. https://tryhackme.com/. Accessed 1 July 2024
15. Web application security forum: hardening project (in Japanese). https://wasforum.jp/hardening-project/. Accessed 1 July 2024

Chapter 7
IoT Security Training

This chapter discusses first the challenges associated with IoT security training in comparison with the general cybersecurity training, both regarding the specific characteristics of IoT devices, as well as from IoT developer and end user perspectives. The main IoT security training approaches are examined next, classified into two categories, hands-on training and theoretical training. This is followed by a case study of two IoT training systems, IoTrain-Sim and IoTrain-Lab, that illustrates the various issues discussed in this chapter.

7.1 IoT Security Training Challenges

IoT security differs from regular cybersecurity in several ways. One main difference, according to [23], is that IoT security also encompasses the monitoring and/or control of the state of physical systems connected over internet, which cybersecurity doesn't consider. Hence, IoT security is more than just applying a set of meta-security rules to networked systems. Instead, it requires to consider the characteristics of each system and system-of-systems in which IoT devices are present. Basically, it can be said that the security of an IoT device is a function of the use of that device, the physical processes controlled by it, and the sensitivity of the systems to which the device connects. This also leads to the fact that the intersection of safety and security engineering must be considered with respect to IoT systems.

Given such differences, IoT security training poses significant challenges in comparison with the typical cybersecurity training activities that we discussed so far. In what follows, we will detail the reasons for these challenges, and further analyze the challenges themselves.

R. Beuran, *Cybersecurity Education and Training*,
https://doi.org/10.1007/978-981-96-0555-2_7

7.1.1 IoT Device Diversity

As the Internet of Things (IoT) has grown tremendously in recent years, IoT devices now come in a variety of sizes and shapes, and they are used in a diversity of contexts. From a consumer perspective, the most typical application is home automation, namely to create the so-called *smart homes*, in which aspects such as lighting, climate, appliances are monitored and controlled in an intelligent manner. Thus, smart homes can include a large assortment of IoT devices, such as smart light bulbs, smart thermostats, smart air conditioners, smart plugs, smart speakers, smart kitchen appliances, smart locks, smart security cameras, and so on.

However, IoT technology is not limited to consumers, and can also be used in various industrial contexts, such as manufacturing, agriculture, infrastructure, environmental monitoring, etc. In particular, the term Industrial Internet of Things (IIoT) is used to refer to manufacturing equipment, sensors and instruments that are connected with computing systems in order to improve productivity and efficiency in an industrial environment.

In this context, it is important to mention the concept of Cyber Physical Systems (CPS). Similar to IoT, CPS refers to systems that integrate physical components with digital ones. In the case of CPS, however, the internet connection aspect is not important, and even absent in many cases. This because the term CPS is often used in industrial fields, such as robotics or avionics, for which the systems are not connected to the internet.

A typical example of CPS are the Industrial Control Systems (ICS) used to control industrial processes in domains such as power generation or chemical processing[1]. One of the most often used types of ICS is SCADA (Supervisory Control and Data Acquisition), which is a standardized control system architecture utilized for large industrial systems in particular.

Given the predominantly industrial background of CPS in general, and ICS in particular, we consider them to be outside the scope of the discussion in this chapter. Nevertheless, ICS have their specific security issues, such as the various potential vulnerabilities of SCADA systems [3]. Therefore, we note that there are dedicated training programs related to ICS, such as the Industrial Cyber Security Center of Excellence (ICSCoE) in Japan [19]. Another example is the ICS training facility and related course discussed in [5] that use open-source hardware and software to provide reconfigurable ICS modules. Moreover, Sifu is a cybersecurity training platform focusing on software development in industrial settings that employs AI-based techniques for challenge assessment and intelligent coaching [13].

There are many other application fields that have their specific type of IoT devices. For example, the Internet of Medical Things (IoMT) refers to the use of IoT devices in the context of healthcare, and the devices that fall into this category include smart wearable devices used for health monitoring and emergency notification purposes,

---

[1] The term Operational Technology (OT) is sometimes used when referring to the control of industrial systems, as opposed to Information Technology (IT) being used in regard to the management of computer systems.

smart medical devices, etc. For various examples of training platforms related to ICS and IoMT, readers should refer to Sect. 11.3.

Some of the challenges related to IoT security training stem from the huge diversity of IoT devices. This means that, while IoT technologies have many high-level aspects in common that can be taught theoretically, there is no "one size fits all" approach that can be taken in terms of the actual devices and technologies used in hands-on exercises. Consequently, instructors need to either consider typical devices (e.g., Raspberry Pi) and technologies (e.g., Wi-Fi communication) when designing the training content, or have very clear use cases (e.g., industrial automation) as models for the creation of the content.

It is also important to point out in this context that, while most training approaches rely on actual devices as hands-on platforms for the training practice, some solutions use simulated virtual devices instead, with some specific advantages and disadvantages, as it will be discussed in Sect. 7.3.

7.1.2 IoT Device Risks

The huge variety of IoT devices creates a large attack surface that has often been exploited for malicious purposes in recent years. One of the most publicized such attacks was the DDoS (Distributed Denial of Service) attack on the DNS (Domain Name System) provider named Dyn that occurred in 2016. The attack used a botnet of tens of thousands of IoT devices infected by the Mirai malware to generate a large amount of DDoS traffic, exceeding 1.2 Tbps, that affected many companies, such as Airbnb, Netflix, and Reddit. Moreover, the subsequent public distribution of the malware source code led to the creation of a large number of IoT botnets worldwide that are still a major cybersecurity threat [17].

Another contributing factor that increases the risks associated with IoT devices is their cyber-physical nature. Thus, many IoT devices include not only sensors, but also actuators, and are thus able to perform actions in the physical world. If such an IoT device would be hacked, this could lead to safety risks for its users. For instance, hacking a smart lock may allow intruders to enter a house, thus leading to potential life-threatening circumstances for its occupants. The risks become even more obvious when referring to IoMT devices, that can directly affect the health of their users. For example, an analysis conducted in [12] has shown that many of the vulnerabilities related to IoMT devices are rated as high or critical, hence with a very high risk associated to them.

Regarding the specific risks associated with IoT devices, given the lack of display capabilities of many of them, the challenge lies on how to convey those risks to trainees. The typical approach in this context is to design training scenarios that make obvious that a given IoT device was hacked by using it to drive an external application with visual features, such as a website, or the digital signage application used in [26]. Alternatively, side effects of the attack on IoT devices can be emphasized, as it was done in the security training scenarios presented in [4].

7.1.3 Developer Issues

When considering the challenges related to IoT security training compared to the regular cybersecurity training in relation with computer systems, it is important to note that there are two perspectives that need to be addressed, each with its specific issues: the developer perspective, and the end user perspective. We focus first on the developer perspective, addressing specific challenges and potential solutions, and a discussion of the end user perspective will follow in the next section.

7.1.3.1 Specific Challenges

IoT developers are the driving force behind the spread of IoT, but there are several issues that create specific challenges in this context. In particular, the issues related to IoT developers emerge from aspects such as the low barrier to entry in the field, and the time to market pressure.

Low Barrier to Entry Developing IoT systems is much cheaper in general compared to computer systems, especially when considering the smaller and simpler of the IoT devices, such as those used for home automation, for example. This is both from a software/firmware development perspective, given the relatively simple nature of the devices, and also from a manufacturing perspective, given the smaller costs of producing the actual devices.

As a consequence, almost anyone with basic technological skills can try to develop IoT devices, which is another reason for their recent proliferation. Such issues are also encountered for regular software development, but do not occur for computer hardware development, which requires a significant larger amount of resources.

Time to Market Pressure The market of IoT devices is a very competitive one. Therefore, the pressure to make the product available for sale as quickly as possible is very high. Consequently, IoT developers will frequently focus mainly on the functionality of the devices, and perhaps their external appearance and design. This means that security and privacy aspects are more often than not neglected.

In contrast, for computer systems the expectations related to security and privacy are already high on the consumer side. Therefore, manufacturers are usually not willing to take any shortcuts in this respect.

7.1.3.2 Potential Solutions

There are several ways in which the above issues can be addressed, and significant efforts have already been conducted in these directions. From an IoT hardware manufacturer perspective, including various security features in their platforms can ease the burden on developers when trying to add security and privacy characteristics into their systems. For example, the ESP32 microcontroller unit (MCU) has some built-in security features, such as secure boot, flash encryption, cryptographic hardware acceleration, and a random number generator. Nevertheless, actually using these features is not always straightforward, and the results are not always as expected; moreover, security and privacy need to be considered in an end-to-end manner, including the communication protocol, cloud storage mechanisms, etc. [22].

From a regulator perspective, various governments and organizations have defined guidelines and requirements pertaining to IoT security. A representative example on the government side are the secure IoT development guidelines released by the European Union Agency for Cybersecurity (ENISA) [14], but similar documents were published in many other countries, such as the U.S., the U.K., etc. On the organization side, the IoT security guidelines and assessment methodology released by the GSM Association (GSMA) is another key example [18].

We note that there are various IoT devices and protocols that include built-in security features, and many countries make available relevant security guidelines. However, whether the developers who use those devices actually utilize their security features, and to what extent they follow the relevant regulations is in the end highly dependent on their security awareness. Consequently, from an IoT developer perspective, general IoT security training, as well as learning from thorough analyses such as that presented in [22], are key to ensure that developers are motivated and technically able to follow safe and competent IoT development practices.

7.1.4   End User Issues

End users are those who put the IoT technologies into actual use. Moreover, they are those who have to suffer the negative consequences in case their IoT systems are successfully targeted by cyberattacks. Therefore, their perspective on IoT is as important as that of developers.

7.1.4.1   Specific Challenges

The specific issues that IoT devices pose from an end user perspective are related to their physical characteristics, such as user interface limitations, but also to other aspects, such as perception and life span, as it will be discussed next.

User Interface Limitations Most IoT devices have very limited user interfaces compared to computer systems, often lacking any form of display and sometimes lacking even input mechanisms. Therefore, interactions with IoT devices are conducted mainly via smartphones apps or web interfaces. Unfortunately, this hides any potential security issues that the devices may have and makes it difficult for users to react in case a device is hacked, for example.

In contrast, computer systems often show more obvious signs of malware activity, for example, via symptoms such as a slower response, undesired messages being displayed, etc. The limited interface of IoT devices also makes it more difficult for users to update the firmware of the device when needed, although many of the IoT devices with network connectivity do have automatic update mechanisms available; this again differs from the case of computer systems, for which the software can always be updated via the internet automatically.

Perception Inertia Many IoT devices are positioned as smart versions of existing devices, such as a smart light bulb being basically a light bulb with intelligent features, such as changing colors and doing other adjustments, which are not available with regular light bulbs. However, in the mind of a typical user, a smart light bulb is often still just a light bulb. This contributes to an inertia regarding the awareness that security and privacy aspects need to be considered when using those IoT devices that need not be considered for their non-smart equivalents.

Short Lifespan IoT devices usually have a much shorter life span compared to computer systems. Some of the reasons for this are related to the physical limitations of the devices, such as the need to use small batteries that are sometimes non-replaceable due to physical or design constraints.

Availability of support is another possible cause of a shorter life span. In some cases, this happens because the manufacturer itself ceases to exist, as bankruptcy can sometimes occur, especially for small manufacturers. Nevertheless, occasionally even big manufacturers can decide to end support for their devices due to economic reasons. For instance, Netgear declared in 2020 that a total of forty-five different Wi-Fi routers and home gateways are "outside security support," and consequently will not get any further security patches, despite these devices having serious security flaws that were already known [29].

7.1.4.2   Potential Solutions

To address the above issues, we believe that the most effective measure that can be taken at the user level is to increase their security awareness in regard to IoT technology. This can be achieved via security awareness education and training methods such as those that be discussed in Chap. 8.

From a regulator perspective, any measures that can help consumers make informed decisions about IoT device security are important. A notable effort in this direction is the cybersecurity labeling for IoT devices and software taken by the U.S. National Institute of Standards and Technology (NIST). While that activity is still ongoing, NIST has already published in the framework of this program a set of recommended criteria for the cybersecurity labeling of consumer IoT products that describe, among others, how a software provider should claim adherence to accepted secure software development practices throughout the software development lifecycle, for example with respect to a secure software development process implementation, secure design and vulnerability remediation, and so on [20].

While the IoT device end user perspective in very important, we consider that by training the IoT developers most of the issues discussed so far can be addressed in a satisfactory manner. Therefore, in what follows we will focus mainly on discussing the technical IoT security training perspective.

7.2 IoT Security Training Approaches

IoT security training is a relatively newer area compared to traditional cybersecurity training. Nevertheless, several types of training approaches have emerged over the years, which we grouped into two classes: hands-on training and theoretical training.

7.2.1 Hands-On Training

Similarly to technical cybersecurity training, the main way in which trainees can acquire deep knowledge and practical skills regarding IoT security is via hands-on training. We have identified three main categories of hands-on IoT security training approaches, as it will be discussed next:

- Academic training.
- Commercial training.
- Training systems.

7.2.1.1   Academic Training

Education activities conducted in academic institutions sometimes include interactive hands-on exercises that students can use to apply into practice the knowledge they have gained in the related lectures. Those exercises are therefore custom designed to support those specific lectures, and being able to solve them requires that students take the lectures first, or already possess equivalent knowledge.

For instance, a set of penetration testing exercises regarding smart home security cameras was presented in [28]. During these exercises, students use the Kali Linux distribution to investigate the vulnerabilities of the real security cameras provided as training platform. However, the exercises are not designed to be done in a standalone manner. Thus, the students must already have an understanding of Kali Linux, a background that is provided in an associated course by the organizing academic institution, the United Arab Emirates University.

Another example of IoT security exercises that are offered in an academic context are those presented in [26]. This set of exercises is more complex, being divided into two classes: basic exercises regarding vulnerability detection and countermeasure techniques, and advanced exercises in relation with pentesting techniques. The basic exercises are implemented using the WebGoat insecure application platform made available by the OWASP foundation [27]. As for the advanced exercises, a real Raspberry Pi device is used as attack target for practicing well-known offensive techniques, such as Cross-Site Request Forgery.

7.2.1.2   Commercial Training

Various training organizations provide commercial IoT training programs that include hands-on activities with actual IoT devices. Typically, these programs have a deep technical nature, and their practical aspect is extremely relevant from a workforce perspective, as it prepares the trainees to handle real-world situations. However, the commercial nature of these programs makes them potentially costly to attend.

For example, Cisco Networking Academy offers a training course named *IoT Fundamentals: IoT Security* [7]. This course makes use of Raspberry Pi devices for hands-on on exercises that target various practical skills. Trainees can learn how to conduct end-to-end security assessments of IoT systems, how to minimize risks via threat mitigation measures, and how to use actual pentesting and vulnerability testing tools. The Cisco Networking Academy training course is conducted in an instructor-led manner and has an estimated completion duration of 50 h.

Another hands-on commercial training program is *IoT Penetration Testing* that is provided by SANS Institute [24]. Although this is an online program, SANS Institute supplies the trainees with the IoT devices necessary for hands-on training upon registration. The course mainly addresses offensive-security topics, such as how to assess the security of IoT web applications, how to discover the functionality of IoT hardware, how to explore IoT device firmware to identify secret information and implementation issues, how to interact with wireless IoT technologies, etc.

7.2.1.3   Training Systems

Another approach to IoT training is to use dedicated hardware platforms for IoT security training. Several companies provide such IoT training systems that include all the necessary components for being able to learn and practice thoroughly with specific IoT technologies. Compared to the other approaches discussed so far, dedicated IoT training systems are more difficult to deploy and scale, and purchase costs are relatively high. Nevertheless, after purchase they can be used repeatedly within an organization at no additional expense.

The company 3 Rocks Technology offers a set of IoT training systems that target engineers in the IoT field [1]. The two key products provided are named *Internet of Things Trainer* and *Embedded IoT Training System*. Both systems can be configured to include hardware components that cover a wide range of sensing aspects, as well as a smart gateway, Raspberry Pi and Arduino devices, etc. The training scenarios make it possible to conduct training in relation with practical IoT systems, including IoT farm management, IoT home appliance control, IoT fire alarm systems, etc.

Another company in the IoT training system area is Scientific & Technical Products (STP). Its systems cover various IoT applications, including home networks and healthcare [25]. An example in the STP training system product family line is the Raspberry Pi 3 based system named *IoT-1000*. Using it, trainees can learn how to configure IoT servers, how to use IoT sensors and actuators and save their data, how to use web cameras, etc. STP also provides a textbook with different scenarios that the trainees can follow to learn the aforementioned skills via hands-on practice.

7.2.2 Theoretical Training

As mentioned already in Sect. 3.1.4 in relation with general cybersecurity training, there are approaches to education and training that focus on knowledge, as opposed to practical skills. Therefore, we will discuss this aspect next in the context of IoT by examining two categories of theoretical IoT security training:

- Online courses.
- Tabletop exercises.

7.2.2.1 Online Courses

While the hands-on training approaches discussed so far are most effective for teaching practical IoT security skills, the range of IoT technologies is very vast, necessitating a large amount of knowledge. A straightforward way to acquire such knowledge is by taking online courses that provide relevant information on IoT security topics. We emphasize, however, that such courses need to be supplemented with hands-on exercises in order to ensure that skill development occurs as well.

One example in the online course category is *Cybersecurity and the Internet of Things*, which is provided by Coursera [9]. The course addressed mainly security and privacy issues regarding IoT technologies, e.g., in relation with consumer wearables and connected homes, that are taught in a practical and interactive manner, such as via case studies and quizzes. The course is provided in an instructor-led manner and has an estimated completion duration of approximately 11 h.

Another related online course is offered on the GetSmarter learning platform under the name *Internet of Things: Business Implications and Opportunities* [16]. Instead of focusing on technical topics, this course provides a business management perspective on IoT, for example, dealing with business strategy and operation aspects in relation with IoT technologies. This course is provided in an instructor-led manner as well and has an estimated completion duration of 36 to 48 h.

7.2.2.2 Tabletop Exercises

The relatively low involvement of learners in online courses is one of their main disadvantages. Therefore, the concept of tabletop training–that is, organizing training sessions in which participants discuss their roles and responses in a given cybersecurity scenario—has also been applied to the area of IoT security training. Specific issues in this context are the fact that in the world of IoT cyber threats can have physical impacts, and physical threats can have cyber impacts, with potentially serious consequences, especially in domains such as industrial IoT.

An example in this case is the card game named *IoT-Poly* [21]. The game uses four types of cards that correspond to IoT systems, attack surfaces, threats and countermeasures. The players use the cards they receive initially, and others they draw from the deck, to conduct a risk assessment on a given IoT system based on three phases: risk identification, risk analysis, and risk evaluation, including aspects such as residual risks. Discussions between players make it possible for them to evaluate each other's decisions and share knowledge within the group.

7.2.3 Approach Comparison

To better clarify the differences between the IoT security training approaches that we discussed so far, we conducted a comparative analysis of their main characteristics from several perspectives: typical target participants, interactivity, and whether an instructor is available or not. The comparison is summarized in Table 7.1, where some comments about each approach are also provided in the last column.

Table 7.1 Comparison of IoT security training approaches

Approach	Type	Participants	Interactivity	Instructor	Comments
Academic training	Hands-on	Mainly students	High	Yes	Typically require student status
Commercial training	Hands-on	Mainly professionals	High	Yes	Potentially high attendance costs
Training systems	Hands-on	Students and professionals	Medium	No	Based on custom hardware, expensive
Online courses	Theoretical	Students and professionals	Low	If yes, remotely	Convenient to attend
Tabletop exercises	Theoretical	Students and professionals	High	Yes	Develop soft skills (team building, etc.)

7.2.3.1 Comparative Analysis

The upper part of Table 7.1 includes the three hands-on training approaches that we discussed. For academic training, the target participants are mainly students, whereas commercial training typically targets professionals. Training systems, on the other hand, can be used both by students and professionals. As for the lower part of the table, which includes the two theoretical training approaches we discussed, both approaches are addressed to students as well as professionals.

Regarding interactivity aspects, hands-on training approaches have in general a high level of interactivity, since the trainees must be deeply involved in the training in order to perform the practical tasks included. However, we have marked the interactivity of academic and commercial training as "high" compared to the "medium" label for training systems to account for the fact that instructors are present in those cases, whereas for training systems the activity is typically conducted by the trainees themselves, without any instructor support. In the case of online courses, interactivity is low, since such courses consist mainly in watching training videos. On the other hand, tabletop training requires active discussions between participants, hence they are also highly interactive.

Instructors are an important part of the training process, and they are available for most academic and commercial IoT security training programs. In contrast, the business model for training systems is to sell those systems to customers, who conduct the training by themselves. This is perhaps the biggest disadvantage of this approach, although it can be compensated by having experienced users in an organization act as instructors for the less experienced trainees. Online courses represent a special case from an instructor involvement perspective. Thus, for many of the online courses, there is no instructor available; but even for those courses that are advertised as "instructor led," the instructor is only available remotely, and interactivity is typically limited to message exchanges, without face-to-face communication. As for tabletop exercises, instructors are generally those who moderate the training activity, provide advice when needed, etc.

We also included in Table 7.1 several comments about each approach that hint at their potential advantages and disadvantages. For academic training, we note that student status is typically required to take those courses, which is a potential barrier to attendance. There are, however, academic courses that are available to non-degree learners (for a fee), thus eliminating this barrier. As for commercial training, the attendance costs are potentially high; one could consider, however, that these costs are counterbalanced by the fact that some of the commercial training programs provide completion certificates that can be used professionally, for example for job hunting or promotion purposes. Training systems are often based, at least partially, on custom hardware, hence purchase costs can be high; these costs can nevertheless be amortized over time if enough members of an organization use the training system. The main advantage of online courses is that they are convenient to attend due to their online nature, and can be done in a self-paced manner, hence are an easier way to gain background knowledge compared to other approaches. With regard to tabletop exercises, their discussion-based nature helps develop soft skills, such as team building, for which there is no equivalent in the other training approaches, which are fundamentally conducted individually.

7.2.3.2   Discussion

We also note that sometimes it is difficult to clearly place a specific system in one of the training categories discussed so far. For example, the training system presented in [6] uses an industrial system physical model to give students a factory-related IoT training experience. For this purpose, the system includes several manufacturing components, such as sensors, motors, and conveyor belts. While this system is developed in the academic world, it is also a hardware-based training system, as those described in Sect. 7.2.1.3. In cases as this one, readers should consider the properties of all the categories to which a system can be considered to belong to, as the specific characteristics of all those categories become relevant.

The comparison we conducted in this section considered the typical properties of training programs that fall into each of the approaches we discussed. Such a generic comparison helps identifying the most suitable approach for a given purpose but does not consider the specificities of a particular training program. For this purpose, a more detailed analysis should be conducted for any specific platform of interest by following the methodology discussed in Sect. 3.1, similarly to the case study taxonomy-based analysis that was summarized in Table 3.1.

7.3   Case Study: IoTrain-Sim and IoTrain-Lab

Two IoT security training systems developed at Japan Advanced Institute of Science and Technology are IoTrain-Sim and IoTrain-Lab [30, 31]. Both systems were released on GitHub in 2020 [10, 11], and their open-source nature makes them very suitable as case studies for the topic of this chapter.

The two mentioned IoT training systems are of the hands-on type, and are part of the academic training system category, being created in a university environment. Both of them target IoT developers via practical tutorials and exercises. In what follows we will review their main characteristics in the context of the concepts discussed so far, then discuss the differences between the two approaches.

7.3.1   IoTrain-Sim

IoTrain-Sim is an IoT security training system that leverages the functionality of the Cooja network simulator to create a simulated IoT network in which trainees can conduct hands-on training activities [11, 30]. Note that Cooja is distributed along with an open-source operating system for IoT devices named Contiki OS [8].

7.3.1.1 System Overview

IoTrain-Sim retrieves IoT training content from the training content database and presents that content to trainees on demand. The training content is either in the form of tutorials, that the trainees can use to gain knowledge about various IoT technologies and security issues, or in the form of Cooja simulation scenarios.

Key Features When using IoTrain-Sim, instructors should prepare the training content in advance, then store and register it into the IoTrain-Sim database. Learners start by consulting the tutorials; upon completion, they can then proceed to conduct the related simulations. For the latter purpose, IoTrain-Sim uses the included simulation scenarios to drive the execution of the Cooja simulator.

Trainees interact with IoTrain-Sim either via a Graphical User Interface (GUI) or via a Command Line Interface (CLI). The GUI makes it possible to access both tutorials and simulations by simply clicking on the corresponding items, as shown in Fig. 7.1.

Main Advantages The fact that it leverages simulation techniques for training purposes is one of the main characteristics of IoTrain-Sim. From an IoT security training perspective, the advantages of this approach are as follows:

- Using a simulation environment for hands-on activities is safe even when using malicious nodes and traffic, which are dangerous to deploy in real environments, especially for beginners.

Fig. 7.1 Screenshot of the IoTrain-Sim graphical user interface

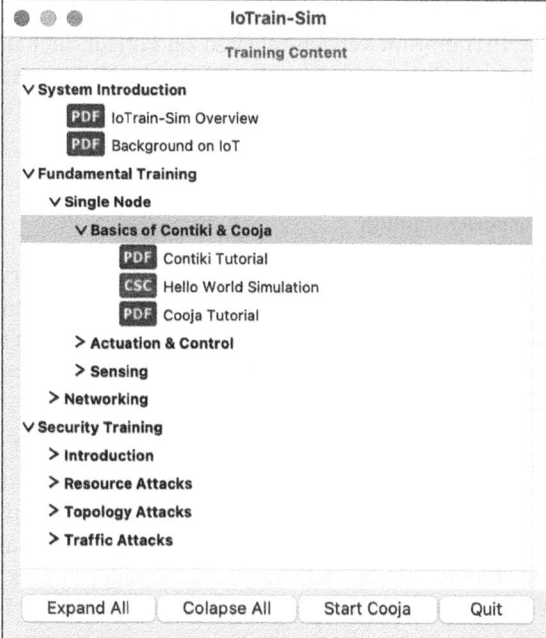

Table 7.2 Overview of the IoTrain-Sim training content

Category	Type	Subtype	Topic
System introduction	Overview	–	Introductory tutorial
Fundamental training	Single node	Basics of Contiki and Cooja	Hello world simulation
		Actuation and control	LED, button, timer
		Sensing	Temperature, humidity, light
	Networking	Communication	Broadcast
Security training	Resource attacks	Direct attacks	Flooding attack
		Indirect attacks	DODAG version attack
	Topology attacks	Isolation attacks	Black hole attack
	Traffic attacks	Misappropriation attacks	Decreased rank attack

- The Cooja simulator reproduces actual IoT hardware, making simulation-based training results applicable to real IoT devices.
- The simulation environment makes it possible to easily conduct large-scale experiments that cannot be easily replicated via real hardware.

7.3.1.2   Training Content

The IoTrain-Sim version released on GitHub includes a set of tutorials in regard to basic IoT knowledge and skills, as well as several security aspects. The three categories of existing training content are (see also Table 7.2 for an overview):

- System introduction.
- Fundamental training.
- Security training.

System Introduction This tutorial provides an overview on IoT technologies and IoT security, and also about the utilization of IoTrain-Sim itself, and is aimed at users of all levels. Trainees are, in general, supposed to start their learning with this module, unless they already have basic knowledge of IoT technologies in general, and IoTrain-Sim in particular.

Fundamental Training These tutorials are aimed at users with a beginner-to-intermediate level regarding IoT technologies and start by introducing the basics of Contiki OS and Cooja. This is followed by hands-on exercises regarding how to operate IoT devices, both in regard to actuation and control, such as via LEDs and buttons, and also with respect to sensing, such as via temperature and humidity sensors. Following that, communication techniques for IoT devices are explained, with focus on broadcast, which is often used in sensor networks.

Security Training These tutorials leverage fundamental training to teach security-specific skills and are aimed at users with an intermediate-to-advanced level in regard to IoT technologies. The focus is on the security of the routing protocol named RPL that is frequently used in low-power and lossy networks such as Wireless Sensor Networks (WSN). In particular, the following types of attacks are considered:

- Resource attacks: These attacks force nodes to perform unnecessary actions in order to deplete their resources, such as processing load and power consumption, thus affecting network operation directly or indirectly.
- Topology attacks: These attacks aim to disrupt the network topology via node isolation or non-optimal routing in order to create communication issues.
- Traffic attacks: These attacks attempt to eavesdrop on other nodes' traffic, or to impersonate the traffic of legitimate nodes by the introduction of malicious nodes into the network.

7.3.1.3 Training Approach

The tutorials about fundamental and security training topics that we discussed include all the information needed to understand those topics, and come with simulation scenarios to experiment with those concepts via Cooja. This is particularly useful in the context of security training, for instance, in order to study specific attack mechanisms, since the attack implementation is already provided. Moreover, the defense mechanisms against each type of attack are also explained, making it possible for trainees to develop the corresponding skills.

For this purpose, the training content of IoTrain-Sim consists of three elements: tutorials in the form of PDF files, Cooja simulation scenarios in the form of CSC files, and C language files that make it possible to modify the behavior of the simulated Contiki nodes. The trainees can access the tutorials and simulations by making use of the IoTrain-Sim interface and can modify the associated C files to change the node functionality as desired. For more details about IoTrain-Sim, see [30].

7.3.2 IoTrain-Lab

IoTrain-Lab is a training system that leverages the functionality of the FIT IoT-LAB testbed to create a network made of real IoT devices with which trainees can conduct hands-on training activities in a controlled environment [10, 31]. The IoT testbed that IoTrain-Lab uses, FIT IoT-LAB, has more than 1500 nodes at nine physical sites across France [2, 15]. The nodes have various hardware architectures (Arduino, Microchip, Nordic, etc.), and support several operating systems (including Contiki) and communication technologies (IEEE 802.15.4, Bluetooth Low Energy, etc.). The fact that FIT IoT-LAB can be used remotely from anywhere in the world in an open-access manner makes it very appropriate as IoT training infrastructure.

7.3.2.1 System Overview

IoTrain-Lab provides a series of training tutorials that trainees can follow to learn about IoT technologies, and facilitates their remote access to the underlying testbed, FIT IoT-LAB, in a multi-user manner.

Key Features The simultaneous access of multiple trainees to FIT IoT-LAB is made possible via the use of container technology. In particular, Docker is utilized to deploy lightweight CentOS Linux containers with all the necessary connection tools and settings. Access management for the Linux containers is done by means of a remote desktop gateway based on Apache Guacamole that runs in another container. To begin the training, learners must first log in into one of the Linux containers, then start using the testbed infrastructure according to the provided tutorials.

IoTrain-Lab does not have any specific user interface, and trainees must conduct the training activity via command line. In particular, they need to connect via the `ssh` command to the FIT IoT-LAB testbed, then start and manage the experiments using the terminal. On the one hand, this makes the access less convenient compared to IoTrain-Sim. However, on the other hand, trainees have more freedom to practice in ways than deviate from the prescribed tutorials, which may be an attractive feature for the more advanced of the users.

Main Advantages The advantages of the testbed-based design of IoTrain-Lab from an IoT security training perspective are as follows:

- Using an isolated testbed environment for hands-on activities is safe even when using malicious nodes and traffic, which are dangerous to deploy in real environments, especially for beginners.
- The use of real IoT devices in FIT IoT-LAB makes testbed-based training results applicable to real-life scenarios.
- The testbed environment makes it possible to easily conduct large-scale experiments that cannot be easily replicated via local setups.

7.3.2.2 Training Content

Similarly to IoTrain-Sim, the current version of IoTrain-Lab that was released on GitHub includes tutorials regarding basic IoT knowledge and skills, as well as some security aspects. The two categories of training content in IoTrain-Lab are described next (see also Table 7.3 for an overview):

- Fundamental training.
- Security training.

Fundamental Training These tutorials refer to basic aspects related to IoT devices, such as node control and radio monitoring/sniffing, and are aimed at users with a beginner-to-intermediate level regarding IoT technologies. Tutorials related to IoT

Table 7.3 Overview of the IoTrain-Lab training content

Category	Type	Topic
Fundamental training	Devices	Node control
		Consumption monitoring
		Radio monitoring
		Radio sniffing
	Protocols	Ping testing
		RPL-based routing
		CoAP protocol
		MQTT protocol
Security training	Resource attacks	Flooding attack

network protocols are also included, both in connection with basic protocols, such as RPL, as well as with regard to more advanced ones, such as CoAP and MQTT.

Security Training This content leverages fundamental training to teach security-specific skills and is aimed at users with an intermediate-to-advanced level in regard to IoT technologies. Only one tutorial is currently included, which focuses on the security of the RPL protocol, in particular when dealing with the network resource attack named *flooding attack*. Via this tutorial, trainees can experiment with this type of attack on real IoT devices, a differentiating factor compared to IoTrain-Sim, which uses only simulated attacks.

7.3.2.3   Training Approach

All the IoTrain-Lab tutorials mentioned so far are available online. They include explanations about the steps needed to conduct the training exercises, accompanied by screenshots and example output data.

Note that the difficulty level of each exercise is specified, and they are ordered according to this level. This makes it possible for trainees to gradually develop their skills if they are beginners, or to jump directly to more challenging exercises, if they already have the required knowledge. For more details about IoTrain-Lab, see [31].

7.3.3   System Comparison

There are many similarities between IoTrain-Sim and IoTrain-Lab. Both of them are mainly targeted at students, but can also be used by professionals, and the training takes place in a tutorial-based, self-paced manner. Moreover, both are available at no cost as free downloads. Lastly, both systems cover fundamental, as well as security training, although the security training content of IoTrain-Sim is richer.

Table 7.4 Differences between IoTrain-Sim and IoTrain-Lab

Features	IoTrain-Sim	IoTrain-Lab
Training type	Local simulation	Remote testbed
Training materials	Tutorials, predefined simulations	Tutorials only
Required knowledge	Low	Low-to-medium
Prerequisite registration	No	For FIT IoT-LAB
Device types	Simulated devices	Real devices
Supported devices	3 sensor types, 1 actuator type	13 IoT board types
Supported OSs	Contiki OS	FreeRTOS, RIOT, Contiki-NG, etc.
Device mobility	Not available	Available via robots

However, there are several important differences as well, as it has been summarized in Table 7.4. Thus, in IoTrain-Sim the training is conducted conveniently via local simulation, whereas IoTrain-Lab requires to access remotely the IoT testbed, which needs to be shared with potentially many other users, hence occasional unavailability may occur. In IoTrain-Sim, in addition to tutorials, predefined simulation scenarios are available, but for IoTrain-Lab only the tutorials are available, and the practical experiments must be created and conducted step-by-step by trainees. While the knowledge level required to use IoTrain-Sim is low, some basic command-line skills and fundamental networking knowledge are required in the case of IoTrain-Lab. No registration is needed to use IoTrain-Sim, but for IoTrain-Lab registering on FIT IoT-LAB is necessary, although this only has to be done in the beginning by the course instructor, and the use is free of charge for academic use.

Regarding the capabilities available during the training, IoTrain-Sim only provides simulated devices, which is a convenient but intrinsically less realistic method compared to the actual IoT devices available in IoTrain-Lab. The types of devices are also richer in IoTrain-Lab, with 13 types of various IoT boards being available on the FIT IoT-LAB testbed; support for operating systems is richer as well, with much more choices compared to the single choice, Contiki OS, of IoTrain-Sim. Last but not least, IoTrain-Lab makes possible mobility experiments, since FIT IoT-LAB also includes several IoT device-equipped robots that can be made part of the hands-on experiments, thus providing much more realistic conditions.

In the case study presented in this section we have focused only on the specific characteristics of IoTrain-Sim and IoTrain-Lab. A more in-depth and general comparison of IoT security training methodologies and tools, including several other systems, is available in [4]. The mentioned paper also examines two practical examples of using IoTrain-Sim and IoTrain-Lab to conduct security training.

References

1. 3 Rocks Technology: Internet of things training systems. https://www.3rockstech.com/index. php/training-systems/internet-of-things. Accessed 1 July 2024
2. Adjih C, Baccelli E, Fleury E, Harter G, Mitton N, Noel T, Pissard-Gibollet R, Saint-Marcel F, Schreiner G, Vandaele J, Watteyne T (2015) FIT IoT-LAB: a large scale open experimental IoT testbed. In: IEEE 2nd world forum on Internet of things (WF-IoT), pp 459–464
3. Alanazi M, Mahmood A, Chowdhury MJM (2023) SCADA vulnerabilities and attacks: a review of the state-of-the-art and open issues. Comput Secur 125:103028. https://doi.org/10.1016/j. cose.2022.103028
4. Beuran R, Wang J, Zhao M, Tan Y (2023) IoT security training for system developers: methodology and tools. Internet Things 24:100931
5. Čeleda P, Vykopal J, Švábenský V, Slavíček K (2020) KYPO4INDUSTRY: a testbed for teaching cybersecurity of industrial control systems. In: Proceedings of the 51st ACM technical symposium on computer science education, pp 1026–1032
6. Cheng JH, Lin HH, Shen JH, Chen BC, He ZL (2020) IoT training system for smart manufacturing education. In: Proceedings of the IEEE international conference on knowledge innovation and invention (ICKII), pp 182–184
7. Cisco networking academy: IoT fundamentals: IoT security. https://www.netacad.com/ courses/cybersecurity/iot-security. Accessed 1 July 2024
8. Contiki development team: Contiki OS GitHub page. https://github.com/contiki-os/contiki. Accessed 1 July 2024
9. Coursera: cybersecurity and the Internet of things. https://www.coursera.org/learn/iot-cyber-security. Accessed 1 July 2024
10. Cyber range organisation and design (CROND): IoTrain-Lab GitHub page. https://github.com/ crond-jaist/iotrain-lab. Accessed 1 July 2024
11. Cyber range organisation and design (CROND): IoTrain-Sim GitHub page. https://github.com/ crond-jaist/iotrain-sim. Accessed 1 July 2024
12. Debar H, Beuran R, Tan Y (2020) A quantitative study of vulnerabilities in the Internet of medical things. In: Proceedings of the 6th international conference on information systems security and privacy (ICISSP), pp 164–175
13. Espinha Gasiba T, Lechner U, Pinto-Albuquerque M (2020) Sifu—a cybersecurity awareness platform with challenge assessment and intelligent coach. Cybersecurity 3(1):24. https://doi. org/10.1186/s42400-020-00064-4
14. European Union Agency for Cybersecurity (ENISA): good practices for security of IoT—secure software development lifecycle (2019)
15. FIT IoT-LAB development team: FIT IoT-LAB website. https://www.iot-lab.info/. Accessed 1 July 2024
16. GetSmarter: Internet of Things: Business implications and opportunities. https://mit-online. getsmarter.com/presentations/lp/mit-internet-of-things-online-short-course/. Accessed 1 July 2024
17. Griffioen H, Doerr C (2020) Examining Mirai's battle over the Internet of things. In: Proceedings of the 2020 ACM SIGSAC conference on computer and communications security, pp 743–756
18. GSM Association (GSMA) (2020) GSMA IoT security guidelines and assessment
19. Information-technology Promotion Agency (IPA): industrial cyber security center of excellence ICSCoE. https://www.ipa.go.jp/en/about/org/icscoe/index.html. Accessed 1 July 2024
20. National Institute of Standards and Technology (NIST) (2022) Recommended criteria for cybersecurity labeling of consumer software. https://doi.org/10.6028/NIST.CSWP.02042022-1
21. Omiya T, Fall D, Kadobayashi Y (2019) IoT-poly: an IoT security game practice tool for learners motivation and skills acquisition. In: Proceedings of the 19th Koli calling international conference on computing education research, pp 1–10

22. Ooi SE, Beuran R, Tan Y (2021) Secure IoT development: a maker's perspective. In: Proceedings of the IEEE international conference on omni-layer intelligent systems (COINS), pp 27–32

23. Russell B, van Duren D (2018) Practical Internet of things security, 2nd edn. Packt Publishing, Birmingham

24. SANS Institute: SEC556: IoT penetration testing. https://www.sans.org/cyber-security-courses/iot-penetration-testing/. Accessed 1 July 2024

25. Scientific and technical products (STP): IoT training systems. https://scitech.com.my/product-category/solution/iot/. Accessed 1 July 2024

26. Shin S, Seto Y (2020) Development of IoT security exercise contents for cyber security exercise system. In: Proceedings of the 13th international conference on human system interaction (HSI), pp 1–6

27. The OWASP foundation: OWASP WebGoat. https://owasp.org/www-project-webgoat/. Accessed 1 July 2024

28. Trabelsi Z (2021) IoT based smart home security education using a hands-on approach. In: 2021 IEEE global engineering education conference (EDUCON), pp 294–301

29. Wagenseil P (2020) These 45 netgear routers can be hacked and will never be fixed—what to do now. https://www.tomsguide.com/news/netgear-routers-no-fixes. Accessed 1 July 2024

30. Wang J (2019) IoT training system using the Cooja network simulator. Master's thesis, Japan advanced institute of science and technology

31. Zhao M (2019) Hands-on IoT security training using IoT testbeds. Master's thesis, Japan advanced institute of science and technology

Chapter 8
Cybersecurity Awareness Training

This chapter discusses first several issues related to cybersecurity literacy, then presents various approaches used for cybersecurity awareness training, such as reading materials, training videos, and e-learning. More advanced methods are presented next, such as phishing simulation and gamification, followed by a comparative analysis of all the examined approaches. Lastly, the cybersecurity awareness training platform CyATP is introduced as a case study of applying the discussed principles into practice.

8.1 Cybersecurity Literacy

In our current world, people of all ages have become more and more reliant on the internet, with the use of smartphones being a sort of democratization mechanism for accessing information. However, while network communication makes daily life more convenient, it also exposes internet users to various kinds of cybersecurity risks, such as malware, phishing, and so on. This has led to the introduction of the concept of *cybersecurity literacy* to denote the basic kind of education that all regular internet users should take in order to ensure that the associated potential cybersecurity risks are minimized [20].

In this book, however, we prefer to refer to this concept by using the alternative name *cybersecurity awareness training*, which emphasizes the practical hands-on aspects that we believe are important to ensure that the learners are able to acquire a correct cybersecurity posture not only from a knowledge point of view, but also in terms of practical skills. For example, the ability to recognize actual phishing emails and websites is more important than the simple abstract knowledge of what phishing emails and websites are.

Nevertheless, as it will be discussed in more detail in Sect. 8.2, not all approaches used for cybersecurity awareness training include such practical aspects. Therefore,

© The Author(s), under exclusive license to Springer Nature Singapore Pte Ltd. 2025   153
R. Beuran, *Cybersecurity Education and Training*,
https://doi.org/10.1007/978-981-96-0555-2_8

distinguishing the characteristics of each type of cybersecurity awareness program makes it possible to determine its suitability for a given purpose. For example, reading material-based training is obviously going to provide only knowledge to learners, whereas phishing simulation-based training makes it possible for learners to acquire practical skills related to phishing by the actual exposure to such issues in a safe and controlled training environment.

One important aspect related to cybersecurity awareness training is that, in contrast with the technical cybersecurity training, it is addressed to people who have little or no interest in low-level cybersecurity issues. Moreover, the target learners have a wide range of ages and backgrounds, including young internet users, potentially even starting in primary school, who have a very limited knowledge about computing and networking. In this context, techniques such as gamification could be used to make the training content more engaging and entertaining.

8.2   Cybersecurity Awareness Training Approaches

As mentioned in the previous section, there are several approaches that can be used to conduct cybersecurity awareness training, as follows:

- Training based on reading materials.
- Training based on video content.
- E-learning technologies.
- Advanced methods: phishing simulation, gamification, etc.

While these approaches are typically used exclusively, they are also combined sometimes with the goal of improving the overall training effectiveness. In what follows we will provide some more details about each approach, then compare their main attributes and practical suitability.

8.2.1   Reading Materials

The most basic form of cybersecurity awareness training is that based on reading materials. For this type of training, trainees in a given organization may receive reading materials in printed or electronic form that describe aspects such as:

- The general dangers associated with the use of IT environments (e.g., malware, phishing, etc.) and possible ways to avoid such dangers (e.g., caution when clicking on links in emails, use of strong passwords, etc.).
- Specific rules about actions that should not be undertaken within that organization's environment (e.g., not to use illegal/cracked software, restrictions on the use of peer-to-peer software, etc.).

- Details about the specific IT environment of that particular organization, and the specific services that are being offered.

This type of training is typically conducted for new members of an organization, such as new employees or new students, before they are allowed access to their computer accounts and the IT environment. Hence, this type of training can be considered as a kind of minimal safety gateway from a personnel perspective to that organization's environment.

Sometimes reading materials are also distributed online for the general public, for example by government organization and police departments in various jurisdictions. As an example, the Cybersecurity & Infrastructure Security Agency (CISA) in the U.S. provides several resource materials as part of their *Secure Our World* program, such as tip sheets, that contain basic information on various cybersecurity awareness topics, including phishing, passwords, and so on [3].

Another example is the online course entitled *Cybercompass* that is made available publicly by Masaryk University, Czech Republic [10]. The course provides a total of five modules, which cover a wide range of topics: device security, passwords, cybersecurity self-defense techniques, secure communication, and incident reporting. *Cybercompass* was evaluated via a questionnaire with more than 130 respondents among the students who took the course in regard to the general impression and usefulness of the modules, whether they have learned something new, whether the course improved their preparedness for everyday security, etc. The assessment produced very positive results, emphasizing the practicality of this type of cybersecurity awareness training method [9].

Nevertheless, although reading materials are very useful as a source of information that can be quickly accessed and easily referenced, being purely text and image based, they are not particularly engaging. Consequently, more modern training approaches have started being used over time, as it will be discussed next.

8.2.2 Training Videos

Training videos are a form of cybersecurity awareness training that uses techniques such as animation and short videos to present the training content in a more attractive and more relatable manner to compared to reading materials. Voice-over, music and sound effects also contribute to making this type of training content more memorable and more effective.

In the most typical scenario, instead of providing new members of an organization with reading materials, they are being shown training videos which convey the same kind of information. In summary, while the content of reading materials and training videos is generally the same, the delivery method changes with the goal of ensuring an improved experience for the trainees.

When the training content is made available online, then the text and image content of the web page is typically combined with training videos, trying to exploit the multimodal nature of delivery made possible by modern technologies. For example, the web site of the CISA *Secure Our World* program mentioned earlier also includes such video content, for instance to provide information on the best cybersecurity practices for staying safe online [4].

8.2.3   E-Learning

E-learning refers to those digital technologies used to deliver educational content via various types of electronic resources. The most typical type of e-learning is being conducted exclusively online, with learners making use of digital devices to access the educational content. In this case learners are able to access the e-learning environment in a flexible and self-paced manner, and can sometimes use features such as discussion forums to interact with the instructors or other learners.

8.2.3.1   Content Types and Features

Compared to the previous cybersecurity awareness training approaches, e-learning has the advantage that it can rely heavily on modern digital technologies. Consequently, most e-learning platforms use a combination of content types and features, as illustrated in Fig. 8.1, although not every platform necessarily includes all the elements that we will discuss below.

Since some of the learners prefer text content and others visual content, e-learning platforms typically combine reading materials and training videos as delivery methods. However, e-learning is more than just the sum of these two types of training content, since by themselves reading materials and training videos only provide a passive training experience. In e-learning, on the other hand, trainees are able to interact with the training content not only to decide the pace of the learning, but potentially also to decide the order in which they learn the topics, for example by exploring those topics that are of more interest at a certain moment.

Fig. 8.1 Overview of the content types and features most commonly used in e-learning platforms

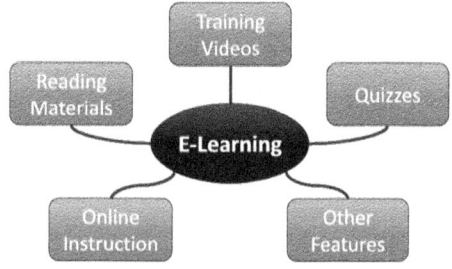

For such reasons related to interactivity, e-learning has gained popularity in recent years as a preferred method of delivering cybersecurity awareness training content, especially in structured environments, such as companies and education institutions, where the identity of the target learners can be easily verified, for example by means of user accounts. Such identity verification allows organizations not only to know which learners are taking the training and what their current progress is, but also to determine the proficiency level they have reached.

This is achieved by means of short quizzes based on the training content that are included with many e-learning platforms, for example, at the end of each learning module. These quizzes serve two purposes: learners are able to determine how well they master the training content, and the organizations they belong to can follow their progress, for example to decide if they have acquired enough knowledge to be considered that they passed the course.

As mentioned already, in some cases e-learning courses include online instruction features that make it possible to interact directly with the course instructors. This allows trainees to ask for clarifications about aspects they may have not understood well, and increases the effectiveness of the education process. Most of the time this type of interaction takes place via electronic communication, such as message forums, but real-time feedback can also be provided for some courses, for example, by scheduling video conference sessions with the instructors.

In addition to all the aforementioned types of content, e-learning platforms may include other features meant to further increase learning effectiveness. One of the most notable such additional features is the use of gamification elements, for example, in the form of badges, to motivate the learners. This topic will be discussed in more detail later in Sect. 8.2.5.

To better illustrate the use of e-learning in the context of cybersecurity awareness training, we introduce below some examples of online training programs that are based on the e-learning paradigm.

8.2.3.2 Udemy Security Awareness Training

Udemy is an education technology company that provides an online learning and teaching platform which includes a multitude of available courses on various subjects. The security awareness training course that Udemy offers consists of a total of two hours of video content that is available on demand; the course is said to take about three hours to complete [19].

The topics covered by the Udemy security awareness training course include phishing, social engineering, data leakage, passwords, safe browsing, personal devices, and general security tips. In a manner typical of e-learning platforms, quizzes are made available at the end of each section as a way for learners to be able to assess the proficiency level they have reached.

8.2.3.3 Coursera Security Awareness Training

Coursera is another education technology company that provides an online learning and teaching platform, and similarly to Udemy many courses are available on it. The security awareness training course offered by Coursera consists of training content that is available on demand and it is said to take about two hours to complete [21].

The topics covered by the Coursera security awareness training course include: the importance of security, data and account security, passwords, networking and mobile security, malware, and social engineering. A course assessment module is made available at the end of the course.

The assessment module makes it possible for trainees to assess the knowledge they have gained, similarly to the quizzes in the corresponding Coursera course. The section-based assessment of Coursera seems, however, to provide a finer granularity, and potentially a quicker and more satisfying type of feedback to the learners.

8.2.4 Simulation

The importance of hands-on practical training has been emphasized extensively in Chap. 3. However, for some types of non-technical content as well, hands-on experience can be essential. Thus, placing the learners in realistic cybersecurity situations makes it possible for them to put their security awareness knowledge into practice, and improve the corresponding non-technical cybersecurity skills.

Such type of interaction is outside the scope of e-learning methodology, in which interaction only take place in relation with the training content itself. In this context, the key technique for making it possible for learners to put their knowledge into practice is to ask them to make decisions regarding cybersecurity issues by simulating the occurrence of those issues.

One of the most common types of cybersecurity issues IT users are confronted with on a regular basis is that of being able to distinguish malicious content, for instance when delivered via phishing emails. This is why one of the most common type of simulation-based cybersecurity awareness training is the *phishing simulation*, as it will be illustrated next via some examples.

8.2.4.1 SecureClick Phishing Simulation

SecureClick is a company that provides employee cyber awareness training by using e-learning methodology to deliver training content on a regular basis, and the training content also comprises tests of knowledge retention. However, one differentiating factor of this training program compared to regular e-learning programs is the phishing simulation service that is included [14].

According to the company, the SecureClick phishing simulation service has several characteristics aimed at improving its effectiveness:

- The phishing content is realistic, being designed based on real-life attacks on IT users that were identified in the past.
- The phishing simulation campaigns are conducted regularly, typically being delivered bi-monthly or monthly.
- The phishing content is tailored to employees according to their department or job role; for example, finance and sales department employees would receive finance and sales themed emails, respectively.
- Detailed reporting is available to make possible for organizations to identify their most susceptible users, and to determine their cybersecurity posture improvements over time.

8.2.4.2   Infosec IQ Phishing Simulation

Infosec is a company dedicated to cybersecurity training, and among their offers is included a security awareness training program named Infosec IQ [8]. One important component of this training program is the phishing simulation service that is being offered in addition to the typical e-learning materials.

The Infosec IQ phishing simulation is conducted using a set of phishing templates that reproduce in practice the topics and attacks covered in the training materials. Phishing simulations are conducted quarterly, and the module makes it possible to assess the rate of success for phishing campaigns, as well as train the phished learners automatically.

8.2.5   Gamification

As mentioned already, the target of cybersecurity awareness training programs are regular IT users that typically lack the motivation to learn concepts that may appear complicated and difficult to master. The fact that such training is mandated by the organizations they belong to also contributes to the lower motivation of the learners, who do not take the training by their own choice.

Gamification refers to the use of game-like features in education in order to better engage and motivate the learners. This concept can, of course, be applied to the field of cybersecurity awareness training, and we distinguish two main classes of gamification features, basic and advanced, as it will be discussed next.

8.2.5.1   Basic Gamification Features

One of the most basic types of gamification features are rewards, such as stars and badges, that are provided to learners as indicators of their progress through a course, for example upon the completion of a module. The visual appearance of those rewards, and other factors, such as the possibility to display them publicly (e.g., on websites), represent the main point of their appeal. Some of the e-learning systems, such as Learning Management Systems (LMS), include this kind of gamification features, for example, by including built-in features related to badges. Moodle [12], which is one of the most widely used LMS, for instance, makes it possible for instructors to add course badges and set the criteria for awarding them. Then, the badges are awarded automatically to learners based on their actions in the system, such as course or activity completion. An example of this approach is represented by the research in [18], where such techniques are used to create a gamification-based cybersecurity awareness course for self-regulated learning within Moodle.

Another basic gamification feature is based on points (or score) that are awarded as the trainees solve the tasks included in the training. In contrast with badges, scores can be used to demonstrate not only the progress, but also the proficiency of the learners. In this case the trainees may be able to track their ranking via leader boards and compare themselves with their peers. Therefore, the main appeal of this type of feature is related to the sentiment of positive rivalry that it inspires. The Moodle LMS mentioned above, for instance, supports a plugin named *Level Up XP* that makes it possible for learners to receive experience points (XP) based on their actions, and compete with each other via a leader board, with the goal of providing a stimulating learning experience [11].

The basic gamification features, such as badges and score, discussed so far are relatively easy to implement in a training program interface. However, their effectiveness is not very high, as these basic features are not enough to make the learning experience similar to that of a good game [15].

8.2.5.2 Advanced Gamification Features

In order to further improve the learning experience, more advanced game design elements are required. For example, features such as story telling that help engage the trainees more deeply and emotionally, are considered very effective in creating aspects of "collateral learning", through which learners are able to gain knowledge in spite of themselves [15].

To achieve such goals, game-like scenarios and interfaces must be used, resulting in a training experience that is similar to an actual computer game. For example, the aforementioned Infosec IQ training program includes a security awareness training games with names such as *Zombie Invasion* or *Deep Space Danger* that provide an experiential learning approach for cybersecurity awareness training [7]. Thus, by using interactive scenarios, decisions and rewards, trainees are able to learn by doing in a fun and safe game environment. The methodology used in these games is said to increase engagement, boost learner retention, and accelerate security behavior changes, which aligns perfectly with the general goals of gamification.

CyberCIEGE is a video game for teaching various computer and network security and defense concepts based on the active learning paradigm [13, 17]. Although no detailed technical skills are needed to play the game, players are able to verify their knowledge, as they try to make a trade-off between budget, productivity, and security. The game includes a wide range of devices the players can utilize, such as workstations, network devices, firewall, biometric scanners, etc. Various attack types are implemented, such corrupt insiders, malware, Denial of Service (DoS) attacks, exploitation of poorly configured systems, etc. An online help system to support players, as well as a scenario-definition language and tools for the creation of new scenarios, are also provided. CyberCIEGE is said to be available at no cost for U.S. government and educational institutions.

Another relevant example of a game-like cybersecurity awareness training experience is described in [6]. In this research, the authors use the Activity Theory-based Model of Serious Games (ATMSG) methodology to design a cybersecurity awareness training game. The game was implemented as a visual novel game, also known as a story game, which is a type of interactive game in which players click on interface elements to make progress through the game, while making narrative choices along the way. The decisions learners make in the game environment help reinforce their cybersecurity awareness skills, which can later be applied in real-life situations.

Applying the real-life *escape room* concept to cybersecurity awareness training is another manner in which gamification elements can be introduced in this type of training. For instance, the authors of [1] use an escape game as a teaching tool, preparing various scenarios that let participants practice their everyday cybersecurity skills. By using techniques such as strong password choices, and phishing email identification, trainees are able to mitigate the damage of the hacks and social-engineering attacks occurring in the game, thus gaining a valuable experience they can apply when faced with real-world security threats.

8.2.6 Approach Comparison

The various cybersecurity awareness training approaches that we presented so far each have different characteristics, which make them more or less suitable under given circumstances. In Table 8.1, we compare these characteristics based on several criteria: form of content, training type, main advantages and disadvantages.

8.2.6.1 Comparative Analysis

Regarding the form of content, we note that some approaches, such as reading materials and training videos, only provide text and images, or video-based content. In the case of e-learning, interactive aspects, such as quizzes are introduced. Additional improvements are present for simulation and gamification, which both include content of hands-on practical nature.

The training type is very much related to the content form. Thus, reading materials and training videos represent passive forms of training, whereas e-learning is

Table 8.1 Comparison of cybersecurity awareness training approaches

Methodology	Form of content	Training type	Advantages	Disadvantages
Reading materials	Text and images	Passive	Easy to reference	Least engaging experience
Video training	Videos	Passive	Impactful delivery	Lack of interactivity
E-learning	Text & images, videos, quizzes	Interactive	Self-assessment possible	Not hands-on experience
Simulation	Hands-on content	Learn by doing	Realistic training experience	Lack of control
Gamification	Game-like hands-on content	Learn by doing	Most engaging experience	High involvement required

interactive. Simulation and gamification approaches take interactivity even further, by making it possible to conduct learn-by-doing type of training activities.

Next we also analyze the main advantages and disadvantages of each cybersecurity awareness training approach:

- Reading materials: Very easy to reference when the information is required, but lack any form of learner engagement.
- Video training: Ensures an impactful and engaging delivery; however, no interaction with the content is available.
- E-learning: Self-assessment, typical via quizzes, is possible, but lacks hands-on experience capabilities.
- Simulation: Provides a realistic training experience; however, learners do not have any control on the delivery of the training.
- Gamification: Offers the most engaging experience, but requires a high level of involvement in the training from the part of the learners.

The analysis we presented demonstrates that there is no single cybersecurity awareness training approach that provides all the necessary features. Our conclusion, therefore, is that combinations of methodologies, such as e-learning and simulation, or e-learning and gamification, are perhaps the ideal solution for ensuring the most engaging and effective learning experience, as it is being done, for instance, in the Infosec IQ training program discussed earlier [8].

8.2.6.2   Detailed Assessment Procedure

In addition to comparing cybersecurity awareness training approaches in general, one may desire to assess in more detail a specific training platform, for example in order to determine how well it is designed and implemented, or how well it is suited for a given purpose.

While there seems to be no widely agreed upon detailed assessment procedure in the context of cybersecurity awareness training, we mention here a possible solution that uses an assessment questionnaire for this purpose [23]. The questionnaire is composed of two parts, as follows.

Likert-scale Evaluation For the Likert-scale evaluation, respondents are asked to select one of the following five choices "Strongly Disagree," "Disagree," "Neutral," "Agree," "Strongly Agree" for each of the nine statements below:

1. The training platform was suitable for learning.
2. The training platform has a clear user interface.
3. You noticed problems with the training platform (dead links, etc.).
4. The training content is sufficiently in-depth.
5. You enjoyed the gamification features in the training (choose "Neutral" if there were not any).
6. The training content addresses real security threats.
7. You felt that the training was engaging.
8. You felt that your knowledge/skills improved by taking the training.
9. The training was practical and/or easy to apply.

The role of the Likert-scale evaluation is to help determine whether the assessed platform, in its current state, is appropriate for learning in terms of various aspects, such as user interface, training content, gamification features, etc.

Open Questions A set of three open questions is used to gather more detailed feedback about the evaluated system for its developers, so that they can improve the system in the future:

1. What are the three most important things that you learned?
2. What were the three biggest strengths and weaknesses of the training?
3. Do you have any suggestions for improving this training program/system?

The above questionnaire was used in [23] to evaluate and compare several cybersecurity awareness training platforms that rely on the different approaches discussed in this chapter. The results of the questionnaire were also used as basis for proposing solutions for the improvement of the evaluated platforms, which emphasizes the possible practical applications of such a detailed assessment procedure.

8.3 Case Study: CyATP

To illustrate the various issues discussed in this chapter, we analyze in what follows a specific cybersecurity awareness training platform, named CyATP [24]. The platform was developed at Japan Advanced Institute of Science and Technology starting from 2020, and CyATP v1.0 was released as open source on GitHub in 2021 [2].

8.3.1 CyATP Overview

CyATP is a cybersecurity awareness training platform that uses a web-based interface to provide various self-study components that support the learning process, as well as gamification components used as part of the evaluation process. CyATP was designed by considering several ways in which the effectiveness of the training can be improved, and we will focus on those specific features in this presentation. For more details about the implementation of the platform, see [24].

The most important education mechanisms that were integrated into the CyATP platform are as follows:

- Interactive learning based on a concept map representation aimed at supporting learners' interest and motivation.
- Content generation as a way to ensure that the training content is rich and varied, and that it can be easily kept up-to-date.
- Quiz interface based on crossword puzzle mechanics as a gamification feature aimed at increasing the learning experience enjoyment.

Each of the above features will be discussed and illustrated in more detail in the next subsections.

8.3.2 Concept Map Based Learning

Most e-learning platforms present the information in a linear fashion, for instance, as a series of modules that the trainees need to go through sequentially in order to learn about the training content. However, this does not account for the differences that exist between learners in terms on knowledge level, interests, etc.

To address this issue, CyATP uses a knowledge graph representation of the training content that makes it possible for trainees to explore the concepts in the training databases by following the logical connections between them in any order they prefer. In this manner, learners are able to prioritize the concepts they are interested it at that specific moment, compared to those concepts they are not interested in or perhaps master already. This capability is achieved via two components of the user interface, named *Concept Map* and *Learn Concepts*.

8.3.2.1 Concept Map Interface

The concept map interface of CyATP displays an overview of all the concepts available in the training database in the form of a hierarchical graph representation. The representation is centered around the top-level concept for which the database was built, surrounded by lower-level concepts (the training content database itself is built automatically, as it will be explained in Sect. 8.3.3.1).

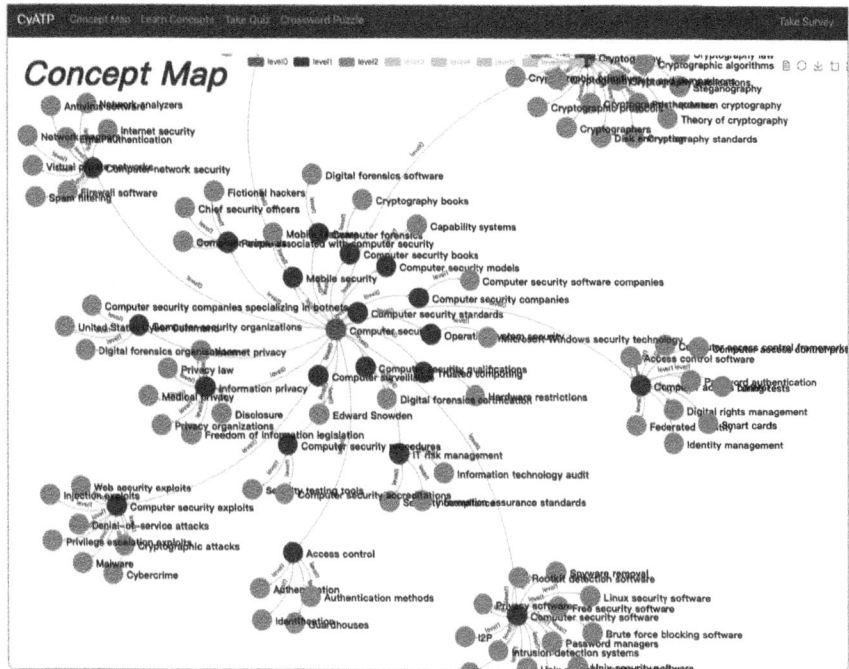

Fig. 8.2 Training content representation in CyATP as a hierarchical concept map

In the example shown in Fig. 8.2, the top-level concept is "Computer security," and the related concepts, such as "Mobile security" or "Information privacy," are shown connected to it in the concept map graph. In their turn, the related concepts of even lower level, such as "Mobile malware" in relation with "Mobile security," or "Medical privacy" in relation with "Information privacy," are also shown connected to the higher-level concepts.

To ease visibility, the logical level on which a concept is located in the logical hierarchy is emphasized via the color of the node. Learners can interact with the graph to navigate through it, zoom in and out, show or hide some of the levels, etc. By exploring the concept map, learners are able to understand the relationship between concepts at several levels of detail, as desired. They can also proceed with the learning process in any order they wish, according to their personal interests.

8.3.2.2 Learn Concepts Interface

The learn concepts interface in CyATP makes it possible for learners to study in more detail any concept they want to know more about. This is achieved via two mechanisms. In the left-hand side, an interface similar to the concept map representation is shown, revealing the relation between the concept of interest and all the

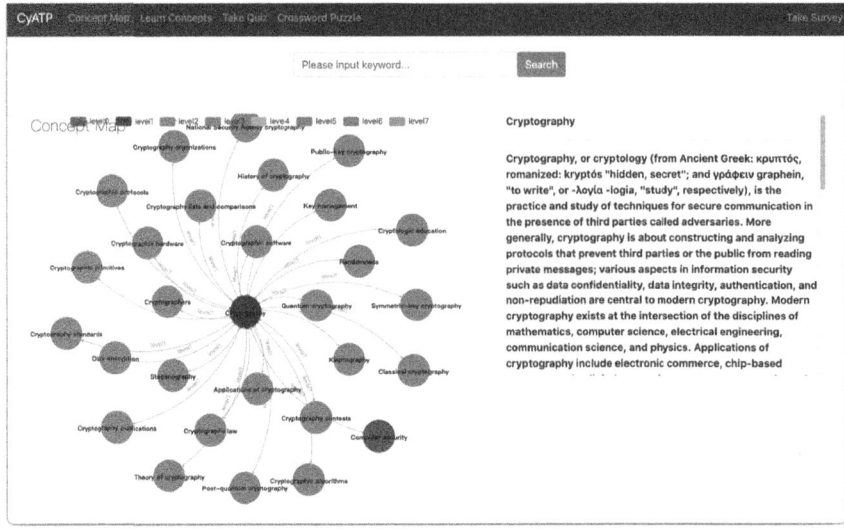

Fig. 8.3 Learn concepts interface in CyATP used for detailed concept understanding

related concepts, both at higher and lower levels in the hierarchy. Secondly, in the right-hand side of the interface, the definition of the concept of interest is displayed, so that learners can gain deeper knowledge about those concepts via their textual description.

In the example shown in Fig. 8.3, "Cryptography" is the concept of interest, and it is displayed in the center of the concept map representation. The higher-level concepts (in this case "Computer security"), as well as the lower-level ones (e.g., "Cryptographic software," "Randomness," etc.) are displayed around it, making the relationships between them very clear. The definition of "Cryptography" is also shown in the right-hand side.

In addition to the above, a search box is available at the top of the interface, making it possible for trainees to find out the definition and relationships for any concept that may be interested in via text search (provided that the search matches at least partially any concept registered in the training content database). This mechanism further adds to the freedom of exploration provided by CyATP.

8.3.3   Content Generation

Creating cybersecurity awareness training content is a tedious task that requires educators to spend a long time creating the necessary educational content, quiz questions, etc. Moreover, since the cybersecurity landscape evolves rapidly, updating the training content requires that extra time is spent to add new content related to the new issues that must be covered, and possibly to remove any unneeded old content. CyATP addresses these issues in two ways:

- Creating the training content automatically by leveraging the DBpedia and Wikipedia public knowledge bases.
- Generating the corresponding quiz content as well automatically by using Natural Language Generation (NLG) techniques.

8.3.3.1 Training Content Generation

For training content creation, the DBpedia knowledge base [5] is queried based on the top-level concept (for example, "Computer security"), and all the relationships between that concept and the related concepts are used to retrieve the associated knowledge graph. In addition, definitions for the concepts are also retrieved automatically from Wikipedia [22]; see [16] for details on the entire procedure.

Using this method, at the time of development, a total of about 2500 cybersecurity concepts and concept definitions were automatically imported into the training database of CyATP. By querying DBpedia at regular intervals, educators can effortlessly update the entire training content, thus benefiting implicitly of any changes in the DBpedia and Wikipedia knowledge bases.

8.3.3.2 Quiz Content Generation

In regard to the quiz content, NLG techniques were used to automatically generate based on the training content a set of pairs of *cloze questions*[1] and answers that are presented in the quiz section of the CyATP user interface. In particular, the SMOTE method was used to train a Bernoulli Naive Bayes model after performing isotonic calibration; see [24] for a detailed description of the approach.

An example of a generated quiz question is shown in Fig. 8.4, along with the four possible answers that were selected, made of the correct answer and three related ones. The screenshot is part of the *Take Quiz* component of the CyATP interface, and it also includes a countdown timer for answering the question, the number of remaining questions, and the current score. Trainees can also provide feedback about the question via the *Question Evaluation* button.

The current version of CyTAP includes a total of 278 cloze questions that were generated using the above method. These questions are presented to learners in the form of a timed quiz that serves as a way for them to verify their proficiency level. Each time a quiz is taken, 10 questions are randomly selected from the quiz question database for that purpose.

---

[1] Cloze questions, also known as *embedded answers questions*, are a type of question in which a portion of text is missing and must be filled in by the learner.

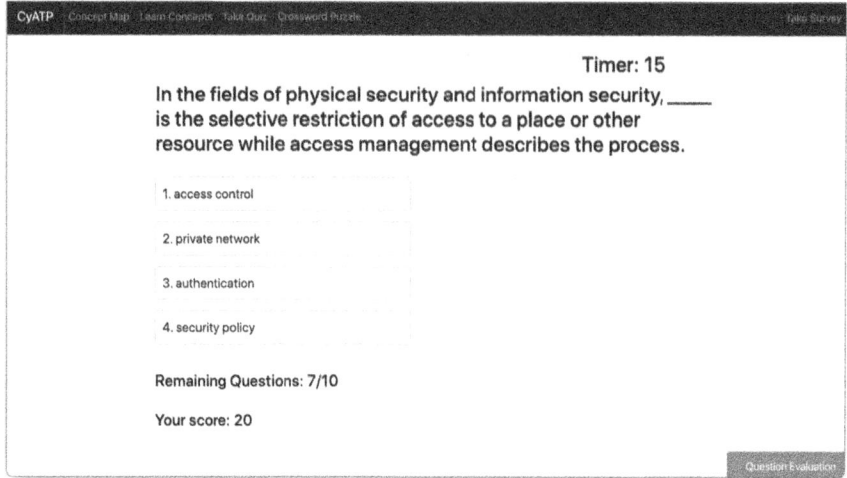

Fig. 8.4 Example quiz question automatically generated by CyATP using NLG techniques

We note that the random question selection in CyATP provides variation in terms of learning experience but does not necessarily support the learning process. For this purpose, more advanced techniques should be used, such as the adaptive learning approach proposed in [16] that prioritizes new content and content that has not yet been learned correctly when selecting the quiz questions.

In addition to being used as quiz questions, the generated cloze questions were also processed for inclusion in CyATP as elements of crossword puzzles. There are currently 28 clues available that make up a total of 10 crossword puzzles, as it will be discussed next.

8.3.4 Crossword Puzzle Quiz

The simple quiz that was discussed above is a very basic form of gamification, as the countdown timer and current score bring a certain excitement to the learning experience of the trainees. However, CyATP also provides a more advanced form of gamification meant to make the learning experience even more enjoyable via the use of crossword puzzle mechanics.

The crossword puzzle component of the user interface displays a crossword puzzle in the left-hand side. Next to it are shown the clues for the puzzle, displayed separately for the across and down directions. The clues consist of cloze questions that represent the definitions of cybersecurity-related concepts. Trainees must input the answer (missing word) of the cloze questions into the crossword puzzle area. Since this requires them to actually type the answer, it is a more challenging process than the simple answer selection from a list of possible choices for the regular quiz mentioned earlier.

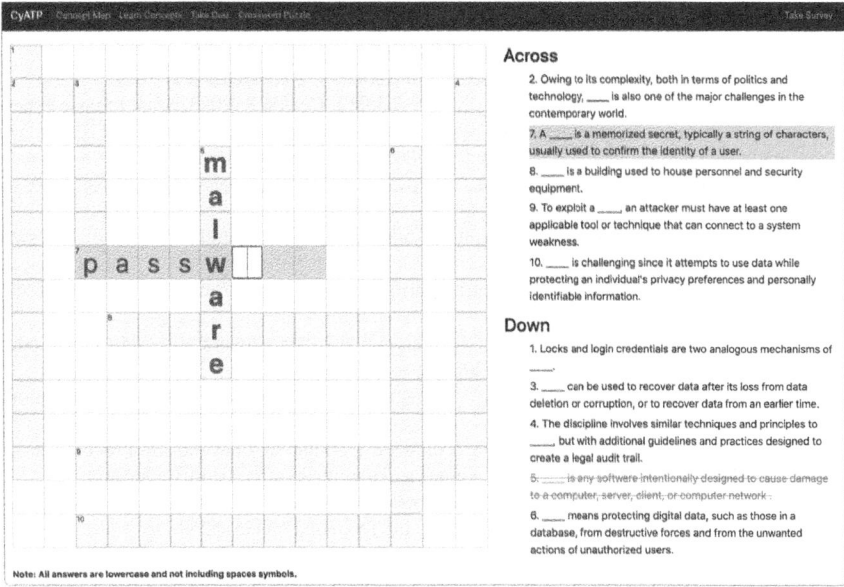

Fig. 8.5 Example crossword puzzle automatically generated by CyATP based on cloze questions

An example of a generated crossword puzzle is shown in Fig. 8.5. Using the crossword puzzle interface in CyATP makes solving the quiz more fun, thus ensuring a balance is achieved between learning and entertainment. The crossword puzzle also exercises the reasoning ability and cultivates the concentration of the learners in ways that cannot be achieved via the usual quizzes in typical e-learning platforms.

References

1. Beguin E, Besnard S, Cros A, Joannes B, Leclerc-Istria O, Noel A, Roels N, Taleb F, Thongphan J, Alata E, Nicomette V (2019) Computer-security-oriented escape room. IEEE Secur Privacy 17(4):78–83. https://doi.org/10.1109/MSEC.2019.2912700
2. Coursera Inc.: security awareness training. https://www.coursera.org/learn/security-awareness-training. Accessed 1 July 2024
3. Cyber Range Organisation and Design (CROND): CyATP GitHub page. https://github.com/crond-jaist/CyATP. Accessed 1 July 2024
4. Cybersecurity and infrastructure security agency (CISA): secure our world resources. https://www.cisa.gov/resources-tools/resources/secure-our-world-resources. Accessed 1 July 2024
5. Cybersecurity and infrastructure security agency (CISA): secure our world. https://www.cisa.gov/secure-our-world. Accessed 1 July 2024
6. DBpedia association: DBpedia website. https://www.dbpedia.org/. Accessed 1 July 2024
7. Huynh D, Luong P, Iida H, Beuran R (2017) design and evaluation of a cybersecurity awareness training game. In: Proceedings of the 2017 IFIP international conference on entertainment computing, pp 183–188

8. Infosec: choose your own adventure meets security awareness. https://www.infosecinstitute.com/iq/cybersecurity-games/. Accessed 1 July 2024

9. Infosec: Infosec IQ. https://www.infosecinstitute.com/iq/. Accessed 1 July 2024

10. Kraus L, Švábenský V, Horák M, Matyás V, Vykopal J, Čeleda P (2023) Want to raise cybersecurity awareness? Start with future IT professionals. In: Proceedings of the 2023 conference on innovation and technology in computer science education, pp 236–242

11. Masaryk   university: cybercompass.   https://security.muni.cz/en/courses/cybercompass. Accessed 1 July 2024

12. Massart F. Level up XP—gamification plugin. https://moodle.org/plugins/block_xp. Accessed 1 July 2024

13. Moodle Pty Ltd: moodle LMS open source learning platform. https://moodle.org/. Accessed 1 July 2024

14. Naval postgraduate school: CyberCIEGE—can you keep the network alive? https://nps.edu/web/c3o/cyberciege. Accessed 1 July 2024

15. SecureClick: phishing   simulation.   https://itsecurityawareness.ie/phishing-simulation. Accessed 1 July 2024

16. Sheldon L (2015) Game-based learning, collateral learning, and beyond. In: Proceedings of the 2015 USENIX summit on gaming, games and gamification in security education

17. Tan Z, Beuran R, Hasegawa S, Jiang W, Zhao M, Tan Y (2020) Adaptive security awareness training using linked open data datasets. Educ Inf Technol 25:5235–5259

18. Thompson M, Irvine C (2011) Active learning with the CyberCIEGE video game. In: Proceedings of the 4th conference on cyber security experimentation and test, pp 1–10

19. Tran TM, Beuran R, Hasegawa S (2023) Gamification-based cybersecurity awareness course for self-regulated learning. Int J Inf Educ Technol 13(4):724–730. https://doi.org/10.18178/ijiet.2023.13.4.1859

20. Udemy Inc.: security awareness training. https://www.udemy.com/course/security-awareness-training/. Accessed 1 July 2024

21. U.S. Congress: American cybersecurity literacy act. https://www.congress.gov/bill/117th-congress/house-bill/4055. Accessed 1 July 2024

22. Wikimedia foundation: wikipedia: free multilingual online encyclopedia. https://www.wikipedia.org/. Accessed 1 July 2024

23. Yuan L (2020) Assessment and improvement of security awareness training methodologies. Master's thesis, Japan advanced institute of science and technology

24. Zeng Y (2021) Content generation and serious game implementation for security awareness training. Master's thesis, Japan advanced institute of science and technology

Part II
Cybersecurity Training Platforms

Part II of the book provides a practical perspective on cybersecurity training via a wide-ranging analysis of many existing training platforms in the Capture The Flag (CTF) and cyber range categories. In addition, we present a detailed case study on the integrated cybersecurity training framework CyTrONE. A capability assessment methodology for cybersecurity training platforms is also discussed before concluding the book.

Chapter 9
Cybersecurity Training Platform Overview

This chapter provides an overview on cybersecurity training platforms, starting by introducing a model that defines the platform components that are used to provide its core functionality and support the training. This is followed by a detailed discussion of the two main components of training platforms: the training content and the training environment. For both components, the most used approaches are examined, and their respective advantages and disadvantages are analyzed.

9.1 Training Platform Model

In this section we will define a generic model for cybersecurity training platforms. The role of this model is to establish a universal framework for the more detailed analysis of training platforms that we will present in the following chapters. Consequently, our model focuses mainly on the common elements that are employed in most currently available training platforms. A simple architecture similar to the model defined here was introduced in the context of the capability assessment methodology discussed in [1]. For a more detailed functional architecture of training platforms, readers can consult the one proposed in the cyber range and security testbed survey discussed in [13].

9.1.1 Model Outline

The generic model for cybersecurity training platforms that we define is shown in Fig. 9.1. The model includes several components that make up the platform, as well as two kinds of actors, as it will be discussed next.

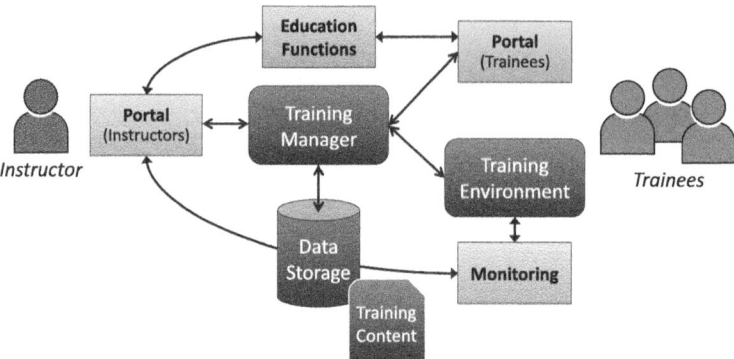

Fig. 9.1 Generic cybersecurity training platform model

9.1.1.1 Model Components

The platform components in our model can be grouped into two classes, according to their main characteristics, as follows:

- Core components.
- Support components.

Core Components The core components are those modules of the training platform that are used for the actual training activities. This includes the Training Manager for managing the training by interacting with the Data Storage and the Training Content stored within, as well as the Training Environment in which trainees can do hands-on practice. The core components are essential in a training platform, as without them no training activity can be conducted. Therefore, all training platforms must include them, at least conceptually, from the point of view of their functionality.

Support Components The support components are those modules of the training platform that provide various usability features in order to support the training activities. This includes the Portal used to interact with the training platform, Education Functions used to support the learning process, and Monitoring for keeping track of the state of the training environment. Basically, the support components are used to facilitate the training activity, such as allowing instructors and participants to more easily interact with or manage the platform. They are, however, not critical for the training activity, and simpler training platforms may omit them. While this omission does not affect the core functionality of the platform, it does reduce its usability.

9.1.1.2 Model Actors

While not components or modules of the training platform per se, we need to discuss the specificities of those who interact with the training platform, which we refer to generically as actors. Specifically, the two types of actors that we consider are:

- Instructors.
- Trainees.

So far we have employed these concepts by relying on the commonly used meaning of the terms, but we will define them more precisely here in order to be able to discuss their interactions with the training platform in the following sections.

Instructors Instructors are those users of a cybersecurity training platform who are in charge of coordinating the training activity. They can be, for instance, faculty members and other academic staff in case the training takes place in a university.

Instructors have enough privileges to perform all the management tasks related to the training activity, such as starting a training session, collecting data regarding the actions of the trainees, scoring them, etc.

Trainees Trainees are those users of a cybersecurity training platform who actually take part in the training activity. Such participants can be, for instance, university students if the training takes place in an academic environment.

Trainees have privileges related to accessing the information about the training activity that they are to perform (e.g., questions, tasks, etc.), and the training environment that they must use to solve those questions/tasks. In addition, they are able to access their own scores, and potentially other forms of detailed feedback about their training performance.

9.1.1.3 Discussion

The cybersecurity training platform model discussed so far is a simple model that has the benefit of being at the same time powerful and generic, as it can be applied to a multitude of training platforms. More detailed models, such as the architecture presented in [13], have a higher granularity, but fail to describe the interactions between components. Moreover, they may include very specialized components, such as those used for testing the functionality of the platform, which we consider having less of a generic nature compared to the modules we defined.

Another important point is that many training platforms typically implement their functionality as separate standalone components that can be mapped directly to those in our model, thus ensuring the highest clarity and flexibility of the design. However, some platforms may aggregate the functionality of two or more components into a single module. A very basic example of this type of aggregation is the case when the training content is hard coded into the training environment. In some implementations the education features could also be included in the Portal component, for example. Other implementations could even replace some functionality with manual operation, such as using scripts to manually execute the training activity instead of relying on a standalone Training Manager module.

As far as actors are concerned, in some training platforms there is an even finer role separation. For example, administrators could be technical personnel that manages the training platform, for example, by setting up the deployment servers, or installing new training content, but without having any role in coordinating the training activities or the education process. In our model these tasks are included in the Instructor persona for simplicity, and also to reflect the fact that such fine role separation is only present for very large training platforms.

Next we will present in more detail each of components of the cybersecurity training platform model introduced in Fig. 9.1.

9.1.2   Component Overview

As mentioned above, we group the training platform components into those components that are used for the actual training activities, the *core components*, and those modules that support the training activities, the *support components*. The main characteristics of the defined components will be detailed next, along with a description of their interactions with each other.

9.1.2.1   Core Components

The core components of a cybersecurity training platform that we define for the purpose of functionality separation are as follows:

- Training Manager.
- Data Storage.
- Training Content.
- Training Environment.

Training Manager The Training Manager module is a software component of the training platform that is used to manage all aspects of the training activity. This includes not only starting and stopping the training activity, but also running actions during the training, such as executing attacks, generating background traffic, etc.

In its simplest form, the Training Manager can be implemented as a set of scripts used to deploy the training content, as well as set up and run the training environment. However, more advanced training platforms use a standalone Training Manager module that has this kind of functionality.

As illustrated in Fig. 9.1, the Training Manager interacts with the Data Storage for the purpose of storing data about the training activities and to retrieve the Training Content. It also interacts with the Training Environment in order to manage it. Optionally, if Portal support components are present, the Training Manager also interacts with them, for example, receiving settings and actions from Instructors, and registering information for Trainees.

Data Storage The Data Storage is the location where all the artifacts related to the training activities are stored. Initially, this refers mainly to the Training Content, such as text and binary files that are needed in order to define the tasks for Trainees and create the Training Environment. However, as training progresses, Data Storage is also used to store any data that may result from the training activity, such as logs of trainees' interactions with the Training Environment, etc.

Data Storage is a passive component of the training platform, and the module that typically accesses it is the Training Manager, as shown in Fig. 9.1. Nevertheless, depending on the implementation, other components can access the Data Storage directly. For example, the Monitoring support component may store data retrieved from the Training Environment, which can then be displayed in the Portal for Instructors or used for further processing.

Training Content The Training Content represents the totality of materials that are used to define a training activity. Depending on the type of training, the Training Content can be in the form of questions the trainees must answer, descriptions of the tasks that they must perform, and so on. Additional types of training content can include an outline of the training activity, hints that help with solving the questions/tasks, etc. The specifications of the training environment that must be used in connection with a given set of training materials can also be part of the Training Content.

The Training Content is typically stored in the Data Storage component of the training platform (see Fig. 9.1). Since it is not a software module, many training platform architectures omit to specify it directly, and consider it as an implicit resource. From our perspective, however, a training platform without training content is basically useless. Moreover, once a training platform is deployed, most of the effort is spent in creating and updating the training content. Consequently, we have defined Training Content as an explicit component of our training platform model. As it is one of the most important components in our model, a more detailed discussion regarding training content will be provided in Sect. 9.2.

Training Environment The Training Environment represents the set of digital assets that are practically used for the hands-on training activity. A Training Environment is first of all composed of one or more computing devices or virtual machines to which the trainees connect to solve the tasks specified in the training content, as well as the network connectivity between them. In addition, the settings and software packages that are included in the computing resource are also part of the Training Environment.

As depicted in Fig. 9.1, the Training Environment is mainly configured and controlled via the Training Manager. However, it can also interact with other modules, such as the Monitoring support component, that extracts trainee activity logs from the environment, for example. It is also important to emphasize that there is a many-to-one dependency between the Training Content mentioned above and the Training Environment. Thus, a given Training Content requires a Training Environment with appropriate specifications in order to be made available for training. Moreover, a Training Environment can be used for hands-on practice in connection with different types of Training Content. The characteristics of training environments will be examined in more detail in Sect. 9.3.

9.1.2.2   Support Components

In addition to the core components of the cybersecurity training platform model that we discussed so far, several support modules can be used to improve the usability of the training platform, as follows:

- Portal.
- Education Functions.
- Monitoring.

Portal The Portal represents the user interface of the training platform. For Instructors, this refers to various training management actions, such as selecting the training content for a given training activity, creating and destroying the training environment, and so on. For Trainees, the Portal constitutes the way in which they can participate in the training via features such as access to the training content and training environment, registration of answers, etc.

The above discussion illustrates the fact that the two types of actors in our model use different features of the Portal. For this reason, in Fig. 9.1 we have represented it as distinct modules for each type of target user, although a particular implementation could use a single Portal component that presents a different interface depending on the role of the logged-in user. As for interactions, the Portal is mainly connected to the Training Manager, to which it delivers user commands, and from which it retrieves status information to be displayed in the interface. In addition, the Education Functions component can be used to add education-related functionality to the Portal, as it will be discussed next.

Education Functions The Education Functions component stands for all the features that add education capabilities to the training platform. Such features can include tutoring, in which e-learning content is presented to Trainees to help them learn related concepts, or hints that can be associated to the provided tasks to assist participants who are stuck when trying to solve them.

Other features are related to the way in which scoring for the solutions provided to tasks is done—including depending on whether hints were used or not—and in which those scores are managed. This can also include the certification of the skill or skills that were required to complete a given task, for example, in connection with skill frameworks such as the NICE Framework (see Sect. 3.2.1).

As shown in Fig. 9.1, Education Functions is basically a support module for the Portal component, hence it interacts with it both in order to assist Trainees, for example, via the tutoring feature mentioned above, and also to support Instructors, for example by making it possible to view and manage Trainee scores.

Monitoring The Monitoring component is a support module that is in charge of collecting information from the hosts in the Training Environment. Such information can be used to better understand the activity of the Trainees. For example, action logs could show which commands the Trainees executed, and in which order, revealing information about how well they master the related knowledge and skills. By ana-lyzing this information, Instructors can refine the training materials in order to better teach those skills, and also refine the training content in order to ensure the target skills are learned according to recognized best practices.

The main interaction of the Monitoring component is with the Training Environment, which is the source of the Trainee action-related information that the module collects, as illustrated in Fig. 9.1. In addition, Monitoring can supply data to the Portal for display to Instructors; the information is also typically saved in the Data Storage for further analysis.

9.1.2.3 Discussion

As mentioned already, the core components of our cybersecurity training platform model are an essential part of any training platform. Hence, all training platforms must include these components in one for, or another. Among the core components, however, Training Content and Training Environment are conceptually the most important, since they represent those components that are intrinsically used in the training activity. This is why we will examine them in more detail in the following two sections of this chapter.

On the other hand, by their nature, all the support components in our model are optional, as training activities can also be conducted without them. However, some of the components are more important than others in terms of the gain in usability they can provide. The Portal is the most important from this point of view, as without a user-friendly interface it can be difficult to make effective use of a training platform, both for Instructors and Trainees.

Education Functions are especially useful in an academic environment, where the main goal of the activity is learning. In contrast, if the main goal of the training platform is skill testing, for example, in a professional environment, such functionality can be omitted. As for Monitoring, it is only required if an in-depth analysis of Trainee actions is desired.

9.2 Training Content

The training content is arguably the most important aspect of a cybersecurity training platform, since it contains all the information that trainees need in order to be able to learn the target skills. However, to create effective cybersecurity training content, instructors need to possess not only technical knowledge, but also an understanding of education approaches. Otherwise, even if the content is technically sound, not presenting it in an attractive manner may decrease the motivation of the trainees, as discussed already in Sect. 2.2.1.3.

This is an important issue because, in practice, cybersecurity training content creators are often simply security experts who were tasked with sharing their knowledge via the training platform. In such cases, developing training content for technical cybersecurity training may pose various challenges. Consequently, in what follows we will provide some guidelines about how to create good cybersecurity training content that is adapted to the characteristics of the trainees.

9.2.1 Training Content Types

The first decision that a cybersecurity training content creator needs to make is about content type. Although the training approaches can differ among various cybersecurity training platforms, training content is typically defined in one of the following three manners that will be discussed next:

- As a quiz made of independent tasks or challenges.
- In the form of a scenario composed of sequential tasks.
- Without following any structure.

9.2.1.1   Quiz-Based Training Content

For quiz-based training, content is organized in the form of questions for which the participants must provide an answer, typically by executing actions and commands in the training environment. The questions are usually grouped by category (such as web, network, cryptography, etc.), but are independent from each other; hence, the order in which they are addressed does not matter.

This type of training content makes it possible to easily assign a score to trainees based on whether they have answered correctly or not the included questions. Moreover, public scoreboards are often integrated in the platforms using this type of content as a gamification element to increase the motivation of the participants.

Quiz-based training content is often found in CTF-style competitions. As an example of a training platform making use of this type of content, we mention the Facebook CTF open-source platform that was released on GitHub (but which has been archived in 2020 and is now read-only) [4]. This type of training content is also called Jeopardy content due to the format similarity with the popular American television game show with the same name. We note that platforms supporting CTFs are a very important type of cybersecurity training platform, and they will be discussed in more detail in Chap. 10.

The main advantage of using quiz-based training content is that the content itself is very easy to create, as each question can be treated independently from all the others, so content can be developed even by multiple creators simultaneously. However, trainee motivation is only stimulated from a competitive perspective, as solving the questions is simply a matter of using the right technical skills. Hence, no higher-level emotional involvement is present.

9.2.1.2   Scenario-Based Training Content

For scenario-based training, training content is organized as tasks that are related to each other, which is the main difference with respect to quiz-based training. As a consequence, scenario-based training tasks typically need to be addressed in the order in which they are presented in order for the participant to be able to progress through the training activity.

In addition to the tasks themselves, scenario-based training includes a story-like description that presents to trainees a fictional background for the training (i.e., the scenario), such as them being secret agents charged with an important mission that involves solving the training tasks. This kind of fictional stories make the training more relatable and fun to conduct from a trainee perspective.

As the trainees advance through the training scenario, they typically have to input some proof of their progress, such as the results of investigative actions that they took in the training environment. The score trainees are assigned when the training activity ends typically indicates how much they have managed to advance through the scenario storyline.

The NetWars family of training programs offered by SANS Institute represents an example of a gamified training experience that uses scenario-based training content [8]. For instance, the training program named *NetWars Core Tournament* covers a wide-range of technical topics, such as Linux and Windows command line, malware reverse engineering, firewall configuration, etc. The interesting part, however, is that the training follows a scenario specifically designed to motivate the trainees. In particular, NetWars Core Version 9 used the following storyline:

> A group of young friends are facing terrible danger, possibly associates with the local Hackins National Laboratory. You can help! Help defend our heroes—find out who's behind all this and maybe even strike back.

Creating scenario-based training content is more difficult compared to quiz content, as creators must intertwine the technical cybersecurity elements of the training with the storyline in a plausible manner. The potential emotional involvement of the trainees in the story is what is aimed for in return, and it constitutes the main advantage of scenario-based training.

9.2.1.3   Unstructured Training Content

The other type of cybersecurity training content is the unstructured one. For this type of training, trainees proceed freely with the activity based on some preliminary information they receive from the instructors. This type of training content is mainly associated with training activities that have as goal exercising the general attack and/or defense skills of the trainees, instead of specific technical skills as in the previous types of training. Consequently, the unstructured training content is most suitable for trainees who already have a sufficiently high cybersecurity skill level.

A typical illustration of unstructured training are the *red team/blue team* exercises, where trainees are assigned as members of one of the two teams. Trainees who are part of the blue team must respond to malicious actions by defending a system from the attacks conducted by the read team. In contrast, trainees who are part of the red team have the role of attacking the system defended by the blue team. An example in this category are the so-called "live fire" red team vs. blue team exercises that are possible using the *SimSpace Cyber Force Platform*, which provides an isolated environment for building the real-world skills of security teams [9].

A related type of cybersecurity training is the so-called *king of the hill* training. In this case the trainees, either individually or as a team, must use both their attack and defense skills, at the same time defending their own system, and attacking the systems managed by the other participants. An example of this type of training is the King of the Hill (KoTH) competitive hacking game made available online on the TryHackMe browser-based cybersecurity training platform [11]. In this implementation, participants compete against 10 other persons to compromise a target machine, and then they must patch its vulnerabilities in order to stop the other players from gaining access. This type of training fundamentally makes it possible for trainees to exercise both their attack and defense skills in a single activity. We note that the Facebook CTF platform mentioned in the context of quiz-based training also supports this type of exercises, in which participating teams compete with each other to gain control over target systems named *bases* [4].

For unstructured training, the training content is less related to learning, as typically there are not many educational materials included. Instead, the focus is laid on the training environment that needs to be created for the training activity, and the types of vulnerabilities to be included, that are related to the target skills that the hands-on practice should focus on. Some support content can be included, however, to assist the trainees. In the case of the Facebook CTF challenges mentioned above, for example, hints can be added to bases (either free or with a penalty associated to them) in order to make it easier for unexperienced trainees to get control of them.

9.2.2 Content Type Comparison

In Table 9.1 we analyze the main characteristics of each type of cybersecurity training content. This kind of analysis can be used as a guideline for instructors when making decisions about what is the most appropriate type of content to create for a given training purpose, or what is the most suitable type of training activity required for improving a certain kind of target cybersecurity skill.

Table 9.1 Comparison of training content characteristics depending on content type

Characteristic	Quiz-based	Scenario-based	Unstructured
Task type	Independent tasks	Task sequence	Implicit tasks
Skill type	Specific individual skills	Individual skills	Various skills
Participants	Low-to-medium experience	Medium experience	Experienced
Motivation	Basic gamification	Advanced gamification	High involvement
Realism	Low realism	Medium realism	High realism

Task Type The first important difference between the forms of training content that we discussed refers to the type of tasks included in the training. These tasks are stated independently from each other for quiz-based training and organized in an ordered sequence for scenario-based training, but in both cases, they are explicitly defined. On the other hand, tasks are typically implicit—such as attack or defense/forensics—for unstructured training.

Skill Type The type of skills that each type of training content addresses is also different. Quiz-based training usually focuses on very specific individual skills (e.g., how to solve a certain cryptographic puzzle). Meanwhile, scenario-based training focuses on more generic individual skills and skill combinations that need to be chained together in order to solve the given task, thus leading to a more realistic type of training. Lastly, unstructured training addresses various types of skills, both as individual skills related attack and defense/forensics techniques, and in the team skill category, as needed to accomplish the realistic system compromise and defense goals of the training activity.

Participants Regarding the typical participants in the three types of training, quiz-based ones are usually attended by young participants with low-to-medium skills that want to improve their abilities. An exception, however, is represented by high-level competitions, such as DEF CON [2], in which this type of content represents a very easy manner of evaluating the raw cybersecurity skills of an individual or team. Scenario-based training typically requires participants with at least medium experience, since the tasks to be solved are more complex. As for unstructured training, due to its nature, only experienced participants can face its challenges and fully benefit from it.

Motivation Next, we will discuss the features aimed at increasing the motivation of the participants, especially via the gamification features corresponding to each type of training content. Quiz-based training only makes possible the inclusion of basic features, such as scoreboards. The storyline included in scenario-based training adds more advanced features, such as motivating the participants to become emotionally involved in the training via the associated scenario, which also serves as a way to establish parallels to real-world situations, thus improving the effectiveness of the training. As for unstructured training, the very time-sensitive and competitive nature of the training involvement stimulates participant involvement even more.

Realism Based on all of the above, we conclude that the realism of quiz-based training is the lowest, since only raw technical security skills are targeted. Scenario-based training has a medium level of realism, as the scenarios used can mimic real-life situations, for example, as encountered by a system administrator. As for unstructured training, it is the most realistic of the approaches from a training content perspective, since it puts participants in conditions that are similar to a real-world scenario, where there is no predefined "script" they can follow.

9.2.3 Education Aspects

Education is a very important aspect of cybersecurity training activities. Thus, there are two main roles of a cybersecurity training activity:

1. Teaching the trainees concepts and skills related to the topics targeted by the training activity.
2. Testing trainees' ability to solve the corresponding tasks included in the training.

Most cybersecurity training platforms cover thoroughly the testing aspects. This can be done by quantifying trainee performance, for example, by scoring trainees based on their answers to quiz questions. Or it can be done by determining their success or failure in conducting a defense or attack exercise. To some extent, some platforms may not even include any education features, and delegate the learning aspects to the implicit effects of hands-on practice. However, we argue that the teaching role of a training platform is at least as important as the testing one. Consequently, education mechanisms that support the learning process are a significant characteristic of training platforms.

In some cases, it can be considered that trainees are supposed to learn the necessary concepts and skills outside the training platform, for example through individual study, or via lectures that are provided by the institution organizing the training. There is, nevertheless, a clear advantage of having the education capabilities integrated directly into the training platform, as the information can be presented together with the task at hand. This is more convenient for trainees, who can refer to it when attempting to solve the task, which helps memorizing the information in context.

To implement such capabilities, the Education Functions component of our training platform model is typically used. However, this is only the technical side of the issue, as the training content is what actually supports the corresponding education features; hence, the role it plays in the learning process is critical. In what follows, we will review as examples some possible education capabilities, and the manner in which they can be implemented in a cybersecurity training platform.

9.2.3.1 Task Hints

A typical way to achieve introduce basic education capabilities in a training platform is to associate hints with the questions and tasks included in the training content. The hints can be displayed on demand by trainees when they are not able to address a particular question themselves. Usually, multiple hints are made available to support the learning process, and trainees can display them one after the other until they become able to solve the task. This is made possible by the fact that the first hints are more generic in nature, to provide only an overall idea for solving the task, then more specific hints follow, to also support the trainees that lack the actual technical understanding for solving it. Since trainees are able to immediately put the information provided via hints into practice, they are able to better understand and memorize it for future use.

We note that for some training activities revealing hints can lead to a penalty being subtracted from the overall score of the trainees, as a mechanism to differentiate between those who were able to solve the task by themselves and those who had to make use of the hints. Nevertheless, even if a penalty is applied, choosing to view the hints is beneficial in case trainees can find no other way of making progress. This is because becoming stuck in the training activity not only has a negative psychological impact, potentially reducing their motivation, but can also impede the progress through the training activity, especially in scenario-based training, in which tasks are dependent on each other, thus causing an overall lower score.

From a technical perspective, the Education Functions component of the platform simply needs to include a mechanism for displaying the hints (buttons, etc.), and a way to account for the hints being displayed in case a penalty is to be applied. The actual content of the hint is developed by Instructors and is stored together with the Training Content in the Data Storage module.

9.2.3.2 Adaptive Learning

The second education capability that we will discuss is of a more complex nature compared to task hints. In particular, we will examine the use of *adaptive learning* features. Adaptive learning, also known as *intelligent tutoring*, is an education approach that provides customized learning activities that take into account the specific needs of learners. To achieve this goal, the interaction of the learners with the training content must be modeled in detail, for example, by using the following elements [6]:

- A set of training materials that are used to teach the target concepts to the learners (also called the *expert model*).
- Information about the learners, such as domain knowledge and learning performance, used to improve the effectiveness of the training process (also known as the *learner model* or the *student model*).

- A mechanism through which the two previous models are combined in order to decide what training content is displayed to the learners (typically named the *instructive model*).

The training materials in the above model are basically the cybersecurity training content in our discussion. What is specific is the use of the learner model, which aims to capture the skill level of each trainee. This model is constructed based on the answers of each individual, iteratively. The training content that is presented at a certain moment is selected by the instructive model based on its level of difficulty in relation to the presumed skill level of the trainee. By adapting the training content to the trainee needs, it becomes possible to create a learning experience that is at the same time engaging and effective, as it was demonstrated in [10].

From an implementation perspective, to support adaptive learning the Training Content must be designed so that information regarding task difficulty is included. Such information can be determined in advance by the instructors creating the content, can be estimated through experimentation with groups of learners, or even computed via a combination of the two methods. The Education Functions component implementation is more challenging though, as both a method for building the learner model, and the instructive model mechanism must be integrated into it.

9.3 Training Environment

In addition to training content, the training environment is the other essential component of a cybersecurity training platform, without each no training activity can take place. The main aspects that need to be discussed in this context are first of all the range of technical solutions that are available in order to implement a training environment. Then, the respective advantages and disadvantages of these solutions must be examined, as their characteristics need to be considered carefully when deciding what is the most suitable solution for a particular training platform, for example, depending on the type of participants and target skills, etc.

9.3.1 Training Environment Types

Training environments are made of a collection of hosts, and their network connections, if any, that trainees use for hands-on practice. There are two ways in which such a setup can be implemented from a technical perspective, as follows:

- Physical environments.
- Virtual environments.

9.3.1.1 Physical Environments

The most basic training environments are those made of physical computing devices interconnected by actual communication networks. The network connectivity in this case can be realized either via wireless technologies, such as Wi-Fi, or via regular wired network technologies, such as Ethernet. In general, wired communication is preferred within the training environment, so as to avoid the possible communication issues that can occur due to wireless interference.

When using physical environments, the setup procedure is relatively straightforward, as only standard host and network administration techniques are required to prepare the training environment. Consequently, only fundamental technical skills that are mastered by most computer science graduates are sufficient to configure the training environment.

Another advantage of using physical environments in a training platform is that all the computing resources of the devices are dedicated to training purposes, hence maximum performance characteristics can be ensured. In addition, the setup of the individual devices can be initially conducted independently of the other parts of the training environment, then they can be put together in later stages to form the desired training environment.

The main disadvantage of using physical devices is related to the cost of acquiring and managing such dedicated devices (unless they are inexpensive devices to start with). Such a cost can be amortized over time if the training platform is used intensively, but if it is only used for occasional training this type of solution may not make much economic sense.

With respect to the type of computing devices used to implement the training environment, we distinguish two main classes:

- High-performance servers.
- Small form factor (SFF) devices.

High-Performance Servers The easiest solution for creating a cybersecurity training environment made of physical devices is to use servers or other high-performance computers that were purchased for this reason, or that were previously acquired and are repurposed for cybersecurity training activities. This solution ensures that enough dedicated computing power can be made available even for the most demanding of the training scenarios.

However, if the training activity does not require a large amount of dedicated resources, there is a possibility of resource waste, and the servers will not be used at their maximum capacity. Therefore, we consider that using dedicated high-performance servers is more suitable as the infrastructure for virtualized training environments, as it will be discussed in Sect. 9.3.1.2.

Small Form Factor Devices A more cost-effective solution is to use SFF computing devices, such as the Raspberry Pi family of compact single-board computers [7]. Not only this type of devices are significantly less expensive compared to high-performance servers, but they are also much easier to manipulate and transport.

One can imagine, for instance, the case of a series of training events organized in an itinerant fashion at various locations. The instructors can then set up the SFF devices in advance at whatever place is convenient for them, including at their home. Then, they simply need to bring the devices to the event venue and connect them to the network infrastructure for integration with the overall system. This approach is used, for example, in some of the SECCON Beginners CTF sessions organized by the Japan Network Security Association (JNSA) [5].

As for disadvantages, SFF devices have limited computing capabilities, hence they are only suitable for simpler training exercises. This is why they are used often in training activities organized for beginners, as the one mentioned above, where a complex training environment is required. Another potential issue is that some of the SFF devices use custom operating systems (OSs), such as Raspberry Pi OS in the case of Raspberry Pi devices, which can represent a challenge for unexperienced instructors. However, these customs OSs are often based on the Unix operating system (in particular the Debian GNU/Linux distribution for Raspberry Pi OS). Consequently, most standard host administration skills can be applied to configure them, lowering the severity of the issue.

9.3.1.2   Virtual Environments

The second type of training environments used in typical cybersecurity training platforms are those made of virtual devices interconnected by virtual networks. The virtual devices are often instantiated on top of physical servers provisioned by the training organizer by relying on standard virtualization technologies, such as virtual machines or containers. For training environments of relatively low complexity, it is also possible to deploy the environment on the devices that trainees already own, such as their own laptops. This reduces the server provisioning and management requirements on the organizer side. As for the network connectivity, it is typically realized by leveraging the functionality of the virtualization technologies in this respect, which make it possible to create virtual networking components.

The main advantage of using virtual environments in a training platform is that the scalability and cost effectiveness of building the training environment are greatly improved. Thus, adding one or more virtual devices into a training environment does not translate into a hardware purchase; instead, only changes to the environment setup procedure are required. Similarly, provisioning for more or less trainees can simply be done by increasing or decreasing the number of training environment instances that are created on a given physical server, in an elastic manner. Consequently, more physical servers need to be acquired only when the cumulative resources of the existing servers become insufficient for the scale of the training activity.

However, using virtualization technologies introduces an overhead both regarding environment setup and computing resources. Concerning environment setup, the necessary tools and skills needed to create virtual environments are different from standard administration skills. Nevertheless, given the popularity of virtualization technologies in recent years, we consider that most specialists have at least some limited experience with them. As for the computing resource overhead, since part of the physical server resources must be used to run the virtualization technologies, the amount of resources available for the training environment instances is reduced. Nevertheless, in normal conditions, this overhead is relatively low compared to the requirements of the training environment, hence it can usually be ignored.

Next let us examine the two types of virtualization technologies that are currently available, namely:

- Virtual machines.
- Containers.

Virtual Machines Virtual machines (VMs) are a virtualized computer that is run on a physical server. A VM is no different from an actual computer in terms of CPU, memory, or disks, but they are all virtualized, albeit often via mapping to the real CPU, memory and disks of the physical server that hosts the VM. An important property of a VM is that it is separated from the physical server OS, meaning that the software inside a VM does not interfere with the physical server functionality. Consequently, multiple VMs can be run on a single physical server independently from each other.

The main advantage of VMs is that they can be used to run almost any OS, no matter what the OS of the physical server that hosts them is. Virtual network infrastructure can also be defined relatively easily. On the other hand, since VMs must emulate the functionality of the computer they are representing, they are a relatively heavyweight form of virtualization technology. Similarly, since the VMs use full copies of OSs, the image files that are used to distribute VMs can be rather large in size, typically are least several gigabytes.

An example of virtual machine technology is that provided by VMware [12], which makes available a suite of tools that make possible the deployment of VMs both on regular end-user hardware (e.g., laptop and desktop PCs), and also on cloud infrastructure servers for large-scale deployments. In addition, the VMware virtualization tools have capabilities of creating a virtual network infrastructure for the deployed VMs, such as virtual switches, and virtual network adapters.

Containers The other form of virtualization are containers, a form of isolated user spaces which can be used to run software applications independently of the other programs running on that server infrastructure. Consequently, for an individual container perspective, it appears as the application runs in an isolated manner, with its own settings and libraries. However, all containers that run concurrently on a server share a common operating system. Container portability derives from the fact that, since it is self-contained, a container instance can be moved to a different server infrastructure, as long as the same containerization technology is present.

The main advantages of containers are their lightweight nature and the fact that they can be packaged in a relatively small standalone file that can be easily deployed on a different physical server. However, the tools required to manage the containers can be quite complex and difficult to learn for beginners. Some restrictions on the type of OS used in the container also apply. Moreover, some of the tools used in cybersecurity training, such as firewalls, rely on the OS kernel functionality. This may render them unusable in containers or may require root privileges for execution; providing such privileges to trainees, however, may not always be feasible, for example, when using shared PCs for training.

One of the most widely used container technology is made available by Docker [3], which provides a complete set of modules and software tools that make it possible to create, manage and run containers. Docker image objects are read-only templates used to distribute the containers, and also to create the processes that represent the actual running containers. Network objects make possible for the applications running in containers to communicate with each other, with the OS on which they are hosted, and with the outside world. However, complex network topologies cannot be built among the containers.

9.3.2   Environment Type Comparison

Given the various choices that exist for creating training environments, we will analyze the main differences between those choices from a cybersecurity training perspective. The discussion is summarized in Table 9.2, where the first characteristic, environment type, is used to remind the nature of each technology.

Scalability The first property we examine is scalability, which is very important for training environments, as limitations in environment size impose constraints on the type of training activities that can be conducted. Physical server-based environments have the lowest scalability given the high costs associated with acquiring them.

SFF devices have better scalability characteristics, since they are relatively cheap; accordingly, acquiring more devices, as needed, is easy. Nevertheless, they are still physical devices that need to be managed; hence, training scale still cannot be extended past a certain limit.

As for the virtual environments, both VM and container technologies provide high scalability properties, albeit containers being even more scalable due to their lightweight nature. Another relevant characteristic, cost effectiveness, follows the same trend with scalability, so we will not discuss it separately.

Table 9.2 Comparison of the main characteristics of the technologies used to create training environments

Characteristic	Servers	SFF devices	VMs	Containers
Environment type	Physical	Physical	Virtual	Virtual
Scalability	Low	Medium	High	Very high
Usability	Very high	High	Medium	Medium
Flexibility	Low	Medium	Very high	High

Usability When considering usability, on the other hand, the training environments based on physical devices are easiest to configure, since only standard administration skills are needed. The physical server solution has a slight edge, however, since SFF devices may have custom OSs that require additional technical skills. As for virtual environment technologies, both VMs and containers require specialized tools for managing them, hence usability is only medium.

We note that when referring to usability in this context we consider the perspective of instructors, i.e., those who must create the training environments. From the perspective of trainees, training environments built using all the above technologies are functionally equivalent, so there are no usability differences between them from this point of view.

Flexibility The next characteristic that we examine is flexibility. Using physical servers leads to a low flexibility, as it is difficult to change the properties of the training environment, especially in terms of network topology.

The small size of SFF devices makes it easier to configure training environments based on them in a flexible manner, but our overall evaluation places this technology at a medium level, since the need to create physical connections can cause some hurdles. Moreover, relying on physical environments makes it impossible to use trainee devices for deployment, further reducing the flexibility.

On the other hand, virtualization technologies offer a much higher flexibility, with the highest level being for VMs, for which the range of choices in terms of OSs and virtual network configuration is superior to that of containers.

References

1. Beuran R, Vykopal J, Belajová D, Čeleda P, Tan Y, Shinoda Y (2023) Capability assessment methodology and comparative analysis of cybersecurity training platforms. Comput Secur 128:103120. https://doi.org/10.1016/j.cose.2023.103120
2. DEF CON cybersecurity conference: DEF CON website. https://defcon.org/. Accessed 1 July 2024
3. Docker, Inc.: what is docker? https://www.docker.com/. Accessed 1 July 2024
4. Facebook, Inc.: platform to host capture the flag competitions. https://github.com/facebookarchive/fbctf. Accessed 1 July 2024
5. Japan network security association (JNSA): security contest (SECCON) beginners (in Japanese). https://www.seccon.jp/2023/beginners/about-seccon-beginners.html. Accessed 1 July 2024
6. Nkambou R, Bourdeau J, Mizoguchi R (2010) Advances in intelligent tutoring systems. Springer, Berlin, Heidelberg
7. Raspberry Pi Ltd.: raspberry Pi. https://www.raspberrypi.com/. Accessed 1 July 2024
8. SANS institute: SANS cyber ranges. https://www.sans.org/cyber-ranges/. Accessed 1 July 2024
9. SimSpace corporation: SimSpace cyber force platform. https://www.simspace.com/cyber-force-platform. Accessed 1 July 2024
10. Tan Z, Beuran R, Hasegawa S, Jiang W, Zhao M, Tan Y (2020) Adaptive security awareness training using linked open data datasets. Educ Inf Technol 25:5235–5259

11. TryHackMe: king of the hill. https://tryhackme.com/games/koth. Accessed 1 July 2024
12. VMware: VMware—delivering a digital foundation for businesses. https://www.vmware.com/. Accessed 1 July 2024
13. Yamin MM, Katt B, Gkioulos V (2020) Cyber ranges and security testbeds: scenarios, functions, tools and architecture. Comput Secur 88:101636. https://doi.org/10.1016/j.cose.2019.101636

Chapter 10
Capture the Flag Platforms

This chapter discusses one of the most important types of cybersecurity training platforms in terms of public perception, the Capture The Flag (CTF) platforms. After examining the two main types of CTF content, which are Jeopardy style and attack-defend, we discuss in detail two categories of CTF platforms, the online and open-source ones. Representative examples in each of the two categories are introduced, followed by a comparative analysis of their main characteristics.

10.1 CTF Platform Overview

Most people who start studying about cybersecurity, especially as young adults, encounter very early the opportunity to have a CTF-type of training experience. The first reason for this is easy access. Since CTF platform management is relatively straightforward, many organizations make available online training platforms that learners can use, often even at no cost, to test their existing cybersecurity skills and learn new ones. The second reason for the popularity of CTF training is the enjoyment they can provide. The gamified training experience provided by most CTF platforms makes it fun for participants to join this type of training, especially via the typical scoreboard feature that allows trainees to compare their results with those of the other participants. Other aspects, such as playful quiz questions and training scenarios, also contribute to the enjoyable nature of CTFs.

The very first CTF is considered to be that organized in 1996 at the annual DEF CON cybersecurity conference [9], but CTF events are currently being held in most countries and for a wide range of participants, including even starting at elementary school level in some cases. CTF attendees can participate to competitions either individually, especially for the easier CTFs that are mainly targeted at beginners, or as a team, in particular for the top-level CTFs, such as the ones organized at DEF CON nowadays, in which even professional security experts compete for fame and/or monetary rewards. Note that a detailed background on cybersecurity competitions, tools, and systems is provided in [3].

As its name indicates, in a CTF type of training the participants are tasked with retrieving digital "flags," which are pieces of information that they can discover by successfully solving a given challenge or accomplishing a given task. The retrieved flag is input via the user interface of the CTF platform; if the flag is correct, then the equivalent number of points is allocated to that individual participant or team.

There are two main types of CTF competitions [21], as it will be described next, although some competitions may combine the two types in a single event, or include slight variations of these types:

- Jeopardy-style CTFs: Competitions that use a quiz format in which participants have to solve a set of provided challenges.
- Attack-defend CTFs: Contests in which the participants compete with each other in attacking and defending one or more target machines.

The two types of CTF competitions will be discussed next in generic terms. Then, in subsequent sections we will also proceed to examine examples of actual CTF platforms. The analysis of their features and characteristics will give readers a more detailed view on how CTF platforms work, and their most common uses. For practical reasons, we will classify the CTF platforms that we will discuss later in two categories, depending on whether they can only be accessed via the web, or their functionality can also be extended:

- Online CTF platforms.
- Open-source CTF platforms.

10.1.1   Jeopardy-Style CTF

The most common type of CTF is the Jeopardy-style one, which is named like this because it is similar to an actual quiz-based Jeopardy game. When participants join a Jeopardy-style CTF training, they are presented with a set of challenges organized in various categories that reflect the main type of skills required to solve those challenges. Typical categories for Jeopardy-style CTF include web, binary analysis, cryptography, and so on, that the participants can choose from depending on the type of skills they want to practice. Often the number of points to be earned for solving one challenge is also displayed, so that trainees can choose easier or more difficult challenges (that yield smaller or larger amounts of points, respectively) depending on their current skill level.

In terms of deployment, a server infrastructure is required to store the digital assets, such as web pages or virtual machines, that are needed to solve the CTF challenges. The information on how to access a web page or virtual machine is provided via the challenge description. Sometimes, the challenge can also contain

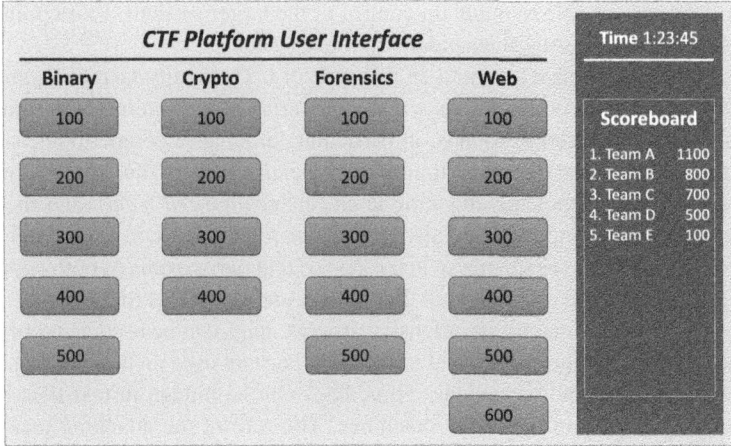

Fig. 10.1 Mockup of a possible user interface for Jeopardy-style CTF platforms that shows a number of challenges and their corresponding amount of points in several categories; the remaining time and the competition scoreboard are also displayed in the right-hand side of the interface

attached files that the participants must download, for example, for binary analysis or cryptography challenges. Ideally, CTF platforms should provide mechanisms to CTF content creators to manage such resources as needed. However, for basic quizzes, all the information needed for a challenge can be included in its text description, and no additional resource is required. Nevertheless, some kind of support for actually creating and displaying the quiz is always necessary.

The duration of CTFs varies according to their difficulty, ranging from a few hours to a few days, or even more. In most cases, a timer will be started when the competition begins and will be prominently displayed in the CTF user interface, given the participants a clear view on the amount of remaining time. When the allocated time elapses, the CTF ends and the team or individual that had most points at that moment wins. Typically, a scoreboard is also displayed during the entire duration of the competition, so that participants can follow in real time the progress of their ranking and see how it compares with that of the other participants. A mockup of a possible CTF platform user interface that illustrates all the specific elements discussed so far is shown in Fig. 10.1.

10.1.2 Attack-Defend CTF

The attack-defend CTF is a type of competition in which a participant or team must perform two types of activities in order to be awarded points: attack the systems controlled by other teams, and defend their own systems from other teams' attacks. The number of points that is awarded is directly proportional with the amount of time participants are able to maintain control of the target systems. Extra points can be awarded for discovering flags hidden in those systems.

The attack and defense activities in this type of CTF usually take place simultaneously, especially for competitions with many participants. Alternatively, the competition can be organized in rounds, in particular for smaller competitions, such as those that are part of the internal training of an organization. In this case, for the first round, one team becomes the attacking team (also called *red team*), and the other team becomes the defending team (also called *blue team*). Then, in the second round of the competition, the two teams switch roles, so that participants of both teams can have the opportunity to exercise both their attack and defense skills.

In CTFs that focus mainly on offensive aspects, flags can be used as proof that a machine has been compromised, and if multiple flags are used on the same machine, how deep that compromise extends. Thus, flags can be hidden in text files placed at strategic locations on the target machines. The role of the attacking team is to attempt to locate and access those flags, then submit them as proof of their success, while the defending team tries to prevent access to those flags. Note that if there is no defense aspect at all in such a CTF challenge, then it can be considered to be of Jeopardy type, typically being classified in the *pwn* category, which refers to the act of gaining ownership of a resource (also known as *pwning*).

In order to ensure a fair competition, various rules are typically put in place for attack-defend CTFs. For example, there may be restrictions on what kind of hacking tools a red team can use. For the blue team as well there are restrictions, such as forbidding actions that cripple the target system, including disabling its network interfaces or turning it off. In case rule violations are detected, the corresponding team will face point penalties or even disqualification.

10.1.3   CTF-Type Comparison

The main advantage of Jeopardy-style CTFs from a participant perspective is that they are relatively carefree to attend, with tasks, as well as required skills, being clearly identified for each challenge most of the time. From an organizer perspective too, the fact that the training environment is relatively easy to set up is an important advantage. For some challenges, all the information can be included in the question text in the form of a quiz, hence no specific environment needs to be created. In other cases, a file attachment can be all that is needed in order to solve the challenge, for example to provide a file that is to be decrypted. Only for the most advanced Jeopardy challenges an actual target environment becomes necessary, but even in that case it is typically just a web site or virtual machine with some specific vulnerabilities, hence the setup is still relatively simple.

As for disadvantages, the fact that a Jeopardy-style challenge only refers to a single technique, or perhaps a limited set thereof, makes it that the challenges can be somewhat disconnected from reality, since a complex set of interrelated skills are usually required to address real-world cybersecurity issues. Nevertheless, we can

Table 10.1 Comparison of the main CTF types

CTF type	Main advantage	Main disadvantage	Suitability
Jeopardy	Easy to attend, and also set up and maintain	Focus mainly on individual techniques	Participants with low-to-medium skill levels
Attack-defend	Similar conditions to real-life scenarios	Challenging to attend, and also to set up and maintain	Participants with medium-to-high skill levels

draw a similarity between Jeopardy-style challenges and exercises done in school, in which each exercise may be of limited practical value by itself, but mastering repeatedly numerous exercises builds problem-solving skills that can later be applied in real life.

On the other hand, when considering attack-defend CTFs, the fact that they are very close to real-world cybersecurity conditions makes them much more useful from a training perspective. Thus, skills practiced by the defender teams can be utilized in a straightforward manner when defending real networks. Similarly, skills practiced by the attacking teams offer a direct perspective on what real attacker actions can be, and prepare professionals both for activities such as penetration testing, and also for becoming more skilled defenders.

Attending an attack-defend CTF, however, is very challenging for participants, as they must perform several tasks, often as quickly as possible, such as exploring the target environment, finding and patching vulnerabilities, detecting attacks and finding ways to stop or prevent them, etc. In addition, from an organizer perspective, the main hurdle is that the target environment needs to be complex enough to make possible a challenging contest that sufficiently tests the skills of the participants. Creating such an environment requires not only a wide range of technical skills from the part of the competition staff, but also a powerful-enough server infrastructure for deploying that environment.

Given all of the above, we conclude that Jeopardy-style CTFs are most suited for beginners who want to hone basic individual skills in a carefree style, whereas attack-defend CTFs are most suited for participants with medium and high skill levels, who can put those skills into practice in realistic scenarios. For these reasons, most currently available CTF competitions are in a Jeopardy or similar style, since they are easier to organize, and the potential target audience is larger. Conversely, only some high-level CTFs that address the needs of advanced cybersecurity professionals use the attack-defend format. Table 10.1 summarizes the key aspects that were discussed in this section in terms of the main advantages and disadvantages of the two CTF types, as well as their suitability.

10.2   Online CTF Platforms

In what follows we will discuss several representative examples of actual CTF platforms, starting with those that fall in the online category. The main advantage of online CTF platforms is that they have the lowest barrier-to-entry from a participant perspective, since usually no setup is required before using them. The examples that we used to illustrate this type of CTF platform also have another common characteristic: they provide all or most training content free of cost, typically after a basic user registration procedure. We decided to focus on online CTF platforms that provide free content as this is how most people interested in cybersecurity begin their learning journey. When applicable, we will discuss the platform features that are only available at a cost, so as to make it clear in which cases the readers may need to explore paid options.

To make it easier to compare platforms, we will separate their presentation by type. First, we will examine Jeopardy-style platforms, as they are the most commonly available type. Then, we also examine several examples of hybrid platforms, that include additional forms of content, such as attack-defend style competitions. We note that there seem to be no platforms exclusively dedicated to attack-defend style CTFs, hence the reason for this classification.

10.2.1   Jeopardy-Style Platforms

Since Jeopardy-style CTFs are most popular with learners, and relatively easy to set up and manage, it is not wonder that most online CTF platforms currently available fall in this category. In what follows, we will review several such platforms, shown below in alphabetical order, and examine their main characteristics.

10.2.1.1   Google CTF

Google CTF is an annual online CTF competition organized by Google since 2016, typically during a couple of days in the month of June [15]. The competition consists of two events: a qualification stage in which the security skills of the participants are tested via a distributed security exercise, and a final stage in which finalists selected in the qualification stage compete in an on-site security exercise.

As with other CTFs, Google CTF participants must solve various challenges within the contest time period in order to earn points. The teams that earn the most points can also receive cash awards. One interesting aspect is that the number of points assigned to a challenge is not decided in advance, but it is calculated based on the number of teams that solved that challenge, so that the point value of a challenge is weighted based on its actual difficulty from a participant perspective. Most of the challenges used in Google CTF since 2017, as well as their solutions, are published on GitHub for reference and study purposes [14]. For 2023, the challenge categories were: *misc*, *crypto*, *pwn*, *reversing*, *web* and *sandbox*.

10.2.1.2 Hacker101 CTF

Hacker101 CTF is an online CTF platform that is made available as part of the Hacker101 online course on web security [19]. Participants of all levels can use the provided training environment to safely practice and improve their cybersecurity skills. The CTF is offered as a complement to the free online resources available on Hacker101, which are organized in several learning tracks that include information and video lessons on various topics, such as web hacking, mobile hacking, cryptography, and so on.

As with other Jeopardy-style platforms, participants have to use their pentesting skills to find flags that are placed in various locations in the target environment, such as within a file, a database, source code, etc. The Hacker101 CTF content is split into several levels, each containing a given number of flags. The levels are tagged with their difficulty level, such as trivial, easy, moderate, hard, and expert, as well as the skills that are required to solve the challenges, such as web, crypto, or math. Participants can select levels in any order, depending on their specific interests in certain topics, for example. Hints are also available for each level to assist those participants who have troubles with a particular challenge. A specific feature is that players can organize themselves in groups to work together through the CTF.

10.2.1.3 HackThisSite

HackThisSite is a free training platform that provides an open learning environment which includes no only hacking challenges, but also articles and various resources regarding the latest information in relation with hacker culture [20]. The training content made available on HackThisSite is divided into two main categories:

- Basic challenges: Aimed at beginners, these challenges are relatively straightforward Jeopardy-style challenges that are designed for building the basic cybersecurity skills of the participants.
- Realistic missions: Activities aimed at more advanced users that ask participants to target websites provided via the platform that contain built-in security flaws which are to be exploited in order to achieve a series of hacking objectives.

Additional training content is included in separate challenge categories that cover various specific areas, such as applications, programming, JavaScript, forensics, and steganography. An extended basic level with more complex introductory content is also made available.

One important characteristic of the HackThisSite platform is the role-playing game approach used for the realistic missions. Thus, when using content in the mission category, participants assume the role of freelance hackers who are contracted by fictitious organizations to hack for social justice causes. After receiving a mission objective, participants have to explore on their own the target website of that mission with the purpose of discovering and exploiting the included vulnerabilities.

10.2.1.4 Pwnable.kr

The pwnable.kr platform is a non-commercial website that provides Jeopardy-style challenges regarding mainly system exploitation topics [27]. The website itself has a fun design, with many graphics aimed at increasing the level of engagement of the participants. The included CTF content covers a wide range of cybersecurity skills, such as programming, reverse engineering, bug exploitation, operating system knowledge, and cryptography.

The pwnable.kr challenges are divided into four categories, depending on their level of difficulty, with the names of each level reflecting the playfulness of the website authors. Thus, the *Toddler's Bottle* level is addressed to the very beginners, *Rookiss* contains typical challenges for rookies, *Grotesque* includes some more advanced challenges, and finally the *Hacker's Secret* level provides challenges that involve special cybersecurity techniques. For each of the included challenges, the intended solution is also provided by the challenge author, so as to help the participants with learning new skills.

10.2.1.5 Smash The Stack

Smash The Stack is a CTF platform that hosts several ethical hacking environments that reproduce real-world software vulnerabilities [31]. These environments are called "wargames" within this platform, and each of them includes a series of levels through which the participants must advance in order to complete the challenge. Access to the environment corresponding to a given challenge is typically done via an SSH client, following the instructions on the challenge web page. Further information about the objective of each level is provided in a README file in the home directory of that level.

The challenges in Smash The Stack cover several cybersecurity areas, such as reverse engineering, web application pentesting, and software exploitation. The vulnerabilities utilized in the challenges are of different types, such as operating system vulnerabilities, network protocol vulnerabilities, application vulnerabilities, etc. The required skill level for each wargame (challenge) is displayed on the main web page of Smash The Stack, such as beginner, intermediate, or advanced, making it possible for participants to select a challenge that matches their abilities.

10.2.1.6   W3Challs

W3Challs in an online CTF platform that hosts a large number of challenges that cover various areas of hacking, albeit being mostly oriented toward offensive hacking [34]. The challenges are organized in six categories: *Crypto*, *Forensics*, *Misc*, *Pwning*, *Reversing* and *Web*. For each challenge within a certain category, the number of points to be gained from solving that challenge is displayed along with the challenge name, representing an indicator of the difficulty of that challenge.

A very useful feature of W3Challs is that the included challenges are labeled with tags that make it possible for participants to filter the challenges based on their preference. Some tags refer to the difficulty level of the challenge, such as *Baby*, and others to the type of challenge, such as *Crypto*, which is helpful especially for challenges that fit into more than one category, as multiple tags can be used per challenge. However, most of the tags refer to the type of skills required to solve a given challenge, such as .NET, Android, ARM, Flash, Java, PHP, Python, etc. Filtering challenges based on such tags makes it possible for participants to focus only on those challenges that are related to the specific type of skills they want to practice, which is a great strategy for beginner learners in particular.

10.2.2   Hybrid Platforms

Some online CTF platforms, in addition to typical content in Jeopardy style, also provide other kinds of content. Most typically, this other form of training is in the attack-defense CTF style. As mentioned already, there seem to be no CTF platforms centered exclusively on attack-defend competitions, hence the reason for using this wider category. In what follows we will present some representative examples of such hybrid platforms, shown below in alphabetical order. We note that given the increased difficulty of managing attack-defense CTFs, only commercial platforms appear to support alternative competition styles.

10.2.2.1   Hack The Box

Hack The Box (HTB) is gamified cybersecurity platform that can be used for skill improvement, certification, and ability assessment [17]. The platform features are organized into several tiers, as follows: *HTB Academy* for learning basic cybersecurity skills, *HTB Labs* for improving existing cybersecurity skills, *HTB Business* for training that targets company employees, and *HTB CTF* for attending or hosting standard CTF competitions.

Each of the tiers has different characteristics that participants should be aware of when making a choice. For example, guided learning and certification are provided for *HTB Academy* tier training. In what follows, we will focus mainly on the *HTB Labs* tier, for which the content is split into two categories:

- *Challenges*: Typical Jeopardy-style content in which light-weight applications are used to practice different pentesting techniques. Challenges are labeled according to their difficulty, as easy, medium, or hard, so that participants can select them based on their current skill level. In the case of challenges, participants' objective is to solve that particular problem, hence it can be used to practice individual skills, as it is always the case with Jeopardy-style content.
- *Machines*: Instances of vulnerable virtual machines that make it possible to practice more complex CTF skills. The VM virtualized hardware, operating systems and services that run on the Hack The Box company servers. Content in this category too is labeled by difficulty level, such as easy, medium, hard or insane, and have various operating systems available (Linux, Windows, FreeBSD, etc.). For this type of training, the objective is to conduct pentesting on the target VMs and use the identified vulnerabilities to access two flags: a user flag demonstrating the ability to access a low-privilege account on the VM, and a root flag proving the ability to access the highest-privilege account.

In addition to the basic types of content mentioned above, there are also several more specialized forms of training, as follows:

- *Battlegrounds*: Virtual environments in which two teams of up to four participants compete with each other for control over the provided environment in accordance with the attack-defend CTF paradigm.
- *Endgames*: Virtual environments that simulate real-world networks of typical organizations, which have multiple entry points and attack paths. The main difference with respect to the *Machines* category mentioned already is that *Endgames* consist of a set of interconnected VMs, not just one VM, thus representing a more realistic environment.
- *Sherlocks*: Scenarios that are aimed at improving defensive skills by providing a gamified narrative in a simulated corporate setting, through which participants can conduct defense-oriented cybersecurity activities, such as malware analysis, threat hunting, etc.

Hack The Box also provides several tools for making participation easier. One of these tools is *Pwnbox*, which is an online version of the Parrot OS Linux distribution that comes with various pre-installed hacking tools, and which can be used to compete in *HTB Labs* without installing any software locally. A discussion forum is also included in the platform, where participants who get stuck with a challenge can ask for hints from other players.

Based on the above discussion, we conclude that Hack The Box is a very mature online CTF platform, with a rich set of features. It is also worth noting in this context that the *HTB Business* tier of Hack The Box has been ranked in 2023 as one of the top training platforms by the Forrester *Cybersecurity Skills and Training Platforms, Q4 2023* report [4].

10.2.2.2 TryHackMe

TryHackMe is a browser-based gamified cybersecurity training platform that provides learning content for participants with various skill levels, from beginner to advanced [32]. A significant amount of the training content is available free of charge, but there are paid premium and business plans that offer additional learning and training capabilities.

The CTF content of TryHackMe is mainly conceived to serve as complement to the learning content on the platform, and it is designed to allow participants to practice the skills they have learned via the online lessons. The challenges are organized in units named "rooms," with each room being labeled with its difficulty level, such as easy, medium, hard or insane. Some of the rooms are of the walkthrough type, providing tutorials on how to achieve various pentesting goals.

The TryHackMe challenges typically include a number of tasks that require participants to answer several questions in order to complete each challenge. In this way the platform directs the learning process so as to provide a more structured learning environment compared to regular CTF challenges. Search functionality is also available, making it possible for participants to select from the more than 800 rooms those that are most interesting to them based on several criteria, such as relevance, difficulty level, room type (challenge versus walkthrough), and plan type (free versus subscription).

Another important feature of TryHackMe is its support for attack-defend competitions in the "king of the hill" format. In this case, participants must compete against several other players with the goal of compromising a target machine. Simultaneously, they should also try to patch the machine vulnerabilities in order to prevent the other participants from gaining access. When using this CTF format, points are awarded based on how long a participant is able to maintain access to the target machine, as well as for the flags that they are able to discover in the process. Thus, participants are able to practice skills that are directly applicable to various real-world scenarios and job roles.

10.2.3 Online Platform Comparison

In Table 10.2 we summarize the main characteristics of the online CTF platforms that we have reviewed. The table is split into two sections, with the upper part presenting the Jeopardy-style platforms, and the lower part the hybrid ones.

Specific Features We first enumerate the specific features of each platform that serve as distinguishing factors. For example, Google CTF is the only platforms to provide monetary rewards, and HackThisSite uses a role-playing game approach to increase participant motivation. The support for filtering by fine-grained skills tags is a specific feature of W3Challs.

Challenge Categories One important criterion when choosing a CTF platform is the type of challenges that it makes available, and this is even more important for

Table 10.2 Comparison of online CTF platforms

Platform	Specific features	Challenge categories	Availability
Google CTF	Cash rewards; Weighted challenge point values; Past event challenges and solutions published	Crypto, Misc, Pwn, Reversing, Sandbox, Web	Annual
Hacker101 CTF	Content organized in levels labeled with tags; Hints available; Support for groups of players	Android, Crypto, GraphQL, Math, Recon, Web	Anytime
HackThisSite	Open learning environment; Basic challenges and realistic missions; Role-playing game approach	Application, Crypto, Forensics, IRC, JavaScript, Steganography, Web	Anytime
pwnable.kr	Challenges organized in levels based on difficulty; Intended solutions made available by authors	Bug exploitation, Crypto, OS, Programming, Reversing	Anytime
Smash The Stack	SSH-based access; Challenges labeled with difficulty levels; Limited number of challenges	Application, Bug exploitation, OS, Reversing, Network	Anytime
W3Challs	Challenges labeled with fine-grained skill tags; Support for detailed filtering by tag	Crypto, Forensics, Misc, Pwn, Reversing, Web	Anytime
Hack The Box	Paid tiers include guided learning and certification; tools that facilitate participation; large number of challenges with search function	Blockchain, Crypto, Forensics, Hardware, Misc, Mobile, Pwn, Recon, Reversing, Web	Anytime
TryHackMe	Paid plans include additional learning capabilities; large number of challenges with search function	N/A (text search)	Anytime

online CTF platforms, where end users cannot typically add new content. For the sake of clarity, in the table we used the same labels for the same concept, even though the documentation of a given platform may use different terms (e.g., *Pwn* versus *Pwning*).

It is clear that some types of challenges, such as *Crypto* or *Web*, are present in almost all platforms. However, we were also able to identify some unique categories, such as *Steganography* for HackThisSite, or *Blockchain* for Hack The Box.

The TryHackMe platform, however, does not label its challenges with categories, so participants need to read their description to estimate what type of skills may be required for a certain challenge; our analysis indicates that typical topics such as *Crypto* and *Web* are covered, but this seems an area in which usability can be improved. On the other hand, a text search function is available, so learners can find challenges that include specific keywords of interest in their descriptions. Moreover, several challenges have the CVE id of the vulnerability that is to be exploited and mitigated in their title and/or description, making it easier to conduct training in connection with a particular vulnerability.

Availability Another important aspect is the availability of the CTF platforms. Almost all the platforms we reviewed are available at any time, although the entire content may not necessarily be accessible all the time. However, platforms such as Google CTF are only used for annual events, hence are more useful to test one's skills and earn recognition, than for actual skill training.

Other Platforms There are several other online CTF platforms that we have not introduced so far in this section, and for which we provide below a brief description for further reference:

- Backdoor CTF[1]: A Jeopardy-style CTF organized annually by the Software Development Section Laboratories (SDSLabs) student-run technical group at IIT Roorkee, India.
- CryptoHack[2]: A fun platform for learning modern cryptography that uses interactive puzzles and challenges to let participants understand deeper ciphers and protocols by trying to hack them.
- Microcorruption[3]: A gamified embedded security CTF that can be used to improve skills related to assembly languages, debugging, and memory corruption vulnerabilities.
- OverTheWire[4]: A collection of gamified challenges that are organized in the form of multi-level "wargames"; each level includes hints (e.g., what commands may be necessary to solve it).
- PentesterLab[5]: A CTF platform with a large number of exercises, although only part of them are free of cost; filtering by difficulty and topic is available.

---

[1] https://sdslabs.co/projects.

[2] https://cryptohack.org/.

[3] https://microcorruption.com/.

[4] https://overthewire.org/wargames/.

[5] https://pentesterlab.com/.

- Root Me[6]: A multi-lingual learning platform regarding hacking and information security with almost 600 challenges and 200 virtual environments.

10.3   Open-Source CTF Platforms

In contrast with online CTF platforms, open-source ones are not intended to be used directly by trainees. Instead, the source code of the platform is made available via a public repository, such as GitHub. Individuals or organizations interested in using a certain platform must download the source code and install it on their own computers or servers. After installation, the CTF platforms become usable, either by the individuals themselves, or by those organizations, for example, in order to conduct a CTF as part of internal training activities.

The need to set up the platform software in advance is an important hurdle in the case of open-source CTF platforms. However, their open-source nature brings a significant advantage compared to online platforms. Thus, by modifying the source code, users can customize the functionality of the platform. More importantly, and perhaps this is the most common use case for open-source platforms, is that organizations can add custom CTF content to them. This is particularly useful when an organization wants to conduct training on very specific tasks related to its internal systems or processes.

In what follows, we will introduce several examples of open-source CTF platforms, which are again organized in two categories:

- Jeopardy-style platforms.
- Hybrid platforms.

10.3.1   Jeopardy-Style Platforms

As mentioned already, Jeopardy-style CTFs are the most typical kind of CTF training, and there are several such open-source platforms, as it will be described next (the platforms are presented next in alphabetical order).

10.3.1.1   CTFd

CTFd is a Jeopardy-style CTF platform developed with the goal of being easy to use and customize [6]. CTFd is implemented using the Python language, and the Flask web framework. The internal database for content and scoring is based on MySQL

---

[6] https://www.root-me.org/?lang=en.

technology. Out of the box, CTFd includes all the basic features that are needed to run a CTF training activity, such as challenge creation, scoreboard and score graphs, email support, team management, etc. In addition, the functionality of CTFd can be easily extended via the use of plugins and themes.

The visualization features of CTFd are very user friendly, including graphs, pie charts and other graphical representations that make it possible for users to understand at a glance what happened during a training event. The platform also includes an administration panel that allows controlling the training activity without any low-level command execution, as well as to create new challenges, categories, hints and flags. We consider that the straightforward mechanism for content creation represents one of the most important features of CTFd.

10.3.1.2 EchoCTF.RED

The echoCTF.RED platform was designed with three main goals: completeness regarding the set of tools and applications for supporting the development, deployment and maintenance of CTF competitions, clear modularity regarding the role of each component, and extensibility in terms of the possibility to easily add new features to the platform components [11]. We note that the commercial company that developed echoCTF.RED also makes it available in the form of an online CTF platform that can be used free of charge at [10].

The features of echoCTF.RED include system settings for configuring the platform, scoreboard settings, team settings, player and registration settings, configurable targets and challenges, etc. One interesting aspect is the concept of "activity streams," which make it possible to view details about the overall activity of players, the activities with respect to a certain target, as well as team-based activities. Moreover, network activity tracking and visualization are also supported. Another interesting feature is the support for publishing competition achievements by means of Twitter (X) and LinkedIn.

10.3.1.3 Haaukins

Haaukins is a virtualization platform for security education developed and maintained by the Network Security Group at Aalborg University and the CyberSkills youth cybersecurity community in Denmark [8]. The platform uses Docker for container virtualization, and VirtualBox for virtual machine creation. The entire functionality of the platform is orchestrated via the Go programming language, which was selected for its support of concurrency and parallelism features. For database functionality, Haaukins leverages PostgreSQL and MongoDB technologies. Additional functionality includes a web client used to control the automated setup of the virtual environment containing the challenges, and support for the Kali Linux and Parrot OS cybersecurity-oriented operating systems as platforms that are to be used by trainees to solve the CTF challenges.

An important aspect of Haaukins is that it has a rich set of documentation that covers not only the architecture of the platform and its installation, but also the included challenges [7]. In particular, the challenges made available in Haaukins are grouped in the following five categories: binary, cryptography, forensics, reverse engineering, and web exploitation. For each challenge, in addition to the challenge description, the number of points to be gained, the difficulty level, the main learning objective, and knowledge prerequisites are also explained. Moreover, the way in which new challenges can be created is also thoroughly documented with clear technical details, making content addition relatively easy, and representing a differentiating factor with respect to other platforms.

10.3.1.4 HackTheArch

HackTheArch is a CTF scoring server implemented using Ruby on Rails by the Military Cyber Professionals Association (MCPA) in the U.S. The goal of the project is to facilitate CTF competitions by providing a generic scoring server that makes it easy to add and modify challenges, and to track statistics of CTF events [24].

The authors created HackTheArch as a tool that allows users to perform tasks that were not possible in other platforms at the time, such as providing hints to participants for a cost, and to create and modify challenges via a web interface. Consequently, the platform implements an optional dynamic hint system that will deduct points from a participant's score when they request hints. Moreover, a web interface is made available in HackTheArch for creating and modifying hints and challenges via a graphical UI.

10.3.1.5 MkCTF

The mkCTF framework was developed to support the creation of Jeopardy-style CTF challenges by using a configurable structure that makes it possible to efficiently integrate and deploy the content on the server infrastructure of the competition [23]. The platform implementation is using the Python programming language. The functionality of the mkCTF framework covers the following main aspects: creation of challenges, their building and deployment, as well as monitoring participants progress in those challenges.

The mkCTF project was initially created as a way to manage the challenges for the CTF held at the INS'hAck 2017 conference that took place at INSA Lyon, France. The challenges and write-ups of the past editions of INS'hAck are also linked via the mkCTF repository, constituting a useful resource both for the creation of CTF content, as well as for preparing for a CTF event.

10.3.1.6   Mellivora

Mellivora is a CTF engine written in PHP for hosting Jeopardy-style competitions [26]. The platform has a rich set of features, such as arbitrary categories and challenges, scoreboard with optional multiple team types, manual or automatic free-text submission scoring, challenge hints, dedicated pages for team progress and challenge overview, a management console with the competition overview, etc. The officially supported configuration for Mellivora is based on the LAMP common software stack for the web applications, namely Ubuntu, Apache, MySQL, and PHP.

In addition to local storage, Mellivora also supports Amazon S3 for challenge file upload. The implementation is considered to be lightweight and fast, making it possible to run even large competitions on an Amazon Elastic Compute Cloud (EC2) micro instance. As a specific feature, the platform provides support for the reCAPTCHA system to protect the competition website from bots. Moreover, the internal logs of the engine can be used to catch any exceptions that may happen during an event, making it possible for administrators to detect any issues with the platform itself. However, Mellivora does not provide graphic tools for monitoring participant progress in a visual manner.

10.3.1.7   PicoCTF

The picoCTF platform was developed as the infrastructure used to run the picoCTF competition organized by Carnegie Mellon University. The platform can be used to host Jeopardy-style CTFs, and it was designed so as to be adaptable to other cybersecurity or programming competitions [5]. Although the development in the public repository was frozen in 2022, picoCTF still represents a very useful resource in the field of CTF platforms.

The picoCTF project is organized in several modules, such as `picoCTF-web` for the website and APIs, and the `picoCTF-shell` utility that is used to create, package, and deploy the CTF challenges. The actual challenges are configured via two modules: `problems`, which contains the CTF challenge source code, and `ansible`, which contains scripts used to configure the corresponding CTF hosts accordingly. Examples of methods for deploying picoCTF are also included, both for local deployment via the Vagrant package for virtualization management, and remote deployment via the Terraform software for defining and provisioning cloud resources.

10.3.2   Hybrid Platforms

Some open-source CTF platforms provide additional features in comparison with the regular Jeopardy-style format, typically in the attack-defense category. In what follows, we discuss some representative examples of such hybrid platforms, which are presented below in alphabetical order.

10.3.2.1   CTF Gameserver

CTF Gameserver is a platform for attack-defense CTFs that is used to host the FAUST CTF, which is run by the CTF team of Friedrich-Alexander University Erlangen-Nürnberg, Germany [13]. The platform is, however, designed so that it can be utilized for other competitions, being scalable and customizable. Note that CTF Gameserver does not include facilities for creating the network infrastructure, setting up the VPN setup, or creating target hosts with vulnerabilities. Consequently, the network facilities need to be prepared independently by following the instructions on the platform webpage regarding expected properties.

The implementation uses a Django-based web application as front end for tasks such as team registration, scoreboard display, and hosting of information pages. It uses a PostgreSQL database for storing the related data, and runs on servers based on Debian OS or derivatives. It also contains the model files, which define the database structure. Other platform components include a controller for coordinating the progress of the competition, a checker that places and retrieves flags, a submission server for captured flags, and so on. Checking the flags is implemented via scripts that support the Python and Go programming languages.

10.3.2.2   Facebook CTF

Facebook CTF (FBCTF) is a platform for hosting both Jeopardy style and "king of the hill" (KOTH) style of CTF competitions that was developed by Facebook [12]. The platform is scalable, and it is said that it can be used to organize competitions with hundreds of participants. The implementation is based on the PHP programming language, and it uses MySQL as database storage technology. A production mode is available for those who only want to use the platform, and the development mode can be used when extensions are planned. Note, however, that the repository has been archived, and is in a read-only state since 2020.

The FBCTF platform has a rich functionality. Some aspects are aimed at competition organizers and facilitate the administration of CTF events via several built-in features, such as a game configuration page, player registration features, team management features, and even LDAP-based authentication. A timer is available for controlling the duration of the competition, although events without a time limit are also possible. Moreover, several languages can be selected via the user interface.

For the Jeopardy-style content, organizers can choose between *Quiz* and *Flag* formats. For a *Quiz* challenge, the quiz title and question must include all the information needed in order to complete the challenge. For a *Flag* challenge, attachments and links can be embedded, such as an image containing steganography information, or a website that is to be exploited. Categories can also be assigned to this type of challenge to allow for their easier identification.

The attack-defend type of challenge is named *Bases*, where a base represents a target system which must be compromised by participants in order to be awarded points. This is a KOTH type of game, where the participating teams must compete over the control of these target systems. Points are awarded both for the initial capture of a base, but also over time, for the period during which the base is controlled by a given team. To make this functionality possible, an agent operating as a scoring bot must be installed on the target system, and report regularly to the scoring server via HTTP the controlling team name and number of awarded points.

The main strength of FBCTF is the high flexibility of the platform that makes it possible to configure a variety of settings via its administration panel. The support for CTFs in multiple languages is also a specific feature of this platform, since most other platforms only provide an English language interface.

10.3.2.3 HBCTF

HBCTF is a hybrid CTF platform developed by the HackBama group of information security industry professionals from Alabama, U.S. [18]. The platform is implemented in Python, and the Apache CouchDB database software is used for the database storage implementation.

The hybrid type of CTF competition that can be conducted using HBCTF combines service hacking and patching aspects, with the search for Jeopardy-style flags. Moreover, the players have to compete with each other for the control of strategic network hosts. Competitions based on HBCTF are carried out as a three-step process. First, players have to check in into the competition server and submit the IP address and port number for the service they are protecting. As the second step, layers receive a score token in return. If they are able to decrypt it, then the token is submitted to receive the corresponding number of points.

HBCTF is basically just a backend server for CTF competitions, and no graphical user interface is available to facilitate management. The development status also seems relatively crude, and no updates have been published in recent years in the public GitHub repository of the platform.

10.3.2.4 iCTF

The iCTF framework was initially developed by the UC Santa Barbara Computer Security Lab to host their own CTF event [33]. The main focus of the platform is on attack-defend type of CTFs, but other formats are also said to be within its scope. The framework leverages virtualization technologies to create the training environment necessary to conduct a competition. In particular, iCTF creates one virtual machine (VM) used by the event organizers to manage the event, and one VM for each participating team that is utilized to solve the CTF challenges.

The main components of the iCTF framework are as follows: a central database for tracking the competition state, a score bot that checks and updates flags for vulnerable services, and a dashboard user interface for showing the scoreboard and allowing players to submit flags. In addition, various tools are provided to manage other aspects, such as routing configuration, VM creation and the built-in services.

10.3.2.5 kCTF

The kCTF platform is not a full-fledged CTF platform, but a Kubernetes-based infrastructure for organizing CTF competitions that is being developed as open source by Google [16]. The main requirement for using kCTF is to have a Linux server on which Docker is installed. Then, it is simply a matter of creating a local Kubernetes cluster in order to be able to run local CTF challenges.

The platform also has various built-in services that address the typical needs of CTF competitions, including mechanisms for creating and verifying proof-of-work challenges to prevent brute-force attacks. Other useful features cover functionality for conducting infrastructure health checks, generating DNS and SSL certificates, sharing files, etc.

The kCTF platform does not provide a web-based GUI neither for administrators, nor for participants. Instead, kCTF is entirely operated via command line, for instance, in order to start and manage challenges, check their status, view the challenge logs, and so on. Consequently, the barrier to entry for using kCTF is higher compared to the other platforms presented.

10.3.2.6 NightShade

NightShade is a simple CTF framework that was designed to make running CTF competitions as easy as possible [1]. The framework is implemented in JavaScript and Python, and uses MySQL for the content and statistics database. The implementation is quite basic, combining the scoreboard with the challenge questions into a single interface panel. NightShade also includes support for displaying user profiles that show relevant information about participants, such as which contests they have joined, which questions they have solved, etc. The list of all competitions hosted by a given administrator can also be viewed.

The NightShade platform makes it possible to organize three types of CTF competitions, as follows:

- Jeopardy style: This mode supports standard Jeopardy-style CTFs, in which the challenge categories are displayed as rows in the left-hand side of the page, and the number of points for each challenge as cells in a matrix; solved challenges are identified via a check mark.

- Traditional style: This mode addresses CTF events in which the challenges take main stage. Thus, the name of a challenge is displayed first, with a check mark in case the challenge was already solved. Related information is shown next to it, such as the category the challenge is part of, the number of points associated to it, and how many people have already solved it.
- Blind style: This mode supports penetration testing-like exercises, in which the challenge page displays the one or more IP addresses of the target hosts, and the participants must first connect to those hosts. By exploring the files and services on each host, trainees must identify any existing vulnerabilities and exploit them in order to retrieve the flags that are placed at unspecified locations. No information about the challenge difficulty (i.e., the number of points to be gained by solving it) is provided for this type of training.

The main strength of NightShade is the support for several CTF competition modes, as it was discussed above. However, the platform user interface is relatively simple, and no information about the event is displayed graphically. This makes it more difficult for organizers and participants to ascertain the status of a competition at a glance.

10.3.2.7 Root the Box

Root the Box is a scoring engine for CTF competitions that can be easily configured and modified for any style of CTF [25]. The platform makes it possible to create an environment with realistic challenges for cybersecurity training and has a customizable and appealing user interface. The implementation is Python based.

The main features of the platform are as follows: support for both individual and team play, real-time animated scoreboard, graphs and status updates, support for chat and file sharing features for teams, etc. Root the Box also makes it possible to use several types of flags, such as static text, regular expressions, date/time, multiple choice flags, as well as files. The platform also supports a wide range of choices with regard to penalties, hints, number of attempts, level bonuses, and so on.

In addition, several other specific features are included in Root the Box. For example, the participants can create in-game botnets by uploading small bot programs to the target machines they have compromised. When using this feature, the teams are periodically rewarded in-game money for each bot in their botnet. The platform also enables the use of in-game money that can be used to unlock new training levels, buy hints for challenges, or even bribe the fictitious in-game police to attack other teams. Moreover, the encrypted bank account passwords for each team are publicly displayed, allowing participants to try to crack them and steal the funds of other participants. All these features make it possible to create a realistic hacker world experience within the game.

Another distinguishing functionality of Root the Box compared to other CTF platforms is the possibility to use an optional story mode in which one can add an introduction message for the competition, as well as messages to be displayed when a flag is captured or a section is completed, with built-in support for graphic files. The use of all the gamification elements described so far increases the entertaining nature of the event, and further motivates the participants.

10.3.2.8   SecGen

Security Scenario Generator (SecGen) is not an actual CTF platform, but rather a CTF support tool. Nevertheless, its functionality is very useful in the CTF context, as SecGen makes it possible to generate randomized vulnerable virtual machines [29]. The VMs are created based on a scenario specification that describes the constraints and properties of the VMs to be generated. SecGen is implemented in Ruby and uses XML as configuration language. The external software tools Puppet for system configuration management and Vagrant for virtualization management are leveraged to provision the required VMs.

According to an example described by the SecGen authors, it is possible to specify generically the creation of a system that has a remotely exploitable vulnerability resulting in user-level compromise, and a locally exploitable flaw resulting in root-level compromise. Based on this scenario, SecGen would create a VM that includes two randomly selected vulnerabilities of the specified type. From a training participant perspective, such a scenario would require discovering and exploiting both vulnerabilities in order to be able to obtain root access to the system. More specific scenario description mechanisms are also available, such as indicating the types of services that should have vulnerabilities (e.g., FTP, SMB, etc.), or even identifying specific vulnerabilities to be included by their CVE id.

10.3.3   Open-Source Platform Comparison

In Table 10.3 we summarize the main characteristics of the open-source CTF platforms that we have reviewed. The table is split into two sections, with the upper part presenting the Jeopardy-style platforms, and the lower part the hybrid ones.

Implementation One important aspect of open-source CTF platforms is what languages and tools are utilized for their implementation. This is because if a potential user does not master those language or tools, using the platform, and especially extending its functionality become hard.

Our comparison shows that most platforms are implemented in Python, with PHP being in second place, and JavaScript is also often used for the web features. However, the Go and Ruby languages are also employed in a few cases, such as Go for Haaukins, and Ruby for SecGen. As for database support, MySQL is by far the most popular choice.

Table 10.3 Comparison of open-source CTF platforms

Platform	Implementation	Last update	Documentation
CTFd	Python, JavaScript, MySQL	2024	Good
echoCTF.RED	PHP, JavaScript	2023	Good
Haaukins	Go, PostgreSQL	2022	Excellent
HackTheArch	Ruby, HTML	2019	Basic
mkCTF	Python	2023	Good
Mellivora	PHP, MySQL	2022	Basic
picoCTF	Python, JavaScript	2021	Good
CTF gameserver	Python, HTML, JavaScript, Go	2024	Excellent
Facebook CTF	Hack (PHP), JavaScript, MySQL	2018	Good
HBCTF	Python	2017	Basic
iCTF	Python	2015	Basic
kCTF	Go	2023	Excellent
NightShade	JavaScript, Python, MySQL	2017	Basic
Root the box	Python, HTML, JavaScript	2024	Good
SecGen	Ruby, Python, XML	2024	Excellent

Last Update Another important issue regarding open-source CTF platforms is whether they are still in active development. The time when a platform was last updated is an important indicator in this sense (the information included in the table was retrieved at the time of writing). For some platforms the status is explicitly mentioned on its page. For example, picoCTF developers mention that it is no longer maintained, and CTFd or kCTF are recommended instead.

For other platforms, however, the year of the last update, such as 2015 for iCTF, and 2017 for HBCTF and NightShade, should be used as indication that no support is to be expected. Nevertheless, if the existing features are sufficient, and one is willing to take on the task of adding new ones if needed, then those platforms can also be selected as potential candidates for deployment. However, if support from the original developers is important, then selecting a platform that has been recently updated is recommended.

Documentation Documentation is also a significant factor when selecting an open-source CTF platform. Several of the platforms we reviewed make have only a minimal amount of documentation available, such as Mellivora, but most of them provide sufficient information to get the users started. Some platforms, however, excel from this point of view, including also information about challenge creation, platform design, and even a security threat model, as is the case for kCTF.

Based on the above analysis, we suggest that interested users select a platform that was recently updated and has good or excellent documentation, such as CTFd, echoCTF.RED, Haaukins, or mkCTF, for the Jeopardy-style platforms, or CTF Gameserver, kCTF or Root the Box, for the hybrid ones. The programming language can be another factor in the decision, depending on one's programming abilities. We note that some of the platforms presented here are not just released for public use, but also utilized by their respective developers to conduct CTF competitions, which further demonstrates their reliability. This is the case for echoCTF.RED, as it was mentioned in its description, but also for Haaukins, for example, that is utilized for the online training events organized by CyberSkills.[7]

10.4   Discussion

In this section we will review several potential issues and some possible solutions regarding CTF platforms, as well as provide additional resources for readers who want to learn more about CTFs.

10.4.1   Potential Issues

Despite their many advantages, the use of CTF platforms also entails several potential issues, that we review below.

Platform Choice Since we have reviewed a significant number of CTF platforms in this chapter, it is important to mention that one potential issue when faced with so many choices for CTF platforms is that it may be difficult to decide which one is most suitable, either to attend as a participant, or to deploy as an organizer.

To address this problem, the report in [2] presents a CTF platform evaluation methodology that relies on two different techniques. For online CTF platforms, usability is evaluated using the system usability scale (SUS) [28], and for open-source ones the criteria-based quantitative software assessment [22] is utilized. We consider that interested parties can apply the methodology described in the mentioned report to evaluate potential CTF platform candidates according to their own requirements.

Intrinsic Problems The relatively low barrier to entry for attending CTFs makes them one of the most common forms of cybersecurity training. However, CTF-based training also has several disadvantages that need to be taken into consideration by organizers, especially when this training format is used to assess the skills of the participants. Some of these issues include:

---

[7] https://www.cyberskills.dk/.

- Flags in CTFs are obtained as the last step of solving the challenge, but their submission provides no information about the method used to obtain the flag, meaning that instructors have no idea regarding the thought processes followed by participants. While this may not be an issue for very basic challenges, more complex ones may require following best practices for the learning to be most effective. To counter this disadvantage, more advanced forms of training, such as those based on cyber ranges, make it possible to save the interactions between the trainee and the environment, such as command shell history, making is possible to evaluate the challenge solving method as well.
- Given that flags are simple pieces of information, it is possible in principle to communicate a flag to other participants, who can submit it and receive the assigned number of points. While this form of cheating is not encountered in competitions that participants are strongly motivated to win, it can happen in company or university training events, in which the results of a participant do not affect those of the others. To prevent such cheating issues, one possibility is to create unique flags that are assigned independently to each participant, so that any given flag is only valid for the corresponding challenge of a certain participant.

Security Issues The nature of CTF platforms leads to a series of security-related issues that can potentially affect their operation, as follows:

- CTF platforms are often used by participants who only provide minimal information upon registration. Consequently, participants with malicious intents may join a competition and try to increase their rewards by cheating, especially when monetary rewards are involved. In worse cases, malicious participants may even try to exploit vulnerabilities in the CTF platform software to gain access to the organizer IT infrastructure.
- For open-source platforms, the code contributions of many developers create risks in the sense that those developers could add source code that contains vulnerabilities, either unknowingly or with malicious intent. Such vulnerabilities could then be exploited by malicious participants to obtain an unfair advantage (e.g., via the use of backdoors).

While several of the platforms we have reviewed mention that cheating will lead to penalties and even disqualification, it is not clear how cheating can be detected in those platforms. As always, security by obfuscation is not an actual solution, and we consider that more transparency is required from this perspective, especially for the open-source CTF platforms.

In addition, we believe that a security threat model should be published for each CTF platform, including the online ones. However, among the platforms we have reviewed, only kCTF developers discuss such a threat model in a dedicated documentation section that covers various security considerations regarding the managed assets, risks, and potential attackers.[8]

---

[8] https://google.github.io/kctf/security-threat-model.html.

10.4.2   Additional Resources

As supplement to the discussion of CTF platforms presented in this chapter, we want to point readers to the wealth of information available in the curated collection of CTF-related resources published in the Awesome CTF repository [30]. That page includes a comprehensive list of online CTF platforms in the section named *Wargames*, and links to open-source CTF platforms in the section named *Platforms*. In addition, the resource collection also includes information about tools that can be used to create and solve CTF challenges, various operating systems, and even a list of free CTF tutorials.

Another very useful resource specifically for those interested in actually attending CTF competitions is the CTFtime website[9] that provides up-to-date information about past and future CTFs. One very helpful aspect of CTFtime is that the listed CTF events are assigned a weight depending on their perceived difficulty. We consider that this weight can be used by potential participants to select an event that matches their skill level, thus ensuring that they make the most out of the competition, both in terms of learning effectiveness, as well as enjoyment.

References

1. Akama, NightShade GitHub page. https://github.com/akama/NightShade. Accessed 1 July 2024
2. Azam MHN, Beuran R (2018) Usability evaluation of open source and online capture the flag platforms. Technical report IS-RR-2018-001. Japan Advanced Institute of Science and Technology
3. Balon T, Baggili IA (2023) Cybercompetitions: a survey of competitions, tools, and systems to support cybersecurity education. Educ Inf Technol 28(9):11759–11791. https://doi.org/10.1007/s10639-022-11451-4
4. Burn J, Blankenship J, Born F, Belden M (2023) The cybersecurity skills and training platforms landscape, Q4 2023. https://reprints2.forrester.com/#/assets/2/2565/RES178480/report. Accessed 1 July 2024
5. Carnegie Mellon University, picoCTF GitHub page. https://github.com/picoCTF/picoCTF. Accessed 1 July 2024
6. Chung K, Skaza M, CTFd GitHub page. https://github.com/CTFd/CTFd. Accessed 1 July 2024
7. CyberSkills, Haaukins documentation. https://docs.haaukins.com/. Accessed 1 July 2024
8. CyberSkills, Haaukins GitHub page. https://github.com/aau-network-security/haaukins. Accessed 1 July 2024
9. DEF CON cybersecurity conference: DEF CON website. https://defcon.org/. Accessed 1 July 2024
10. Echothrust Solutions, echoCTF hacking laboratories. https://echoctf.red/. Accessed 1 July 2024
11. Echothrust Solutions, echoCTF.RED GitHub page. https://github.com/echoCTF/echoCTF.RED. Accessed 1 July 2024
12. Facebook, Inc., Platform to host capture the flag competitions. https://github.com/facebookarchive/fbctf. Accessed 1 July 2024

---

[9] https://ctftime.org/ctfs.

13. FAU Security Team, CTF gameserver GitHub page. https://github.com/fausecteam/ctf-gameserver. Accessed 1 July 2024
14. Google LLC, Google CTF GitHub page. https://github.com/google/google-ctf. Accessed 1 July 2024
15. Google LLC, Google CTF website. https://capturetheflag.withgoogle.com/. Accessed 1 July 2024
16. Google Open Source, kCTF GitHub page. https://github.com/google/kctf. Accessed 1 July 2024
17. Hack the Box, Hack the box website. https://www.hackthebox.com/. Accessed 1 July 2024
18. HackBama, HBCTF GitHub page. https://github.com/osteth/HBCTF. Accessed 1 July 2024
19. HackerOne, Hacker101 website. https://www.hacker101.com/. Accessed 1 July 2024
20. HackThisSite, HackThisSite website. https://www.hackthissite.org/. Accessed 1 July 2024
21. Harmon TD (2024) Cyber security capture the flag (CTF): what is it? https://blogs.cisco.com/perspectives/cyber-security-capture-the-flag-ctf-what-is-it. Accessed 1 July 2024
22. Jackson M, Crouch S, Baxter R (2011) Software evaluation: criteria-based assessment. Tech. rep, Software Sustainability Institute
23. Koromodako, mkCTF GitHub page. https://github.com/koromodako/mkctf. Accessed 1 July 2024
24. Military Cyber Professionals Association (MCPA), HackTheArch GitHub page. https://github.com/mcpa-stlouis/hack-the-arch. Accessed 1 July 2024
25. Moloch, Root the box GitHub page. https://github.com/moloch--/RootTheBox. Accessed 1 July 2024
26. Nakiami, Mellivora GitHub page. https://github.com/Nakiami/mellivora. Accessed 1 July 2024
27. Pwnable.kr, pwnable.kr website. https://pwnable.kr/. Accessed 1 July 2024
28. Sauro J, Measuring usability with the system usability scale (SUS). https://measuringu.com/sus/. Accessed 1 July 2024
29. Schreuders ZC (2024) SecGen GitHub page. https://github.com/cliffe/SecGen. Accessed 1 July 2024
30. Singh A (2024) Awesome CTF GitHub page. https://github.com/apsdehal/awesome-ctf. Accessed 1 July 2024
31. Smash the Stack, Smash the stack website. https://www.smashthestack.org/main.html. Accessed 1 July 2024
32. TryHackMe, TryHackMe website. https://tryhackme.com/. Accessed 1 July 2024
33. UC Santa Barbara Computer Security Lab, The iCTF framework GitHub page. https://github.com/diegorusso/ictf-framework. Accessed 1 July 2024
34. W3Challs, W3Challs website. https://w3challs.com/. Accessed 1 July 2024

Chapter 11
Cyber Ranges

This chapter discusses cyber ranges, which are dedicated network environments used for cybersecurity training purposes. We divided our presentation into two categories, depending on the type of targeted skills: general cyber ranges, which are employed for generic cybersecurity training, and specialized cyber ranges, which are dedicated to specific application areas. For each category, we first provide several representative examples, followed by a comparative analysis of the main characteristics of those cyber ranges.

11.1 Cyber Range Overview

The term *cyber range* is traditionally used to refer to network environments that are employed for cybersecurity training purposes, and it was defined via analogy with the term *shooting range*, which denotes facilities used for firearm training. One of the first such training environments for which the term cyber range was used was that introduced by the U.S. Air Force in 2002 for training its personnel [37].

Initially, the term cyber range was mainly employed to refer to the actual training environment that mimics host and network configurations and that is used during the training activity. However, over the years, the complexity of cyber ranges has increased, with the addition of components for managing the training process, facilitating instructor and trainee access, and so on. Consequently, the modern meaning of the term cyber range is generally equivalent to the term *cybersecurity training platform* discussed in Chap. 9, that we prefer to use in this book for clarity purposes. Nevertheless, many training platforms use "cyber range" in their name, so in this chapter we will use both terms with an equivalent meaning.

As for the difference with respect to the CTF platforms discussed in Chap. 10, in general, cyber ranges have more advanced features than those platforms, such as support for large-scale training environments and traffic generation capabilities.

© The Author(s), under exclusive license to Springer Nature Singapore Pte Ltd. 2025   221
R. Beuran, *Cybersecurity Education and Training*,
https://doi.org/10.1007/978-981-96-0555-2_11

However, most cyber ranges can also be used for CTF competitions. Therefore, readers can consider cyber ranges to be a partially overlapping but more powerful form of training environment in comparison with CTF platforms.

11.1.1   Cyber Range Significance

Cybersecurity training platforms, hence cyber ranges, are a critical component of cybersecurity training, as they make it possible to acquire and practice hands-on skills. Consequently, the number of cyber ranges has also increased over the years.

We consider that this proliferation is connected to the development of the NICE Workforce Framework for Cybersecurity (NICE Framework) [40]. As discussed in Sect. 3.2.1, NICE is a program dedicated to advancing cybersecurity education and workforce development that described various characteristics of the cybersecurity workforce, such as work roles and competency areas, and defined a large set of related tasks, knowledge, and skills.

However, in addition to defining the NICE Framework, NICE has also recognized the outmost importance of cyber ranges for cybersecurity training. One of the most relevant NICE deliverables in this context is *The Cyber Range: A Guide*, which is a guideline on the use cases, features, and types of cyber ranges in connection with cybersecurity education, certification, and training [37].

The NICE cyber range guide covers a wide variety of topics, including why cyber ranges are necessary, and who needs them. Regarding the need for cyber ranges, the guideline states that cyber ranges "provide a safe and legal environment for acquiring hands-on cyber skills and offer a secure setting for product development and security posture testing." As for the potential cyber range users, a non-exhaustive list of use cases is included in the guide, such as:

- Educators who want to implement cybersecurity education courses and curricula.
- Organizations or individuals who require initial training or continuing education for cybersecurity-related fields and positions.
- Organizations who plan to conduct realistic testing of new products and organizational restructuring.
- Organizations or individuals who need to perform skill validation as part of the evaluation of candidates for cybersecurity-related positions.

11.1.2   Cyber Range Categories

In the rest of this chapter, we will proceed to review a series of cyber ranges in order to offer a better understanding of the overall landscape of these training platforms. However, due to the relatively large number of examples, for clarity reasons, we consider that it is important to categorize them.

Thus, based on the type of cybersecurity training activities that are possible with a given training platform, we distinguish two categories of cyber ranges:

- General cyber ranges: Cyber ranges that are used for standard cybersecurity training activities in connection with regular computer networks.
- Specialized cyber ranges: Cyber ranges that are used for cybersecurity training activities in specific areas, such as IoT, or Industrial Control Systems.

In what follows, we will discuss several representative cyber range examples from each category. When a cyber range has both general and specialized features, we included it in the category which we considered to be mainly covered by that cyber range. Interested readers can also consult the survey of cyber ranges and testbeds in [17] for additional examples, although given that the survey was conducted in 2013 some of the information included is out-of-date. The more recent surveys presented in [10, 49, 56] are also useful references in this context.

11.2 General Cyber Ranges

From the very beginning, cyber ranges were used for cybersecurity training in relation with regular computer networks. Due to the nature of the training, the first cyber ranges originated from a military/government background, as mentioned previously. Nevertheless, both the private sector and academia made significant progress in this area, with more and more cyber ranges being established over the years.

Since the nature of the organization managing a cyber range influences the type of training activities that are conducted, we will further categorize the general cyber ranges into three classes, for which we will present examples in alphabetical order:

- Government cyber ranges.
- Private-sector cyber ranges.
- Academia cyber ranges.

11.2.1 Government Cyber Ranges

In the government cyber range category, we include those cyber ranges that were created mainly with government funding, either at a local, federal, or national level. These cyber ranges are often located on the premises of regional universities. Note, however, that in many cases private-sector companies are strongly involved in the construction of those cyber ranges and may even manage them as government contractors. Given the type of funding, the target audience for most of the cyber ranges in this category is education institutions and government professionals.

11.2.1.1 AIT Cyber Range

The AIT Cyber Range is a cyber range developed by the Austrian Institute of Technology (AIT) as a virtual environment for the simulation of critical digital IT systems [5, 34]. The facility can accommodate up to 24 participants on-site, who are able to access the training environment located on the AIT premises in Vienna. Hands-on exercises with Industrial Control System (ICS) equipment can also be conducted in the training room.

While the initial focus of the available training scenarios seemed to have been enterprise environments, ICS-oriented scenarios have also been made available, such as those for energy distribution systems, nuclear facilities, and manufacturing systems. As for the threat scenarios, they include elements of advanced ransomware attacks, as well as those targeted at ICS.

The AIT Cyber Range is managed by means of a web-based control interface with two main components: the Game Maker Control interface for the creation of training scenarios and the Game Maker Runner module for executing the training scenarios on the provisioned infrastructure. As for the cyber range itself, its architecture consists of three modules based on open-source technology. The functionality of the three modules is as follows:

- Computing platform: The infrastructure for the deployment of the training environment, mainly in the form of a self-hosted OpenStack cluster that uses Ubuntu-based nodes. A recent expansion has also made it possible to use cloud deployment for improved scalability.
- Infrastructure provisioning: Creation of network configurations, and their orchestration on the computing platform. The key tool in this context is Terraform that uses the infrastructure-as-code paradigm to define reusable configurations.
- Software provisioning: Adding the virtual machines that are part of the training environment, and configuring their functionality. This module leverages the configuration management tool Ansible, using which it is possible to define software deployments and configurations as template code.

11.2.1.2 Arkansas Cyber Range

The Arkansas Cyber Range is a cyber range deployed at the University of Central Arkansas in the U.S. with support from the Arkansas Department of Higher Education [4]. The Arkansas Cyber Range training modules currently cover the following cybersecurity topics:

- Introduction to the cyber range platform and hacker techniques.
- How to recognize regular and irregular traffic patterns?
- How to conduct network traffic shaping and manipulation?
- Training on information logging and monitoring.
- Specific aspects related to Windows and Linux hosts.

- Training with regard to network services.
- Training in relation with digital forensics.

Even though the Arkansas Cyber Range is hosted physically at the University of Central Arkansas, it is stated that Arkansas public schools and teachers who want to use the above training modules in their curricula can do it at no cost.

11.2.1.3 CR14 Cyber Ranges

Foundation CR14 is an organization established by the Ministry of Defense of Estonia that provides several cyber range solutions which are used for cybersecurity training, exercises, testing, validation, and experimentation [20]. More details about the cyber ranges managed by CR14 are provided below.

Open Cyber Range The Open Cyber Range (OCR) was developed as a collaborative project between Estonia and Norway Green. It is important to note that the base functionality of the OCR hardware and software platform is free of charge. OCR provide tools that simplify cybersecurity exercise creation by using a purpose-built software platform and scenario definition language.

Estonian Cyber Range The Estonian national cyber range is one of the earliest national cyber ranges, and it is used for national and bilateral cyber defense exercises. Moreover, it is employed for some of the largest international cybersecurity training exercises, namely Locked Shields and Crossed Swords.

The Estonian cyber range is also used for research and development purposes by CR14 and the North Atlantic Treaty Organization (NATO) Cooperative Cyber Defense Centre of Excellence (CCDCOE). In addition, its infrastructure serves as basis for the NATO Cyber Range discussed next.

NATO Cyber Range The NATO cyber range is a training platform used for the largest cyber defense exercises and training conducted by NATO, such as the Cyber Coalition, and the Coalition Warrior Interoperability Exercise.

Classified Cyber Range As its name implies, this is a specialized cyber range used for classified cybersecurity training exercises.

11.2.1.4 CRATE Cyber Range

CRATE is a cyber range developed by the Swedish Defense Research Agency (FOI) as a training platform for practical cybersecurity exercises [47]. For this purpose, CRATE provides a controllable environment in which participants can learn cybersecurity skills by combining the technical insight of cyber threats, actors, and vulnerabilities with education perspectives. CRATE can also be used to conduct experiments regarding cyber threats, such as how artificial intelligence techniques can be used in connection with cyberattack and defense, or how to identify and interpret the traces left by cyberattacks.

The infrastructure of CRATE is represented by a cluster of more than 500 virtualization servers. The servers are connected to two separate subnets, one for administration purposes, and one for exercise and experiment purposes. CRATE provides a series of automation mechanisms that facilitate the setup of training activities and also increase their realism [21]:

- Range provisioning: Prepare the virtualization servers and training environment.
- System and service configuration: Configure the training environment virtual machines and their services.
- Exercise management: Manage the exercises in terms of scenario creation and control, performance scoring and evaluation, etc.
- Action execution: Perform various actions, such as simulated cyberattacks, in a reliable and repeatable manner.
- User emulation and traffic generation: Emulate user behavior by executing user actions, such as sending and receiving emails, opening attachments, and accessing web pages, in order to generate realistic traffic during the training.
- Data collection: Perform traffic monitoring and intrusion detection to improve situational awareness during exercises and experiments.

An interesting feature of CRATE is the support for interfacing with hardware devices, which can be integrated with the emulated environment. This capability was used to create replicas of critical infrastructure environments with ICS and SCADA components, such as energy production and distribution, a railroad system, and a water purification plant, in the so-called CRATE City environment. In particular, software-based Programmable Logic Controller (PLC) solutions are utilized to emulate the railroad system, for which more than 70 such PLCs are used.

11.2.1.5 Florida Cyber Range

The Florida Cyber Range is a cybersecurity training environment managed by the University of West Florida [51]. The goal of this cyber range is to serve as platform for a wide variety of purposes, such as cybersecurity education and training via hands-on exercises, competency-based skill development, as well as research, test and evaluation in the cybersecurity domain.

Some of the key features of the Florida Cyber Range include realistic network traffic generation, support for common network protocols, attack modeling based on threat intelligence, etc. Moreover, the cyber range can be customized according to the needs of other organizations.

The Florida Cyber Range is used for a training program open to participants from all backgrounds and includes several courses and certifications, such as Network Defense, Cloud Security Basics, Incident Response, Malware Analysis, ICS and SCADA Security, and CompTIA Security+. The program content is also said to be aligned with the work roles in the NICE Framework.

11.2.1.6 Michigan Cyber Range

Michigan Cyber Range is the name for a cybersecurity training program that leverages a physical cyber range for conducting training exercises targeted both at individuals and teams [50]. The range and program are operated by Merit Network, Inc. in the form of a public-private collaboration between government, education institutions, and private industry.

The Michigan Cyber Range was conceived as a regional cyber range hub in Michigan, with a total of six cyber range training centers that provide professional development opportunities for individuals, and training facilities that employers can use to train their new and existing employees. Thus, the three main uses of the Michigan Cyber Range are:

- Teaching: Provides hands-on learning and certification for various compliance requirements and frameworks, with a total of about 40 industry-recognized certifications being available, including for the NICE Framework, U.S. National Security Agency, U.S. Department of Defense, etc.
- Testing: Offers software tools and penetration testing capabilities that local companies can use to test their systems in a cost-effective and scalable manner.
- Training: Hosts live exercises regarding cybersecurity attack and defense skills for educations institutions, and the public, private, defense, and military sectors.

11.2.1.7 National Cyber Range

The National Cyber Range (NCR) is a cyber range managed by the U.S. Department of Defense (DoD) that is dedicated to testing, training, and mission rehearsal for military personnel [45]. NCR is a closed-loop network system based on technologies developed under the supervision of the Defense Advanced Research Projects Agency (DARPA). The cyber range can be used to recreate cyberspace environments that are custom tailored and operationally realistic, including features such as traffic generation that models the traffic of real-world applications and protocols, and emulation of real cyberattacks and threats.

A wide range of supporting services are also provided, such as customized instrumentation and data analysis. Typical use cases for NCR include experimentation with cybersecurity-related technologies, evaluation of system architecture, security control assessment, cooperative vulnerability and penetration assessment, etc.

NCR is organized in the form of a cyber range complex with facilities at different physical locations, each with a specific focus area. For instance, the Eglin cyber range is used by the Air Force, the Charleston one is dedicated to sea-based technologies on submarines and ships, and the Orlando cyber range supports the DoD operational mission force training. The newest cyber range in this complex, located at the Naval Air Station Patuxent River, was inaugurated in 2023 [38]. All the mentioned cyber ranges are part of an integrated network and use a common core architecture and tool set. This makes it possible to use NCR to conduct a wide variety of distributed exercises of different scales.

11.2.2 Private-Sector Cyber Ranges

Private-sector cyber ranges are those training platforms that are created and managed by private-sector commercial companies. Access to training is provided as a paid service; hence, anyone can in principle benefit from the training, although the training costs are relatively high, in general. In what follows, we will provide several examples in this cyber range category.

11.2.2.1 Airbus CyberRange

Airbus CyberRange is an advanced simulation and training solution for conducting hands-on training regarding cyber threats [2]. This cyber range makes it possible to:

- Build complex virtual systems similar to an organization's network environment.
- Replicate network activities regarding the operation of an organization.
- Conduct penetration testing in the isolated environment that is created.
- Simulate realistic training scenarios, including cyberattacks.

Given its flexibility, the Airbus CyberRange can be used in several different manners, as explained next:

- Preproduction testing: Test new equipment and cybersecurity processes in a realistic environment that mimics the organization network.
- Educational activities: Raise cybersecurity awareness and learn how to apply cybersecurity policies by means of gamified challenges.
- Operational testing: Evaluate the impact of cyberattacks on an organization infrastructure by using a similar but isolated environment.
- Training activities: Conduct operational exercises in a realistic environment, and assess the efficiency of security practices for handling a cyber incident.

We note that Airbus CyberRange is available in various forms, such as Software as a Service (SaaS), on-premise deployment, or as a mobile box that the organization can deploy as needed.

11.2.2.2 ATCorp CYRIN

CYRIN is a cyber range provided by Architecture Technology Corporation (ATCorp) [3]. The platform uses an e-learning style web-based interface that participants use to conduct the training. Its most significant features are:

- High-fidelity training: Training exercises are designed to let participants practice various cybersecurity offensive skills, such as performing active network scans, and discovering server vulnerabilities, but also defensive ones, including by competing against each other.
- Exercise creation capabilities: By using a patented Exercise Builder module, users can easily create customized exercises to meet specific needs, including via real-time modifications and updates. The CYRIN software layer can also be integrated with an existing cloud-based or hardware-based training infrastructure.
- Comprehensive participant evaluation: Real-time participant evaluation is used instead of the conventional post-training evaluations. The automated progress metrics make it possible to determine where trainees encounter difficulties in the training, so that additional exercises can be conducted for those areas. The assessment is conducted by mapping high-level learning objectives to actions performed by participants by using agents to monitor the exercise and determine whether a given skill has been demonstrated or not.

CYRIN provides an online catalog of the available exercises that can be filtered not only by training category, or the tools used, but also based on NICE Framework work roles or MITRE ATT&CK attack techniques. At the time of writing, out of 62 scenarios, 48 are in the *Labs* category, meaning that they teach basic skills, such as how to use various cybersecurity tools. Out of the remaining training scenarios, eight are grouped in the *Exercises* category and refer to more complex activities, such as intrusion analysis, CTF challenges, and even a red team versus blue team exercise. The other six scenarios are in the *Attacks* category and focus on defense training. It is significant to note that four of these scenarios refer to the ICS and operational technology (OT) domain, including application-level and network-level attacks.

11.2.2.3 Cisco Talos Cyber Range

Cisco Talos Incident Response (Talos IR) is a company providing various cybersecurity services, one of them being cyber range training [12]. The training consists of three-day hands-on exercises conducted on a cyber range platform. The cyber range is used to run training scenarios that expose the participants to real-world threat tactics, techniques, and procedures (TTPs), so that they can learn advanced incident response best practices.

The first two days are dedicated to solving an initial training scenario under the guidance of the instructors. Following an introduction to the overall training methodology and incident response concepts, participants use the cyber range to conduct a wide variety of analysis activities related to Windows event logs, disk structure, Windows registry, memory, and so on. A Linux forensics component is also included in this training activity.

The third day uses a different scenario in which participants have to autonomously perform incident response tasks based on the acquired skills, with instructors providing support as needed. This allows trainees to practice the use of the tools they

mastered during the first two days, such as the memory forensics tool Volatility, as
well as the incident response methodologies they learned, and the knowledge they
acquired, for example, regarding the MITRE ATT&CK knowledge base.

11.2.2.4 Cyberbit Cyber Range

Cyberbit is a cybersecurity training company that was designated a leader of cybersecurity training platforms in the Forrester *Cybersecurity Skills and Training Platforms,
Q4 2023* report [8]. Cyberbit Cyber Range is a realistic cybersecurity training environment the company provides, in which live attacks are simulated in conditions
similar to real-world security incidents [16]. Its main characteristics are:

- A large catalog of cyberattacks is available, making it possible to experience a wide
  variety of attacker techniques, tactics, and procedures. Simulated attacks specific
  to cloud native and hybrid environments are also included.
- The training scenarios correspond both to attack and defense training and range
  in difficulty from beginner to advanced. Industry best practices, such as the NIST
  Incident Response Framework, the NICE Framework, and MITRE ATT&CK, are
  also integrated with the platform.
- Widely-used commercial tools are available within the platform, so that participants can gain experience with tools they can actually use on their job, such as
  specific firewall systems by Palo Alto Networks or CheckPoint.
- The network topologies for the training exercises are based on corporate networks
  for increased realism. Moreover, the complex network architectures make it possible for participants to experience attacker behaviors encountered in real life,
  including lateral movement and data exfiltration, so that they are ready to apply
  the acquired skills on their job.
- Trainee progress is assessed automatically, depending on the real-time performance of the participants during the training exercise. The evaluation is conducted
  from several perspectives, such as the correctness of the identified artifacts, or the
  success in terminating a malicious process or deleting a malicious file.
- Attacks on ICS/OT networks are also supported, making it possible to conduct
  training regarding critical physical infrastructure, including power grids, manufacturing lines, oil and gas plants, etc. The emulated OT network includes human-
  machine interfaces, hardware controllers, and physical devices, and attacks from
  the IT to the OT domain can be simulated.

A specific category of exercises consists of Cyber Labs, which are similar to CTF
challenges. These exercises are meant as foundational building blocks that teach
individuals the theory and tools of cybersecurity, as well as attacker tactics, in the
form of short sessions. Upon their completion, participants are then ready to proceed
to team-based cyber range exercises. Even though this type of training content makes
Cyber Labs similar to a CTF platform, we decided to include Cyberbit in this chapter
due to the significance of the cyber range training services it provides.

In addition to the aforementioned training content, the Cyber Crisis Simulator program of Cyberbit provides a mechanism for running crisis simulation scenarios in which the management teams and incident response teams participate in collaborative exercises. An extensive exercise catalog is provided, covering topics such as ransomware, data leakage, and web defacement.

We note that many of the cyber ranges deployed in government or education institutions are based on private-sector solutions. For example, the multimillion-dollar Regent University cyber range, which is in use since 2017, is said to be based on the Cyberbit technologies described here [48].

11.2.2.5   IBM X-Force Cyber Range

IBM X-Force Cyber Range is a cybersecurity training platform that uses realistic cybersecurity breach scenarios in an immersive environment to prepare participants to respond to and recover from security incidents, manage vulnerabilities, and improve the overall security culture of an organization [22]. The cyber range exercises can be conducted using predefined simulated breaches and can also be customized based on customer requirements. Workshops and executive briefings are also organized to help participants assess their security strategies and identify any potential gaps, as well as to educate teams about best practices for cybersecurity crises.

One important aspect about the IBM X-Force Cyber Range is that the training exercises are conceived in such a way as to make possible the participation of personnel with various non-technical roles regarding cybersecurity, who can work together with the IT teams during the exercise. Examples of such non-technical roles include legal and risk management leaders, Chief Information Security Officers (CISOs), finance department personnel, human resource leaders, communications and PR leaders, and even chief executive officers (CEOs).

11.2.2.6   Immersive Labs Cyber Range

Immersive Labs is a company that provides a wide range of cybersecurity training services, and that was labeled a cybersecurity training platform leader in the Forrester *Cybersecurity Skills and Training Platforms, Q4 2023* report [8]. The flagship training program of Immersive Labs is called Cyber Team Sim, and it uses cyber range exercises to assist with the development and evaluation of technical cybersecurity skills [23]. The exercises employ realistic preconfigured cyber range environments that include the latest cyber threats and that are easy to deploy. The key features of the program are as follows:

- Relevant training content: The provided prebuilt scenarios simulate real-world conditions both for offensive and defensive circumstances.

- Risk-free training: The sandbox cyber range environment makes it possible to safely practice both offensive and defensive skills in settings similar to a work environment, but without affecting production networks.
- Data-driven assessment: The training results are visualized both at individual and team levels to provide an accurate evaluation of the training progress.
- Distributed training support: Team members can engage in the same training scenarios from globally distributed locations.

A catalog of all the currently available scenarios is provided, both for Cyber Team Sim and the other training forms that will be discussed below, giving a clear view of the training platform potential [24]. A total of 22 prebuilt scenarios is included in Cyber Team Sim, such as *The Heist* and *APT43*. The scenarios are classified in the Offensive or Defensive category, with 7 and 15 scenarios in each, respectively. Their difficulty level, Beginner, Intermediate, or Advanced, is also specified.

An additional training service, named Cyber Ranges, is also available from Immersive Labs. Using Cyber Ranges, organizations can build complex network environments that meet their own specific requirements. By emulating their production networks in a cyber range, organizations are thus able to achieve the most realistic cyber training experience for their teams.

Moreover, a series of Labs—training exercises similar to CTF challenges—is also provided, with thousands of readily available exercises in several categories, such as Fundamentals (368 labs), Defensive Cyber (786 labs), Offensive Cyber (676 labs), Application Security (563 labs), Cloud Security (290 labs), and Cyber Threat Intelligence (503 labs). Note that, although this aspect brings the Labs program close to a CTF platform, we included Immersive Labs in this chapter due to the strong weight of cyber range training in its offer.

Yet another training program offered by Immersive Labs is Cyber Crisis Simulator, which is a platform for digital tabletop exercises intended for executive management and crisis management teams. The goal of this program is to help participants make better decisions in real situations by providing engaging scenarios that evolve in dynamic manner based on every decision made. A total of 54 scenarios were available at the time of writing, with names such as *Phishing Compromise* and *Network Abduction*. Note that, in addition to general cybersecurity, several scenarios focusing on the healthcare and critical infrastructure domains are included. Moreover, scenario customization is also possible, with several templates being provided.

11.2.2.7 JYVSECTEC Cyber Range

JYVSECTEC, short for Jyväskylä Security Technology, is cybersecurity research, development, and training center in Finland that is operated commercially as part of the Institute of Information Technology of JAMK University of Applied Science. The company operates a cyber range that combines virtualization techniques, physical devices, and business-specific systems to create environments tailored to specific training, testing, or research and development needs [26]. The JYVSECTEC cyber range can be used for many purposes, including:

- Individual training for cybersecurity experts, analysts, and pentesters, as well as in connection with Digital Forensics and Incident Response (DFIR).
- Cybersecurity training and capability development for organizations and teams, including the assessment of procedures regarding cyber incident response.
- Evaluation of new cybersecurity solutions before they are deployed in production environments.

These uses are made possible by the various capabilities of the cyber range environment, for which the name Realistic Global Cyber Environment (RGCE) is also used. In particular, RGCE emulates the real internet in a closed and control environment that provides the following services and features:

- Internet Service Providers (ISPs) with BGP routing and public IP addresses.
- A realistic name service architecture and hierarchy.
- An infrastructure for time synchronization and PKI certificates.
- Virtualized mobile devices and app store.
- Controlled software repositories for various operating systems.
- A Tor Onion anonymous communication network infrastructure.
- General services, such as news sites, social media, and instant messaging.

A key characteristic of RGCE is the support for user and traffic simulation that makes it possible to recreate realistic traffic patterns and service usage [30]. This capability refers to the emulation of two main aspects, as follows:

- Actor simulation: Human and configuration errors, hackers of different skill levels, insiders and disgruntled employees, nation or state sponsored actors, etc.
- Attack vector and technique simulation: Various types of DDoS attacks, malware attacks, ransomware attacks, supply chain attacks, APT campaigns, botnets, phishing campaigns, website defacements, etc.

11.2.2.8 Keysight Cyber Range

Keysight Cyber Range is a training platform that provides real-life settings for cybersecurity training activities [29]. The key features of the cyber range are:

- Comprehensive software platform that provides functionality related to cyber range orchestration, reporting, platform administration, and data export.
- Set of tools for making the training more realistic, such as traffic generators (i.e., BreakingPoint), Security Information and Event Management (SIEM) tools, web servers, firewalls, and cybersecurity tools and frameworks.
- Library of predefined training scenarios based on real-world threats, as well as the ability to create customized scenarios either from scratch, or by modifying any of the predefined ones.

- Support for gamification-based scenarios, either predefined or custom, for gamified training activities such as CTF.
- Learning content, such as educational and instructional materials, included with each predefined training scenario.

The aforementioned BreakingPoint traffic generator is an optional component of the cyber range solution that constitutes an important differentiating factor in comparison with other cyber ranges. Specifically, BreakingPoint can be used to simulate more than 490 real-world application protocols and recreate over 60,000 cyberattacks and malware threats. Note that BreakingPoint is also available as a standalone product for network security training.

In addition to the above, consulting services are provided to support organizations in customizing the training according to their needs, both in terms of the training scenarios and also regarding the tools used during the training. Specific training for tools provided by Keysight is also available.

11.2.2.9   NetWars Cyber Ranges

SANS Institute makes available a series of cyber ranges with the NetWars label that are intended to address different cybersecurity training needs [43], as follows:

- Core NetWars: The most comprehensive of the NetWars cyber ranges, this training platform covers topics such as hardware hacking, mobile app analysis, threat hunting, and web application pentesting.
- Cyber Defense NetWars: A cyber range focused on prevention, analysis, and defense against real-world attack scenarios, such as brute-force and ransomware attacks. Training topics include log and packet analysis, cryptography and steganography, and network security monitoring.
- DFIR NetWars: A cyber range that targets digital forensics, incident response, threat hunting, and malware analysis skills. Training topics include database analysis, media exploitation, and rapid triage of cyber threats and damages.

The other cyber ranges in the SANS NetWars suite, which have specialized training targets—GRID NetWars, Healthcare NetWars, and ICS NetWars—will be introduced in Sect. 11.3. Additional services provided by SANS Institute in regard to cyber range training include:

- Custom cyber ranges: SANS can create customized cyber ranges to meet the specific needs of an organization, including the definition of learning objectives, development of a training score card, and custom configuration of the training content and environment.
- NetWars Tournament: A 6-hour practice competition version of NetWars that covers the content of the following cyber ranges: Core, Cyber Defense, DFIR, GRID, ICS, and Healthcare.

- NetWars Continuous: An online 4-month hands-on training solution that covers the topics of the Core and DFIR cyber ranges. The training content is designed with tasks and hints that support a continuous knowledge and skill development.

11.2.2.10 Project Ares Labs

Project Ares Labs is a cyber range-based training program provided by the company Circadence [11]. The program uses realistic network environments and hands-on exercises to enable an interactive learning experience. The key features of Project Ares Labs are as follows:

- Cyber learning games: Basic cybersecurity concepts, such as the cyber kill chain, network ports and protocols, or regular expressions techniques, are taught through arcade-style game experiences.
- Cyber range practice: Foundational cybersecurity labs based on hands-on practice are used to introduce skills related to topics such as Linux Basics and Windows Fundamentals and tools such as Nmap, Kali Linux, PowerShell, Snort, and Wireshark. A built-in hint system is used to support the learning process.
- Specialized labs/scenarios: Missions based on offensive and defensive real-world scenarios are used to teach trainees how to handle complex threats, such as botnets, data exfiltration, phishing, and ransomware. In-game rewards, such as badges and coins, are used to motivate participants, who can play individually, or as a team.

11.2.2.11 RHEA Next-Generation Cyber Range

The company RHEA System S.A. provides a wide range of services on its Next-Generation Cyber Range platform [42]. Its main training targets are as follows:

- Governments and large enterprises, who can train their cybersecurity professionals in a safe and controlled training environment that can be set up using a GUI. Through a series of included templates, various cyberattack scenarios can be modeled corresponding to the specific nature of those organizations.
- Critical infrastructure and heavy industry, who can use the platform to conduct training related to the protection of critical infrastructure and heavy industry facilities. The training environment can emulate assets in relation with SCADA, ICS, and IoT technologies.
- Academic institutions, who can use the cyber range as a cybersecurity education platform for training their students. Training scenarios can be customized to meet the requirements of the education curriculum.
- Small businesses, who can use the cyber range in a SaaS manner that makes it possible to conduct customized training activities remotely.

11.2.2.12   Silensec CYBER RANGES

Silensec CYBER RANGES is a cybersecurity training platform that uses a series of advanced technologies to deliver realistic training and capability development exercises [44]. The training is conducted in life-like environments using real-world scenarios to make it possible for participants to learn how to handle real cybersecurity threats. The key features of CYBER RANGES are as follows:

- Realistic environment: The training environment is built based on an extensive library of predefined training scenarios that replicate corporate network infrastructure and use real-world systems and applications. The scenarios leverage the MITRE ATT&CK knowledge base, including CVE-based vulnerabilities, and can scale to thousands of virtual machines simultaneously.
- Team-based participation: The training is conducted for teams that have access to their own virtual training environment, with the outcome of the training depending on participants' performance as a team.
- Custom scenarios: Organizations can use a scenario composer to create custom scenarios that reflect their specific needs by leveraging a library of systems and applications that serve as scenario building blocks. Existing scenarios can also be modified in order to meet specific training objectives.
- Training activity features: Training activity effectiveness is improved via the use of several realistic features, such as agent-based cyberattacks, user traffic simulation, and red team automation. The attack library is based on MITRE ATT&CK information, and the attacks are automatically executed via live injections based on sets of configurable IP addresses.
- Training orchestration: The user interface of the training platform can be used to manage the training activities, with one-click creation of large-scale exercises that use multiple isolated or shared networks, and automated execution of attack injections. The exercises can be in the form of red team versus blue team training, but also in the form of participant competency assessment testing.
- Scoring and reporting: A rich set of features regarding scoring and reporting is provided. Thus, scoring can be done at individual and team level, as well as per category; a timeline for scoring is also available. Custom performance criteria can also be defined, and the scoring system can be integrated with third-party tools, such as learning management systems.

CYBER RANGES earned several recognitions, for instance, being the official cyber range for International Telecommunication Union (ITU) cybersecurity training exercises. In addition, the platform was endorsed by MITRE ATT&CK, and it can be used to conduct training in relation with the attack techniques defined in the knowledge base. Moreover, NICE Framework work role competency and progression tracking are available.

11.2.3   Academia Cyber Ranges

In the academia cyber range category, we include those cyber ranges that are developed and mainly deployed in an academic or research environment. Consequently, the main target audience of these cyber ranges is students, even though some of them are also used to train professionals. In what follows, we will provide a series of representative examples in this cyber range category.

11.2.3.1   CyTrONE

CyTrONE is an integrated cybersecurity training framework that was designed as a flexible and comprehensive solution for cybersecurity training [6, 13]. CyTrONE was designed with a modular architecture that makes it possible to replace or add components as needed, which contributes to the flexibility of the framework. Its modules include a web UI, a management module (named CyTrONE, as well), a cyber range creation module (CyRIS), a scenario progression management module (CyPROM), and so on. Training activities are conducted via the Moodle LMS, which is integrated with the framework by means of another dedicated module (CyLMS). CyTrONE will be examined as a detailed case study in Chap. 12, so readers should refer to that information for more details.

11.2.3.2   KYPO Cyber Range Platform

KYPO Cyber Range Platform (KYPO CRP) is a cloud-based cyber exercise and research platform that enables security experts to emulate computer networks for the purpose of performing hands-on cybersecurity exercises and experiments safely, without the danger of threatening the real network infrastructure [36, 54]. KYPO CRP provides an interactive learning environment that was designed to support multiple simultaneous training sessions, each having their own exercise assignments and learner assessments. The platform covers various cybersecurity training use cases, ranging from individual assignments with step-by-step instructions, or that are to be solved independently by trainees, to long-term team training or gamified training, such as CTF exercises.

The management of the training sessions in KYPO CRP is handled via two key modules. The first one, named Training Service, is in charge of the training session life cycle. The second one, Sandbox Service, is responsible for the creation and management of the training environment. The modules rely on a set of three human-readable definition files that describe the training content.

Thus, the Training Definition specifies the set of tasks that participants have to solve. It uses a JSON-format description that includes introductory information, training tasks, optional hints or detailed solutions, questionnaires about the exercise, etc. The training environment is described via the Sandbox Definition, which consists of two separate files that use the YAML format. The first file, named Topology Definition, specifies the network topology of the training environment, such as routers, hosts, and network mapping information. The second one, Provisioning Definition, specifies the configuration of the individual host VMs in a format compatible with Ansible, which is employed as software configuration management system.

Participants' activities within the training environment are monitored via software probes that gather activity data on-the-fly and store it for further use. The access to the cyber range is mediated via the KYPO web portal, which supports several types of data visualization and web-based interaction features that enable learning data exploration. These features make possible, for example, the formative assessment of trainees with individual feedback for a particular exercise, but also a summative assessment, that is, overall trainee grading at the end of an instructional unit.

To learn more about KYPO CRP, interested readers can consult [7], where KYPO CRP modules are mapped onto a generic cybersecurity training platform model, and the functionality of the platform is evaluated via a capability assessment methodology. A comparative analysis with respect to the CyTrONE cybersecurity training framework that we will present in Chap. 12 is also available in that paper.

11.2.4 General Range Comparison

In this section, we will compare the main characteristics of the general cyber ranges that we presented so far, for which an overview is displayed in Table 11.1. Note that the table is organized in three sections, corresponding to the classes of cyber ranges we have discussed, namely government, private-sector, and academia cyber ranges, respectively. The following analysis criteria are used in the table:

- Focus: The main focus of the training activities on a given cyber range:
    - Education: Education and training for various types of participants.
    - Military: Training of military personnel.
    - Commercial: Training is provided as a service by a commercial company.
    - Research and education: Research regarding cyber ranges, as well as their use for education and training.

- Distinctive features: Characteristics that mostly distinguish a cyber range with respect to other cyber ranges.
- Specialized training: Support for conducting training in specific application domains aside from general training (if available).

11.2.4.1 Government Cyber Ranges

Regarding government-supported cyber ranges, we note first that their main focus is either general education and training, sometimes restricted to educational institutions

Table 11.1 Comparison of general cyber ranges

Name	Focus	Distinctive Features	Specialized Training
AIT Cyber Range	Education	Based on open-source technologies	ICS, power grid, nuclear plant, manufacturing
Arkansas Cyber Range	Education	Wide range of training modules	N/A
CR14 Cyber Ranges	Military	Collection of cyber ranges that share components	N/A
CRATE Cyber Range	Military	Support for user emulation and traffic generation	ICS, SCADA, power grid, railroad system, water plant
Florida Cyber Range	Education	Wide range of training modules; NICE Framework support	ICS, SCADA
Michigan Cyber Range	Education	About 40 industry-recognized certifications available	N/A
National Cyber Range	Military	Cyber range complex that includes four locations	N/A
Airbus CyberRange	Commercial	Multiple forms of access (SaaS, on premise, mobile box)	N/A
ATCorp CYRIN	Commercial	Automated trainee progress assessment; Detailed exercise filtering (tools, work roles, etc.)	ICS, SCADA
Cisco Talos Cyber Range	Commercial	Three-day hands-on training program	N/A
Cyberbit Cyber Range	Commercial	Large catalog of scenarios; Automated trainee progress assessment; Crisis simulation	ICS, power grid, manufacturing, oil and gas plants
IBM X-Force Cyber Range	Commercial	Participation of non-technical personnel possible	N/A
Immersive Labs Cyber Range	Commercial	Large catalog of scenarios; Automated trainee progress assessment; Crisis simulation	N/A
JYVSECTEC Cyber Range	Commercial	Emulates real internet services; Support for human actor and traffic simulation	N/A
Keysight Cyber Range	Commercial	Traffic generation for over 490 application protocols and 60,000 cyberattacks	N/A
NetWars Cyber Ranges	Commercial	Set of six cyber ranges; Tournament and continuous training programs available	ICS, power grid, healthcare
Project Ares Labs	Commercial	Gamified training experience (badges, coins, etc.)	N/A
RHEA Next Generation	Commercial	Wide range of training services	ICS, SCADA
Silensec CYBER RANGES	Commercial	Various features regarding scoring and reporting	N/A
CyTrONE	Research and education	Open source; Modular architecture with standalone components; YAML-based definition	N/A
KYPO CRP	Research and education	Open source; Training facilitation features; JSON/YAML-based definition	N/A

within the same geographic area (e.g., Arkansas Cyber Range), or military training (e.g., National Cyber Range).

In general, these cyber ranges provide a wide variety of training modules and offer industry-recognized certifications, sometimes even supporting skill frameworks such as the NICE Framework (e.g., Michigan Cyber Range). Some organizations reuse hardware and software components in their cyber ranges in order to make it possible to conduct training for different purposes (e.g., CR14 and National Cyber Range). Moreover, some cyber ranges may even have advanced training capabilities, such as support for user emulation and traffic generation (e.g., CRATE).

It is important to note that the organizations that make available cyber ranges from this category usually provide few details about the technologies used to construct them. One reason could be that many of these cyber ranges are built using technologies provided by private-sector companies, even if the names of those companies are not always disclosed. Two exceptions in this regard are AIT Cyber Range and CRATE, for which several academic publications are available that present technical information about their architecture and capabilities. This is due to the fact that these systems are developed in-house by the research institutes that operate them.

A consequence of the use of proprietary technologies, either from private-sector companies or developed in-house, is that the source code of the cyber range platforms is not made publicly available. This is the case even when the platform is developed by the organization managing the cyber range itself, such as for the AIT Cyber Range and CRATE mentioned above, and also for CR14, presumably due to the military nature of the training conducted on them.

We observe that some of the government cyber ranges also provide support for specialized cybersecurity training, mostly in relation with ICS and SCADA technologies. For some of these systems, critical infrastructure domains are also covered, such as the power grid or the railroad system.

11.2.4.2 Private-Sector Cyber Ranges

The cyber ranges in the private-sector category are the most numerous, given the commercial incentive of providing training for profit. However, we noticed a certain level of churn in this category, with some cyber ranges we were familiar with not being advertised anymore, such as the Raytheon Cyber Range, or the Boeing Cyber Range. We can imagine that some of those technologies have been integrated in other solutions of their corresponding companies, but it can also be assumed that market conditions have eliminated some of the more expensive solutions, as new competitors entered the marketplace.

Most private-sector cyber ranges provide a large training catalog—that of Cyberbit Cyber Range being one of the largest—with detailed exercise filtering being available in some cases (e.g., ATCorp CYRIN). The forms of training are diverse, ranging from several-hour tournaments to three-day training programs, and even months long continuous training. Moreover, many training programs include support for the NICE Framework; this demonstrates that leveraging the association of work roles, tasks, knowledge, and skills, as defined in various workforce and skill frameworks, is an important aspect of cybersecurity training (see Sect. 3.2 for a more detailed discussion of this issue).

In terms of distinctive features, several of the cyber ranges we presented (e.g., Cyberbit Cyber Range) provide automated trainee progress assessment capabilities, which makes it easier to quantify the exact skill level a participant has attained.

Creating a training environment as realistic as possible is also important for many companies, and most of them accomplish this by using realistic network topologies. However, emulating real internet like services, as well as human actor actions and traffic generation are also important capabilities in this respect, as provided by the JYVSECTEC Cyber Range. Another standout in this regard is the Keysight Cyber Range, which can use the optional BreakingPoint traffic generator to reproduce over 490 application protocols and 60,000 cyberattacks and malware threats.

We note that IBM X-Force Cyber Range includes a distinctive feature that is not often encountered for cybersecurity training platforms, which mainly focus on technical training. Thus, the exercises available on this cyber range are designed in such as manner as to make it possible for personnel with non-technical roles, such as legal and risk management leaders, finance department personnel, or human resource leaders to work together with the IT teams during the exercise. This contributes both to an increased security awareness of the non-technical personnel and also to an improvement in the incident response capabilities of the organization as a whole. The crisis simulation platforms from Cyberbit and Immersive Labs play a similar function, although they do not appear to integrate an actual technical training aspect, as it is done in IBM X-Force Cyber Range.

Another important remark is that, as expected, private-sector cyber ranges do not provide any source code for their platforms. Moreover, the details made available focus predominantly on the end-user experience and features and rarely on the technologies used to implement those capabilities. In fact, in some cases the amount of information provided was so low that we decided to exclude certain cyber ranges from our analysis; this was the case for the GLESEC Cyber Range,[1] for which only a very simple overview of the available services is made public.

However, the JYVSECTEC Cyber Range is an exception in this respect, since even though its source code is not public, several scientific publications related to its capabilities and the underlying concepts are available, such as [28]. The reason for this is that JYVSECTEC is a university spin-off company, and cyber range development is still conducted as part of a research institute.

Several of the private-sector cyber ranges also include specialized cybersecurity training capabilities regarding ICS and SCADA technologies. In addition, some of them cover also the power grid, oil and gas plants, and even the healthcare domain.

---

[1] https://www.glesec.com/cyber-range/.

11.2.4.3   Academia Cyber Ranges

The cyber ranges we included in the academia cyber range category are those developed primarily in an academic research environment; hence, the focus in this case is both research and education. As the surveys we mentioned in Sect. 11.1.2 indicate, there are many such cyber ranges that have been implemented over the years. However, their development often finishes when the corresponding research projects end. Therefore, we have focused here on two cyber ranges that have been developed for a decade or more and are still in active use, namely CyTrONE and KYPO CRP. We note that the scope of KYPO CRP training activities is the largest of the two, ranging from education to military training.

The most important characteristic of the two cyber ranges we presented is that the source code needed to deploy them is publicly available. This means that interested organizations can utilize them on their own premises as well and also modify the source code to extend their functionality as needed. Therefore, the names of these two cyber ranges refer not only to the actual cyber range deployment, but also to the corresponding cyber range platform software that can be used by anyone.

One distinguishing feature of CyTrONE is that the components used in its modular architecture can also operate in a standalone manner, which increases their applicability and overall flexibility. As for KYPO CRP, it has several training facilitation features, such as trainee activity monitoring and learning data exploration capabilities, as well as support for both formative and summative assessments.

A point of similarity for the two platforms is that the training content and environment definition is done by means of human and machine-readable representation formats, such as YAML and JSON. This allows instructors to directly analyze and update the definitions if needed.

11.3   Specialized Cyber Ranges

Specialized cyber ranges are those training platforms that cover other technologies than those associated with regular computer networks. Although there can be many such technologies, in what follows, we will cover the following types of specialized cyber ranges that we consider the most significant, and for which we will provide a series of representative examples shown in alphabetical order:

- Internet of Things (IoT) cyber ranges.
- Industrial Control System (ICS) cyber ranges.
- Critical infrastructure cyber ranges.
- Internet of Medical Things (IoMT) and healthcare cyber ranges.

11.3.1 IoT Cyber Ranges

IoT cyber ranges make it possible to conduct cybersecurity training related to IoT devices and networks, often by using simulation and emulation techniques to create training environments that reproduce those systems' characteristics.

11.3.1.1 IoT-CR

IoT Cyber Range (IoT-CR) is an IoT testbed intended for research and training related to IoT security [39]. The training environment is represented by a customizable IoT network, made of both virtual and physical devices, and supports the concurrent execution of multiple scenarios.

Although the IoT-CR cyber range is said to include twenty RE-MOTE IoT devices developed by Zolertia,[2] most of the discussion in the cited paper refers to the use of virtual devices for improved scalability and flexibility. For this purpose, IoT-CR leverages the Cooja IoT network simulator, which is run in headless mode, and delivers to participants the simulation results.

The scenario that is discussed consists of a realistic network topology, IoT device configuration, and IoT applications developed in Contiki-NG. The use of IoT-CR was demonstrated via a red team versus blue team simulation scenario involving a man-in-the-middle (MITM) attack variant for IoT devices.

11.3.1.2 IoTrain-Lab

IoTrain-Lab is an IoT security training platform that uses the FIT IoT-LAB testbed as training infrastructure [14, 57]. The cyber range is composed of the real IoT devices in the testbed and can be used by trainees to conduct hands-on training activities in a controlled environment. The training content of IoTrain-Lab focuses on fundamental IoT training exercises, but IoT security training is included as well. Since IoTrain-Lab was already described in detail in Sect. 7.3.2, readers should consult that section for more information.

11.3.1.3 IoTrain-Sim

IoTrain-Sim is a companion training system for IoTrain-Lab. However, different from IoTrain-Lab, IoTrain-Sim relies on simulation techniques and leverages the Cooja IoT network simulator to enable a wide variety of training exercises [15, 55]. The training content of IoTrain-Sim includes both fundamental IoT training exercises and security training ones. For the security training exercises, the focus is on attacks specific to Wireless Sensor Networks (WSNs), such as resource attacks, topology

---

[2] https://github.com/Zolertia/Resources/wiki/RE-Mote.

attacks, and traffic attacks. IoTrain-Sim was previously introduced in Sect. 7.3.1, which should be referred to for more details.

11.3.1.4 Leaf

Leaf is a cybersecurity training platform intended for realistic IoT training exercises, with focus on edge IoT scenarios [19]. The term *edge IoT* refers to the convergence of IoT technologies with edge computing, that is processing and analyzing data on the edge of the network, closer to the IoT devices, instead of performing it in the cloud. Thus, Leaf is intended as a solution for organizing training exercises for various edge IoT application domains, as well as an experiment platform for validating solutions for the prevention, detection, mitigation, and recovery from edge IoT specific cyberattacks.

Leaf has two main components, a training support application and the cyber range. The training support application is a web application implemented in PHP that relies on the Zend Framework, which is an open-source web application framework, and CoreUI, which is an open-source UI library and administration panel template that supports the development of responsive web applications.

The cyber range in Leaf is designed in an agnostic manner with respect to the actual implementation technologies. This makes it possible to represent heterogeneous IoT assets by relying on simulation and virtualization techniques to support a variety of scenario components and network topologies. In particular, the IoT nodes and the wireless connections between them are simulated using event-based simulators, such as OMNET++ and Ns-3. On the other hand, the edge nodes are recreated by using emulation techniques that rely on the OpenStack and Chef virtualization technologies.

11.3.1.5 SPIDER

SPIDER is a cyber range dedicated to cybersecurity training in relation with 5G networks [41]. To achieve this, the training environment replicates a custom 5G network that emulates a realistic 5G infrastructure. The infrastructure for SPIDER is represented by two 5G testbeds, namely MATILDA and Mouseworld. Both testbeds rely on the European Telecommunications Standards Institute (ETSI) open-source network function virtualization management and orchestration software stack named MANO to provide 5G network emulation functionality. The key features of SPIDER are as follows:

- Emulation scenario definition: Configure the assets in the 5G environments, including any possible vulnerabilities.
- Management and orchestration: Coordinate the 5G network slices and the deployment of vertical applications in the network.

- Tracing and progress tracking: Use log extraction agents, aggregators, and an indexing engine to gather all the relevant information regarding training activities.
- Cyber risk assessment engine: Track cyber risk evolution in real time during the training in function of the occurring attacks and mitigation deployments.
- Training scenario orchestration: Manage the execution of the training scenarios, such as crypto mining malware detection, and DNS attack.
- Synthetic attack generation: Use machine learning techniques to generate synthetic network traffic that mimics both cyberattack and normal traffic to create realistic training conditions.

By using the features described above, SPIDER makes it possible to conduct various types of activities, such as cybersecurity risk assessment of 5G networks, and cybersecurity training for defending 5G networks from cyberattacks. This type of hands-on exercises in which participants are able to interact in real time with the 5G environment and gather feedback from the emulated network equipment enables them to develop advanced procedures for defending 5G networks from cyberattacks.

11.3.2 ICS/SCADA Cyber Ranges

Industrial Control Systems (ICSs) are conceptually similar to IoT devices and networks. However, the industrial setting of ICS can be said to cause an increase in the risks associated to them, given the potential huge consequences and disruptions that attacks on ICS can cause. One type of ICS that is often used in practice is Supervisory Control and Data Acquisition (SCADA), a standardized control system architecture utilized for large industrial systems. Cybersecurity training in relation with ICS in general and SCADA in particular are very important given the related risks. In what follows, we will review several examples in this context.

11.3.2.1 ICS NetWars

One representative ICS cyber range is ICS NetWars by SANS Institute [43]. This cyber range is focused on factory machinery operations, and it recreates an experience similar to a factory floor. In ICS NetWars, trainees are exposed to challenges related to the defense of physical equipment and manufacturing components from cyberattacks. Example training topics include asset discovery and infrastructure mapping, detection of ICS-specific malware, endpoint forensics, process restoration, and use of engineering applications.

11.3.2.2 ICSCoE

The Industrial Cyber Security Center of Excellence (ICSCoE) is a center managed by the Information-technology Promotion Agency (IPA) in Japan [25]. ICSCoE was established in 2017 with the purpose of development of human resources, systems, as well as technologies aimed at dealing with cybersecurity risks in regard to industrial infrastructure.

Since human resource development is a key part of the program, the activities of the center consist of exercises in environments that reproduce real plants, including practical attack-defense training. In particular, trainees utilize realistic process control networks to gain firsthand experience of the effects of cyberattacks on Industrial Control Systems and devices. Thus, they become familiar with architectures of control systems, ICS security vulnerabilities, and mitigation measures specific to ICS.

11.3.2.3 KYPO4INDUSTRY

KYPO4INDUSTRY is a training facility dedicated to teaching ICS security concepts and skills [9]. The training environment is built using open-source hardware and software that are leveraged to provide reconfigurable ICS modules. The components of the training platform include Programmable Logic Controllers (PLCs), input/output modules, a touchscreen display, a linear motor actuator, as well as a communication gateway.

The associated course is based on the flipped-classroom format, in which participants work on hands-on projects that replicate real cyberattacks on ICS in the form of educational games. This experience makes it possible for trainees to understand the ICS-specific risks and to gain practical skills regarding mitigation techniques for cyberattacks that target ICS.

11.3.2.4 Other ICS/SCADA Capable Cyber Ranges

In addition to the examples we have mentioned so far, the following general cyber ranges that we discussed in Sect. 11.2 also provide ICS and/or SCADA-related training functionality in addition to general cybersecurity training:

- Government cyber ranges

  - AIT Cyber Range (see Sect. 11.2.1.1).
  - CRATE Cyber Range (see Sect. 11.2.1.4).
  - Florida Cyber Range (see Sect. 11.2.1.5).

- Private-sector cyber ranges

  - ATCorp CYRIN (see Sect. 11.2.2.2).

– Cyberbit Cyber Range (see Sect. 11.2.2.4).
– RHEA Next-Generation Cyber Range (see Sect. 11.2.2.11).

The fact that both government and private-sector cyber ranges have dedicated training capabilities for this domain demonstrates that ICS/SCADA-related cybersecurity training is indeed of high importance.

11.3.3 Critical Infrastructure Cyber Ranges

Critical infrastructure refers to that infrastructure of a country that is considered essential for the functioning of the society. Consequently, governments put in place special strategies and protection measures regarding such infrastructure, including against cyberattacks. Cybersecurity training with respect to critical infrastructures is one key component of these strategies.

One of the most important types of critical infrastructure is the power grid. While the power grid itself is associated already with a series of specific cybersecurity risks, the enhancements related to smart grid technologies, that include both flows of electricity and information, lead to an even greater attack surface, as it was discussed in detail in [35]. Consequently, in what follows we will provide several examples of power grid related cyber ranges, followed by a more generic one.

11.3.3.1   GRID NetWars

One cyber range that addresses power grid cybersecurity training needs is GRID NetWars, which is made available by SANS Institute [43]. In particular, this cyber range targets technologies used in electrical generation and distribution systems. Accordingly, the challenges included in the training are themed around power system scenarios, protocols, and architectures, but the skills gained are said to be applicable to other critical infrastructure sectors too. Some of the training topics covered in this program are stages of ICS cyberattacks, credential theft, process manipulation, cyberattack effects on reliability and system integrity, etc.

11.3.3.2   GridAttackSim

As discussed for other cyber ranges in the IoT domain, leveraging simulation techniques can help with creating cybersecurity training environments that, despite a certain loss in realism, are nevertheless very useful for improving cybersecurity skills. This also applies to the critical infrastructure sector, since conducting training on real critical infrastructure limits the scope of the training scenarios and is dangerous in case any mistakes are made.

One system that leverages simulation is GridAttackSim, which is a smart grid attack co-simulation framework [31]. GridAttackSim is implemented by combining the functionality of Framework for Network Co-Simulation (FNCS), with that of the GridLAB-D power distribution simulator, and the Ns-3 network simulator to make it possible to simulate smart grid infrastructure.

The framework includes a set of built-in attack profiles that make it possible to conduct experiments in a variety of scenarios and visualize the consequences of the cyberattacks. GridAttackSim is open source, which means that in addition to deploying it freely, users can also add by themselves custom attack profiles and smart grid architectures in order to explore new scenarios and conditions.

We note that using analytical modeling is an approach that makes it possible to quantify the effects of cyberattacks on critical infrastructure at a much lower cost than using a cyber range, even though it is an even more abstract model of reality compared to simulation. Thus, the analytical modeling approach was used in the context of smart grids by GridAttackAnalyzer, a cyberattack analysis framework that uses graph-based security modeling techniques for the numerical analysis of smart grid cyberattacks [32]. For a comparison of the simulation and analytical modeling approaches used by the two systems discussed here, see [33].

11.3.3.3   Soteria ARENA

Soteria ARENA is a cybersecurity training platform for SCADA and IoT-operated Industrial Control Systems [46]. However, the training scenarios disclosed online refer not to general factory operation, but to critical infrastructure components, such as water plants and power plants. Therefore, we decided to include this cyber range in the critical infrastructure category. In fact, other elements are also present in the training scenarios, such as streetlights and airport infrastructure, differentiating it even more from the typical industrial settings of ICS/SCADA.

The training activities used in ARENA are based on real-world threats regarding critical infrastructure and use as training environment models of the target systems. Participants conduct hands-on exercises with those emulated systems, for example, to perform penetration testing attacks intended to disturb their operation.

A key characteristic of ARENA is that the training platform allows participants to see the physical impact of their actions for a better understanding of ICS and their vulnerabilities to cyber and physical threats. Thus, in addition to the simulation models, miniature physical models are also available for some of the exercises, which provide immediate feedback to participants. This aspect of ARENA makes it possible to conduct realistic training both for attack and defense techniques.

11.3.3.4 Other Critical Infrastructure Cyber Ranges

Note that the following general cyber ranges that we have discussed previously also provide critical infrastructure-related training functionality in addition to their main cybersecurity training capabilities:

- Government cyber ranges

  - AIT Cyber Range (see Sect. 11.2.1.1).
  - CRATE Cyber Range (see Sect. 11.2.1.4).

- Private-sector cyber ranges

  - Cyberbit Cyber Range (see Sect. 11.2.2.4).
  - RHEA Next-Generation Cyber Range (see Sect. 11.2.2.11).

The critical infrastructure sector that most of the above cyber ranges cover is the one that we mainly discussed in this section, namely the power grid. This signifies that energy production and distribution are arguably considered the most important domain by all critical infrastructure training providers. Other sectors covered by the mentioned cyber ranges include power plants (e.g., oil, gas, nuclear), water treatment plants, the railroad system, as well as heavy industry facilities.

11.3.4 IoMT and Healthcare Cyber Ranges

The Internet of Medical Things (IoMT), also known as healthcare IoT, refers to those medical devices and applications that are connected to healthcare systems via computer networks, for instance, by using technologies such as Wi-Fi. Given the sensitive area of IoMT applications, security threats must necessarily be considered. Moreover, the quantitative study presented in [18] has demonstrated that there are many vulnerabilities related to IoMT devices that are rated as high or critical from the point of view of the security risk associated to them. For this reason, in what follows we will discuss several cyber ranges in the healthcare domain.

11.3.4.1 Healthcare Cyber Range

Healthcare Cyber Range (HCCR) is a project that extended the functionality of the JYVSECTEC RGCE cyber range discussed in Sect. 11.2.2.7 to the healthcare domain by adding support for healthcare systems and processes [27]. HCCR aims to increase the resilience of healthcare actors regarding cybersecurity issues and to ensure patient safety in the context of digital healthcare through a range of specific cybersecurity education and training activities:

- Developing and testing cybersecurity exercises for the healthcare domain.
- Identifying specific cybersecurity skills for healthcare actors.
- Developing cybersecurity processes for the healthcare domain according to its specific requirements.

The training activities in the HCCR environment contribute to the improvement of cybersecurity skills and competence of healthcare actors in order to meet the stringent requirements of the healthcare domain. For this purpose, HCCR includes the following components that model virtual hospitals and equipment, social and health information systems, as well as national services:

- Patient information systems: Various aspects, such as medical records, prescriptions, laboratory results are modeled.
- Patient records: Realistic information regarding elements such as personal data, disease classifications, drug pack sizes, and reference values are provided.
- Intensive care unit: A physical patient simulator as well as medical equipment (a ventilator and a patient monitor) is included in addition to virtual systems.
- Integrated national services: Models of Finnish national healthcare services, pharmacies, and prescription centers are available, along with an authentication service.

11.3.4.2   Healthcare NetWars

Another example in this category of cyber ranges is Healthcare NetWars, provided by SANS Institute [43]. This cyber range is used for training related to techniques for securing technologies and systems in the medical field. For this purpose, participants must solve tasks related to device vulnerability scanning, web application assessments, and ransomware threat response. The training topics include telemedicine and web application security, Electronic Medical Records (EMR) and incident analysis, medical device IoT security, and ransomware analysis and decryption.

11.3.5   Specialized Range Comparison

In this section, we will compare the main characteristics of the specialized cyber ranges that we discussed so far, for which an overview is provided in Table 11.2. The table is organized in four sections, corresponding to the categories of ranges we presented, namely IoT, ICS/SCADA, critical infrastructure, as well as IoMT and healthcare cyber ranges. The following analysis criteria will be considered:

- Focus: The main focus of the training activities on a cyber range:

  - Research and education: Research regarding cyber ranges, as well as their use for education and training.

Table 11.2 Comparison of specialized cyber ranges

Name	Focus	Scenario	Device Type	Distinctive Features
IoT-CR	Research and education	WSN	Simulated and real	Leverages the Cooja IoT network simulator
IoTrain-Lab	Research and education	WSN	Real	Deployed on the FIT IoT-LAB testbed; Open source; Includes training exercises
IoTrain-Sim	Research and education	WSN	Simulated	Leverages the Cooja IoT network simulator; Open source; Includes training exercises
Leaf	Research and education	Edge IoT	Simulated and emulated	Leverages OMNET++ and Ns-3 simulators and virtual machines
SPIDER	Research and education	5G	Emulated	Leverages the MANO 5G software stack; ML-based traffic generation
ICS NetWars	Commercial	Factory operation	Emulated	Wide range of topics
ICSCoE	Education	Factory operation	Emulated and physical models	Basic and advanced practical exercises; Realistic process control networks
KYPO4INDUSTRY	Research and education	Factory operation	Emulated and physical models	Used for ICS cybersecurity course; Relies on open-source hardware and software
GRID NetWars	Commercial	Power grid	Emulated	Wide range of topics
GridAttackSim	Research and education	Smart grid	Simulated	Co-simulation framework; Open source; Includes attack profiles and grid scenarios
Soteria ARENA	Commercial	Plant operation	Emulated and physical models	Hands-on experience with real-world devices and physical automation systems
Healthcare Cyber Range	Commercial	Healthcare	Emulated and physical models	Models hospital and equipment, social and health information systems, national services
Healthcare NetWars	Commercial	Healthcare	Emulated	Wide range of topics

- Commercial: Training is provided as a service by a commercial company.
- Education: Education and training for various types of participants.

• Scenario: The main type of training scenario that a cyber range targets.
• Device type: The type of devices and other components of a cyber range:

- Simulated: Logical models are used to represent the devices.
- Emulated: Software implementations of real devices are used.
- Real: Actual physical devices are employed.
- Physical models: Real devices set up in the form of miniature physical models are utilized.

• Distinctive features: Characteristics that mostly distinguish a cyber range with respect to other cyber ranges.

11.3.5.1   IoT Cyber Ranges

Typical IoT devices are mainly targeted to end users, which are the consumers; hence, they are less used in commercial settings. This explains, perhaps, why the IoT cyber ranges that we were able to identify originate all from an academic environment; hence, they were mainly developed for research and education purposes. Possibly as a consequence, the cyber ranges we presented do not appear to be in use for actual training activities. Moreover, the present status of some of the described projects is relatively hard to ascertain.

The training scenarios for several of the cyber ranges in this category are related to general IoT uses, such as Wireless Sensor Networks in the case of IoTrain-Lab and IoTrain-Sim. However, other domains are also covered, such as edge IoT for Leaf, and 5G networks for SPIDER.

Since creating training environments for such heterogeneous scenarios is difficult, most cyber ranges use either simulated or emulated IoT devices. For simulation, some cyber ranges rely on the Cooja IoT network simulator, and one of them, Leaf, on OMNET++. For emulation purposes, virtualization techniques, as well as software implementations of the IoT functionality are employed.

In the case of IoT-CR, however, interfacing with real IoT devices is also supported. Another special case is represented by IoTrain-Lab, which leverages an IoT testbed, FIT IoT-LAB, to make possible training with a wide variety of real IoT devices.

Among the presented cyber ranges, IoTrain-Lab and IoTrain-Sim are remarkable for the fact that their source code is publicly available. Hence, interested organizations can deploy them on their own server infrastructure and even extend their functionality if necessary. Moreover, both of them include a set of training scenarios, both for fundamental and security training, that makes them readily usable in comparison with the other systems.

A specific feature of SPIDER, which we have not encountered for other cyber ranges, is that it leverages machine learning techniques to provide network traffic generation capabilities. By mimicking both cyberattack and normal traffic to create realistic training conditions, SPIDER makes it possible to conduct both cybersecurity risk assessments of 5G networks, as well as cybersecurity training for defending 5G networks from cyberattacks.

11.3.5.2 ICS/SCADA Cyber Ranges

Among the cyber ranges that are dedicated to ICS and/or SCADA-related cybersecurity training, some are from the private sector, such as ICS NetWars, others from government organizations, such as ICSCoE, and some even from the academia, such as KYPO4INDUSTRY. This illustrates the wide variety of needs that must be addressed when conducting training in this domain.

All the cyber ranges we presented in the ICS/SCADA category use factory operation as training scenario, which is the most typical scenario for this domain. Emulation techniques are generally used to recreate the factory setting, but for ICSCoE and KYPO4INDUSTRY this is combined with physical models of the system that include real human-machine interfaces, as well as sensor and actuation devices. This considerably improves the realism of the training, as participants are able to experience directly the effects of their actions.

As a commercial system, ICS NetWars includes a wide variety of training topics, such as asset discovery and infrastructure mapping, detection of ICS-specific malware, and use of engineering applications. ICSCoE also includes various practical exercises ranging from basic to advanced, with the basic exercises providing introductory knowledge on all topics, and the advanced exercises providing more practical training on specific elective topics selected by participants. As for KYPO4INDUSTRY, the cyber range is used for a full ICS cybersecurity course taught at the academic institution where it was developed.

Another distinctive feature of ICSCoE is that it uses realistic process control networks that are built using actual network equipment for an increased realism of the training. In KYPO4INDUSTRY, on the other hand, a strong emphasis was laid on the use of open-source hardware and software, so that the cyber range setup can be replicated at other institutions.

We note that, as we have mentioned already, several of the general-purpose cyber ranges support ICS/SCADA training as well. This makes us conclude that following general cybersecurity training, ICS/SCADA-related training is next in terms of importance from an overall perspective.

11.3.5.3 Critical Infrastructure Cyber Ranges

Two of the examples of critical infrastructure cyber ranges that we presented target power grid cybersecurity training. The power grid is also a training scenario included in several other cyber ranges that provide critical infrastructure training support, as mentioned when discussing this topic in Sect. 11.3.3. We consider that the reason for the prevalence of this domain is that the potential consequences of cyberattacks on this type of critical infrastructure are more severe than for other types of systems.

GRID NetWars is a commercial system using emulation of power systems based on virtualization technologies to make it possible to conduct training related to power distribution and generation. A wide variety of training topics are included, such as stages of power grid cyberattacks, process manipulation, and cyberattack effects on reliability and system integrity.

For GridAttackSim, which is an academia system, the training target is actually the smart grid, which is a power grid that integrates communication technologies to improve power delivery. This actually increases the attack surface of the system, hence the pressing need to address cybersecurity training for this specific domain. GridAttackSim uses a co-simulation approach to integrate the power grid and communication network simulation into an overall smart grid simulator. The source code of the framework and several attack profiles and smart grid scenarios are publicly available, meaning that anyone can use and modify it.

The third example we provided, Soteria ARENA, on the other hand, has a different approach. In that cyber range, a comprehensive scenario is used that includes a water plant, a power plant, and even an airport infrastructure. Combined with miniature physical models of the systems, Soteria ARENA enables realistic critical infrastructure training through a hands-on experience with real-world devices and physical automation systems.

We note that several of the ICS/SCADA cyber ranges we presented also include training in connection with critical infrastructure, such as oil and gas plants, or the railroad system. Therefore, we conclude that even though only keywords such as ICS or SCADA are shown in the description of some cyber ranges, the actual training content may be related to critical infrastructure as well. Consequently, interested learners should always check in detail the available information to determine the types of training scenarios that are actually available in a cyber range.

11.3.5.4 IoMT and Healthcare Cyber Ranges

The healthcare domain is undoubtedly a very important area for cybersecurity, given the obvious associated risks. However, there are many challenges in setting up dedicated cyber ranges, which may explain the smaller number of systems in this category. Nevertheless, the two examples we provided, which are both from the private sector, clearly demonstrate the commercial interest that exists for conducting cybersecurity training in this area.

The cyber ranges we presented both rely on emulation techniques to create the healthcare-related training environment. For Healthcare Cyber Range, for instance, replicas of patient records and other social and health information systems, as well as national services are included in the environment. Moreover, an intensive care unit model with a physical patient simulator, as well as medical equipment is also available in addition to the virtual systems.

Healthcare NetWars, on the other hand, relies solely on emulation techniques, with the focus being apparently almost exclusively on the cyber aspects of healthcare systems. Nevertheless, a wide range of training topics is available, such as telemedicine and web application security, Electronic Medical Records (EMR) and incident analysis, and medical device IoT security.

Another example of a healthcare cyber range is AERAS, although the practical results of the project are only expected in 2025 [1]. Thus, AERAS is an ongoing EU Horizon 2020 project that aims to develop a realistic and adaptable cyber range platform for systems and organizations in the healthcare sector. The solution will be delivered at technology readiness level TRL-7, namely via a system prototype demonstration in two pilot operational environments. We look forward to the deliverables of this project, which promises to bring a significant contribution to the research in the field of cybersecurity training for healthcare.

11.4 Discussion

In what follows, we will discuss several key aspects regarding the general and specialized cyber ranges that we have presented in this chapter. This will be followed by several recommendations regarding cyber ranges that we consider to be the best overall in terms of training scope breadth and training content richness.

11.4.1 General Cyber Ranges

The general-purpose cyber ranges we introduced in Sect. 11.2 were selected based on their characteristics of being cybersecurity training platforms that make it possible to conduct training activities that are more complex and realistic in comparison with the CTF platforms discussed in Chap. 10. Nevertheless, in some cases, even if the words "cyber range" appeared in the name of a training platform, we decided to exclude it from our presentation if the training activity complexity seemed insufficient from this point of view.

For example, Virginia Cyber Range is a cloud-based cybersecurity training platform used by thousands of students and faculty from hundreds of high schools and universities in the Commonwealth of Virginia [52]. However, an examination of the available courses showed that the content seems to be very close to that of online CTF platforms. The same can be said about the U.S. Cyber Range at Virginia Tech, which is a cyber range providing similar albeit paid courses for students and educators all over the U.S. (we do note, however, that more advanced training environments are reportedly planned for Fall 2024 [53]).

Some of the cyber ranges introduced in this category, in addition to general cybersecurity training, make it possible to also conduct specialized training activities (e.g., regarding ICS and SCADA). This demonstrates that the breadth of training scope is an important characteristic of a comprehensive training platform.

11.4.2   Specialized Cyber Ranges

For the specialized cyber ranges presented in Sect. 11.3, many of the examples we provided rely on the use of simulation techniques, sometimes in combination with emulation, in order to create the necessary training environment. In some cases, this was done to reduce the construction cost and to increase the experiment scale for the cyber range. In other cases, such as for critical infrastructure, the difficulties related to conducting training on real systems were another deciding factor. Despite the complex nature of such systems, modeling their physical characteristics makes it possible to conduct training in conditions that cannot be realized when using actual systems, for example, because of the possible damage that can occur.

However, in the case of ICS/SCADA and critical infrastructure systems, their actual operation is specific to the particular systems used in a given application area. Consequently, when the most realistic type of training is required, we consider that a dedicated cyber range that mimics as closely as possible the real systems, including via physical components, is the most appropriate solution.

11.4.3   Overall Recommendations

Among the cybersecurity training companies that we have surveyed, SANS Institute has the widest range of training domains via its NetWars training platforms, that encompass both a variety of general cybersecurity training activities, as well as many specialized areas, such as ICS, power grid, and health care. For this reason, we consider that this company represents a good starting point for learners, no matter what their domain of interest may be.

Another training provider that covers a wide range of training domains, both for general and specialized training is Cyberbit. Moreover, as mentioned previously, Cyberbit has been designated as one of the leaders of cybersecurity training platforms in the Forrester *Cybersecurity Skills and Training Platforms, Q4 2023* report [8], scoring highest in the strategy and current offering categories. Hence, we also recommend Cyberbit as a training provider for various application domains.

While the coverage of the specialized training domain is relatively weak, Immersive Labs is another strong contender, with a catalog of thousands of general cybersecurity training exercises. In addition, other methods than cyber range training are available, such as the Cyber Crisis Simulator digital tabletop exercise. Note that Immersive Labs as well has been named a cybersecurity training platform leader in the Forrester *Cybersecurity Skills and Training Platforms, Q4 2023* report [8], with an overall evaluation close to that of Cyberbit.

References

1. A cyber range training platform for medical organisations and systems security. https://cordis.europa.eu/project/id/872735. Accessed 1 July 2024
2. AIRBUS: CyberRange: advanced simulation and training solution. https://www.cyber.airbus.com/products/cyberrange/. Accessed 1 July 2024
3. Architecture Technology Corporation (ATCorp): CYRIN cyber range. https://cyrin.atcorp.com/. Accessed 1 July 2024
4. Arkansas Department of Higher Education: Arkansas cyber range. https://dese.ade.arkansas.gov/Offices/ar-comp-sci-initiative/arkansas-cyber-range-project. Accessed 1 July 2024
5. Austrian Institute of Technology (AIT): AIT cyber range. https://cyberrange.at/. Accessed 1 July 2024
6. Beuran R, Tang D, Pham C, Chinen K, Tan Y, Shinoda Y (2018) Integrated framework for hands-on cybersecurity training: CyTrONE. Comput Secur 78C:43–59. https://doi.org/10.1016/j.cose.2018.06.001
7. Beuran R, Vykopal J, Belajová D, Čeleda P, Tan Y, Shinoda Y (2023) Capability assessment methodology and comparative analysis of cybersecurity training platforms. Comput Secur 128:103120. https://doi.org/10.1016/j.cose.2023.103120
8. Burn J, Blankenship J, Born F, Belden M (2023) The cybersecurity skills and training platforms landscape, Q4 2023. https://reprints2.forrester.com/#/assets/2/2565/RES178480/report. Accessed 1 July 2024
9. Čeleda P, Vykopal J, Švábenský V, Slavíček K (2020) KYPO4INDUSTRY: a testbed for teaching cybersecurity of industrial control systems. In: Proceedings of the 51st ACM technical symposium on computer science education, pp 1026–1032
10. Chouliaras N, Kittes G, Kantzavelou I, Maglaras L, Pantziou G, Ferrag MA (2021) Cyber ranges and testbeds for education, training, and research. Appl Sci 11(4):1809. https://doi.org/10.3390/app11041809
11. Circadence: project ares labs. https://circadence.com/project-ares-classroom-labs/. Accessed 1 July 2024
12. Cisco Talos incident response: cyber range training. https://talosintelligence.com/incident_response/cyberrange. Accessed 1 July 2024
13. Cyber Range Organisation and Design (CROND): CyTrONE GitHub page. https://github.com/crond-jaist/cytrone. Accessed 1 July 2024
14. Cyber Range Organisation and Design (CROND): IoTrain-Lab GitHub page. https://github.com/crond-jaist/iotrain-lab. Accessed 1 July 2024
15. Cyber Range Organisation and Design (CROND): IoTrain-Sim GitHub page. https://github.com/crond-jaist/iotrain-sim. Accessed 1 July 2024
16. Cyberbit: cyber range. https://www.cyberbit.com/platform/cyber-range/. Accessed 1 July 2024
17. Davis J, Magrath S (2013) A survey of cyber ranges and testbeds. https://apps.dtic.mil/sti/pdfs/ADA594524.pdf
18. Debar H, Beuran R, Tan Y (2020) A quantitative study of vulnerabilities in the Internet of medical things. In: Proceedings of the 6th international conference on information systems security and privacy (ICISSP), pp 164–175
19. Ficco M, Palmieri F (2019) Leaf: an open-source cybersecurity training platform for realistic edge-IoT scenarios. J Syst Arch 97:107–129. https://doi.org/10.1016/j.sysarc.2019.04.004
20. Foundation CR14: multiverse of cyber ranges. https://www.cr14.ee/. Accessed 1 July 2024
21. Gustafsson T, Almroth J (2021) Cyber range automation overview with a case study of CRATE. In: Asplund M, Nadjm-Tehrani S (eds) Secure IT systems. Springer International Publishing, Cham, pp 192–209. https://doi.org/10.1007/978-3-030-70852-8_12
22. IBM: IBM X-Force cyber range. https://www.ibm.com/services/xforce-cyber-range. Accessed 1 July 2024
23. Immersive Labs: cyber team sim: cyber range exercising. https://www.immersivelabs.com/platform/cyber-team-sim/. Accessed 1 July 2024

24. Immersive Labs: Lab content catalogs. https://immersivelabs.zendesk.com/hc/en-us/categories/12462363480465-Lab-Content-Catalogs. Accessed 30 Aug 2024
25. Information-Technology Promotion Agency (IPA): Industrial cyber security center of excellence ICSCoE. https://www.ipa.go.jp/en/about/org/icscoe/index.html. Accessed 1 July 2024
26. Jyväskylä Security Technology (JYVSECTEC): cyber range. https://jyvsectec.fi/cyber-range/overview/. Accessed 1 July 2024
27. Jyväskylä Security Technology (JYVSECTEC): healthcare cyber range (HCCR). https://jyvsectec.fi/healthcare/. Accessed 1 July 2024
28. Karjalainen M, Kokkonen T (2020) Comprehensive cyber arena; the next generation cyber range. In: 2020 IEEE European symposium on security and privacy workshops (EuroS&PW), pp 11–16. https://doi.org/10.1109/EuroSPW51379.2020.00011
29. Keysight Technologies, Inc.: Keysight cyber range. https://www.keysight.com/us/en/products/network-test/cyber-range-services.html. Accessed 1 July 2024
30. Kokkonen T, Hämäläinen T, Silokunnas M, Siltanen J, Zolotukhin M, Neijonen M (2015) Analysis of approaches to Internet traffic generation for cyber security research and exercise. In: Balandin S, Andreev S, Koucheryavy Y (eds) Internet of things, smart spaces, and next generation networks and systems. Springer International Publishing, Cham, pp 254–267. https://doi.org/10.1007/978-3-319-23126-6_23
31. Le TD, Anwar A, Loke SW, Beuran R, Tan Y (2020) GridAttackSim: a cyber attack simulation framework for smart grids. Electronics 9(8). https://doi.org/10.3390/electronics9081218
32. Le TD, Ge M, Anwar A, Loke SW, Beuran R, Doss R, Tan Y (2022) GridAttackAnalyzer: a cyber attack analysis framework for smart grids. Sensors 22(13). https://doi.org/10.3390/s22134795
33. Le TD, Thanh Nguyen HP, Huynh KT, Beuran R (2022) Smart grid cyber-attack analysis and countermeasures. In: 2022 RIVF international conference on computing and communication technologies (RIVF), pp 590–595. https://doi.org/10.1109/RIVF55975.2022.10013873
34. Leitner M, Frank M, Hotwagner W, Langner G, Maurhart O, Pahi T, Reuter L, Skopik F, Smith P, Warum M (2021) AIT cyber range: flexible cyber security environment for exercises, training and research. In: Proceedings of the 2020 European interdisciplinary cybersecurity conference, pp 1–6. https://doi.org/10.1145/3424954.3424959
35. Luo B, Beuran R, Tan Y (2020) Smart grid security: attack modeling from a CPS perspective. In: 2020 IEEE computing, communications and IoT applications (ComComAp), pp 1–6. https://doi.org/10.1109/ComComAp51192.2020.9398878
36. Masaryk University: KYPO cyber range platform. https://crp.kypo.muni.cz. Accessed 1 July 2024
37. National Institute of Standards and Technology (NIST): the cyber range: a guide (2023). https://www.nist.gov/document/cyber-range. Accessed 1 July 2024
38. Naval Air Systems Command: Navy unveils new national cyber range to bolster defense cybersecurity. https://www.navair.navy.mil/news/Navy-unveils-new-national-cyber-range-bolster-defense-cybersecurity/Mon-10162023-1509. Accessed 1 July 2024
39. Nock O, Starkey J, Angelopoulos CM (2020) Addressing the security gap in IoT: towards an IoT cyber range. Sensors 20(18). https://doi.org/10.3390/s20185439
40. Petersen R, Santos D, Wetzel KA, Smith MC, Witte G (2020) Workforce framework for cybersecurity (NICE framework), NIST special publication 800-181 revision 1. https://doi.org/10.6028/NIST.SP.800-181r1
41. Rebecchi F, Pastor A, Mozo A, Lombardo C, Bruschi R, Aliferis I, Doriguzzi-Corin R, Gouvas P, Alvarez Romero A, Angelogianni A, Politis I, Xenakis C (2022) A digital twin for the 5G era: the SPIDER cyber range. In: 2022 IEEE 23rd international symposium on a world of wireless, mobile and multimedia networks (WoWMoM), pp 567–572. https://doi.org/10.1109/WoWMoM54355.2022.00088
42. RHEA System S.A.: next generation cyber-range services. https://www.rheagroup.com/services-solutions/security/cybersecurity/cyber-range/. Accessed 1 July 2024
43. SANS Institute: SANS cyber ranges. https://www.sans.org/cyber-ranges/. Accessed 1 July 2024

44. Silensec: CYBER RANGES. https://www.cyberranges.com/. Accessed 1 July 2024
45. Simulation Training and Instrumentation Organization: National cyber range (NCR). https://www.peostri.army.mil/national-cyber-range-ncr. Accessed 1 July 2024
46. Soteria: Soteria ARENA. https://www.soteria-int.com/product_arena/. Accessed 1 July 2024
47. Swedish Defence Research Agency (FOI): CRATE—Sweden's national cyber training facility. https://www.foi.se/en/foi/research/information-security/crate---swedens-national-cyber-training-facility.html. Accessed 1 July 2024
48. Tate E (2017) Regent University opens stand-alone cyber range. https://edscoop.com/regent-university-opens-stand-alone-cyber-range/. Accessed 1 July 2024
49. Ukwandu E, Farah MAB, Hindy H, Brosset D, Kavallieros D, Atkinson R, Tachtatzis C, Bures M, Andonovic I, Bellekens X (2020) A review of cyber-ranges and test-beds: current and future trends. Sensors 20(24):7148. https://doi.org/10.3390/s20247148
50. University of Michigan-Flint: cybersecurity training center. https://cybersecurityumflint.com/. Accessed 1 July 2024
51. University of West Florida: Florida cyber range. https://uwf.edu/centers/center-for-cybersecurity/florida-cyber-range/. Accessed 1 July 2024
52. Virginia cyber range. https://www.virginiacyberrange.org/. Accessed 1 July 2024
53. Virginia Polytechnic Institute and State University: U.S. cyber range. https://www.uscyberrange.org/. Accessed 1 July 2024
54. Vykopal J, Čeleda P, Seda P, Švábenský V, Tovarňák D (2021) Scalable learning environments for teaching cybersecurity hands-on. In: 2021 IEEE frontiers in education conference (FIE), pp 1–9. https://doi.org/10.1109/FIE49875.2021.9637180
55. Wang J (2019) IoT training system using the Cooja network simulator. Master's thesis. Japan Advanced Institute of Science and Technology
56. Yamin MM, Katt B, Gkioulos V (2020) Cyber ranges and security testbeds: scenarios, functions, tools and architecture. Comput Secur 88:101636. https://doi.org/10.1016/j.cose.2019.101636
57. Zhao M (2019) Hands-on IoT security training using IoT testbeds. Master's thesis. Japan Advanced Institute of Science and Technology

Chapter 12
Detailed Case Study: CyTrONE

This chapter presents a detailed case study on the cybersecurity training framework named CyTrONE. An overview of the framework is given first, explaining the key details of its architecture. The training content and training environment representation are analyzed next, examining the corresponding representation syntax, and several illustrative examples for each case. Lastly, the most important lessons learned from designing and implementing CyTrONE are reviewed, which are intended to serve as a reference for future training platform developers.

12.1 Motivation and Target

So far, in Part II of this book, we have discussed cybersecurity training platforms in general in Chap. 9, and we have reviewed a selection of CTF and cyber range platforms in Chaps. 10 and 11, respectively.

As a complement to those discussions, in this chapter we will examine in detail a particular cybersecurity training platform, CyTrONE [4]. The goal of this extensive case study is to illustrate possible manners of addressing the following two issues:

1. How to design a cybersecurity training platform in order to achieve the functionality needed in order to meet various training goals and requirements?
2. How to implement the key capabilities of a training platform, namely the training content and training environment, in a flexible and powerful way?

The reasons why CyTrONE was selected as the target of this detailed case study are as follows. First of all, CyTrONE is a full-fledged cybersecurity training platform, having a wide variety of capabilities that cover all the feature categories that training platforms need. Moreover, we were closely involved in its design and implementation by the Cyber Range Organization and Design chair at Japan Advanced Institute of

© The Author(s), under exclusive license to Springer Nature Singapore Pte Ltd. 2025
R. Beuran, *Cybersecurity Education and Training*,
https://doi.org/10.1007/978-981-96-0555-2_12

Science and Technology. This in-depth connection makes it possible to present a thorough analysis of the design and implementation of CyTrONE to our readers.

Given the scope of this chapter, we consider that it is mostly relevant to training organizers, who will find clear illustrations of possible manners of addressing the aforementioned issues. Nevertheless, advanced trainees who are curious about the ways in which the various features of a training platform can be implemented may find it of interest as well.

12.2   Framework Overview

CyTrONE is an integrated cybersecurity training framework that was designed as a flexible and comprehensive solution for cybersecurity training [4]. The framework is intended as a versatile answer to the two main challenges that are related to the implementation of cybersecurity training platforms, which are:

1. Representing the training content in a flexible way that also makes it possible to update and manage it in an easy manner.
2. Representing the training environment in a way that is powerful enough, while allowing for easy updates and management.

In what follows, we will first introduce the general architecture of CyTrONE, and illustrate how it can be mapped onto the training platform model discussed in Sect. 9.1. Then, we will describe in more detail the approaches used to address each of the aforementioned challenges.

12.2.1   CyTrONE Architecture

CyTrONE was designed with a modular architecture that makes it possible to replace or add components as needed, contributing to the flexibility of the framework. The overall architecture of CyTrONE is pictured in Fig. 12.1. Next, we will briefly examine each framework component by following the left-to-right order of the components in the figure, namely:

- Web UI.
- CyTrONE.
- Training Database.
- Training Content.
- CyLMS.
- Moodle LMS.
- CyPROM.
- CyRIS.
- Cyber Range.

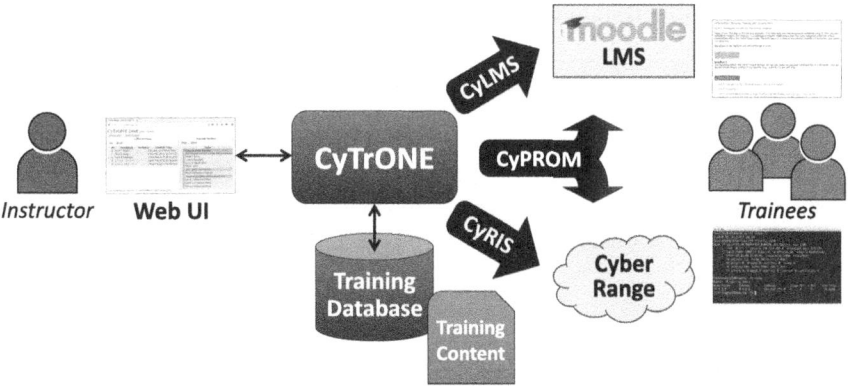

Fig. 12.1 Overall architecture of the integrated cybersecurity training framework CyTrONE

12.2.1.1 Web UI

The web user interface (UI) component of the framework is primarily targeted at instructors and makes it possible for them to control the execution of CyTrONE. The Web UI has two main functions currently:

- Create a training activity based on training content representations stored in the training database; the number of trainees/teams must be specified at this point, so that the framework knows how many replicas of the corresponding training environment should be created.
- End an ongoing training activity by removing the associated training content from the Learning Management System (LMS) and destroying all the training environment instances associated to that activity.

12.2.1.2 CyTrONE

The module called CyTrONE, which also gives the training framework its name, serves as a general management module for the entire framework. This is achieved via several key functions, as follows:

- Mediate the interactions between users and the framework, either via the command line or via the web user interface.
- Control the other framework modules, namely CyLMS, CyRIS, and CyPROM.
- Retrieve from the training database the training content and corresponding training environment representation for a particular training activity.

12.2.1.3   Training Database

The Training Database component of the framework mainly stores the training content, and all the files associated to it, as it will be described in the next section.

In addition, several auxiliary configuration files are stored, which provide the information needed for each instructor to be able to access the framework UI and create training activities. This includes usernames and passwords, details about the servers that are to be used for cyber range creation, etc.

12.2.1.4   Training Content

The Training Content component of CyTrONE refers to three main types of information that are needed to create training activities, as follows:

- Training content representation: The tasks that participants must address during a given training activity.
- Training environment description: The composition of the training environment that participants must use in order to address those tasks.
- Auxiliary files: Any other files that are required to conduct the training, such as images that are to be displayed in the LMS, binary files, and scripts needed to set up the training environment.

The CyTrONE training content representation, its specific syntax, and several illustrative examples will be discussed in Sect. 12.3. Similarly, the training environment description syntax and examples will be presented in Sect. 12.4.

12.2.1.5   CyLMS

The module named CyLMS serves as a control module for the LMS that in the architecture of CyTrONE plays the role of interface with the trainees [5], more specifically the Moodle LMS. The main functions of CyLMS are as follows:

- Register the training content in the LMS, so that trainees can access the tasks they were assigned for the training activity.
- Remove the training content from the LMS when the training activity ends.

Note that the SCORM format for e-learning content representation [1] is used in CyLMS for allowing it to seamlessly import training content into Moodle, without the need for Moodle-specific customizations. This makes it possible, in principle, to integrate CyLMS with a different LMS with only a minimal implementation effort.

12.2.1.6 Moodle LMS

Moodle is one of the most widely used LMSs, with almost 50 million courses being currently available [10]. Consequently, many participants have already experienced using Moodle before conducting a training via CyTrONE, which facilitates their adaptation to the user interface. Due to these considerations, we have selected Moodle as training UI in CyTrONE, where it plays several roles:

- Make it possible for trainees to access the training content for any of the available training sessions.
- Allow trainees to submit answers for the challenges they solved, and check the correctness of their answers.
- Let instructors manage which trainees are allowed to access training activities and to check their training results.

12.2.1.7 CyPROM

The module called CyPROM enhances the functionality of CyTrONE via a feature named *scenario progression*. This feature makes it possible to orchestrate training activities in which the training environment is changing in a dynamic manner, making the training more realistic [2].

The main function of CyPROM is to manage the scenario progression for each training environment instance independently, according to the actions of each trainee, and the ever-changing state of their environment. This function is achieved via three types of scenario elements:

- Triggers: Timers and signals that make it possible to trigger specific actions in a scenario after a time interval passed, or based on predefined events.
- Actions: Operations to be executed in a training environment; the actions can be related to the interaction with the trainees, such as displaying messages, hints, or questions, or can be related to security operations, such as conducting specific attacks in the target environment.
- Branching: Mechanism for taking decisions regarding which scenario action should be executed next based on the outcome of the previous action.

Most CyPROM actions are executed directly in the cyber range, as needed in order to dynamically change the state of the environment depending on the current place in the predefined training scenario. However, those elements that are related to the interaction with trainees can also be displayed via the LMS interface.

12.2.1.8 CyRIS

CyRIS is a key component of the CyTrONE framework, being in charge of auto-matically creating cyber ranges based on specific descriptions [3]. The cyber range creation process is composed of the following three stages:

1. Base VM preparation: This refers to preparing virtual machine (VM) images made available in advance so that they are ready for the next stage. For this purpose, the disk images are first copied into the working directory, and the corresponding VMs are started. Then, the basic setup of the VMs is conducted, such as configuring access via SSH and setting up the hostname and network interfaces.
2. Content installation: This stage sets up the content of the cyber range VMs according to the cyber range description file via two types of processes:

   a. Environment setup operations: Managing user accounts, installing any spec-ified software, copying any required files, executing programs or scripts as needed for custom setup, configuring the network settings, etc.
   b. Security-related operations: Configuring the firewall, starting emulated mal-ware, executing emulated cyberattack actions, capturing network traffic, etc.

3. Guest VM cloning: The final stage consists in creating clones of the prepared VMs in order to start multiple instances of the same cyber range environment for multiple trainees or teams of trainees. This is done by copying first the configured base images to all the servers on which the cyber range is to be instantiated. The cloned VM instances are then started, and user accounts and passwords for accessing each cyber range instance are set up. In addition, the subnets made of cloned VMs are configured according to the cyber range description.

12.2.1.9 Cyber Range

The cyber range shown in Fig. 12.1 denotes the training environment in which the training activity takes place. When using CyTrONE, one cyber range instance is created for each participant or team by using CyRIS, as discussed above. The number of instances to be created is decided by the instructor when starting the training activity, and the actual composition of each instance is based on the cyber range description file that CyRIS receives as input.

The main technology used to create the cyber range is the open-source virtual-ization technology built into the Linux kernel named Kernel-based Virtual Machine (KVM). However, we have also implemented the necessary support to make it pos-sible to deploy cyber ranges in the Amazon AWS EC2 cloud [7]. The available cyber range features, as well as the associated cyber range description format will be discussed in more detail in Sect. 12.4.

12.2.2 Training Platform Model Mapping

By comparing the architecture of CyTrONE shown in Fig. 12.1 with the generic training platform model presented in Fig. 9.1, it is relatively easy to draw a parallel between the two. The details of this mapping, which will be discussed below, demonstrate that the training platform model that we introduced in Chap. 9 is indeed a useful tool for analyzing the architecture of any specific training platform, and for understanding how its functionality maps onto the model in order to better ascertain the role of its components.

12.2.2.1 Model Mapping Details

In what follows, we will present in detail the result of the training platform model mapping for the case of CyTrONE. For each of the model components defined in Sect. 9.1.2, the module or modules that correspond to it in the CyTrONE architecture that was introduced in Sect. 12.2.1 will be indicated, with their names emphasized as bold text for clarity. Similarly to what we did when defining the training platform model, we will distinguish between the core components of the model and the support ones.

Core Components The mapping of the core components of the training platform model with respect to the corresponding CyTrONE modules is as follows:

- Training Manager: Overall management functionality is handled by the **CyTrONE** module of the framework, with support from the **CyLMS**, **CyPROM**, and **CyRIS** modules for specific functions.
- Data Storage: This model component is equivalent to the **Training Database** element in CyTrONE.
- Training Content: This model component corresponds to the homonymous **Training Content** element in CyTrONE.
- Training Environment: This model component is equivalent to the **Cyber Range** element in CyTrONE.

Support Components As for the support components of the training platform model, their mapping to CyTrONE components is presented below:

- Portal: This functionality is split in CyTrONE between the **Web UI** for instructors to manage the training activity, and the **Moodle LMS** component for trainees to conduct the training, and instructors to check their progress.
- Education Functions: This functionality is entirely delegated to the **Moodle LMS** component of the framework.
- Monitoring: The equivalent of this functionality is handled by the **CyPROM** module in CyTrONE.

12.2.2.2   Design Decision Insights

The model mapping that we conducted above helped emphasize two specific design decisions in CyTrONE whose significance we will discuss next. This is another role that training platform model mapping can play, as the insights gained illustrate the thought process behind a given platform design. These insights can also assist with decisions regarding the implementation of a new training platform, or with respect to planned extensions of an existing one.

Modular Architecture The training management functionality in CyTrONE is split between several modules, in accordance with the modular architecture paradigm of the framework that we mentioned previously. This makes it possible to separate the framework module functionality in order to make the source code easier to understand and facilitate extensions when needed.

However, the CyTrONE modules are not just logical components, they are actually standalone modules that can also be used independently. For example, it is possible to use CyRIS to create a cyber range environment, while using completely different components as Portal and Education Functions, or even completely omitting those components for a leaner execution, depending on the organizer requirements. The implications of the modular architecture of CyTrONE will be discussed in more detail in Sect. 12.5.1.

Moodle LMS Reliance As indicated in the above mapping, Moodle LMS is used both as Portal in CyTrONE, mainly with regard to trainees, as well as for the Education Functions aspect. The main advantage of this decision is that CyTrONE can leverage the wide variety of capabilities of Moodle, with the only development effort being related to the implementation of the communication between the framework and the LMS. Moreover, since Moodle is very well known, many trainees are already accustomed to it; hence, the amount of effort required to get used to the CyTrONE UI is minimal in many cases.

On the other hand, not having a fully custom solution may limit sometimes the decisions regarding user interface aspects. If a desired feature is not already provided, it can only be added by modifying the source code of Moodle, which is a relatively complex task (however, not impossible, given the open-source nature of Moodle). Nevertheless, we consider that the advantages outlined above surpass these issues for most circumstances related to cybersecurity training. The implications of the reliance on Moodle LMS will be detailed in Sect. 12.5.2.

12.3   CyTrONE Training Content

The training content is used to define the details of training activities. Therefore, the manner in which it is represented has a significant impact on the usability of a training platform. In what follows, we will first explain training content representation in CyTrONE, then we will discuss several training content samples that illustrate how the representation format can be used in practice. Note that in this section we will focus on those aspects related to the tasks provided to trainees; everything related to the training environment will be examined later in Sect. 12.4.

12.3.1 Training Content Representation

CyTrONE training content is represented in a text-based format that is easy to read and modify, as it will be discussed next. The training content representation syntax will also be introduced to indicate how specific training content elements can be represented in practice.

12.3.1.1 Representation Overview

In CyTrONE, training content is represented using the YAML data serialization language, which was selected due to the various advantages it presents. An example will also be shown below for illustration purposes.

YAML Advantages Using YAML as representation format has several advantages in regard to training platform development, as follows (for a more detailed discussion, see Sect. 12.5.3):

- Human and machine readable: The most important aspect of YAML is that files using this representation format can be easily read and modified by people, while in the same time, YAML files can also be easily processed via software libraries, both for reading and writing. This facilitates content creation tasks for instructors, as well as internal file handling by the platform.
- Easy to compare files: Since YAML uses a text-based representation, two YAML files can easily be compared to examine their differences. This is very useful in relation with training content creation, as one can clearly determine how the training content was changed between two content versions.
- Support for comments: Comments can be included in YAML files to explain the meaning of certain syntax elements. These comments can be referred to by content creators when updating or extending the training content, so that content creation based on existing files becomes easier.

Representation Example As an example of CyTrONE training content representation, we present in Fig. 12.2 an excerpt of an actual training content file. This excerpt originates from a sample file included in the CyTrONE distribution released on GitHub [8], namely `database/NIST-level1-content-en.yml`.

The sample training content representation file defines a training activity inspired by the U.S. NIST *Technical Guide to Information Security Testing and Assessment* [11]. For this activity, the trainees are asked to investigate the security of a desktop computer, the training activity consisting in a total of ten tasks. The first

```
1     ---
2     - training:
3       - id: NIST-L1-EN
4         title: Investigate the security of a desktop computer
5         overview: >
6           <p>Today is your first day on the job as a sysadmin. Your boss
7               tells you that he suspects somebody tried to hack into your
8               company's network, and asks you to investigate a possible
9               cyberattack that may have happened when the system
10              administrator was a guy called Daniel Craig. The boss sits
11              you in front of the previous sysadmin's computer, and wishes
12              you good luck.</p>
13          <p>You glance at the machine and reluctantly get to work.</p>
14        level: 1
15
16        questions:
17        - id: L1-EN-001
18          body: The operating system and kernel release number can tell you
19                about the possible vulnerabilities of a computer. Find out
20                the full kernel release number of the machine (e.g.,
21                3.4.5-6.7.8.abc.x86_64).
22          answer: 3.10.0-957.12.2.el7.x86_64
23          hints:
24          - You can use the command <code>uname</code> to find out OS details.
25          - $ uname -r
26          - An alternative solution is to get the required information from
27            the <code>/proc/version</code> file.
28          ...
```

Fig. 12.2 Excerpt from a CyTrONE training content representation file

task is included in the excerpt, and it is related to determining information about the operating system kernel of a target machine. The representation syntax will be described in the next section, and this particular description file will be introduced in more detail later in Sect. 12.3.2.1.

12.3.1.2 Representation Syntax

In what follows, we will provide an overview of the training content representation syntax in CyTrONE. Note that we only included here those syntax elements that are necessary to understand the training content representation sample shown in Fig. 12.2, which will be used as a reference to explain how this syntax is used in practice. The CyTrONE User Guide should be consulted for information on the complete representation syntax [8].

The first part of the training content representation file provides an overall description of the training activity, which is followed by a list of questions that the trainees must address, as explained next.

Table 12.1 Overview of training content representation syntax for the training description

Element	Meaning
id	Identifier for the training activity
title	Title of the training activity
overview	Detailed description of the training activity
level	Optional label for the training activity sequence/difficulty
questions	List of questions or tasks that are to be solved by trainees

Table 12.2 Overview of training content representation syntax for the question description

Element	Meaning
id	Identifier of the question/task
body	Explanation of the question/task to be addressed
answer	Correct solution for the question/task
hints	Optional hints to assist trainees

Training Description Training content definition in CyTrONE requires that information about the training activity is provided first by following the syntax summarized in Table 12.1. The function of each syntax element is as follows:

- id: Identifier of the training activity, which is displayed in the Moodle LMS for easy reference, but is also used internally to manage the training database.
- title: Short description of the training activity that is displayed as activity title in the Moodle LMS user interface.
- overview: Detailed description of the training activity that provides the background for trainees to understand the tasks that follow. It plays a particularly important role when using gamified content, as it establishes the necessary background story (see lines 5–13 in Fig. 12.2). HTML code can be used within this element for text formatting, and even to include images in the description.
- level: Optional label that is used to identify their order for training activities that are part of a series; this label can also be used as an indication of the difficulty level of an activity.
- questions: List of questions or tasks that the trainees must address; each question is represented using the syntax explained below.

Question Description For each question that trainees must answer or task that they must solve, detailed information about that question or task must be provided in CyTrONE according to the syntax summarized in Table 12.2. The meaning of the syntax elements used to define questions is as follows:

- id: Identifier of the question; this is currently used only internally to refer to that question for processing purposes.
- body: Explanation of the question/task to be addressed, which should provide enough information so that trainees can attempt to solve it (see lines 18–21 in Fig. 12.2). HTML code can be used within this element for text formatting purposes, for instance, in order to highlight some keywords.
- answer: Correct solution for the question/task; this information is used only internally to check whether the answer provided by a trainee is correct or not.
- hints: Optional hints to assist those trainees who encounter troubles solving the corresponding question/task; multiple hints can be provided for one question (see lines 23–27 in Fig. 12.2). Depending on the goal of the training, the hints can be very specific or vague; hints can be even omitted if the training is conducted for trainee examination purposes. HTML code can be used in hints for text formatting, e.g., in order to emphasize command names.

Multiple blocks composed of the above syntax elements can be included in order to have an arbitrary number of questions in a training activity. While not discussed here, it is also possible to include multiple-choice questions in the training content, as well as multiple correct solutions for a question.

12.3.1.3 Representation Processing

The processing flow of the training content representation discussed so far involves mainly the sequence of steps explained below.

1. CyTrONE reads the training content representation file from the training database and sends it to CyLMS.
2. CyLMS processes the representation file and converts it to SCORM format.
3. Then, CyLMS creates a new activity in the Moodle LMS, which employs the SCORM format file as its content.

The most complex step in this workflow is step 2, as it requires parsing the representation format and converting it to the specific syntax used by SCORM. This step is very important in our framework, as it makes it possible to leverage the overall functionality of Moodle, and it isolates the internal representation syntax of CyTrONE from that of SCORM.

Note that the workflow presented above is relatively generic. Based on the same paradigm, a conversion to representation formats different than SCORM that may be specific to other LMSs is possible. However, the relative universality of SCORM makes this unnecessary, in principle. Moreover, the only step in the workflow that would need to be modified if another SCORM-compatible LMS is used in step 3, which is Moodle dependent.

12.3.2   Training Content Examples

Now that we have seen how the training content is represented in CyTrONE, we will discuss two sets of training content that we developed for this framework by using two different content creation perspectives. These two sets of training content are available for download free of charge on the Cyber Range Organization and Design (CROND) web page [9].

In addition to illustrating the general characteristics of cybersecurity training content, and the capabilities of CyTrONE, this discussion will also illustrate how the concepts we have discussed in Sect. 9.2 can be put into practice when designing training content for two typical use cases.

- Gamified training content.
- CTF-style training content.

12.3.2.1   Gamified Training Content

The first training content set that we will introduce uses a gamified approach to make the training activity more enjoyable. In particular, a role-playing scenario is used that has trainees assume the role of a newly appointed system administrator who needs to investigate a possible cybersecurity incident, followed by an assessment of the company's network security.

Content Overview The tasks included in this training set are inspired by the U.S. NIST *Technical Guide to Information Security Testing and Assessment* discussed in Sect. 4.3.2.1. Each task was designed to make it possible for trainees to practice one of the techniques mentioned in that guide. This design principle enables organizers to make sure that they cover all the necessary techniques related to a given goal, such as security testing and assessment in this case. Other guidelines that we examined in the context of attack, forensics, and defense training could be used in a similar manner to design training content that is well targeted and effective.

The content we created is organized into two sections that we named *levels*, so as to emphasize the gamification approach. Thus, the training activity starts with easier tasks for *Level 1*, and continues with more challenging ones for *Level 2*. The training content includes a total of 20 questions that provide an almost complete coverage of the types of techniques mentioned in the NIST guideline. An overview of the two levels is presented in Table 12.3, which also shows the task count per level; a more detailed description of each level follows.

Level 1 The first level of the gamified training content entrusts a new system administrator with the task of investigating a suspected cybersecurity incident that may have occurred recently. The story for this gamified scenario is conveyed to trainees in the description of the level, which is shown below.

Table 12.3 Overview of the gamified training content set created for CyTrONE

Name	Level description	Count
Level 1	As the new sysadmin of a company, you are asked to investigate a suspected cybersecurity incident	10
Level 2	As a follow-up assignment, you are now tasked with assessing the security of the company network	10

Table 12.4 Overview of the *Level 1* tasks in the gamified training content set

Id	Task description	NIST assessment technique
1	Retrieve information about the OS kernel	System Configuration Review
2	Determine the IP address of a computer	Network Discovery
3	Determine the IP address of the gateway	Network Discovery
4	Identify the name of a user account	System Configuration Review
5	Review unsuccessful login attempts	Log Review
6	Use a simple password guessing method	Password Cracking
7	Check the settings in the sudoers file	System Configuration Review
8	Identify the origin of an attempted intrusion	Network Sniffing
9	Find out an open port number	Network Port and Service Identification
10	Identify the name of a suspicions program	Vulnerability Scanning

Today is your first day on the job as a sysadmin. Your boss tells you that he suspects somebody tried to hack into your company's network, and asks you to investigate a possible cyberattack that may have happened when the system administrator was a guy called Daniel Craig. The boss sits you in front of the previous sysadmin's computer, and wishes you good luck.

To finish this assignment, trainees must answer a sequence of 10 questions that are ordered according to best practices for incident investigation. Answering each question makes it possible to move forward through the assignment, hence their order is also important from this point of view.

For illustration purposes, the tasks in this level are summarized in Table 12.4, which also indicates the corresponding NIST assessment technique for each task.

The tasks are designed to cover several important security assessment techniques from the NIST guideline technique categories named *Review Techniques* and *Target Identification and Analysis Techniques*, such as configuration review, log review, network discovery, and vulnerability scanning. Given that this level is considered to be an introductory one, only a single task in the higher-risk category *Target Vulnerability Validation Techniques* is included, namely password cracking.

Level 2 The second level of the gamified training content set is a continuation of the first level, and it tasks the participants, who are assuming the same role of system administrator, with assessing the security of their company's network. The description of this gamified scenario, as displayed to trainees in the Moodle interface, is shown below.

> Your boss invites you to his office and congratulates you for your achievements so far. He says he has a new task for you: investigating the security of the company network.
>
> You would have preferred to have a break—or even a short holiday—after completing your previous assignment, but security issues are not something that can wait, so you get back to your desk and start working again.

This level too presents a sequence of 10 questions that the trainees must answer. As before, the tasks are ordered according to best practice considerations, and solving them in order allows participants to advance through the assignment.

Some of the questions in *Level 2* cover the *Review Techniques* and *Target Identification and Analysis Techniques* NIST guideline categories, such as ruleset review, documentation review, network sniffing, and wireless scanning. However, this level is targeting more advanced techniques as well, namely in the *Target Vulnerability Validation Techniques* category. Applying these techniques, such as password cracking, penetration testing, and even social engineering, makes it possible for trainees to have an experience similar to an actual pentesting engagement.

12.3.2.2   CTF-Style Training Content

The second set of training content created for CyTrONE was designed in the style of CTF competition content. Note that the details that we provide below correspond to v1.1 of this training content set.

Content Overview As it is typical for CTF content, the challenges in this training set are organized in several categories, namely *Binary*, *Crypto*, *Network*, *OS*, and *Web*. The training content is provided both in English and Japanese, and the total number of challenges included in this set is 38. A summary of each content category is presented in Table 12.5, including the number of challenges in each of them; additional details about each category are discussed next.

Binary This category includes challenges related to the analysis of binary files. Some of the provided binary files are executable programs that contain flags embedded in the machine code representation. The other ones are a variety of non-executable files, such as images and archives. To solve such challenges related to binary files, trainees

Table 12.5 Overview of the CTF-style training content set created for CyTrONE

Name	Category description	Count
Binary	Analyze executable and non-executable binary files	7
Crypto	Decipher messages encoded with various techniques	8
Network	Investigate network traffic and network services	8
OS	Practice the use of OS management and utility commands	7
Web	Exploit various types of web server vulnerabilities	8

must examine their content, determine their type, attempt to execute the files, modify them as needed, try to decompress them, etc.

Crypto The challenges in this category task trainees with deciphering messages that have been encoded using various encryption techniques. For some challenges, very basic techniques are used, such as the Caesar cipher. However, most challenges require trainees to use tools such as `openssl`, to attempt brute-force cracking, use knowledge of standard ciphers and algorithms (e.g., RSA), interact with web servers that provide encryption services and try to crack them, and so on.

Network In this category are included challenges related to network protocols and services. Some of the challenges require trainees to examine the content of the provided network packet capture files by using network analysis tools to investigate the content of protocols such as SMTP, FTP, and DNS. For other challenges, trainees must interact with various network services and try to obtain the flags by using techniques such as port knocking or even Denial of Service (DoS) attacks.

OS In order to let trainees practice the use of typical operating system commands, we have created several specific challenges in this category. Some of the challenges require knowledge of OS management commands, such as `ps`, top, `netstat`, and so on. Other challenges require abilities regarding various OS utility commands, such as `cat`, grep, and `file`.

Web This category includes challenges related to attack techniques that can be used to target web servers. The techniques that trainees must master to be able to solve some of the challenges are relatively standard, such as Cross-Site Scripting (XSS), SQL injection, and directory traversal. However, several challenges require deeper knowledge about web technologies, such as JavaScript, HTTP, PHP, and so on. Since the skills required to address the challenges in this category are the most advanced among those in the CTF-style training content set, we provide a summary of all the *Web* category challenges in Table 12.6 for illustration purposes.

Table 12.6 Overview of the *Web* category challenges in the CTF-style training content set

Id	Challenge description
1	Exploit a web server with an XSS vulnerability
2	Exploit a web server with a directory traversal vulnerability
3	Learn about the robots exclusion protocol (REP)
4	Exploit a JavaScript vulnerability in a login page
5	Learn about the HTTP basic access authentication protocol
6	Exploit a vulnerability in the code of an HTML form
7	Perform an SQL injection attack on a web server
8	Exploit a vulnerability in an insecure PHP application

12.4 CyTrONE Training Environment

For CyTrONE, the term *cyber range* is used to denote the training environment used in the framework. Note that this is a more limited scope in comparison to cyber range platforms, for which it often refers to the entire training system, including education features, etc. However, we will keep the original meaning in our presentation to maintain compatibility with all CyTrONE research papers and documentation.

With this distinction in mind, in what follows, we will examine the manner in which cyber ranges are described in CyTrONE and review several representative cyber range examples.

12.4.1 Cyber Range Description

CyTrONE uses a cyber range description in text format to represent the environment that must be created for a given training activity. The cyber range description in CyTrONE is considered to be one of a pair of files, alongside the training content representation discussed already, that together provide all the information needed to conduct the training activity.

The reason why this information is separated into two distinct files in CyTrONE is that it facilitates the reuse of cyber range descriptions. This is because the same training environment can be used for different training activities, with different associated tasks, depending on goals and circumstances. For instance, one can imagine a set of easy questions with detailed hints for beginners, and a set of more complex questions with minimum hints for more advanced trainees, although both sets of tasks are associated with the same cyber range.

An overview of the CyTrONE cyber range representation format will be discussed next, followed by details of the corresponding file syntax, in order to illustrate how cyber range elements can be represented in practice.

12.4.1.1 Representation Overview

Similar to the way in which training content is represented, the cyber range description also uses YAML as file format. Again this makes it possible to leverage the advantages the YAML format offers, as discussed in connection with the representation of training content in Sect. 12.3.1.1.

As an example of a cyber range representation in CyTrONE, we display in Fig. 12.3 an excerpt of an actual cyber range description file. This excerpt originates from a sample file included in the CyTrONE distribution released on GitHub [8], namely `database/NIST-level1-range.yml`.

The sample cyber range description file that we provided corresponds to the training content inspired by the U.S. NIST *Technical Guide to Information Security Testing and Assessment* [11] mentioned earlier in Sect. 12.3.1. For this activity, trainees are asked to investigate the security of a desktop computer, and this cyber range description file is used to create the virtual machine corresponding to the desktop computer in the training activity.

12.4.1.2 Representation Syntax

In what follows, we will provide an overview of the cyber range representation syntax in CyTrONE. Note that we only included below those syntax elements that are necessary to comprehend the cyber range description sample shown in Fig. 12.3, which will be used as reference to explain how this syntax can be used in practice. The CyTrONE User Guide should be consulted for information on the complete representation syntax [8].

A cyber range description file in CyTrONE is composed of three sections that provide information with regard to the various aspects needed to create the cyber range, namely *host settings*, *guest settings*, and *clone settings*, as explained next.

Host Settings The term *host* is used in CyTrONE to refer to the server on which cyber range instances are to be created. The first section of the cyber range description file, named `host_settings`, includes the settings needed to define information about that host, as summarized in Table 12.7. The syntax elements used in the host settings section have the following functions:

- `id`: Identifier of the host, which is used in the subsequent `guest_settings` and `clone_settings` sections to refer to it.

```
1    ---
2    - host_settings:
3      - id: host_1
4        mgmt_addr: {{ host_mgmt_addr }}
5        virbr_addr: {{ host_virbr_addr }}
6        account: {{ host_account }}
7
8    - guest_settings:
9      - id: desktop
10       basevm_host: host_1
11       basevm_config_file: /home/cyuser/images/basevm.xml
12       basevm_type: kvm
13       tasks:
14       - add_account:
15         - account: daniel
16           passwd: JamesBond
17           full_name: Daniel Craig
18       - install_package:
19         - package_manager: yum
20           name: wireshark
21       - emulate_attack:
22         - attack_type: ssh_attack
23           target_account: daniel
24           attempt_number: 54
25           attack_time: 20170328
26       ...
27
28   - clone_settings:
29     - range_id: {{ clone_range_id }}
30       hosts:
31       - host_id: host_1
32         instance_number: {{ clone_instance_number }}
33         guests:
34         - guest_id: desktop
35           number: 1
36           entry_point: yes
37         topology:
38         - type: custom
39           networks:
40           - name: office
41             members: desktop.eth0
```

Fig. 12.3 Excerpt from a CyTrONE cyber range description file

- mgmt_addr: The network address used for accessing the host in order to deploy the cyber range on it.
- virbr_addr: The network address of the virtual bridge used to access the VMs deployed on a host.
- account: The user account to be used when accessing the host defined in the current block.

Note that multiple hosts can be defined in the host settings section by using a sequence of blocks that follow the above syntax. Moreover, for several settings,

Table 12.7 Overview of the cyber range description syntax for host settings

Element	Meaning
id	Identifier of the defined host
mgmt_addr	Management address of the host
virbr_addr	Virtual bridge for accessing the VMs on the host
account	User account for accessing the host

Table 12.8 Overview of the cyber range description syntax for guest settings

Element	Meaning
id	Identifier for the guest
basevm_host	Host on which the VM base image is stored
basevm_config_file	Configuration file for the VM base image
basevm_type	Type of the VM base image
tasks	List of tasks to be executed for preparing the guest

double curly bracket symbols '{{ }}' are used to denote that the values for those configuration variables are to be filled in by CyTrONE at runtime (see lines 4–6 in Fig. 12.3). This makes it possible to create generic cyber range description files that can be deployed on a variety of servers, with the specific details being filled in directly by CyTrONE when the range is created.

Guest Settings The term *guest* is used in CyTrONE to refer to the VMs that are used to construct a cyber range. The second section of the cyber range description file, named guest_settings, contains the information about all the guests, as summarized in Table 12.8. The meaning of the syntax elements used in the guest settings section is as follows:

- id: Identifier of the guest, which is used in the subsequent clone_settings section to refer to that guest.
- basevm_host: Id of the host on which the VM base image is stored; the VM image will be copied from that host as part of the cyber range creation process.
- basevm_config_file: Configuration file that is used to define the base VM associated to the guest.
- basevm_type: Type of the VM base image, which is used internally to select the correct functions needed during the creation process.
- tasks: List of tasks that must be executed on the guest in order to prepare it for use in the cyber range.

A complete description of task syntax is out of scope for this presentation, but several examples will be provided below. Thus, the tasks that are defined in the example shown in Fig. 12.3 are as follows:

Table 12.9 Overview of the guest configuration tasks supported for guest settings

Task type	Name	Meaning
Account setup	`add_account`	Add user account
	`modify_account`	Modify user account
Incident emulation	`emulate_attack`	Emulate a cyberattack
	`emulate_traffic_capture_file`	Emulate and capture a cyberattack
	`emulate_malware`	Emulate malware symptoms
Program setup	`install_package`	Install a software package
	`copy_content`	Copy a file or directory
	`execute_program`	Execute a script or program
Firewall setup	`firewall_rules`	Configure firewall rules

- `add_account`: Create a user account on the guest with the specified account username, password, and full name.
- `install_package`: Install a package on the guest by using the specified package manager and package name.
- `emulate_attack`: Emulate a cyberattack on the guest, such as an SSH attack. Each attack has its specific parameters, such as target account, number of connections attempts, or the time that should be associated to the attack in the generated PCAP file (see lines 21–25 in Fig. 12.3).

Note that the original cyber range representation file contains several other tasks that were omitted for the sake of brevity, as indicated via the ellipsis symbol '…' appearing on line 26 in the figure. For a summary of all the tasks supported for guest configuration, see the overview presented in Table 12.9, in which they were grouped by task type. By combining these predefined tasks, it is possible to create guests with a wide variety of settings, as described in [4].

Clone Settings The term *cloning* is used in CyTrONE to refer to the creation of multiple cyber range instances from the guest base VMs that were set up according to the guest settings section in the description file. This is achieved in practice by using the disk images of those VMs as *backing files*, a mechanism in the KVM virtualization system that records for every newly created VM only the differences with respect to those files. This makes it possible to create VM copies with effectively the same content as the base VMs in a simple and efficient manner.

The clone settings section of the cyber range description file provides the information needed for the cloning process, as summarized in Table 12.10. The following syntax elements are used to convey this information:

- `range_id`: Identifier of the created cyber range, which is used internally to manage it, such as retrieving the creation information or destroying it.

Table 12.10 Overview of the cyber range description syntax for clone settings

Element	Meaning
range_id	Identifier of the cyber range
hosts	List of hosts on which the cyber range is to be deployed
guests	List of guests that make up the cyber range on each host
topology	Topology for connecting the guests in a cyber range

- hosts: List of hosts on which the cyber range is to be deployed, with each host being identified by its id. The number of cyber range instances to be deployed on each host must also be specified, followed by a list of guests, as described next.
- guests: List of guests that should be included in each cyber range instance. Each guest is identified by its id, and the number of guests of that type must also be specified (see lines 33–36 in Fig. 12.3). The key named entry_point is used to indicate whether a particular guest is to serve as landing point when trainees access the cyber range instance.
- topology: The network topology is used to interconnect the specified guests. Its main component is a list of subnets, with each subnet being given a name and a list of members, which are the network interfaces of the guests that are to be connected to that subnet (see lines 39–41 in Fig. 12.3).

12.4.1.3   Representation Processing

The processing flow for the cyber range representation consists mainly in the following sequence of steps:

1. CyTrONE reads the cyber range description file from the training database, and fills in the values for the configuration variables in that file (see Sect. 12.4.1.2). The values are determined based on the settings corresponding to the instructor creating the cyber range, and the creation command received via the UI.
2. CyTrONE then sends the standalone cyber range description file to CyRIS.
3. CyRIS uses the received description file to create a cyber range with the guest composition and number of instances specified in that file.

Step 1 in the workflow above is critical to ensure that cyber range description files can be prepared in advance in an agnostic manner and can be used independently by several cyber range creators who share the same platform. This is because different settings regarding the deployment hosts and accounts can be associated to each instructor in the CyTrONE database. Moreover, the number of cyber range instances to be created is configured at runtime via the CyTrONE UI.

The creation of the actual cyber range at step 3 is the most complicated step in the processing flow we described. However, since this functionality is delegated to the CyRIS module, the corresponding functionality in the CyTrONE management module can be kept lightweight. Nevertheless, we can clearly state that CyRIS is the most complex module of the framework, and its implementation represented the most challenging aspect of the entire development process.

12.4.2 Cyber Range Examples

To illustrate the characteristics of CyTrONE cyber ranges, we will discuss two types of cyber ranges that refer to different use cases. These examples will also serve as a reference for the manner in which the concepts discussed in Sect. 9.3 can be put into practice when designing a suitable cybersecurity training environment for the following two typical situations:

- Simple cyber ranges.
- Complex cyber ranges.

12.4.2.1   Simple Cyber Ranges

For a vast majority of cybersecurity training activities, the training environment is relatively simple in terms of network topology, especially for CTF competitions. Often, only a single host needs to be set up, typically as a virtual machine, with all the content required for a relatively small set of challenges. This means that the focus for this type of simple cyber ranges is on training content installation on that VM.

To illustrate how this type of cyber range can be created via CyTrONE we will discuss two simple environments that are associated to the gamified training content sets described in Sect. 12.3.2.1. The actual cyber range description files that serve as a reference for the explanation below are included in the corresponding archive available for download on the CROND web page [9].

One-VM Environment For the first level of the training content set, named *Level 1*, a single guest VM is required for each participant, which CyTrONE needs to deploy. Therefore, the topology of this environment is very basic, as shown in Fig. 12.4a. Thus, the cyber range contains one VM named desktop, which is connected to the office subnet. The key elements that must be defined in this case in the cyber range description file are those guest setup tasks that are needed to prepare the environment, namely:

- Create a user account for the desktop VM.
- Emulate an SSH attack on that user account.
- Capture network traffic in PCAP format for another SSH attack.

office

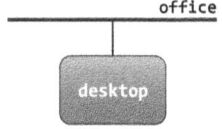

external_servers

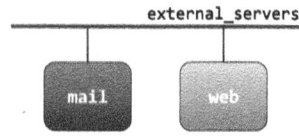

(a) Cyber range with one VM corresponding to the *Level 1* training content

(b) Cyber range with two VMs corresponding to the *Level 2* training content

Fig. 12.4 Simple cyber range examples

- Install the packages `wireshark`, `GeoIP` and `lsof`.
- Emulate a malicious program that leads to an increase in CPU load.

All the above setup actions are required for trainees to be able to solve the questions that are included in the *Level 1* training content representation file. For an example of the actual syntax used in the corresponding cyber range description file to specify the first three of these tasks, please refer to lines 13–25 in Fig. 12.3.

Two-VM Environment The second level of the training content set, named *Level 2*, is slightly more complicated in terms of network topology, since two guest VMs are required to solve the included questions, a mail server and a web server. These two VMs, named `mail` and `web`, respectively, are deployed by CyTrONE according to the topology presented in Fig. 12.4b, where they are both connected to the subnet named `external_servers`. The key aspects to be defined in this case as well are the tasks needed to set up the training environment, as follows:

- Setup of `mail`

  - Create two user accounts, and modify the password for the `root` account.
  - Capture network traffic in PCAP format for an emulated DDoS attack.
  - Install the packages `wireshark` and `nmap`.
  - Copy and execute the script needed to install the password cracking tool John the Ripper, and the Wi-Fi cracker software Aircrack-ng.
  - Copy a Wi-Fi PCAP file that was prepared in advance.
  - Configure the firewall rules for this VM.

- Setup of `web`

  - Modify the password for the `root` account.
  - Install the packages `httpd` and `php`.
  - Copy the necessary resources, and execute a script to set up the web server.
  - Configure the firewall rules for this VM.

The two-VM environment was necessary for this scenario because the questions in the associated training content ask participants to conduct a wider variety of tasks. Thus, several initial tasks are related to the investigation of a possible attack on the mail server. However, other tasks are related to penetration testing activities that are

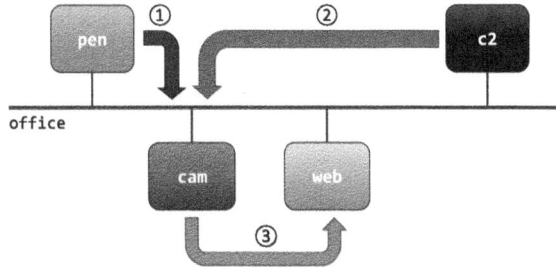

Fig. 12.5 Cyber range for the IP camera scenario

specific to web servers, such as *Local File Inclusion* or *PHP Shell Upload* techniques. In addition, a task related to network discovery must also be completed. For all these reasons, this more complicated two VM environment must be created.

Note that changing the password for the `root` account is generally needed for guest VMs in CyTrONE since the password used in the base VM is predetermined, so as to make possible the initial automatic setup. Modifying the password when the cyber range is created ensures that participants cannot use `root` privileges, even if they are familiar with the predetermined password, as doing that would make solving some of the tasks easier.

12.4.2.2   Realistic Cyber Ranges

For the next two examples, we will present more realistic cyber ranges that have a composition similar to actual company networks. Such cybersecurity training environments are required when organizers intend to place participants in conditions that mimic more closely real-life situations.

IP Camera Scenario The first realistic cyber range example, which uses the network topology shown in Fig. 12.5, is inspired by the content of one of the written tests included in the *Registered Information Security Specialist Examination*[1] conducted by the Information-technology Promotion Agency (IPA) in Japan.

In this scenario, trainees assume the role of pentesters that are tasked with reproducing a security incident that occurred in an organization. To start the training, they need to connect to the pentesting machine, named `pen`, where all the tools needed for the investigation are installed. Then, they have to carry out the following three main steps, which are also depicted in Fig. 12.5 for clarity:

1. Trainees use the pentesting machine `pen` to connect to a guest VM playing the role of an IP camera, named `cam`, via the TELNET protocol, which is the method allegedly employed by attackers in the security incident (step ① in the figure).
2. Next, trainees download an attack tool, `slowhttptest` in this case, from a guest VM that plays the role of a Command and Control (C&C) server, named `c2`, to the `cam` guest VM (step ②).

---

[1] https://www.ipa.go.jp/en/it-examinations/reference.html.

3. Finally, trainees use the downloaded attack tool to conduct an attack on another guest VM representing the web server of the organization, named web (step ③).

The following tasks are used in the cyber range description file to set up the training environment needed to enact the above scenario:

- Setup of pen

  - Install the packages nmap and telnet.
  - Copy and execute a script to install the Metasploit pentesting framework.
  - Modify the password for the root account.

- Setup of cam

  - Install the packages httpd, telnet-server, and wget.
  - Copy and execute scripts to configure all the packages and the firewall.
  - Modify the password for the root account.

- Setup of web

  - Install the package httpd.
  - Copy and execute scripts to configure the httpd package and the firewall.
  - Modify the password for the root account.

- Setup of c2

  - Install the package httpd.
  - Copy and execute scripts to configure the httpd package, the slowhttptest DoS attack tool, as well as the firewall.
  - Modify the password for the root account.

This cyber range example is relevant due to the realism of the training scenario, with a sequence of steps that are inspired by an actual cybersecurity incident. On the other hand, the realism of the cyber range network topology is relatively low, as the topology was simplified for the purposes of the training activity, with all the VMs being connected to a single subnet (even though in reality several internal subnets and an external internet connection would be required).

Company Network Scenario For the second realistic cyber range example, we present a more complex network topology, which mimics that of a company network. As shown in Fig. 12.6, this example uses a firewall to separate the external-facing servers, which are placed in a so-called Demilitarized Zone (DMZ), from the other servers and PCs located in the internal LAN. The following three subnets are used to define the topology for this scenario:

- external: Subnet including servers that are accessible from outside the company, in this case a server providing DNS and email services named dnsmail.

Fig. 12.6 Cyber range for the company network scenario

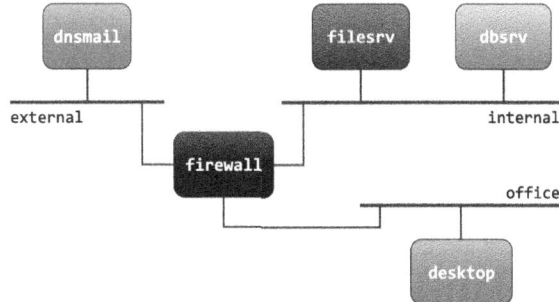

- `internal`: Subnet which contains servers that are accessible only from inside the company, in our scenario a file server and a database server, named `filesrv` and `dbsrv`, respectively.
- `office`: Subnet that includes office computers, which in this scenario are represented by a single machine named `desktop`.

In addition to the four machines mentioned above, the firewall device, named `firewall`, plays a significant role in the described topology. In particular, the firewall allows the machines in the three subnets to connect with each other, while preventing unrelated traffic from the DMZ from reaching the intranet.

The main point of interest of this example scenario is the manner in which such a network topology is represented in the CyTrONE cyber range description file. The excerpt shown in Fig. 12.7 presents the clone settings section of the file that is used to represent the cyber range discussed above.

The excerpt makes it clear how the composition of the cyber range is defined in terms of which guests, and how many of them are to be included, as specified on lines 6–21 in the figure. As for the network communication and topology, the two most notable aspects regarding the custom syntax included in the representation shown in Fig. 12.7 are explained next:

- The element `forwarding_rules` is used to configure the firewall so as to allow access from the `office` subnet to the MySQL database (port 3306) and SMB file server (ports 139 and 445) in the `internal` subnet, as well as the SMTP server (port 25) and DNS service (port 53) in the `external` subnet (see lines 9–12).
- The subsection `networks` is employed to define the actual network topology (see lines 24–33); for example, on lines 28–30, for the `internal` subnet, `filesrv` and `dbsrv` interfaces are connected as subnet members, and the interface `eth1` of the firewall is configured as the gateway for that subnet.

```
1   - clone_settings:
2     - range_id: {{ clone_range_id }}
3       hosts:
4       - host_id: host_1
5         instance_number: {{ clone_instance_number }}
6         guests:
7         - guest_id: firewall
8           number: 1
9           forwarding_rules:
10          - rule: src=office,external dst=internal.dbsrv dport=3306
11          - rule: src=office,external dst=internal.filesrv dport=139,445
12          - rule: src=office dst=external dport=25,53
13          entry_point: yes
14        - guest_id: dnsmail
15          number: 1
16        - guest_id: filesrv
17          number: 1
18        - guest_id: dbsrv
19          number: 1
20        - guest_id: desktop
21          number: 1
22        topology:
23        - type: custom
24          networks:
25          - name: external
26            members: dnsmail.eth0
27            gateway: firewall.eth0
28          - name: internal
29            members: filesrv.eth0, dbsrv.eth0
30            gateway: firewall.eth1
31          - name: office
32            members: desktop.eth0
33            gateway: firewall.eth2
```

Fig. 12.7 Clone settings section of a cyber range description file defining the topology for the company network scenario

12.5 Lessons Learned

The implementation process of the CyTrONE framework and its modules began in 2016, starting with the core component, the cyber range instantiation system CyRIS. During the many years of development, we have understood deeply the positive and negative aspects related to the various design decisions we made, as it will be explained below. We note here that interested readers can also consult [6] for a discussion of lessons learned in the context of cybersecurity training platform development from various perspectives.

12.5.1 Modular Architecture

Let us first discuss our experience with designing and implementing the CyTrONE framework by using a modular architecture. This paradigm signifies that a system is composed of a set of standalone modules that can be developed and tested independently. Therefore, modularity is considered to be one of the key approaches aimed at sound system engineering.

As explained in Sect. 12.2.1, we implemented a total of five software modules in the CyTrONE framework that interact with each other: Web UI as user interface, CyTrONE for overall management, CyLMS for interaction with the LMS, CyRIS for cyber range creation, and CyPROM for dynamic scenario progression management. In addition, the external module Moodle provides LMS functionality to the framework (cf. Fig. 12.1).

12.5.1.1 Advantages

In what follows we will summarize the main advantages that the modular design of CyTrONE had from our perspective.

Function Separation Given that each module of CyTrONE is in charge of functionality that has a limited scope, the design and implementation of each module were done independently and sometimes even in parallel. The only constraints during the development process were related to the interactions between modules. For this purpose, we defined a communication protocol based on the HTTP/HTTPS protocol, which is a highly flexible solution.

Distributed Execution Since the interaction between CyTrONE modules relies on a standard network protocol, it is possible to execute each module in a distributed manner on different servers. This not only makes the architecture more flexible, but also allows distributing the processing load.

This capability is particularly useful for cyber range creation. Thus, when the total number of instances cannot be created on a single server, we have taken advantage of this flexibility to have several CyRIS modules running on multiple hosts, each being in charge of creating cyber range instances on those hosts.

Standalone Module Use Since CyTrONE modules can operate independently of each other, they can also be executed in a standalone manner. Independent testing is one straightforward use of this feature. However, the possibility for training organizers to choose only the module or modules that are necessary for a particular task is another important advantage. Such an approach conveniently reduces the complexity of the setup procedure and also decreases the execution load on the host.

For example, we have heard of a university that used only the CyRIS module of the framework to create a training environment for teaching OS operation skills. In that case, no LMS features were required, with the education tasks being handled directly by the course instructor, hence the simplified setup.

12.5.1.2   Disadvantages

Adopting a modular architecture for CyTrONE also made us realize several disadvantages of this approach, as it will be explained next. Nevertheless, we consider that the advantages greatly exceeded disadvantages in this case; hence, using such a modular architecture was an overall positive decision.

Development Complexity One main issue regarding the development of the standalone modules in CyTrONE is that communication protocols between them had to be designed and implemented, as mentioned above, instead of simply making direct function calls between software modules.

In particular in the beginning of the development process, whenever a new feature that affected module interaction was to be added, the communication protocol implementation had to be updated for both the sending and receiving modules. Fortunately, such changes became less frequent as the implementation matured, when most functionality changes were done internally to the modules.

In addition to the above issue, the possibility of standalone execution of modules also meant that their core features had to be accessible via basic user interfaces, such as command line. This also slightly increased the implementation effort required to develop each module.

User Guide Complexity Making it possible for end users to execute the CyTrONE modules in a standalone manner had another consequence. Thus, each module required a separate user guide to explain its functionality and features. Maintaining the user guides for all the modules and describing the interactions with the other modules (especially in the CyTrONE user guide) are relatively challenging tasks that required careful thinking.

12.5.2   Moodle LMS Reliance

The next CyTrONE feature that we will discuss is its reliance on the Moodle LMS. This refers first of all to the Portal functionality, which is used both by trainees and instructors, but also to the Education Functions aspect, for instructors to follow the progress of trainees, for example (see Sect. 12.2).

12.5.2.1   Advantages

Integrating the Moodle LMS as a CyTrONE component had several advantages from our perspective, as follows.

Rich Capabilities As an LMS that is widely used, and that has been developed for more than 20 years, Moodle has very rich capabilities regarding learning management. Some of these capabilities include user account management, learning activity management, learning activity scoring, score management, etc. Through the integration with the framework, CyTrONE can leverage all those capabilities with a minimum development effort (which is mainly related to the implementation in CyLMS of the communication mechanism with Moodle).

Familiar UI In addition, since Moodle is a very well-known LMS, many instructors and trainees are already familiar with its interface and functions. This means that the amount of effort that is needed for new CyTrONE users to get used to the training UI is minimal in many cases.

SCORM Compatibility The compatibility of Moodle with the generic SCORM format is another important advantage. Since we use SCORM for importing training activities into Moodle, we can say that our framework is not tightly coupled with Moodle, as any other LMS that supports the SCORM format could be integrated with CyTrONE in case a certain organization prefers a different LMS.

12.5.2.2 Disadvantages

As seen below, there are not many disadvantages of using Moodle LMS, and we consider that reliance on it was also a good framework design decision.

Lack of Full Control One drawback of having an external module, such as Moodle, as part of the CyTrONE framework is that developers do not have full control over its functionality. For instance, this leads to possible limitations in terms of the user interface, as that provided by the LMS must be employed as such.

Code Porting Concerns Adding a desired feature that is not already provided by Moodle requires either developing a plugin for it, or even modifying the original source code of Moodle. Although code changes are possible due to the open-source nature of Moodle, this task is not only challenging in terms of programming, but the need to port that feature to newer versions of Moodle makes updates difficult.

12.5.3 YAML Representation

Both for training content and training environment representation, CyTrONE uses the YAML text-based format, as explained in Sects. 12.3 and 12.4. This format was selected after considering several other alternatives, such as XML and JSON. The advantages and disadvantages of this choice will be examined next.

We note at this point that using a binary representation format was not considered as an alternative for CyTrONE, since supporting that format would have required a significant implementation effort for developing and maintaining the graphical user interface that would have been needed to generate files in that format. This implementation cost would have, then, prevented our dedication to the development of the core functions of the framework.

12.5.3.1   Advantages

The use of YAML format for training content representation has several important advantages, as follows.

Readability When considering the ease that we envisaged for training content creation and update, readability is a key aspect. Compared to other text-based formats, such as XML and even JSON, YAML is much easier to read, and content creators can easily add new text or syntax items to it without any special procedures.

Easy Processing YAML files are easy to process, since dedicated libraries exist in Python, which is the main language used to implement CyTrONE, as well as in many other languages. In particular, the library that we used is called PyYAML.[2] This library provides a complete parser for YAML v1.1, support for Unicode, and other features, representing an excellent solution for our use case.

Moreover, the syntax of YAML files makes it possible to also check that all the keywords used in a representation file are correct. This makes it possible to verify the input files and avoid possible execution errors during the training activity creation stage, which can be costly.

Easy Generation YAML files are also easy to generate, as the PyYAML library mentioned above supports the output of Python objects in YAML format. In fact, we have used this feature to output a human-readable representation of the properties of the cyber ranges created by CyRIS, so that instructors can verify the settings, and also use them for additional purposes (e.g., cyber range visualization).

12.5.3.2   Disadvantages

As shown below, we were not able to identify many disadvantages of using the YAML format in CyTrONE. Consequently, we consider that relying on this format for content representation was also a beneficial decision.

No Built-in Support YAML is not available as a standard built-in feature of Python. Therefore, an appropriate library, such as PyYAML, needs to be installed before using this format, which is somewhat cumbersome, and it increases the number of dependencies of the platform.

Whitespace Issues In the YAML format, indentation is used to indicate to which upper-level element a certain element belongs to. If multiple users employ different editors to modify the same file, sometimes it is possible to have a mixture of tabs and spaces used together as whitespace characters to represent such indentation.

This situation can cause issues with parsing those files, and the errors indicated by the parser are typically hard to understand. Consequently, one must take care not to mix whitespace characters in YAML files (note that this issue is also encountered for Python files, which use indentation in a similar manner).

---

[2] https://pypi.org/project/PyYAML/.

12.5.4 Other Concerns

In what follows, we will discuss several other aspects related to our experience with designing and implementing the CyTrONE framework.

Guest OS Choice Cybersecurity training platforms must provide several choices of OSs for the machines in the training environment, i.e., guest VMs in the case of CyTrONE. Without such choices, the instructors may not be able to create the desired training content, as many cybersecurity issues are OS dependent. In CyTrONE, CentOS is the fully supported guest OS, but the use of Ubuntu as well as Windows is also possible to a large extent, with several versions being supported for each OS.

However, the implementation effort that is required to support a new OS must be carefully considered in order to make an informed decision on whether support for it should be added or not. In particular, supporting all the custom cyber range creation tasks in CyTrONE required non-trivial programming skills.

Host OS Choice The balance between OS choice and implementation effort is also important for the case of the host OS, although to a lesser extent, since only platform administrators are affected by this decision. For CyTrONE, we decided to support exclusively Ubuntu Long-Term Support (LTS) as a host OS. This is because Ubuntu is a sufficiently user-friendly operating system, and the LTS releases only occur once every two years.

Nevertheless, a dedicated implementation effort was required even with this restrictive choice, since CyTrONE was in continuous development over a long period. Specifically, this meant supporting the four OS versions from Ubuntu LTS 16.04 to Ubuntu LTS 22.04, each time fixing the functionality that stopped working because of minor specification differences (e.g., the behavior of the KVM libraries).

Sample Content Learning how to create cybersecurity training content for a new training platform can be quite challenging. The best way to facilitate this process is to provide sample training content and related resources (such as VM base images), so that instructors can experiment with training environment creation, and understand the features of the platform. Moreover, the sample content can be used as a starting point for creating new training content by extending the included samples.

We also envision that, if a cybersecurity training platform is used in multiple organizations, those organizations could share the training content with each other to create an ecosystem of training content sets that can be used by others either as it is, or can be adapted to the needs of each organization.[3]

Security Assessment As discussed already in the context of CTF platforms (see Sect. 10.4.1), given that cybersecurity training has a sensitive nature, the training platform itself needs to be assessed from a security perspective, and ideally a security threat model should be built for it.

---

[3] Although not supported in CyTrONE, we note in this context that a user-friendly GUI is also a powerful manner of supporting training content creation.

In the case of CyTrONE, intermodule communication was secured via the use of the HTTPS protocol, and passwords are securely encrypted when stored on disk. As for the training content representation, some issues were discovered that made it possible to conduct "command injection" like attacks. While those issues were fixed, it is possible that other such injection vulnerabilities still exist. However, our threat model is that the content representation files are only accessible to instructors, who are assumed to have no malicious intentions; hence, we consider the security risk to be limited from this point of view.

In general, although there is no dedicated methodology for securing cybersecurity training platforms, we recommend following well-known best practices from the area of secure software development for this purpose, including secure web application development techniques, if necessary.

References

1. Advanced Distributed Learning (ADL) Initiative: SCORM overview. https://adlnet.gov/past-projects/scorm/. Accessed 1 Jul 2024
2. Beuran R, Inoue T, Tan Y, Shinoda Y (2019) Realistic cybersecurity training via scenario progression management. In: IEEE European symposium on security and privacy workshops (EuroS&PW 2019), workshop on cyber range applications and technologies (CACOE'19), pp 67–76
3. Beuran R, Pham C, Tang D, Chinen K, Tan Y, Shinoda Y (2018) Cybersecurity education and training support system: CyRIS. IEICE Trans Inf Syst E101-D(3):740–749
4. Beuran R, Tang D, Pham C, Chinen K, Tan Y, Shinoda Y (2018) Integrated framework for hands-on cybersecurity training: CyTrONE. Comput Secur 78C:43–59. https://doi.org/10.1016/j.cose.2018.06.001
5. Beuran R, Tang D, Tan Z, Hasegawa S, Tan Y, Shinoda Y (2019) Supporting cybersecurity education and training via LMS integration: CyLMS. Educ Inf Technol 24(6):3619–3643. https://doi.org/10.1007/s10639-019-09942-y
6. Beuran R, Vykopal J, Belajová D, Čeleda P, Tan Y, Shinoda Y (2023) Capability assessment methodology and comparative analysis of cybersecurity training platforms. Comput Secur 128:103120. https://doi.org/10.1016/j.cose.2023.103120
7. Beuran R, Zhang Z, Tan Y (2022) AWS EC2 public cloud cyber range deployment. In: IEEE European symposium on security and privacy workshops (EuroS&PW 2022), workshop on cyber range applications and technologies (CACOE'22), pp 433–441
8. Cyber Range Organisation and Design (CROND): CyTrONE GitHub page. https://github.com/crond-jaist/cytrone. Accessed 1 Jul 2024
9. Cyber Range Organization and Design (CROND): Achievements. https://www.jaist.ac.jp/misc/crond/achievements-en.html. Accessed 1 Jul 2024
10. Moodle Pty Ltd: Moodle LMS open source learning platform. https://moodle.org/. Accessed 1 Jul 2024
11. Scarfone K, Souppaya M, Cody A, Orebaugh A (2008) Technical guide to information security testing and assessment. National Institute of Standards and Technology Special Publication 800-115

Chapter 13
Training Platform Capability Assessment

This chapter discusses a capability assessment methodology for cybersecurity training platforms. We first provide an overview of capability assessment and define the relevant stakeholders and their perspectives. The capability assessment methodology is introduced next, with a detailed explanation of the assessment criteria and assessment procedure. Last, we present the capability assessment results for the CyTrONE training framework, illustrating the potential uses of capability assessment from the perspective of the stakeholders defined previously.

13.1 Capability Assessment Overview

Capability assessment methodologies, also known as Capability Maturity Models (CMMs), are not something specific to the field of cybersecurity. However, there are several important aspects that need to be considered in the particular context of cybersecurity training, as discussed next.

13.1.1 Motivation and Background

We have introduced in Sect. 3.3 a set of requirements and necessary features that cybersecurity training programs and training platforms must meet in order to ensure the effectiveness of the training. However, those requirements were defined at a very high level, which makes it difficult to use them for a detailed analysis.

In order to be able to evaluate and compare cybersecurity training platforms in a thorough manner, their wide variety of functions related to the training content and environment, end-user support, and so on must be considered. One of the first efforts in this area was the capability maturity model for cyber ranges proposed

R. Beuran, *Cybersecurity Education and Training*,
https://doi.org/10.1007/978-981-96-0555-2_13

in [1]. The model defines 19 core capability elements that are to be assessed on a five-level scale. However, the elements are defined in a relatively abstract manner, such as Management System, Threat Library Capability, and Monitoring System. Moreover, no information on how to decide the specific capability level for each of the identified elements is provided. Consequently, we consider that this model has insufficient detail for a comprehensive assessment of training platforms.

A more suitable cybersecurity training platform capability assessment methodology is that introduced in [3], which is much finer grained. The methodology presents a total of 58 assessment criteria, and for each of them, the requirements to assign a specific level are clearly defined. By using this methodology, which we will present later in this chapter, training platform stakeholders can assess objectively the capabilities of training platforms. This can serve, for example, to determine how suitable a given training platform is for a certain organization or training activity.

We note in this context that the CMM approach has also been applied to the field of cybersecurity training, more specifically as a way to determine the current cybersecurity competence level of the personnel of an organization [4]. The goal of that research was to make it possible to choose target cybersecurity training activities that are the most suitable for each person in that organization. We consider that this type of strategic decisions is important in the context of cybersecurity training in order to further ensure training effectiveness.

13.1.2 Cybersecurity Training Platform Stakeholders

Before going into the details of the capability assessment methodology, let us define the three categories of stakeholders with regard to cybersecurity training platforms, and what their perspectives on capability assessment are.

Organizers As we have discussed previously, training organizers are those stakeholders who deploy training platforms in view of organizing training activities. This category actually includes several subclasses of stakeholders, as follows:

- Decision-makers: Managers who are in charge of deciding what training platform is to be deployed, or what kind of training platform should be developed, if an existing solution cannot be used.
- Administrators: Engineers who will actually deploy and manage the training platform, its training content, and so on.
- Instructors: Teaching staff who will effectively conduct the training activities, and create training content (if needed).

This distinction between types of organizers is important because members of each subclass have different requirements concerning the capabilities of a training platform, as it will be discussed in Sect. 13.1.3.

Trainees The participants in cybersecurity training programs are those who use the corresponding training platforms as part of their learning process. Consequently, trainee experience is strongly influenced by the capabilities of those training platforms. However, they usually have no decision power regarding the selection of the actual platform that is used in a given program, and their influence is at most indirect, for example, by means of feedback surveys.

Developers Training platform developers have a firsthand involvement in the design and implementation of the training platforms. Although some of the requirements regarding the features that a training platform should have may originate from organizers, most of the design and implementation decisions are made by developers. This means that they role regarding the capabilities of training platforms is crucial and cannot be neglected.

13.1.3 Capability Assessment Perspectives

Each of the three categories of stakeholders mentioned above has different interests and requirements in terms of cybersecurity training platform capability assessment, as it will be discussed next.

Organizer Perspective From the perspective of training organizers, there are two main issues that the capability assessment methodology can help address, as follows:

- When considering the *deployment* of a training platform, the capability assessment method makes it possible to objectively evaluate alternative solutions in order to select the one that best matches the organizer needs in terms of the intended goals of the training program.
- When planning the *development* of a training platform, the capability assessment criteria can be used as a blueprint for formulating the specifications of the platform that developers should be asked to implement, so as to meet various levels of functionality or usability requirements.

Trainee Perspective The trainees are the "customers" of cybersecurity training programs. Therefore, at first sight, the most relevant kind of assessment for them is that of the training program as a whole, as it was done in the taxonomy-based analysis of Hardening Project that we presented in Sect. 3.4.

Nevertheless, knowing how advanced the functional capabilities of the training platform used in a given program are can increase the motivation of the participants. Moreover, it can also interest them in tackling new challenges that are made possible by the various features of the training platform. Furthermore, the usability characteristics of a training platform have a direct influence on the trainee user experience, thus affecting their motivation and enjoyment of the training activity.

Developer Perspective As mentioned above for organizers, developers too can leverage capability assessment criteria to decide the initial requirements for a cybersecurity training platform. In addition, there are several other ways to use the capability assessment methodology for an ongoing implementation when considering the bottom-up perspective of developers:

- The methodology can help identify the most important missing features of the platform, in order to support decisions on what new capabilities should be added as necessary improvements during the next development cycle.
- The methodology can also help determine those features that are not yet sufficiently developed, and whose addition would increase the capability level of the platform in the most cost-effective manner.

Based on the above discussion, we conclude that those who can make the best use of a capability assessment methodology are training organizers and platform developers—those stakeholders who are in charge of deploying and operating the platforms, as well as those involved in their design and development. However, trainees may also find some elements of interest in the capability assessment results. All these aspects will be discussed from a practical point of view in Sect. 13.4, with reference to the assessment of the CyTrONE training framework.

13.2   Capability Assessment Methodology

In this section we will explain the cybersecurity training platform capability assessment methodology introduced in [3], starting with an overview of the methodology and a summary of the assessment criteria. Then, we will also describe the procedure that one should use in order to assess an actual training platform.

13.2.1   Methodology Outline

The assessment methodology proposed in [3] relies on a *capability assessment tool*, which is provided in PDF format as supplementary material to that paper. The assessment tool presents a list of criteria that are grouped into several categories, as it will be explained in detail in Sect. 13.2.2. The total number of criteria for v1.0 of the capability assessment tool is 58.

Each assessment criterion has an identifier and a description that summarizes its scope, such as criterion "*TD-1: Types of training supported in training definitions*" defined in regard to training definitions, which is a type of assessment related to training content representation capabilities. A set of choices follow the description, which is ordered based on the platform capability level, from the least to the most capable (see the example in Fig. 13.1).

For each choice, the capability level associated to it is indicated. Level 1 represents the minimal requirement for having a certain functionality. Level 3 is the maximum capability level defined in the current version of the tool, although for some criteria only choices up to Level 2 are provided. For some choices, alternatives that are associated to the same capability level exist if they are equivalent in terms of complexity. As a special case, the Level 0 capability is to be assigned if a particular functionality is missing completely from a training platform.

For most assessment criteria, the explanation of the conditions that must be met to reach that capability level is given as plain text. However, additional information is provided for several criteria, such as images of network topologies, or even equations to be used to decide specific performance-related capabilities. Such supplementary information is an important feature of that capability assessment tool that makes it easy to assess the correct level for those criteria.

The various characteristics of the capability assessment methodology that we discussed so far enable training platform stakeholders to assess the capabilities of training platform in an objective manner, a task that is further facilitated by the practical assessment details that are provided.

We note that overall design of the capability assessment tool that we introduced was inspired by the SIM3 Self Assessment Tool [7], which is an online tool for assessments in connection with the Security Incident Management Maturity Model (SIM3) developed by the Open CSIRT Foundation. The model defines a set of maturity parameters for computer security incident response teams (CSIRTs), which in SIM3 v2 are divided into four categories. The provided tool makes it possible to conduct the assessment online and visualize the maturity level of a CSIRT in the form of a radar chart.

13.2.2 Capability Assessment Criteria

The capability assessment methodology groups the evaluation of the characteristics and features of cybersecurity training platforms into three categories of assessment criteria, which we will discuss below in detail:

- Training content representation (training definition and sandbox definition).
- Network environment management.
- Training activity facilitation.

An overview of the capability assessment criteria is shown in Table 13.1. Note that the first category, training content representation, includes two subclasses, training definition and sandbox definition. For clarity, we have shown in the table the information separated by class, having a total of four main elements. For each criterion class, criteria are further grouped based on their scope, and we show that information as well in the table, along with the number of criteria for each case.

13.2.2.1 Training Content Representation

The training content representation category of assessment criteria refers to those characteristics and features of cybersecurity training platforms that are related to the following two aspects:

Table 13.1 Overview of the capability assessment criteria

Criterion class	Criterion group	Count
Training Definition (TD)	Functional	6
	Usability	6
	Total	**12**
Sandbox Definition (SD)	Functional	7
	Usability	6
	Total	**13**
Environment Management (EM)	Functional	5
	Performance	3
	Usability	5
	Total	**13**
Activity Facilitation (AF)	Pretraining setup	6
	Training execution	12
	Post-training assessment	2
	Total	**20**
Total number of criteria		**58**

- The manner in which the tasks that the participants must solve are represented, for which the term *training definition* (TD) is employed.
- The description of the network environment that must be used to solve the above tasks, for which the term *sandbox definition* (SD) is used.

We note at this point that the order in which the two classes, TD and SD, are presented in the capability assessment tool is the opposite from that we use here, with SD criteria being defined first in the tool. Nevertheless, the order of the classes is not important during the actual assessment procedure, and we prefer to introduce the training definition criteria first, as this matches the order in which the related concepts were discussed in this book.

Training Definition Criteria There are 12 criteria in total in the training definition class, which are organized logically into two groups based on their scope:

- Functional capabilities: Criteria related to the functionality provided via training definitions, which includes supported training types, how to structure the training, supported types of questions and answers, etc. (TD-1 through TD-6).
- Usability capabilities: Criteria that refer to the usability of the training definitions, including the creation of the definitions, their representation and validation, the availability of documentation, etc. (TD-7 through TD-12).

Figure 13.1 depicts the full description of the assessment criteria TD-1 through TD-3 as an example. Note the clear explanations that are included to support the assessment process. We remark that for all the criteria in this example, two alternatives

---

TD-1: Types of training supported in training definitions

☐ Level 1 – Task-based training: questions are presented ordered or unordered via a GUI, and trainees' answers are validated, but the GUI does not interact with the sandbox; similar to a jeopardy CTF game.

☐ Level 1 – Milestone-based training: the platform checks the status of the sandbox (network services or data stored on hosts) to automatically determine whether milestones defined by instructors are met or not; similar to attack-defense or King of the Hill CTFs, or cyber defense/offense exercises.

☐ Level 2 – Both task-based and milestone-based modes are supported.

TD-2: Structuring of individual tasks/milestones

☐ Level 1 – No relationships can be defined, and all tasks/milestones are available at once.

☐ Level 1 – Task/milestone relationships can be defined, so that completing one task/milestone is a prerequisite for presenting another task/milestone.

☐ Level 2 – Both modes above are supported.

TD-3: Types of questions supported in training definitions

☐ Level 1 – Only short-answer questions are supported.

☐ Level 1 – Only multiple-choice questions are supported.

☐ Level 2 – Both short-answer and multiple-choice questions are supported.

Fig. 13.1 Example of training definition capability assessment criteria

are provided for Level 1 capability, and supporting both alternatives is considered to denote a Level 2 capability.

Sandbox Definition Criteria There are 13 criteria in the sandbox definition class, which are also organized logically into two groups, similar to the case of the training definition class:

- Functional capabilities: Criteria concerning the functionality provided via sandbox definitions, which includes sandbox customization, supported types of hosts and operating systems, security features, etc. (SD-1 through SD-7).
- Usability capabilities: Criteria related to the usability of the sandbox definitions, including the creation of definitions, their representation and validation, the availability of documentation, etc. (SD-8 through SD-13).

We note that for criterion SD-7, which refers to network topology capabilities, figures are used in the explanation for the sake of clarity. The figures depict the topologies mentioned in the text, such as bus, star, tree, and hybrid topologies. This ensures that there is no misunderstanding when evaluating this particular capability.

Discussion The total number of criteria in the two classes that make up the training content representation category is 25. This relatively large number of criteria emphasizes the importance of training content representation for a training platform, an aspect that we believe is often overlooked by training platform developers.

13.2.2.2 Network Environment Management

The network environment management (EM) category of assessment criteria includes those characteristics and features of cybersecurity training platforms that are used in relation with the network environment used for training. This includes creating the network environment, orchestrating the actions that are needed to modify it during the training, and destroying the environment when the training ends.

Environment Management Criteria The total number of criteria in this category is 13, and they are organized into three groups, based on their scope:

- Functional capabilities: Criteria regarding network environment management functionality, including environment creation and control, support for executing action and network attacks, etc. (EM-1 through EM-5).
- Performance capabilities: Criteria that refer to network environment management performance, namely the reliability and efficiency of environment creation, and resource consumption (EM-6 through EM-8).
- Usability capabilities: Criteria related to network environment management usability, such as the type of user interface, the degree of automation, and monitoring features (EM-9 through EM-13).

Note that for criteria EM-6 through EM-8, which refer to performance assessment, the following information is also provided along with the text-based explanation to ensure that the assessment can be conducted objectively:

1. The reference network topology that is to be used when conducting the capability assessment tests.
2. Equations that describe mathematically the conditions that must be met to reach a certain capability level.

Discussion We consider that the criteria related to the performance capabilities of a training platform are an important contribution of this assessment category, as they provide objective numerical metrics for evaluating the performance characteristics of the platform. Nevertheless, since the training platform must be deployed in order to be able to conduct those measurements, these criteria are more difficult to assess compared to all the other criteria that can be evaluated only based on platform specifications and/or source code.

13.2.2.3   Training Activity Facilitation

The training activity facilitation (AF) category of assessment criteria refers to those characteristics and features of a cybersecurity training platform that make it easier to use. The capabilities in this category include aspects such as: how tasks are assigned to participants via the training platform, how instructors can follow trainee progress during the training activity, how to record participant results, and so on.

Activity Facilitation Criteria This category includes a total number of 20 criteria, which are organized into three groups, as described below:

- Pretraining setup capabilities: Criteria in relation with pretraining setup activities, including automation of the deployment, import of the training content, visibility and access time control for training sessions, etc. (AF-1 through AF-6).

- Training execution capabilities: Criteria regarding various training execution characteristics, for instance, the use of an LMS or intelligent tutoring system (ITS), educational features such as scaffolding or cheating prevention and detection (AF-7 through AF-18).
- Post-training assessment capabilities: Criteria related to post-training assessment activities, namely the export of training data, and result analysis across different training sessions (AF-19 and AF-20).

Discussion The training activity facilitation category includes a large number of criteria compared to the other classes we discussed so far. This is because there is a wide variety of features that a platform can provide in order to facilitate training activities from many perspectives.

We note, however, that the criteria in this category are not essential for a cybersecurity training platform to function. Therefore, we suggest considering them initially simply as optional capabilities that would make the platform easier to use. Nevertheless, some activity facilitation features can become a requirement, for instance, if organizers decide they should be present as a differentiating factor of their training platform. In that case, those specific features and the corresponding capability levels should be examined in a rigorous manner.

13.2.3 Assessment Procedure

Now that we have introduced the capability assessment methodology, we will also provide some practical advice on how to actually assess the capabilities of a given cybersecurity training platform.

13.2.3.1 Preparation Steps

Before proceeding with the assessment, it is necessary to conduct several preparation steps, as it will be explained next.

Acquire Documentation First of all, it is important to retrieve the available documentation about the cybersecurity training platform that is to be assessed. For some platforms, this could mean collecting information from the related websites, but obtaining a detailed user guide, if available, is best.

Deploy Platform The information available in documentation and user guides may be somewhat vague, making it difficult to correctly assess the actual capabilities of a training platform. Deploying the platform on the organization servers is the best way of trying its features in view of a detailed assessment. Moreover, it also allows those who deploy the platform to determine how good the documentation is.

We remark that, due to the overhead and practical challenges of training platform deployment, trying to conduct the assessment exclusively based on documentation is possible, especially if more than a few platforms are to be evaluated. However, for assessing the criteria related to platform performance, which require measurements, deployment cannot be avoided.

Acquire Source Code Although the documentation and platform deployment should provide, in general, enough information for the general assessment of a training platform, for an even more accurate appraisal of some of the capability assessment criteria it may be necessary to get hold of the actual source code of the platform. If one has enough technical expertise, this additional source of information makes it possible to determine precisely the exact capability level for any platform feature.

Decide Assessment Profile Before starting the assessment, evaluators should also decide which of the assessment criteria are most relevant for a given purpose. Even though all the criteria could be assessed each time, some of them may not be of interest for a given target.

To facilitate this task, the concept of *assessment profile* was introduced in [3], with several examples being provided, such as *Simple Training Activity* or *Unsupervised Training Activity*. Those profiles state the criteria that must necessarily be evaluated when the corresponding types of activities are being planned. Defining a custom profile that meets the specific requirements of an organization is also possible, thus further reducing the assessment load.

13.2.3.2   Assessment Process Suggestions

Once the preparations for assessment are completed, the capability assessment tool should be used to conduct the actual assessment. In this context, we provide below several suggestions on how to proceed with this task so as to minimize the effort needed to conduct the assessment.

1. As the initial step of the assessment, one should go through all the relevant assessment criteria, possibly by using an assessment profile, and try to evaluate the corresponding capability level based on the available documentation, as this is the approach that requires the least amount of work.
2. For those criteria that could not be assessed based on the available documentation, one can try to contact the developers of the platform. However, for open-source platforms, obtaining detailed answers may be difficult due to the volunteer nature of the developers.
3. If there are still any assessment criteria for which the capability level is undecided, one should deploy the platform, and evaluate those criteria directly by using it. This alternative has the advantage that it will also provide a direct experience with that platform, at the cost of having to deploy it.
4. For performance capability assessments, the platform must necessarily be deployed; if deployment was not required at the previous step, then it must be done now. Since these criteria can also be evaluated at the end, delaying the deployment is acceptable. Moreover, if a precise assessment is not absolutely

necessary, obtaining estimated hardware requirements and performance metrics from platform developers is also a possibility.

Next we will illustrate how the capability assessment can be conducted in practice, and how its results can be interpreted, through a case study on the cybersecurity training platform we discussed in Chap. 12, CyTrONE.

13.3 CyTrONE Capability Assessment

In this section, we will present in detail the capability assessment that we conducted for the integrated cybersecurity training framework CyTrONE [2, 5] by using the methodology discussed so far.

As developers of CyTrONE, the assessment was based mainly on our firsthand knowledge of the framework. In some cases, however, we referred to the module user guides and source code to determine what features are available to end users, as some features of CyTrONE are still under implementation, and not fully ready for use or documented. In addition, we have performed the experiments required to access the performance-related capabilities of CyTrONE.

In what follows, we will examine the results of the capability assessment by looking at each of the three categories of assessment criteria that were defined in the methodology, namely training content representation, network environment management, and training activity facilitation.

13.3.1 Training Content Representation

For the training content representation category, the two aspects to assess are the capabilities related to training definition and sandbox definition. The results of the assessment are plotted in the form of radar charts in Figs. 13.2 and 13.3, respectively. Since the maximum values that can be assigned for each assessment criterion are not the same, the maximum capability levels are also plotted with a lighter color as reference.

Training Definition We will first analyze the results for the training definition capability assessment. Regarding criteria TD-1 through TD-6, which are related to functionality, we consider the values to be acceptable in general. We note that for criterion TD-3, which is related to the types of supported questions, the platform achieved the maximum score. However, for criterion TD-5, which is related to the ability to specify a trainee's role in the training, the level is 0, as this functionality is missing from CyTrONE.

As for criteria TD-7 through TD-12, which are related to usability, we note an even better overall score, with maximum scores for three of the criteria, namely

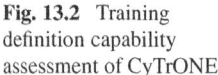

Fig. 13.2 Training
definition capability
assessment of CyTrONE

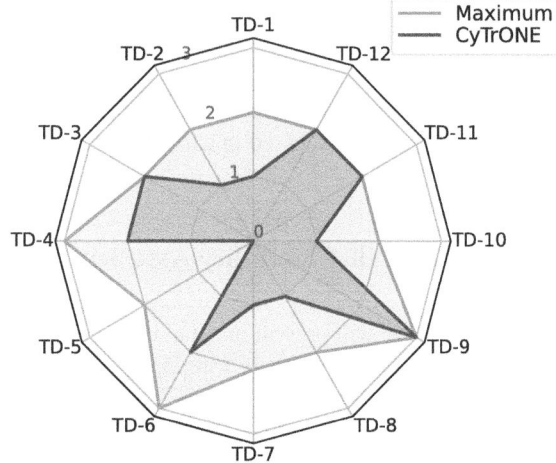

Fig. 13.3 Sandbox
definition capability
assessment of CyTrONE

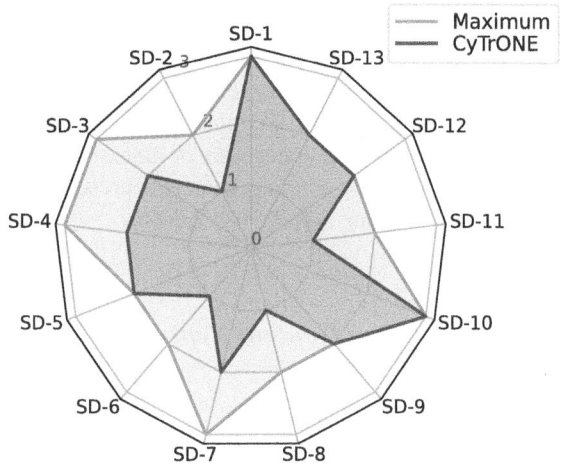

TD-9, TD-11, and TD-12, which are related to the representation format, and the availability of documentation and training content samples, respectively.

Sandbox Definition Let us examine next the results for the sandbox definition capability assessment. Regarding criteria SD-1 through SD-7, which refer to functionality, we note again that the capability levels are generally acceptable. There are even two maximum scores, namely for criteria SD-1 and SD-5, which are related to the overall customization capabilities for sandboxes, and support for security-related sandbox configuration, respectively.

The usability criteria SD-8 through SD-13 were assessed even higher, with four of the criteria receiving maximum score. Specifically, this is the case for criteria SD-9, SD-10, SD-12, and SD-13, which are related to security measures for isolating sand-

Fig. 13.4 Network
environment management
capability assessment of
CyTrONE

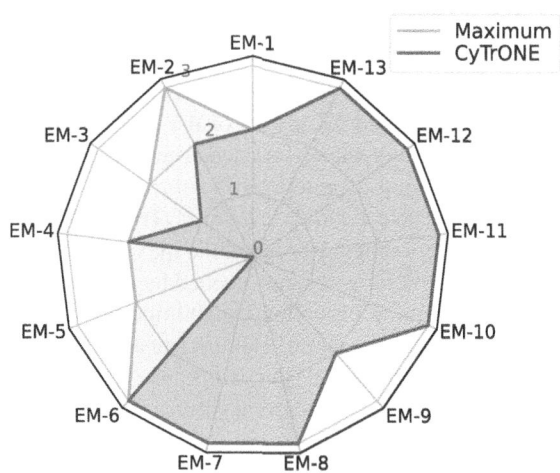

boxes, the representation format for the sandbox definition, as well as the availability
of documentation and sample sandbox definition.

13.3.2 Network Environment Management

For the network environment management category, the results of the capability
assessment are plotted as a radar chart in Fig. 13.4. Again, the maximum values for
each criterion are shown with a lighter color.

   With regard to the criteria related to functionality, EM-1 through EM-5, we remark
an overall satisfactory level. Noteworthy are criteria EM-1 and EM-4, for which
maximum scores were assigned, as they are related to the support of environment
creation for parallel training activities, and for network attack execution, which are
important functions of a training platform. One aspect that is not at all supported in
CyTrONE, however, is background traffic generation, as illustrated by the Level 0
score for criterion EM-5.

   Criteria EM-6 through EM-8 refer to performance characteristics, and CyTrONE
scored maximum capability levels for all of them. The same can be said for criteria
EM-9 through EM-13, which are related to usability. This brings the general capability of the CyTrONE framework to a relatively high level from a network environment
management perspective.

13.3.3 Training Activity Facilitation

For the third category of capability assessment criteria, training activity facilitation category, we plotted the results of the assessment in radar chart form in Fig. 13.5, with the maximum values for each criterion represented with a lighter color.

The first group of criteria, AF-1 through AF-6, are related to pretraining setup capabilities. The capability level of CyTrONE is not very high in this respect, with only one criterion being assigned the maximum value, AF-6, which is related to the degree of instructor assistance needed by trainees.

For the training execution capabilities, AF-7 through AF-18, the evaluation is relatively similar in general. There is one criterion, however, for which the capability level is 0, namely AF-10; this is because CyTrONE lacks cheating prevention and detection features in the current release (although some research has already been done in this respect). On the positive side, the assessment yielded maximum values for criteria AF-11, AF-12, and AF-13, which are related to host access manner and experience, including support for accessing in-use hosts by instructors.

The last group of criteria refers to post-training assessment capabilities, namely AF-19 and AF-20. The capability level of CyTrONE is average from this perspective, with Level 1 rating for both of them, for a maximum Level 2 capability.

13.4 Capability Assessment Applications

There are several manners in which the capability assessment results for a given cybersecurity training platform can be used, with the main two cases being:

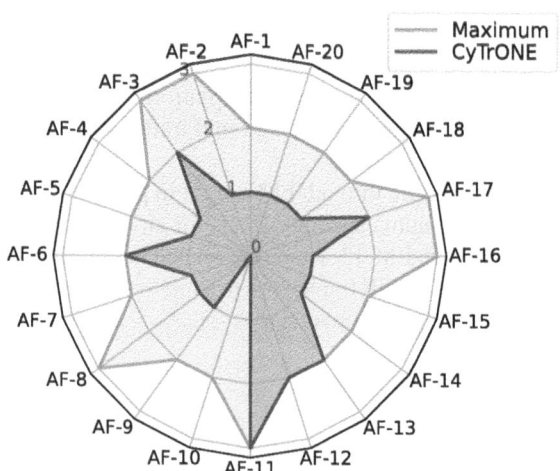

Fig. 13.5 Training activity facilitation capability assessment of CyTrONE

1. Assess the target training platform to determine how good it is with regard to the capability categories that were defined in the assessment methodology.
2. Compare two or more training platforms by examining the differences in their capabilities to decide which platform is more suitable for a given purpose.

In what follows, we will discuss how the results of the capability assessment can be used in practice for the above goals by considering the perspectives of the three types of stakeholders defined in Sect. 13.1.2. The discussed applications will be illustrated with examples based on the results obtained for CyTrONE that were presented in the previous section.

13.4.1 For Developers

The radar charts presented in Figs. 13.2 through 13.5 provide a very detailed view on the capabilities of a training platform. This makes them most useful for training platform developers, so we will first look at their perspective. Thus, developers can use those results to identify features that should be added to the platform implementation, or existing functionality that should be extended.

Feature Addition If a capability is deemed to be at Level 0 for a certain criterion, then adding the corresponding feature would improve the overall capabilities of the platform. For example, criterion TD-5 in Fig. 13.2 indicates that CyTrONE content representation cannot be used to specify the roles of trainees. Adding support for trainee roles, such as attacker or defender, would be beneficial from this perspective.

Feature Extension On the other hand, a given capability may be present in the platform, but its assessment score can be low. For instance, criterion AF-2 in Fig. 13.5 is evaluated as Level 1, but the maximum score for that capability is Level 3. This indicates that support for importing training content is relatively poor in CyTrONE, since instructors must update the content database themselves. Consequently, adding the feature of importing training content via CLI or GUI would improve the overall capability of the framework.

13.4.2 For Organizers

As it was discussed when introducing organizers, this stakeholder category has several subclasses, so we will distinguish between them when discussing the capability assessment applications from an organizer perspective.

13.4.2.1 Instructors

Instructors are those who use cybersecurity training platforms most closely among all the organizers. Consequently, they can make use of the radar charts we discussed

Table 13.2 Capability assessment results per groups of criteria

Criterion class	Criterion group	Capability level (%)
Training Definition (TD)	Functional	57.14
	Usability	76.92
	Overall	**66.67**
Sandbox Definition (SD)	Functional	72.22
	Usability	84.62
	Overall	**77.42**
Environment Management (EM)	Functional	63.64
	Performance	100.00
	Usability	100.00
	Overall	**88.24**
Activity Facilitation (AF)	Pretraining setup	57.14
	Training execution	57.14
	Post-training assessment	50.00
	Overall	**56.52**
Total capability level		**71.01**

already to determine, for example, to what extent a certain required feature is supported by the training platform.

However, if a training platform is to be evaluated overall, and maybe even compared to another training platform, a higher-level view is preferable, that aggregates the results of the assessment. To illustrate this idea, we present in Table 13.2 statistical information about the capabilities of CyTrONE per group of assessment criteria. The statistics are shown as percentages to compensate for the fact that the maximum capability level can differ from a criterion to another, since percentages offer an easy-to-understand metric that can also be used to compare two different platforms.

We note that Table 13.2 offers some insights that are not readily available from the radar charts. For training definition capabilities, for instance, the functional capabilities are at around 57%, whereas usability is rated higher, at around 77%, with the overall capabilities in this class being at around 67%. Similarly, although the functional environment management capabilities are only at around 63%, performance and usability both reach the value of 100%, for an overall of around 88%.

In the table, we have also included the total overall capability for CyTrONE computed across all the assessment criteria. The value of about 71% can be considered as an overall estimate of the capabilities of the framework. This value can also be used to compare CyTrONE to other cybersecurity training platforms.

Table 13.3 Capability assessment results per type of criteria

Criteria type	Capability level (%)
Functional capabilities	65.12
Performance capabilities	100.00
Usability capabilities	87.50
Facilitation capabilities	56.52
Total capabilities	**71.01**

13.4.2.2 Administrators

Administrators are not involved in the actual use of training platforms, but in their management. For this reason, they may disregard some of the information in the radar charts and only focus on those aspects that are related to platform management.

Thus, similar to the concept of assessment profile mentioned in Sect. 13.2.3.2, administrators could ignore most of the features regarding training definition, but need to consider carefully those related to sandbox definition. This is because technical effort on their side is needed to implement support for sandboxes, for instance with regard to host categories (see SD-2), such as bare metal, VMs, or containers, and CPU architectures (see SD-3), such as x86 or ARM.

Another point of significant interest for administrators is the performance-related criteria regarding network environment management, namely EM-6 through EM-8, as administrators are those who need to make those assessments and also handle any technical issues that may arise.

For these reasons, we consider that administrators can benefit from an even higher-level view than the information shown in the previous table by focusing only on the type of assessment criteria. Therefore, in Table 13.3 we show the corresponding statistics from this perspective. The table indicates that the overall functional capabilities of CyTrONE are medium, whereas performance capabilities are excellent, and usability capabilities are overall high. The facilitation capabilities are lowest, at just 56%, but they are not of much concern to administrators.

13.4.2.3 Decision-Makers

The third type of stakeholders in the organizer category are the decision-makers. Capability assessment provides them with objective metrics that can be used to support their decisions. However, we consider that the detailed information shown in the radar charts is too low level for this purpose.

Consequently, for decision-makers, we propose using a view that emphasizes the capability levels of the assessed training platform for each class of capability criteria. Such information is visualized in Fig. 13.6, which shows the capability levels in percentage for the four classes of capabilities defined in the assessment methodology. The total capability level is also plotted, since it can serve as an overall metric.

Looking first at the training content representation classes, namely training definition (TD) and sandbox definition (SD), we observe they have acceptable values that both exceed 60%, with SD capabilities being higher, close to 80%. This means that the overall capability of CyTrONE regarding training content representation is over 70%, which on the whole is a good score.

For network environment management capabilities (EM), CyTrONE scores even higher, with the overall level for that class being close to 90%. On the contrary, training activity facilitation capabilities (AF) have the lowest score of all the classes, being less than 60%. From this metric, decision-makers can understand that this is the weakest point of the training platform.

In Fig. 13.6, we also observe that the total capability level of CyTrONE is around 70%, and this global metric can be used to compare it to other platforms in an objective manner. However, we consider that a more detailed analysis that considers the average capability level for each class of criteria is a better approach, as it allows highlighting the specific advantages and disadvantages of each platform. This kind of detailed comparative analysis was conducted in [3], where CyTrONE was compared with the KYPO Cyber Range Platform [6, 8].

The fact that the capability assessment methodology we discussed makes possible such a comparative analysis represents one of its strongest potential applications. Moreover, this type of comparison is the most effective use of the methodology from the perspective of decision-makers.

Fig. 13.6 Capability assessment per class of criteria: training definition (TD), sandbox definition (SD), network environment management (EM), training activity facilitation (AF), and the overall level (Total)

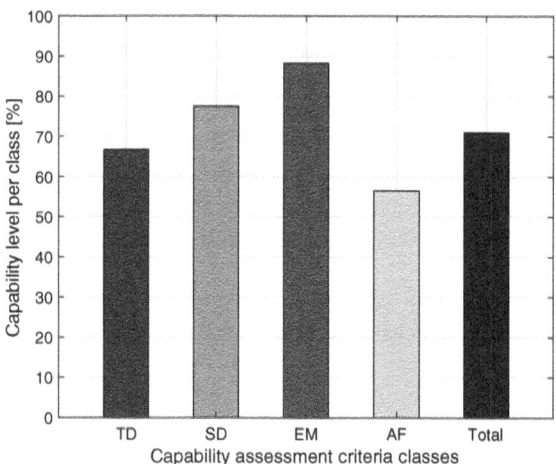

13.4.3 For Trainees

Typically, trainees do not have a direct control over what training platform is used in a cybersecurity training course. Therefore, the kind of detailed assessment results as those shown in the radar charts are not very relevant to them. However, trainees may be interested in the high-level assessment information that we have presented, such as that included in Table 13.3 or Fig. 13.6, as it gives them an overview of the capabilities of the training platform.

Moreover, training organizers could use that type of high-level information for the purpose of attracting trainees into a training program, for instance, by showing potential participants how good the capabilities of the training platform are. Organizers could also choose to present comparative assessment data to emphasize the characteristics of their training platform in comparison with those of the platforms used by other cybersecurity training providers.

Note that if someone is trying to select a training platform for themselves, such as one of the online CTF platforms discussed in Chap. 10, then their role is not only that of a trainee. Consequently, they should also refer to the organizer perspective discussed earlier in Sect. 13.4.2 for examples of how the capability assessment results can be utilized from that point of view.

Acknowledgements The author would like to acknowledge the contributions of Jan Vykopal, Daniela Belajová, and Pavel Čeleda from Masaryk University, Czech Republic, to the development of the training platform capability assessment methodology that was presented in this chapter. Moreover, Jan Vykopal implemented the initial version of the script used to plot the radar charts that we have presented.

References

1. Aschmann MJ (2020) Towards a capability maturity model for a cyber range. Master's thesis. Rhodes University, Faculty of Science, Computer Science
2. Beuran R, Tang D, Pham C, Chinen K, Tan Y, Shinoda Y (2018) Integrated framework for hands-on cybersecurity training: CyTrONE. Comput Secur 78C:43–59. https://doi.org/10.1016/j.cose.2018.06.001
3. Beuran R, Vykopal J, Belajová D, Čeleda P, Tan Y, Shinoda Y (2023) Capability assessment methodology and comparative analysis of cybersecurity training platforms. Comput Secur 128:103120. https://doi.org/10.1016/j.cose.2023.103120
4. Chockalingam S, Nystad E, Esnoul C (2023) Capability maturity models for targeted cyber security training. In: Moallem A (ed) HCI for cybersecurity, privacy and trust. Springer Nature Switzerland, Cham, pp 576–590
5. Cyber Range Organisation and Design (CROND): CyTrONE GitHub page. https://github.com/crond-jaist/cytrone. Accessed 1 Jul 2024
6. Masaryk University: KYPO cyber range platform. https://crp.kypo.muni.cz. Accessed 1 Jul 2024
7. Open CSIRT Foundation: self assessment tool. https://sim3-check.opencsirt.org. Accessed 1 Jul 2024
8. Vykopal J, Čeleda P, Seda P, Švábenský V, Tovarňák D (2021) Scalable learning environments for teaching cybersecurity hands-on. In: 2021 IEEE frontiers in education conference (FIE), pp 1–9. https://doi.org/10.1109/FIE49875.2021.9637180

Chapter 14
Conclusion

This chapter summarizes first the content of the book by highlighting the main contributions of each chapter. Following that, a set of key takeaways is provided to emphasize the most significant insights of this book. Last, we discuss trends and future prospects with regard to cybersecurity education and training.

14.1 Book Summary

In this section we will briefly review the content of the book and highlight the most important aspects of each chapter. The presentation follows the book structure, in which the first part addressed training methodologies, and the second part discussed training platforms.

14.1.1 Part I: Training Methodologies

In Part I of this book, we have examined the general methodologies related to cybersecurity education and training in order to provide readers with a comprehensive understanding of this topic.

Background and Overview Discussion We started the book by introducing in Chap. 1 its background and motivation, and discussing its key contributions and intended audience. Then, in Chap. 2, we gave an overview on cybersecurity education and training, and emphasized the distinction between technical cybersecurity training, aimed mainly at cybersecurity professionals, and cybersecurity awareness training, aimed at regular IT users.

Technical Cybersecurity Training We continued with an in-depth discussion of technical cybersecurity training in Chap. 3, introducing its purpose, approaches and characteristics, and examining the Hardening Project training program as a motivating example. This was followed by a detailed presentation of the three forms of technical cybersecurity training in the subsequent chapters.

Thus, Chap. 4 discussed attack training, which focuses on offensive techniques, and introduced fundamental attack training and pentesting training methodologies. In Chap. 5, we examined forensics training, which refers to digital forensic procedures, and we outlined the principles of fundamental forensics training and forensic methodology training. The third form of technical cybersecurity training, defense training, was considered in Chap. 6, which included an overview of fundamental defense training and defense methodology training. For all the tree forms of technical cybersecurity training, a comprehensive set of additional resources, such as related knowledge bases and guidelines, was provided.

Other Forms of Training As a complement to generic technical cybersecurity training, the Internet of Things (IoT) security training discussed in Chap. 7 is a methodology that takes into account the specificities of IoT devices and networks. Two training systems, IoTrain-Sim and IoTrain-Lab, were used to illustrate possible solutions for the IoT security training challenges.

Then, in Chap. 8, we proceeded to examine the completely different paradigm of cybersecurity awareness training, which uses techniques such as e-learning, simulation, and gamification to increase training appeal and effectiveness. The case study of CyATP served as an example of how to put these techniques into practice.

14.1.2 Part II: Training Platforms

In Part II of the book, we focused on more practical aspects related to cybersecurity training, so that readers can complement the more theoretical discussion in Part I with clear examples of how the general methodologies are applied in real life, so as to gain a full mastery of the topic.

Training Platform Outline First, in Chap. 9, we presented an overview of cybersecurity training platforms, starting with the introduction of a training platform model to be used as reference for understanding the general characteristics of training platforms. Moreover, the two essential components of a training platform, training content and training environment, were analyzed in detail.

Training Platform Review We then began the review of actual cybersecurity training platforms, starting with Capture The Flag (CTF) platforms in Chap. 10. CTF platforms are those platforms that most participants encounter when they set about to attend cybersecurity training activities. Our focus was on online CTF platforms and open-source ones, as they are the most accessible.

This was followed by an examination of cyber range platforms in Chap. 11. Cyber ranges are the most advanced type of cybersecurity training platform, as they provide training environments that are the most realistic in terms of structure and content. We first analyzed general cyber ranges in government, private sector, and academia, followed by more specialized cyber ranges in domains such as IoT, Industrial Control Systems (ICS), and Internet of Medical Things (IoMT).

Detailed Case Study The detailed case study of the CyTrONE integrated cybersecurity training framework in Chap. 12 was used to demonstrate how a training platform can be designed to meet various training requirements. Moreover, the training content and training environment used in CyTrONE illustrated how these important aspects of a training platform could be implemented.

As a complement to the detailed case study, we introduced a training platform capability assessment methodology in Chap. 13. This methodology was then used to assess the characteristics of CyTrONE with a twofold purpose: clarifying the capabilities of the discussed framework, and illustrating how the assessment methodology can be applied in practice.

14.2 Key Takeaways

In what follows, we will present several insights that we consider to be the key takeaways of this book:

1. **Technical Versus Awareness Training**: Technical cybersecurity training and cybersecurity awareness training have different targets and intrinsic characteristics. Consequently, suitable approaches must be used for each of them in order to achieve the most effective training results.
2. **Interdependency of Training Forms**: The three forms of technical cybersecurity training—attack, forensics, and defense training—can be discussed separately, and are often conducted as such. However, the strong interdependency between them is an essential aspect that needs to be considered thoroughly by trainees and organizers alike.
3. **Training Methodology Recommendations**: For all the forms of cybersecurity training that we discussed, a distinction between basic and advanced skills can be made. Fundamental training focusing on practical hands-on exercises is most suitable for acquiring general-purpose basic knowledge and skills. On the other hand, standards-based training that relies on top-down processes is required for acquiring the advanced skills needed by cybersecurity professionals.
4. **Need for Defense Training**: Many cybersecurity training platforms that focus on attack and forensics training are available. Nevertheless, since defense skills are the most important in a professional setting, more defense-oriented training platforms and programs, such as Hardening Project, are needed to fill the current cybersecurity workforce gap.

5. **Training Platform Development**: To design an effective cybersecurity training platform, modeling its functionality is a powerful mechanism for ensuring that all the required features are present. Furthermore, using a capability assessment methodology makes it possible to determine what features the implementation effort should focus on.

14.3 Toward the Future

Bridging the cybersecurity workforce gap that we have mentioned on several occasions in this book will take years. To achieve this critical goal, relevant organizations must relentlessly conduct education and training activities in ever more compelling and diverse forms. Some possible steps in the context of the EU cybersecurity education have already been highlighted in [6], such as the enrichment of the curriculum for the poorly covered knowledge areas, and the more effective use of cyber ranges for skill building. In this final section, we will endeavor to analyze what is to be expected in the future with regard to cybersecurity education and training.

14.3.1 Cybersecurity Training Prospects

Let us start by discussing some of the current trends and future perspectives in connection with cybersecurity education and training that we consider most consequential for defining a general outlook.

14.3.1.1 Current Trends

The present tendencies in cybersecurity education and training are a good indicator of the short-term evolution of the field. The International Information System Security Certification Consortium, Inc. (ISC2) has highlighted several important trends in this regard, as follows [8]:

- Growing demand for specialized training programs that focus on hot topics, such as threat hunting, incident response, cloud security, AI and blockchain.
- General shift toward online learning platforms, as well as virtual cybersecurity training environments, which are used in a self-paced style, and are combined with self-study materials.
- Increased recognition of the advantages of ethical hacking and offensive security training for helping organizations identify and mitigate various security threats and vulnerabilities.

- Significant need to integrate compliance-focused training in the cybersecurity education curriculum in order to address relevant data protection laws and regulations, such as GDPR.
- Increasing popularity of scenario-based training that mimics real-world cyber threats, an approach that keeps the trainees engaged, and makes the training more effective, including via the use of gamification techniques.
- Noticeable expansion of vendor-neutral certifications and training that provide a broad view on a wide variety of cybersecurity concepts.

The above considerations can help cybersecurity training organizers make informed decisions about the features and characteristics that should be added in the short term to the training programs they manage. However, over the years, the cybersecurity landscape will evolve as well, as we will discuss next.

14.3.1.2 Future Prospects

Cybersecurity education and training are long-term efforts. Therefore, considering the future prospects of cybersecurity in general, and education and training in particular, is very important as a way to support training organizers when considering future development strategies.

The Future of Cybersecurity Predicting the future is not an easy task, especially for a dynamic field such as cybersecurity. Although not all opinions regarding the future of cybersecurity can fully agree, a relative consensus of several experts was reported in [11], as summarized below:

- Cloud computing is expected to still be in high demand due to its convenience, even though this will only perpetuate the security risks associated with it. However, peer-to-peer networks based on blockchain may emerge as an alternative to the cloud that provides better security—at least for some applications.
- Passwords, which are one of the oldest and biggest security risks, may still be in existence in the foreseeable future due to their high usability. Nevertheless, we note that passkey technology, which has become more widely spread recently, may represent a viable and secure alternative, depending on its adoption rate.
- The adoption rate of AI technologies, both in the society at large, but also in the field of cybersecurity will keep increasing. This makes very plausible a scenario in which threat hunting bots will fight against malicious ones, with humans fine tuning their behavior from behind the scene.
- As more and more data is stored online, it is expected that the number of data breaches will increase. The size of the data breeches is expected to grow as well, a prediction that has already been confirmed by the record-breaking leak of 10 billion stolen passwords that were shared online in July 2024 [9].
- Major threats, such as supply chain and infrastructure attacks will become even more significant in terms of scale. In particular, nation-state attacks targeting the critical infrastructure are expected to multiply considerably.

Cybersecurity Training of the Future Cybersecurity training needs to address the needs of the organizations that request the training, which will definitely evolve alongside the forseen changes in the cybersecurity landscape discussed above.

Consequently, it is difficult to create a future-proof training program, and the best strategy is to have high flexibility in adapting the content and methodologies of the training programs and platforms to the evolving training targets. Some possible approaches for reaching this goal, based on the suggestions in [8], are as follows:

- Provide training modules that can be accessed online anytime and anywhere, including on mobile devices, and which are continuously updated.
- Make use of interactive, game-based learning methods that engage participants and render the training more effective.
- Design specialized training modules that take into account the particular risks of the various departments in an organization, as well as those specific to the organization as a whole (e.g., critical infrastructure attacks, etc.).
- Employ AI technologies in the training platform to create personalized training paths that adapt to the characteristics of the trainees, their results to date, etc.

Another aspect that we consider of great significance for the future of cybersecurity training is to achieve some form of "standardization" regarding the manner in which training content and training environments are represented in cybersecurity training platforms. This would make it possible to create ecosystems in which content creators and training organizers can share their content, either free of charge or at a cost, and that content would function on any training platform that accepts that standard format as input. Unfortunately, efforts so far, including by the author [3], have failed to gain traction in the research community. Nevertheless, we still hope that it will happen one day.

14.3.2 Cybersecurity Training in the Age of AI

As mentioned already, given the more and more widely spread use of AI technologies in our society, the implications of AI have started becoming evident in the field of cybersecurity training. There are two main perspectives that we need to examine regarding this topic—how AI could be used for cybersecurity training, and what cybersecurity training should be used for in relation with AI—as discussed next.

14.3.2.1 AI for Cybersecurity Training

AI technologies have already been used to support cybersecurity education and training in various manners. For instance, research on improving penetration testing via the use of reinforcement learning, and awareness training through the use of natural language processing, was presented in [4].

This trend will definitely continue, especially by employing AI to automate those tasks that are too demanding for security experts in terms of effort, skills, or even just time. Some possible examples when considering the three forms of cybersecurity training that we discussed in this book are provided below.

Attack Training When conducting attack training activities, an AI-based cyber defense agent could be used to actively defend the target system. This would make it possible to provide a realistic training environment in which trainees can practice penetration testing skills in conditions similar to real life, as opposed to the typical statical environments that are currently employed when human defenders are not involved in the training.

Forensics Training In the case of forensics training, an AI-based cyberattack agent could be used to target the training environment as one step of the environment creation phase. The trainees could then investigate the consequences of the cyberattack to analyze its mechanisms, as well as compare their conclusions to the actual attack techniques that were used.

Defense Training Defense training too can make use of an AI-based cyberattack agent, in particular to reproduce live attack scenarios. In this case, participants would be able to conduct hands-on exercises in realistic cybersecurity training conditions by practicing their defense skills against the AI agent in real time. Moreover, such a scenario could also be used to evaluate the effectiveness of defense techniques, since if an attack fails it signifies the defense was successful, which can be recorded automatically, similar to the interactive methodology described in [12].

14.3.2.2 Cybersecurity Training for AI

The advent of AI means that, in the very near future, AI technologies will permeate all layers of the society. However, AI technologies bring their intrinsic risks related to cybersecurity. In fact, various offensive techniques from the field of cybersecurity are already being used on large AI models, which are subject to threats such as:

- Prompt injection attacks that use maliciously crafted prompts to compromise the output of an AI model.
- Data poisoning attacks that rely on malicious training data for the same purpose of compromising model output.
- Backdooring attacks, which in the case of AI refer to creating a model that behaves as expected for typical input data, but produces malicious output for specific inputs selected by the attacker.

Moreover, red teaming methodology has also been adapted to the field of AI, where AI red teams try to use attack techniques such as those described above to compromise AI models developed by their own organization. In this scenario, the developers of the AI models are those who play the role of the blue team, trying to defend their models. The idea that the developers will also need to protect the society from the potential harms caused by the AI models they created, which become the "attackers," has also been suggested [1].

Consequently, it is absolutely necessary for cybersecurity training to integrate AI-related training activities within its scope. For example, we can imagine including an attack training section dedicated to prompt injection attacks, forensics training activities teaching how to identify attacks on AI models, and defense training focused on mitigating those types of attacks.

14.3.3 From Cybersecurity to Trustworthiness

Throughout this book, we have discussed issues related to cybersecurity and cybersecurity training. However, according to the Society 5.0 vision put forward by the Japanese government, we are advancing toward a human-centered society that will use a highly integrated cyberspace and physical space structure to address a wide range of economic development and social issues [7]. This tight integration of the cyberspace and physical space means that disturbances originating from the cyberspace will no longer be limited to it, and could have potential consequences in the physical space. Hence, pure cybersecurity approaches will become insufficient for addressing the entire range of issues that will arise.

Trustworthiness Efforts aimed at dealing with the inadequacy of approaches based only on cybersecurity strategies first started in the field of Industrial IoT, being spearheaded by the Industry IoT Consortium (IIC). Thus, IIC has proposed a definition for the broader concept of *trustworthiness* that emphasizes the multitude of aspects that need to be considered in this context, as follows [2]:

> **Trustworthiness** Degree of confidence one has that the system performs as expected with characteristics including safety, security, privacy, reliability and resilience in the face of environmental disturbances, human errors, system faults and attacks.

Also focusing on the area of Cyber Physical Systems (CPS) and IoT is the trustworthiness assurance framework for IoT systems defined in [5], which attempts to establish a generic methodology based on trustworthiness assurance levels for managing trust with regard to IoT/CPS. Based on the work done in this ares, we consider that the shift from cybersecurity to trustworthiness approaches is a possible solution for coping with the challenges to be expected in the future society.

Trustworthiness Training Given the transition from cybersecurity to trustworthiness, the scope of cybersecurity training will need to be extended to also cover issues related to trustworthiness. In particular, it will be important to conduct training regarding the possible consequences of cyberspace incidents in the physical space, as well as the expected effects in the reverse direction, combined with teaching appropriate mitigation techniques for both these cases.

It can be said that current security training programs focusing on Industrial Control Systems (ICS), such as the *ICS410: ICS/SCADA Security Essentials* course provided by SANS Institute [10], are a good start in this direction. However, they lack the breadth that will be required to address all the needs of Society 5.0.

We conclude by saying that the road ahead for improving cybersecurity education and training is still long, and challenges abound. We hope that this book will become a useful instrument in this context, and urge our readers to join us in the effort of pushing forward toward this shared goal, thus contributing to the creation of a better and safer society for everyone.

References

1. Bajema N (2024) Why are large AI models being red teamed? https://spectrum.ieee.org/red-team-ai-llms. Accessed 1 Jul 2024
2. Baudoin C, Bournival E, Buchheit M, Simmon E, Zarkout B (2024) Industry Internet of things vocabulary. https://www.iiconsortium.org/wp-content/uploads/sites/2/2022/04/Industry-IoT-Vocabulary.pdf. Accessed 1 Jul 2024
3. Beuran R (2019) Towards an open exchange format for cybersecurity training content. In: Usenix security symposium, lightning talks presentations
4. Beuran R, Hu Z, Zeng Y, Tan Y (2023) Artificial intelligence for cybersecurity education and training. Springer International Publishing, Cham, pp 103–123. https://doi.org/10.1007/978-3-031-15030-2_5
5. Beuran R, Ooi SE, Barbir AO, Tan Y (2022) IoT system trustworthiness assurance. In: 17th ACM Asia conference on computer and communications security (AsiaCCS 2022), pp 1222–1224. https://doi.org/10.1145/3488932.3527287
6. Blažič BJ (2022) Changing the landscape of cybersecurity education in the EU: will the new approach produce the required cybersecurity skills? Educ Inf Technol 27(3):3011–3036. https://doi.org/10.1007/s10639-021-10704-y
7. Cabinet Office, Government of Japan: society 5.0. https://www8.cao.go.jp/cstp/english/society5_0/index.html. Accessed 1 Jul 2024
8. ISC2 (2023) Past, present and future of cyber training. https://www.isc2.org/Insights/2023/10/Past-Present-Future-of-Cyber-Training. Accessed 1 Jul 2024
9. Petkauskas V (2024) Rockyou2024: 10 billion passwords leaked in the largest compilation of all time. https://cybernews.com/security/rockyou2024-largest-password-compilation-leak/. Accessed 1 Aug 2024
10. SANS Institute: ICS410: ICS/SCADA security essentials. https://www.sans.org/cyber-security-courses/ics-scada-cyber-security-essentials/. Accessed 1 Jul 2024
11. Stone M (2021) The future of cybersecurity: what will it look like in 2031? https://securityintelligence.com/articles/future-of-cybersecurity-2031/. Accessed 1 Jul 2024
12. Tang D, Pham C, Chinen K, Beuran R (2017) Interactive cybersecurity defense training inspired by web-based learning theory. In: 9th IEEE international conference on engineering education (ICEED 2017), pp 90–95. https://doi.org/10.1109/ICEED.2017.8251171

The manufacturer's authorised representative in the EU is Springer
Nature Customer Service Centre GmbH, Europaplatz 3, 69115 Heidelberg,
Germany. If you have any concerns regarding our products, please
contact ProductSafety@springernature.com

Printed and bound by CPI Group (UK) Ltd, Croydon, CR0 4YY

27/04/2026

02097572-0008